The Politics of Desire

The Joan Palevsky  Imprint in Classical Literature

In honor of beloved Virgil—

"O degli altri poeti onore e lume . . ."

—Dante, *Inferno*

The Politics of Desire

Propertius IV

Micaela Janan

UNIVERSITY OF CALIFORNIA PRESS
Berkeley   Los Angeles   London

University of California Press
Berkeley and Los Angeles, California

University of California Press, Ltd.
London, England

© 2001 by the Regents of the University of California

Library of Congress Cataloging-in-Publication Data

Janan, Micaela Wakil.
The politics of desire : Propertius IV / Micaela Janan.
   p.   cm.
Includes bibliographical references (p.) and index.
ISBN 0-520-22318-7 (alk. paper)—ISBN 0-520-22321-7 (pbk. : alk paper)
1. Propertius, Sextus. Elegiae. Liber 4. 2. Elegiac poetry, Latin—History and criticism.
3. Psychoanalysis and literature—Rome—History. 4. Politics and literature—Rome—History. 5. Desire in literature. 6. Rome—In literature. I. Title.
PA6644.B43 J36 2001
874'.01—dc21
                                                                                        99-055385
                                                                                             CIP

Manufactured in the United States of America

09 08 07 06 05 04 03 02 01 00

10 9 8 7 6 5 4 3 2 1

The paper used in this publication meets the minimum requirements of ANSI/NISO Z39.48-1992 (R 1997) (*Permanence of Paper*).

The following chapters are revised versions of materials published elsewhere: chapter 4: " 'Beyond Good and Evil': Tarpeia and Philosophy in the Feminine (Propertius 4.4)," *Classical World* 92.5 (1999): 433–47; and chapter 8: "Refashioning Hercules: Propertius 4.9," *Helios* 25.1 (1998): 65–77. They are published here with the kind permission of the editors.

For Orest
The Book of Ruth 1:16–17

CONTENTS

ACKNOWLEDGMENTS / ix
A NOTE ON CITATION / xi

Introduction / 3

1. Theoretical Preliminaries / 11

2. "Shadow of a Doubt": Framing the Subject in the Gallus Poems / 33

3. The Ethics of Evil: Arethusa to Lycotas (4.3) / 53

4. "Beyond Good and Evil": Tarpeia and Philosophy in the Feminine (4.4) / 70

5. The Return of the Dead: The Acanthis Elegy (4.5) / 85

6. "The Book of Revelation": Cynthia's Truth (4.7) / 100

7. Cynthia Returns from Lanuvium (4.8) / 114

8. Hercules in Rome (4.9) / 128

9. The Phenomenology of the Spirits (4.11) / 146

10. Dreaming Rome / 164

NOTES / 169
BIBLIOGRAPHY / 215
GENERAL INDEX / 237
INDEX OF PROPERTIAN POEMS CITED / 243

ACKNOWLEDGMENTS

David Konstan offered the initial spark of inspiration for this book when he suggested to me in 1992 that the beguiling peculiarities of Propertius' enigmatic corpus deserved attention from a Lacanian perspective. He was kind enough to read the initial draft of the manuscript that surfaced almost three years later, and to offer helpful comments on the whole, as did Joy King and Paul Allen Miller. Professor Miller has continued generously to offer his unerring gift for clarifying insight to successive drafts; not only intellectual exchange, but friendship with him have greatly improved this book and my life.

Good fortune has placed me in Duke University's Classical Studies department, whose intellectual attainments and warm support for colleagues' endeavors make it an earnest of Scholar's Heaven. In particular, Peter Burian and Diskin Clay read numerous versions of the manuscript; their observations greatly helped to clarify and improve the final product. Kent Rigsby, John Oates, Mary T. Boatwright, and Lawrence Richardson, Jr., all gave generously of their historical and archaeological knowledge whenever I asked (which was often, and probably inconveniently—although their unfailing readiness to help never made me feel as much). Of course, I owe an incalculable debt to Lawrence Richardson's learned and sensitive commentary on Propertius' poems; as my many citations of his *Propertius: Elegies I–IV* indicate, without his work on Propertius, my own would be very different, and much impoverished.

Thanks are due also to Maria Wyke, Marilyn Skinner, and two anonymous readers, all of whose reports helped the manuscript make its way into print. I have benefited greatly from their careful readings.

At the University of California Press, Katharine Toll's ready encouragement, exemplary efficiency, and unfailing good humor have been crucial to seeing the book to completion while minimizing its author's pain. Rachel Berchten's and Elizabeth Ditmars' eagle eyes will have helped ease the reader's pain, by purging the text of many obscurities and solecisms.

The Arts and Sciences Research Council of Duke University provided funds over several years for bibliographic research that greatly aided the book's completion. Christopher Spelman, Denise McCoskey, and David Banta all lent their able hands and even abler minds to the task of hunting down the necessary scholarship in print.

Finally, my greatest debt is owed to Orest Pelech, both for his mind and his heart. He brought his exquisitely accurate editorial sense to bear upon countless redactions of the work, rescuing me from error on numerous occasions. He uncomplainingly endured my late nights, amorphous anxieties, and tedious dwelling on a topic he already knew too intimately for any mortal's comfort. Without his love and support, this book would not have been possible.

No doubt errors remain in this book, even after the help so generously given by all the people named above. For these, I have only my own obstinacy to blame.

A NOTE ON CITATION

In my text, I have cited both ancient and modern works according to the conventions of classical philology (and provided my own translations). The abbreviations for ancient texts are taken from *The Oxford Classical Dictionary;* those for journals, from *L'Année Philologique.* My text for Propertius (unless otherwise noted) is that of E. A. Barber (*Sexti Properti Carmina*, 2nd ed. [Oxford, 1960]); for Freud, *The Standard Edition of the Complete Psychological Works of Sigmund Freud*, ed. and trans. James Strachey. Citations from the *Standard Edition* of Freud appear as "*SE,*" then the volume number, followed by a colon, then page numbers: thus, "*SE* 23:209" = "Standard Edition, volume 23, page 209."

For Lacan, to avoid cumbersome citations in the text, the bibliography lists in full the works I have used; only brief citations will be given in my discussions. These will chiefly be to Lacan's orally transmitted work (which constitute the bulk of his legacy), his *Séminaires* given between 1953 and 1980. The texts of these seminars are being slowly edited from student notes and tape recordings of the sessions by Lacan's son-in-law, Jacques-Alain Miller. "S" followed by a Roman numeral refers to a *Séminaire*; a double-page citation following such a symbol, with the two numbers separated by a solidus, refers to the original French edition and to the corresponding passage in its English translation, both cited in the bibliography (accordingly, "SVII 44/34" = "page 44 of *Séminaire VII* in the French edition, page 34 in the English translation"). A page citation alone refers to Lacan's single essay collection, *Écrits*; a double-page citation refers to the original French edition of *Écrits* and to the corresponding passage in Sheridan's English translation of selected essays from *Écrits* (thus, "101/8" = "page 101 in the French edition of *Écrits*, page 8 in Sheridan's translation").

OTHER ABBREVIATIONS:

Pf. (or Pfeiffer) = Rudolf Pfeiffer, ed., Callimachus, 2 vols. (Oxford, 1949–1953).

OLD = P. G. W. Glare, ed., *Oxford Latin Dictionary* (Oxford, 1982).

The Politics of Desire

Introduction

This study rests upon the simple premise that the various kinds of Latin poetry require various critical approaches. A search for the methodology most suited to reveal the innermost workings of a particular genre supports best our endeavors to interpret Rome's legacy. Specifically, I argue, psychoanalysis—crafted as it is to address what is fragmented, occluded, and in tension within human consciousness and culture—can best examine the incoherences that characterize Roman elegy: the logical contradictions and unexplained emotional *volte-face*, the mystifying ellipses of narrative, the at times abrupt changes in speakers and addressees, the oscillations between self-condemning love and self-justifying loathing for the Roman ethos that contemns *amor*. In particular, Jacques Lacan's focus on desire as the principal force that shapes subjectivity lends itself well to tracing intimately the eddies of longing across a genre that self-avowedly turns on love as its theme.

My previous book, *When the Lamp Is Shattered*, focused upon Catullus' poetry from the late Republic as the earliest known reasonably complete body of Roman lyric poetry. Its purpose was to fashion a basic vocabulary with which to discuss the emergence of divided erotic subjectivity[1] from the tantalizingly elliptical narrative of Latin lyric. I concentrated on the poems addressed to Catullus' lover Lesbia (the "Lesbia cycle") as the fullest account of a love affair available from his corpus. In order to throw into relief the significant details of lover's and beloved's intimate exchanges within these poems, I used those aspects of Lacan's thought best suited to explicating what seems innermost (most private, most personal) to the subject and the intrinsic scission of that "intimate core." Lacan's concept of the subject divided by desire is helpful in addressing the difficulties of constructing a single, logically coherent subject from Catullus' portrait of a lover rent by various dichotomies (duty versus love, the beloved's idealization versus her debasement, the lover's "divinization" under love's power versus his amorous enslavement). These difficulties correlate to the equally perplexing rigors of extracting a rationally unified narrative from the text's fragmentary glimpses of Catullus' and Lesbia's love affair. From these related enigmas, I produced in *When the Lamp is Shattered* a conceptually unified analysis of the relatively interiorized concerns recorded in Catullus' Lesbia poems—poetry crucial, as precursor, to Roman love elegy, the field of inquiry for the present book.

This second book seeks to build upon the earlier work by expanding the scope both of its methodology and area of inquiry, and by articulating more broadly the social and political forces that shape the subject within Roman erotic poetry. Lacan's focus on desire always evokes the horizon of the political within the personal by showing how cultural institutions engage the subject's longing to be "whole" as strongly as lovers do (and by the same psychic means). The present study again takes advantage of Lacanian insight to offer an analysis of Propertius' corpus, but from a perspective that takes fuller account of the poetry's historical context.

I have again made use of Lacan's concept of the divided subject as an inherent cleavage that presses human beings to seek "unity" or "wholeness," but here I examine the way that widely various cultural signifiers can captivate that desire. The lure of "model citizen" or "great statesman" can be as strong as that of "devoted lover"—and is just as surely doomed: first, because division founds subjectivity: the subject cannot be healed without being abolished altogether; second, because the cultural icons under whose auspices we seek integrity themselves participate in the logical impasses that give rise to subjectivity. They are no less intrinsically flawed than the subject.[2] Propertius deeply interests himself in the allure, and the betrayal, of these seductive promises of unity offered by cultural symbols; the poet's fascination, even in its deep skepticism, aligns him more closely with "official" Rome than is usually suspected.

THE FORUM AUGUSTUM

The audience that read Propertius' poetry witnessed during the principate of Octavian—known after January 16, 27 B.C.E. as "Augustus"—a particularly fierce grappling with tensions among cultural elements evident in Rome's representation of itself; consciously or unconsciously, they brought that intensified awareness of their culture's internal contradictions to their reading of the Propertian corpus.[3] As Paul Zanker's analysis of the imagery of Augustan Rome shows (surveying not only monumental architecture, but the myriad humbler vignettes that emblazoned coinage, rings, and other quotidian objects), the public vision of the empire that Augustus' regime offered her citizens was an attempt to coax a totality from the division and incoherence of Roman cultural identity. Augustus' efforts to impose unity upon Rome's eclectic heritage are most purely evident in the Forum Augustum, the great colonnaded square containing the temple of Mars Ultor ("Mars the Avenger") that was built on the emperor's personal property (*privato solo*)[4] as an expression of his own ideas and emblazoned with a decorative program designed to educate the Roman people in the emperor's new vision of Rome.[5] The Forum Augustum contains several images that awkwardly undertake to reconcile irreconcilables, such as the status of the Roman as both immigrant and native (descended from Trojan exiles and Latin aborigines), as Alban and Roman (Alba Longa being Rome's progenitor and, notwithstanding, its bitter enemy in a virtual civil war),[6] citizen of a nominal republic and a de facto monarchy.[7]

The Forum's very attempt to integrate the various parts of Roman mythic history—principally the myth cycles of Romulus and Aeneas—accentuates the tensions and contradictions within Rome's image of itself inherited from the past. For example, the Forum's alcoves symmetrically balance the famous image of Aeneas fleeing the burning ruins of Troy, carrying his father on his shoulders and leading his son Ascanius by the hand, against the figure of Romulus, hoisting on *his* shoulder the enemy commander's armor to be dedicated as *spolia opima*.[8] The juxtaposition, as Zanker points out, makes good enough sense as images of *pietas*[9] and *virtus*[10] respectively—except that Aeneas' protective loyalty toward his family throws into sharp relief Romulus' singular affront to such loyalty. Romulus founded the honor of the *spolia opima* when he killed King Akron of Caenina; the king had himself tried to avenge an infraction against *pietas*, namely the abduction of Caenina's women that Romulus engineered on the occasion of Rome's first Consualia.[11] The criteria that elevate both Romulus and Aeneas to venerable status cannot logically be reconciled.

Equally odd is the iconographic lifting of Romulus' counterpart, Aeneas and his family, above the logic of time and place. While Ascanius appears in the costume of a Phrygian shepherd, Anchises sports the garb of a Roman priest, and Aeneas wears Roman armor with the elaborate footwear appropriate only to a Roman patrician (an apparent reference to his status as progenitor of the noble Julii). Categories of foreigner and native, past and future, secular and sacred, noble and commoner jostle each other uneasily in this forcible blend of what Troy's exiles were with what they became.

And yet the Forum's parade of notables who articulate this divergent history—Aeneas, the Alban kings, and the Julii on one side, opposite Romulus and his fellow *triumphatores*,[12] the *summi viri*[13] of Rome's past, on the other—frame Augustus' controlling presence, implied by his triumphal chariot that commands the very center of the forum. Though the Senate dedicated this *quadriga* to Augustus as "father of the country" (*pater patriae*) after the Forum's completion, Augustus' obvious pride in the chariot and its inscription[14] shows that the Senate's inspiration fit his own vision of the Forum as an image of Rome's future—a harmonious "golden age" of peace that he himself had wrought and continued to preserve. Zanker argues cogently that the images of the Forum are carefully orchestrated to support Augustus' implicit claim to the power to unify the diverse threads of Roman identity, by uniting in his bloodline the peaceful and fertile heritage of Venus (his mythical ancestor, through Aeneas) and the martial heritage of Mars (from whose son Romulus he, like all Romans, claimed descent). Augustus surpasses Romulus' *virtus*, the iconography implies, at the same time that he exemplifies *pietas* better than Aeneas; he unites the dual heritage of Rome in one person.

Yet Augustus' presence as the greatest of the *triumphatores* and generals who line the Forum's colonnades—a pre-eminence implied by his centrally-placed triumphal vehicle—ironically underlines the desperate need to overcome the centrifugal forces adumbrated, not only in the odd contradictions of Rome's mythical progenitors (Venus and Mars, Romulus and the Aeneadae), but in the Forum's gallery of history's great Romans. Mortal enemies line up together in the statue niches of the Forum's alcoves: Sempronius Gracchus with Scipio Aemilianus Africanus,[15] Marius with Sulla, Pompey with Lucullus.[16] Moreover, some of these imperialists evoke a social ethos and history specifically inimical to Augustus' strategic exaltation of his clan, the *gens Juliorum*, above all others in his conspectus of the Roman past, and to the monarchic and dynastic ambitions intimated in the assimilation of the Julians to the Alban kings in the north colonnade. For example, Scipio Aemilianus' enmity toward Sempronius Gracchus' son, Tiberius Gracchus the tribune, evidently stemmed from fear that Tiberius' proposed agrarian reforms were but instruments of demagoguery designed to advance their author's popular influence well beyond that of his oligarchic peers.[17] Similar alarm apparently motivated the *summus vir* Caecilius Metellus Numidicus' vigorous opposition to the "demagogues" Glauca and Saturninus.[18] When, on the other hand, the power that demagoguery seeks so avidly comes to rest *nolens volens* in the hands of another *summus vir*, M. Furius Camillus, he manifests a diffidence equally out of tune with Augustan ambitions. Though appointed dictator more than once (five times, according to Plutarch), Camillus assumed this office with reluctance, eager to lay it aside at the earliest opportunity.[19] He receives praise for always exercising his authority in common with his compeers, even when the power to propose and dispose was his alone.[20] By contrast, the Forum makes clear that Augustus' ambitions do not lie in the direction of a self-effacing equality with his peers.

I have lingered upon this description of the Forum Augustum in order to highlight the contradictions that shape the conceptualization both of Roman identity and of the state that shaped that identity. Assuredly some, if not all, of these contradictions existed before the principate and endured afterward, but the tensions they exert upon *Romanitas*[21] are greatly dramatized and hence the more forcibly impressed upon Rome's consciousness precisely through the principate's brave but futile attempts (like the Forum Augustum) to reconcile them out of existence. This consciousness of identity in tension conditions the audience for whom Propertius writes; accurately and precisely understanding the mechanism by which it operated is crucial to our fully understanding his poetry.

THE POET IMAGINES ROME

Lacan (as I shall argue with greater detail in chapter 1) offers us the best tools with which to approach this evident crisis in conceiving *Romanitas*, because his model of subjectivity pivots upon an internal contradiction and division. That split is the very condition of subjectivity, driving all the subject's thoughts and actions insofar as he attempts to close the gap by identifying with one or another icon of ostensibly unproblematic and "whole" identity his society offers. The range of possible icons is vast and varied, even though all "work" according to the same principles. Accordingly, the wide embrace of Lacan's view of subjectivity can address within a single conceptual model the stark, seemingly contradictory division of Propertius' fourth book into erotic and political elements, along with the dichotomies of private versus public and individual versus social suggested by the principal divide. In his conceptualization of the subject's relation to society and history, Lacan refuses to regard such oppositions as fixed and stable; his thought therefore best corresponds to the complexities of Propertius' verse—to the way that hidden commerce between seeming antitheses colors the tensions that traverse its historical context and shapes the subjectivity it records.

Propertius' poetry, his fourth and last book especially, figures crucially in a debate lately sparked within the study of Latin poetry in general and Roman elegy in particular, chiefly owing to increased awareness within classical scholarship of Foucault's theory of *épistémè*—the historically distinct structures of explanation available to any given cultural formation. This debate attempts to seize the meaning of Roman poetry through its complex layers of ambiguity and contradiction by placing the poems within a sharply demarcated historical context alien (it is said) to the modern world.[22] Paul Veyne's *Roman Erotic Elegy* is the best known example of this type of scholarship applied to elegy; Veyne claims that an epistemic shift obscures from us, the heirs of Romanticism, the pure gamesmanship of elegiac inconsistency.[23] In this view, the elegists—all members of the Roman male elite—assume narrative positions of passionate enslavement to a flinty mistress and docile submission to a code of erotic debasement quite foreign to their social stratum purely out of a desire to amuse their equally elite audience. Accordingly, we can simply dismiss, with a knowing smile, the puzzling representations of *mollitia*[24] and *servitium amoris*[25] in their poetry as "empty" signifiers.

Yet Duncan Kennedy has recently objected that Veyne vastly oversimplifies when he discounts these signifiers heretical to Roman elite masculinity as pure *divertissement*.[26] Kennedy points out that ideological paradigms and the semantic possibilities they admit never cleanly give way one to the other; the contradictions Veyne sees as purely formal moves in a game are rather competing ideological paradigms coexisting in productive tension. In turn, Paul Allen Miller cogently argues that such tension—"semiotic slippage," in his words—itself makes elegy possible:[27] historical conditions that foregrounded a widening gap between the Roman male subject's basic sense of self and his cultural recognition *as a subject* in the world of codified, signifying practices gave rise to new forms of self-representation—including elegy and its torturously ambiguous relation to the "way of the ancestors" (*mos maiorum*). Miller translates that tension into Lacanian terms as a gap between the Imaginary and the Symbolic realms (roughly, between the realm of ego identifications that falsely, imperfectly assure the subject of his fixity and consistency, and the realm of cultural symbolization systems). Accordingly, Miller sees Latin elegy's genesis as revolving around the problematization of subjectivity—the slipping of the claims of traditional Roman ideology on the subject that takes place, non-coincidentally, as the Roman Republic dies and the Augustan principate supplants it (the very problematization that the Forum Augustum represents so clearly in the sharp self-contradictions of its civic vision).

Miller's convincing and fruitful analysis of elegy's historical conditions of possibility indicates Propertius' crucial importance to understanding the genre as a whole. His poetry centrally engages the liminal period between Republic and Empire, recording the fact that he lived out his boyhood and youth in the Republic's endgame (watching his personal fortunes crumble in the shadow of its demise), yet became Augustus' client in the emerging principate. The other Roman elegists occupy historical and intellectual positions at a greater distance from this transition. Catullus never lived to see the principate;[28] Tibullus engaged only obliquely the political issues raised by its ascendancy.[29] Ovid writes chiefly when the new regime is already well established, the republic a dim memory of his childhood.[30]

Miller discusses skillfully and with great sensitivity Propertius' role in shaping elegy; he discloses whole new vistas of interpretation, especially in the poet's first three books. However, his account of Book IV, though also thought-provoking and rich, strongly emphasizes those elements of the last-published poems that align themselves with dominant ideology, and consequently misconstrues (to my mind) the true nature of their subversion. Miller notes that Propertius IV consists to a surprising extent of narratives in voices other than the familiar lover-narrator's on historical themes toward which the poet's attitude (patriotic, derisive, wistful, or any other) cannot be ascertained with certainty. This contrasts starkly with the lover-narrator's subjective monologues on the difficulties of his love life assembled in Books I-III. Miller sees irony, the determinedly elusive dominant trope of Book IV, as indicating the Augustan principate's ultimate triumph: with the new regime establishing itself more and more strongly, the gap between the subject's self-identification and his cultural recognition as a subject narrows to the point that a determinate space for opposing Rome's dominant ideology can no longer be imagined. Only irony remains, Miller says, the trope wherein one can only determine with certainty what the speaker is *not* saying—what stance he ironically undercuts—but not what he *is* saying, from what *point de repère* he as a subject speaks. In Miller's words, "the compulsive deconstruction of elegy's own aesthetic and subjective structures that this irony enacts retains within it the oppositional kernel that characterizes the subgenre, but now recontains it within a series of seemingly objective and hence unchanging frames."[31] He assigns Propertius IV (along with Ovid's *Amores*) to elegy's "sunset" period, when the possible coigns of vantage outside the Augustan ideological system have been all but foreclosed.

I disagree with this assessment in part because—for all the astuteness of Miller's interpretation—it fails to account satisfactorily for crucial details in Propertius IV, such as Propertius' insistence on zeroing in on the embarrassments of Roman history: the costly futility of endlessly defending the empire's borders (4.3), the recently controversial *spolia opima* (4.10), or even the penchant of the Ara Maxima's patron god, Hercules, for cross-dressing (4.9).[32] Surely an apologist for Rome, or even a poet infected with indifference, would steer clear of such flashpoints. But in addition, the smothering power Miller grants to the Symbolic as the Real's "(re)container" unduly minimizes the fact that Lacan always clearly located the Real *within* the Symbolic, in its gaps and fissures, the places where the Symbolic "breaks down" in failing to disambiguate itself.[33] That the Symbolic should frame the Real hardly robs the latter of its disruptive power—to the contrary, it increases the Real's power to act as the worm in hegemony's heart. Although Miller acknowledges Lacan's implication of the Real with the Symbolic, he undervalues the full significance of this interweaving. He declares that Book IV's contextualization of the Real by its particular historical Symbolic—by the elements drawn from Roman nationalistic discourse that seem to overshadow any "personal" viewpoint of the poet's—co-opts elegy's subversiveness. I shall argue the contrary in the following pages: the way Book IV emphatically situates the Real in the very heart of a Symbolic that denies and suppresses it at every turn underlines the false pretensions of cultural symbolization systems to represent the world objectively, transparently, accurately. The powerful analysis that Miller has launched by locating elegy's genesis in the widening gap between the Symbolic and the Imaginary—a gap pried open by the Real—nonetheless misses the Real's mutinous effects as a gap within the Symbolic itself. Lacan subsumed the Symbolic's esoteric gap under the idea of Woman *qua* icon of impasse in cultural symbolization systems; significantly, Propertius cedes much of his fourth book's narration to a motley assortment of female speakers with disturbing things to say about Rome, women whose stories cause us to question the logical foundations of Rome's self-conceptualization. Book IV is not only thoroughly subversive,[34] but paradigmatically so: Propertius IV's studied entropy ironically seems *de trop* precisely because it grants the most dramatic form to the discordant forces that call elegy into existence.

Each chapter in this book (save the first two, devoted to laying the conceptual groundwork for the whole) focuses on a poem or poems drawn from the Propertian corpus. In part, I examine representative readings by modern critics, paying close attention to where and how they uncover the most interesting facets of the poem and also where and how they miscarry. In particular, why various critics identify, and negotiate, "faults" in the poem, whether attributed to a corrupt manuscript tradition or to the poet's nodding, interests me. Every chapter presses hard the conceptual assumptions behind the methodologies used to locate these poetic "flaws," arguing that many a so-called blemish discovered in these poems proceeds from attempting to impose upon them a unifying and straightforward rationale oblivious to Propertius' strategic use of unreason (e.g., anacolutha, abrupt narrative transitions, and vividly incongruous imagery). All such gaps and fissures in logic dramatize in a principled fashion fundamental aporiae in the early principate's cultural symbolization systems, the Symbolic that intimately shaped both Propertius' poetry and its audience. I have drawn upon Lacanian psychoanalysis to fashion perspectives on the various poems with dual purpose: to complement the best discoverable in the critical tradition (while illuminating some of its blind spots); to render better account of what is (tellingly) missing from the text, as well as what is there. Although this book focuses on Propertius, it should interest the student of ancient Latin *litterae humaniores* in general, given that it critically examines fundamental methodologies commonly used in interpreting ancient literature and the assumptions behind them. Moreover, since the argument critically engages the topics of psychoanalysis, history, ideology and hegemony, subjectivity, and the role that language plays in all these, it should also appeal to those interested in contemporary literary theory and cultural studies.

The general scholarly reader will find that this book requires no previous knowledge either of Propertius studies, Lacanian psychoanalysis, or any other subdiscipline. I have summarized the relevant critical debates in discussing each poem and explained all specialized terms used in my argument, explicating Lacanian thought in the plainest language compatible with precise and accurate representation of his theory. Though Lacan's startling and counterintuitive thought usually will not allow the substitution of synonyms for his terminology, I have explained the latter's provenance and meaning. All the Latin in the main text has been translated into English. Since the argument unfolds as a whole built progressively on its parts, the reader will benefit most who avails herself of the entire book. However, anyone interested in my exegesis of a single poem from Propertius IV can make sense of the relevant chapter if she reads through the introduction and chapter 1 beforehand. These chapters systematically unfold all theoretical knowledge and terminology necessary to understanding the book's approach to Propertius (aside from matters that pertain only to individual poems and that are, accordingly, addressed only in the relevant chapters). It is my hope that these measures will make interest, rather than prior expertise, the only passport my readers need into Propertius' world.

CHAPTER ONE

Theoretical Preliminaries

These contrasts, these extravagancies, these fluctuations and incoherencies, these half-formed or misshapen thoughts, what do they signify? What is the secret of this chaos?

J. P. POSTGATE

Postgate's eloquent frustration pinpoints the difficulties for Propertius scholars: the demanding nature of the poet's verse has robbed him of an understanding audience. Indeed, these profound difficulties in interpreting his verse have been encountered by readers of his elegies from the time of Rome's chaotic transition from Republic to Empire through the present. Some of these may be laid to the account of a manuscript tradition plagued by ill fortune:[1] the twelfth-century Neapolitanus on which we chiefly rely comes to us—like Odysseus suffering Polyphemus' curse—"late, in bad case, with the loss of all companions."[2] It lacks the authority of true antiquity or of multiple independent traditions to attest its readings.

Yet how much of our perplexity can be blamed on Propertius' untidy transmission remains a matter of hot debate. James Butrica points out that Karl Lachmann banished from both his highly significant editions "obtrusas Propertio elegantias," conjectures foisted upon Propertius that falsely made him mirror the elegance of his contemporaries.[3] Butrica's own exhaustive study of the manuscript tradition produces little in his sample text that differs from Barber's conservative Oxford Classical Text, though he will radically change the *apparatus criticus* of future Propertius editions; his work indicates that we cannot appeal to the manuscript's authority to solve our difficulties.

Lachmann saw what other scholars preferred to deny: many of the difficulties in understanding Propertius' compressed and imagistic thought are owed not to the faults of his manuscript tradition, but to a style far more disjunctive than "mainstream" classical poets (Horace, Catullus, or Vergil, for example) would have countenanced. Received wisdom in Propertius studies has often tried to organize these discontinuities under a presumed tension between "the erotic" and "the political"

Postgate 1881, lxxii.

(a tension that subsumes the "private" versus "public" and "individual" versus "collective").[4] However, this interpretive dichotomy does less to render the rifts in the poetry intelligible than to reify them as effects of a simplistically conceived "anti-Augustan" disaffection: all becomes clear (so the explanation runs) if we see Propertius as pitting a lover's personal agenda against the principate's moral austerities and political hypocrisies.[5] This explanation fails to take into account the complexity of Propertius' position: three-quarters of his verse was written while he was the recipient of quasi-official imperial patronage from Augustus' informal "Minister of Culture," Maecenas—a fact that sorts badly with a portrait of the artist as young Jacobin.

By contrast, I shall argue in the following pages that Propertius' idiosyncratic disjunction responds more broadly to a social crisis characterized by the disintegration of an ideologically secure sense of self. This has classically made his poetry difficult to read for ages in which a seemingly assured identity formed the basis of consent to the social order.[6] Yet we moderns have oddly benefited from the deterioration of intellectual faith that has shaped our century. Conditions of our own time and of its intellectual roots in the nineteenth century peculiarly correspond to the upheaval of Rome's transformation from republic to empire (as I shall explain further below); consequently, contemporary methodologies forged in the modern crucible uncannily offer the best approach to Propertius' verse.

The work of Jacques Lacan in particular suits the study of these elegies insofar as he offers the best conceptual tools with which to examine the relation between political upheaval and the disintegration of apparently stable selfhood. Lacan sketches a subject essentially divided—principally between Conscious and Unconscious realms, but also between other polarities; displacements precipitated by social and political convulsions merely exacerbate, and so make visible, an intrinsic condition.[7] The subject dissimulates this division by identifying with some master signifier that guarantees his place in the interconnected symbols and meanings generated by his culture's institutions. He reconciles or opposes himself to what constitutes, e.g., a "good man," "good lover," "model citizen," and the like. The divided psychoanalytic subject can thus function as a coherent whole (as "I"), but can only do so via ideological commitments that make the various parts of being (anatomy, intellect, desire, cultural ideals) cohere in an apparently natural fashion. These commitments make possible such everyday self-defining statements as "I am Gaius," "I am a man," "I am a Roman citizen."[8] Whatever the signifier that promises to locate the subject and thus make him whole—be it Woman, *Romanitas*, Augustus' call to "return to our ancestors' ways"[9]— the relation desire creates between subject and signifier is the same; social upheaval and institutional transmutation render this appeal both more seductive and less plausible.[10] Lacan's formulation of the subject as essentially divided among social and psychic polarities— a division that both love and civic fealty offer (falsely) to heal—aligns public and private desire along the axis of the subject's division, seen as *both* a political *and* erotic dilemma.

CALLIMACHUS ROMANUS

The axis of the present discussion passes through Book IV, the chief riddle of the Propertian corpus; a wealth of study and (at times wild) speculation have been trained upon the fourth book's oddities. No common viewpoint organizes Book IV in the way that Propertius' lover-narrator acts as unifying voice for the first three books. Its poems veer from one vantage to another, often assuming women's narrative voices and ranging across class distinctions from lowly procuress to aristocratic matron. The book oscillates, without obvious rhyme or reason, between principally erotic and principally political poems, a mode of organization so obscure that it has misled some to declare it the careless work of a posthumous editor (or even of a *pasticheur*).[11]

Worse, the erstwhile poet of love does a *volte face* in his fourth book and declares himself the "Roman Callimachus" ("Romani . . . Callimachi," 4.1.64), whose reflections upon Rome will assume distinctly aetiological form as he examines "ancient rites and their appointed days, and the ancient names of places" (*sacra diesque canam et cognomina prisca locorum,* 4.1.69).[12] His program strongly recalls that of the third-century B.C.E. Hellenistic poet in his *Aetia,* a verse collection of legends purporting to explain Greek customs, rites, and history. Scholars have rightly seen the growing influence of Callimachus in general, and the *Aetia* in particular, not only in Book IV's antiquarianism and its jettisoning of a unifying authorial narrative voice, but in its experimental incorporation of various different generic elements into elegy.[13] Of course, Propertius was hardly the first Roman elegist to take the *Aetia* as his model: a generation earlier, Catullus drew upon its organizing conceit by translating the *Plokamos Berenikes* (*Aetia* IV, fr. 110 Pf.) into Latin elegiac couplets. But it is instructive to compare Catullus' use of the *Aetia* with Propertius' in order to gauge the distance between the former poet, who laid the groundwork for Roman subjective love elegy, and the latter, whose final book constitutes nearly the last word in this short-lived genre's *floruit*. Measuring that distance will indicate Propertius' particular role in "pushing the envelope" of the elegiac genre during its rapid, multifarious evolution into new, virtually unrecognizable forms.

I set aside the broader sway Callimachus' poetics wielded over Catullus and Catullus' successors, the Augustan poets, all at pains to realize the Callimachean ideal of finely-wrought, erudite, playful poetry, to concentrate on aetiology, the *Aetia*'s specific organizing conceit and the startlingly new focus of Propertius IV. As a thread that binds beginning to near-end of the elegiac tradition aetiology can help us assess both the originality of Propertius' reshaping of that tradition and the effect of his innovation.

Catullus' *Coma Berenices*, his single foray into aetiology, translates into quite faithful Latin Callimachus' droll poem on the supposed catasterism of Queen Berenike II's lock of hair, dedicated as a thank-offering for her husband's (Ptolemy Euergetes') safe return from invading Syria. The lock itself speaks, lamenting its separation from Berenike and the envy generated by its berth among the stars. As

Kathryn Gutzwiller has recently reminded us, the poem had distinct political significance when Callimachus composed it as a flattering court toy in the third century B.C.E.; it favorably (if wittily) portrays the queen's passion for her husband. The poem thereby conforms to the history of Ptolemaic attempts to make palatable to Greek subjects the monarchy's emulation of Egyptian models of rule that gave prominence to queens.[14] Reciprocal passion between the two regal spouses figured and justified this power-sharing arrangement. Callimachus' favorable sketch of royal desire also palliates the problematic fact of "brother-sister" marriage the Ptolemies had adopted in Egypt.[15] Nonetheless, by the time Catullus translated this poem approximately a century and a half later, it had no distinct political resonances for the contemporary Roman scene: only its playfulness, its wit, and its focus on separated lovers and on erotic passion in marriage remain.

Book IV's second elegy offers the closest Propertian parallel to Catullus' *Coma Berenices:* once again, an inanimate object speaks—a quondam Etruscan, now Roman, statue of the minor god Vertumnus. Propertius borrowed this specific conceit from such poems as *Aetia* fr. 114 Pf. (a statue of Apollo answers Callimachus' questions) and *Iambi* VII fr. 197 Pf. (Hermes' statue relates its own origins). The Vertumnus elegy shares with Catullus' poetic translation an interest in Callimachean cleverness and playfulness, even some of its interest in the erotic.[16] Yet clearly the simple rendering of a Greek original into Latin—even to produce a tour de force comparable to the *Coma Berenices*—did not exhaust Propertius' ambition. Rather, he takes Callimachean aetiology as the broad outline of a form into which he may pour his particular concern, which is (as Maria Wyke has pointed out) to represent Rome past and present, its history and contemporary observance—but not as a comforting whole, a divinely sanctioned *kosmos*.[17] Rather, Book IV borrows from Callimachean aetiology its most disturbing impetuses in order to reinvent the genre for another historical context.

Vertumnus' comically garrulous address to the passerby would seem, at first glance, an unlikely vehicle for subversive ambitions, yet the elegy abounds in complex allusions to Roman politics both of Propertius' day and of centuries past. The god mentions *en passant* his arrival in Rome, the result of M. Fulvius Flaccus' *evocatio*[18] as he pursued—and won—victory over the Etruscans of Volsinii in 264 B.C.E. The god proclaims himself content with his translation, but disdains "an ivory temple," happy merely to gaze upon the forum (4.2.5–6); his demur (as Paola Pinotti reminds us) glances at the majestic temple on the Aventine that contained a statue of Fulvius Flaccus arrayed as *triumphator* (Festus 228L), a temple that should have been Vertumnus' proper place. Pinotti convincingly argues that the god's disdain for this temple—his rejection of a perfect venue for encomiastic reflection on Rome's past heroes and her monuments—and his allusion to Rome's historically belligerent, brutal treatment of her neighbors imply skepticism toward both militarism and its self-congratulation.[19] Book IV repeats that disenchanted perspective throughout, even in elegies 4.6 and 4.10, which superficially laud Rome's military triumphs while sowing doubts equally about these triumphs' nobility and their efficacy.[20] The very fact that Propertius organizes half his last published book around original aetiological compositions—as opposed to Catullus' single, exquisite translation from the *Aetia* to gratify a friend's request—indicates that he finds in Callimachus' poetry a particularly congenial form. When grafted onto subjective love elegy, aetiology proves flexible enough to keep tension between the political and the erotic, the objective and the subjective, alive and taut throughout Book IV.

The programmatic first poem of Book IV—whose duplicitous agenda many scholars have pointed out, though they disagree at times on the exact nature of its polarities—exemplifies the workings of these thought-provoking tensions.[21] Elegy 4.1 takes shape around stark contradiction: no sooner does Propertius propose to mirror Rome in his verse (4.1.55–57) within an aetiological agenda (commemorating *sacra diesque* and *cognomina prisca locorum*, 4.1.69) than a strange voice, belonging to the astrologer Horos, mocks this enterprise as folly. Horos claims that Apollo—Callimachus' *and* Propertius' particular patron god—looks upon the Roman poet's contemplated agenda with disfavor (4.1.73); he urges the poet to cleave to his wonted metier, erotic elegy inspired by Apollo (4.1.133–36). The poem ends abruptly without reconciling these two disparate programs; the Vertumnus elegy comes next in Book IV and increases rather than resolves the dissonance. Despite articulating an aetiology conformable to Propertius' Roman agenda, Vertumnus' garrulous statue itself embodies both poles of discourse in its protean capacity to emulate "a girl who's not hard" in silks ("non dura puella," 4.2.23) as well as a bearer of arms who has won glory (27). Its duplicity does not stop there.

Elegy 4.2 exemplifies the aetiological elegy as form par excellence in which Propertius can create a reflection of Rome and of Roman history—and that on a scale, and of a scope, unprecedented in Roman elegy. Yet Alain Deremetz argues that the Vertumnus elegy expands upon Propertius' promise to examine *cognomina prisca locorum* by aligning itself with the philosophical tradition that saw in etymology the royal road to truth. Propertius turns the derivation of "Vertumnus"—the divine name most closely associated with the *Vicus Tuscus*—into an apparently scrupulous search for reality.[22] The god rounds upon "Lying Rumor" as though its false etymologies of his name were pernicious heresies ("mendax fama, noces!"—"lying rumor, you do harm!" 4.2.19). Yet—as Deremetz also recognizes—the quintessence of himself Vertumnus reveals is that he has no quintessence: he can emulate anything. The search in his name for the core of truth round which his being crystallizes founders on the discovery of a "core" with a protean capacity always to be something else.

The same baffling double-take on origins and truth colors the other five aetiological elegies of Book IV. Three take shape around etymologies—sometimes implicit,[23] sometimes explicit—and, like the Vertumnus elegy, probe for a derivation that reveals some essential feature of the thing named. Similarly equivocal success marks their searches: in 4.10, for example, Propertius cannot decide whether *Iuppiter Feretrius* derives from *ferre*, "carry," or *ferire*, "wound," while in 4.9, Hercules' cult name *Sanctus* arises "quoniam manibus purgatum sanxerat orbem" ("because he had consecrated and purified the world with his own hands")—a derivation difficult to square with the elegy's focus on Hercules' desecration of the Bona Dea shrine. Clearly, doubt as to whether tracing the inception of a monument, a sacred ritual, or other contemporary phenomenon can reveal a significant causal link between the origins of the object under investigation and its present manifestation marks these three elegies, but such uncertainty darkens Book IV's non-etymological elegies as well. Propertius inherits that ambivalence from Callimachus—indeed, from the Alexandrian poets in general: anxiety, rather than certainty, over cultural continuity with the Greek literary past fueled the Alexandrians' intense literary interest in aetiology. Peter Bing and Graham Zanker have both recently argued that the Alexandrians treated aetiology as a peculiarly double-edged tracing of the link between past and present—a tracing that simultaneously draws attention to the abyss between past and present and attempts to bridge it.[24]

The ambivalence and uneasy sense of cultural discontinuity felt by the Alexandrians when confronting their Greek past—a past tied to another land, another political system, almost another culture—would have found a responsive chord among many of Propertius' contemporaries, as Garth Tissol has pointed out.[25] They inhabited an empire with such extended boundaries, so generous an embrace of different ethnic and cultural groups, and such fresh memories of political and social upheaval as to baffle its denizens of any sure grasp of what it meant to be Roman. That bafflement provides the necessary exegetical background (as I have argued above and also, at greater length, in chapter 2) to the fragmenting of identity noticeable in the Monobiblos' Gallus poems. But the problem of identity returns in Book IV in expanded form, encompassing not just an individual's slippery prosopography, but a nation's tenuous link to its defining foundations. While tracing the clew that promises to link Rome's past to her present and to contemporary Roman observances in a meaningful way, Propertius severs that causal link by showing the construction of the past to be fictive. Book IV, more starkly and relentlessly than anywhere else in the corpus, reveals truth to be not just irrecoverable but in fact nonexistent, unthinkable, inconceivable. Elegy 4.4, for example, takes shape around a spring claimed by the enemy Sabines from which the Roman Tarpeia draws water—a spring mysteriously accessible, and inaccessible, to her; elegy 4.9 shows the Velabra of Hercules' day to be simultaneously Tiber's everglade and dry land. Propertius describes dream-landscapes untroubled by the principle of non-contradiction, thus reinforcing the barrier to the past's recuperation announced when he declared that the present-day Roman shared nothing with Rome's past except his name (4.1.37).

Even the elegies in Book IV that evoke no aetiology fall under the shadow of doubt about the truth supposedly available in a survey of the past. Private and recent histories prove as intractable as national mythology: Cynthia (in elegy 4.5) suddenly develops a past governed by a *lena* ("bawd"), when she never had one before—a *lena* who moreover appears in the poem dead, but not really dead, insofar as she wields power over mistress and lover-poet from beyond the grave. In 4.7,

Cynthia flatly contradicts her past as recorded by Propertius by revealing his unfaithfulness and her fidelity. These logical contradictions in the elegies' "historical record" simply dramatize the fact that as subjects in language, we always *reconstruct* our past—we cannot bear direct witness to it. Neither the past nor any feature of it can be conceived until already gone—until the present displaces and opposes the past as a matter purely of *logical*, rather than temporal, priority.

The past's fictive and retrospective status flows logically from Lacan's model of the desiring subject that I have sketched earlier in this chapter, a subject aboriginally divided by language and thus made to desire the "wholeness" that alignment with various cultural signifiers appears to offer. The fissure Lacan traces in the subject's self-conception also generates an unconscious narrative—a reconstructed history—to rationalize that desire. The "split" the subject putatively sustains as a subject-in-language returns as a narrative of a lost whole, arranged in a temporal relationship of origin and succession. This narrative posits a happiness of which we have always been robbed before we knew we had it and to which we long to return. We "reread" our past to construct a narrative of a fall from grace and thereby supplant logical priority with temporal priority: out of the division and lack that imbue the present moment emerge (lost) unity and plenitude. We all construct a past congenial, if melancholy, to recall: thus our *present* creates our *past* as a retrospective narrative to account for who we are and what we want. The seemingly clear distinction between past and present blurs and nearly disappears under the force of rigorously scrutinizing that rereading.

A PRELIMINARY TEST CASE: THE GALLUS POEMS

In the following pages, I shall argue that the fourth book's distinctive features point to the political-erotic subject's incoherence as its chief theme. To elucidate the import of its anomalies with maximum precision, I have focused upon the elegies in Book IV most clearly preoccupied with the logical impasses that bedevil the construction of those seeming polar opposites, sex and the state—all poems that, noncoincidentally, prominently feature feminine voices. (Lacan especially helps us here, insofar as he construes Woman both as gender position and figure for conceptual deadlock; I shall explain further below.) I have accordingly devoted chapters individually to the following elegies: 3 (Arethusa's letter to Lycotas), 4 (Tarpeia's betrayal of Rome), 5 (Acanthis' hetaira-catechism), 7 (Cynthia's return from the dead), 8 (Cynthia's return from Lanuvium), 9 (Hercules' attacks on Cacus and the Bona Dea shrine), and 11 (Cornelia's defense before the Underworld).

I do not, however, begin with the fourth book, but rather with the first—with the Gallus poems—in order to lay out in brief compass the general themes of my project before essaying the individual poems of Book IV at greater length. While that might have been done by drawing on almost any of Propertius' books, the Monobiblos' problematic structure makes it particularly germane: its apparent sharp division between erotic emphasis in 1.1–1.20 and political emphasis in

1.21–1.22 raises *in nuce* the same problem of coherence that Book IV's thematic oscillation between love and the state poses, a problem irresolvable by any approach that sees *amor* and *Roma* as antitheses. The Gallus poems also demonstrate Book IV's focus on problematic subjectivity and the logical consequences thereof to be rooted in Propertius' earliest thought.

When applied to the Monobiblos' six poems that prominently feature the tantalizingly elusive "Gallus" (1.5, 1.10, 1.13, 1.20, 1.21, and 1.22), Lacan's model of the divided subject allows us to take account of the way Propertius' text "fractures" precisely where it leads us, as readers, to expect a unified subject; where the text reneges on the promise, it forces us to rethink our expectations' conceptual premises.[26] The series deploys rapidly displaced images, each linked to a single name: "Gallus" designates a callous womanizer, one woman's devoted slave, a pederast near foundering in his affair, a pro- and an anti-Augustan soldier. Any logical relation between images remains unarticulated. These poems' details resist summation under the history of a coherent "Gallus."[27] Equally, they resist clean separation one from another, so as to produce discrete "Galluses." The Gallus poems thwart the smooth coherence of their protagonist(s): details of these elegies, no matter how apportioned among semiotic histories, cannot conjure up any coherent, discrete subject (or subjects). Textual evidence strongly urges identifying the "Gallus" of 1.5, 1.10, 1.13, and 1.20 with Cornelius Gallus, Augustus' soldier and elegiac poet-lover of "Lycoris"—the very Gallus Vergil has dying for his mistress' love in *Eclogue* 10.[28] But Propertius stresses Gallus' "nobility" and aristocratic "ancient deathmasks of the ancestors" (1.5.23–24), when we know that Cornelius Gallus was a mere provincial knight who could claim neither. At the same time, the verses that attribute such marks of high rank to 1.20's "Gallus" are virtually quoted from Cornelius Gallus' own work.[29] Moreover, though 1.21's "Gallus" fights *against* Augustus, his age, military status, and dying devotion to a woman all curiously align him with Cornelius Gallus. Propertius teases and frustrates us by evoking, then denying, the numinous biography of his principal elegiac predecessor. Why?

These overlapping-but-not-quite-alignable "Galluses" eliminate the possibility of drawing *any* coherent subject out of these poems; they thus figure a resistance to the promise of a coherent self with which ideology procures our institutional loyalty. Propertius' "Gallus" demonstrates the ultimate incommensurability between the subject's being and the signifier that represents him within any discursive network—precisely the gap that his ideological commitments seek, and persistently fail, to close. Yet Propertius does not thus interrogate only Augustan ideology; more radically, he scrutinizes the very foundations of ideology per se, and of its sinister empty promises.[30]

Seen in this light, the political dimension of Propertius' work actually parallels his erotic project—which helps explain why judicious attention to his verse has burgeoned during the last two centuries. The age to whose thought we are the most immediate heirs offered Propertius his first sympathetic listeners in almost two millennia precisely because his elegies mirrored the nineteenth century's own deep skepticism—a loss of faith to which the efforts of Marx, Nietzsche, Darwin, and Freud heavily contributed, and that has left its deep impression on contemporary thinkers from Heidegger to Deleuze.[31] The martial conflicts of Propertius' era had ushered in a similar pyrrhonism: the Roman Republic's chaotic final years witnessed wars between Rome and her Italian allies, armed conflicts among Roman citizens, and the jockeying of the powerful for supreme control of the state—events that radically undermined faith in the ability of human beings to will or reason their way to "the good" either individually or collectively.[32] Propertius' poetry bears witness not only to this agony of disbelief, but to Augustus Caesar's concerted attempt in the early Empire to paper over such doubts via his neo-conservative moral and political program for Rome. Comparative peace and government radically reconceived follow the upheaval of the Republic's last years, but so does a project of social regeneration: Augustanism represents an attempt to synthesize an all-embracing mythology to cement the social and political framework that supports the emperor's reign, and to knit up what previous decades of upheaval had unraveled.[33] Hence the emperor's unprecedented interest in fostering poets who might produce helpful propaganda; no political leader before him needed a Maecenas to offer artists patronage while suggesting patriotic themes for their work.[34]

From the perspective offered by the Gallus poems—haunted by their fragmentary ghosts of lover, soldier, romantic, cynic—the emperor Augustus emerges less the Propertian Antichrist (as prevailing critical wisdom would have it) than as the lover's uncanny double, insofar as Augustus represents a desperate and determined effort to make "wholeness" possible, to locate a redeemed and healed subject in a purified, coherent Roman state. The success or failure of the *princeps'* enterprise—even the ruthlessness with which he pursued it—do not negate the symmetry: the impossible object for which lovers and emperors strive makes both bankrupt idealists.[35]

CITIZENS AND LOVERS

My brief sketch of the mechanism whereby the divided subject strives for identity raises a question: why does assimilation to a signifier never really "work" in the sense of permanently producing a unified, coherent subject? Even if the subject is inherently divided, why can that rift not be made trivial beneath the organizing influence of the signifier in which he places his faith? To answer that question, I must expand my schema to address "bad faith" on the side of the signifier as well as the subject; logical incoherence intrinsic to language equally prevents his lasting integration. The signifiers "Man," "Roman," "good lover," "good citizen" attain meaning (as do all signifiers) not positively by their content, but negatively by their difference from other elements of the system. Yet in determining their meaning, we are caught at the conjunction of two contradictory rules of language. We must simultaneously assume the inexhaustibility of meaning—that another signifier will always come along to change retroactively the meaning of all that have come before—and presuppose the totality of "all other signifiers" as the milieu necessary to the meaning of one. Language demands—impossibly—that we determine the totality of an infinite progression.[36]

The grouping of terms into implied binaries regularly obscures this paradoxical necessity by narrowing the field of interpretation: "Man" comes to mean what it does construed as the *opposite* of "Woman," "Roman" as the *opposite* of "non-Roman," and so on.[37] Yet the paradox of the two rules of language I have just cited shows that this move is, strictly speaking, logically illegitimate: another signifier can and will inevitably come into play to change the relation between the original two ("Man's" clean opposition to "Woman," for example, wavers and blurs under the gravitational pull of such terms as "transvestite," "homosexual," "hermaphrodite," "Amazon," and the like). The signifying system cannot ever constitute itself as coherent and closed, a collection of signifiers to which nothing can be added and whose relations to one another are therefore fixed; consequently, the signifiers with which the subject identifies are as riven by doubt as he or she is.

The sexual dyad Man/Woman, as the "master-case" of incoherent binaries (particularly for Propertius' erotic poetry), demands to be probed first in order to trace exactly how it exemplifies the production, and the failures, of meaning and identity. (The dyad Roman/non-Roman next receives attention as a parallel, secondary case, one Roman cultural configurations intimately connect to the opposition Man/Woman.) We must note, first of all, that we do not confront a neutral pair: "Man" is the privileged term, a fact that extends the meaning of "Man" from "male of the species" to "human being per se." Ancient thought from philosophy to biology to ethics asymmetrically constitutes Man and Woman as universal "norm" and particular "deviation" respectively. Plato, for example, traces the origin of women's souls to the souls of men who have proven deficient in reason; Aristotle views the male as the normative example of the human species, the female as a "deformed" man; Cicero considers moral excellence (*virtus*) properly to belong to the man (*vir*), seeing etymology as evidence of a more fundamental truth; the highest praise Valerius Maximus and Seneca can offer a woman's conduct is that it shows her to have "a man's spirit" or to lack all feminine flaws.[38] Examples could be multiplied, but the instances cited make sufficiently clear the overall pattern of creating Man as a whole, a universal, precisely by positing Woman as exclusion.

The Pythagorean table of opposites exemplifies this operation in a particularly pure form that, though far removed from Propertius in time, reflects intellectual scaffolding essential to his poetry. Genevieve Lloyd summarizes the table's basic conceptual dichotomy:

> The Pythagoreans saw the world as a mixture of principles associated with determinate form, seen as good, and others associated with formlessness—the unlimited, irregular or disorderly—which were seen as bad or inferior. There were ten such contrasts in the table: limit/unlimited, odd/even, one/many, right/left, male/female, rest/motion, straight/curved, light/dark, good/bad, square/oblong. Thus "male" and "female," like the other contrasted terms, did not here function as straightfor-

wardly descriptive classifications. "Male," like the other terms on its side of the table, was construed as superior to its opposite; and the basis for this superiority was its association with the primary Pythagorean contrast between form and formlessness.[39]

The Pythagorean table of opposites expresses with especial clarity not only the set of moves that produces Man as the subject of thought, but also sketches the conceptual basis of that construction's collapse. Fundamentally, the table is a peculiarly terse signifying system, with the consequence that each term attains meaning only differentially; none can gain a purchase on some pre-symbolic grounding and claim transcendent status. While the binary arrangement and implied hierarchy of the Pythagorean system appears, at first glance, to circumvent groundlessness, this move to privilege one half the terms as normative inherently dooms itself. For example, the Pythagoreans align Man with all the elements grouped under the implied rubric "determinate form," Woman with the undesirable deviations that accrue to "formlessness"; yet She thereby becomes the circumscribing conceptual boundary necessary to his definition as norm, ideal. He, the supposedly prior term from which She "deviates," depends on her deviation for his self-definition.

The intellectual moves of the Pythagoreans find a canny mimicry in Lacan's work, which deliberately draws upon the most offensive representations of Woman as lacking to construct Her conceptualization, but systematically exposes these as attempts to inscribe the conceptual shortcomings of pure binarity onto Woman. Lacan notes that all the failings of cultural symbolization systems (in Lacanian shorthand, the Symbolic) accrue to Woman's side of the account; yet he also perceives that, ipso facto, She exposes the Symbolic's shortcomings, not least because it can produce no cogent account of Her.[40] Woman thus prevents Man's smooth integration as universal, paradigmatic being; in Slavoj Žižek's words, "Woman *qua* object is nothing but the materialization of a certain bar in the Symbolic universe."[41] She is posited as the site of all that Man disowns because it will not conform to strict rules of rationality, order, logic—posited as "not-all," in Lacanian terms, a heterogeny of phenomena that cannot be grasped on the basis of a single, coherent principle.

From this perspective, the bafflingly contradictory characterizations of Woman in the Propertian corpus conform to an odd rationale, beginning with Cynthia's infinite variety that unfolds with particularly dizzying rapidity in the *Monobiblos*: she is now chilly and aloof "pure young woman" (*casta puella*, 1.1), now fashionable coquette (1.2), now faithful wifely companion (1.3), now demimondaine vampire (1.5), now common greedy doxy (1.8), now grand courtesan (1.11).[42] Even in Book IV, where Woman fully exfoliates into a wide spectrum of women's voices from every stratum of Roman life—faithful wife (4.3), aristocratic matron (4.11), beggared procuress (4.5), Vestal Virgin (4.4)—multiplying the *dramatis personae* does not simplify the problem. Rather, it exposes the roots of Woman's paradox in Roman culture's conceptual shortcomings; each of these portraits centers upon a crucial contradiction that organizes women's lives precisely because they face a symbolization system whose categories of thought cannot adequately evaluate them.

The dyad Roman/non-Roman is a parallel, secondary, case of binarity's incoherence, one that comes to grief in exactly the same ways Man/Woman does. The category "Roman" also finds itself embarrassingly dependent upon its "rejected," "inferior" counterpart, "non-Roman," and accordingly finds it equally impossible to constitute itself as universal paradigm. Propertius' poetry consistently plays out the consequences of this unreliability: wherever the barbarian manifests itself (as a scented enemy commander in 4.3, or Antony's motley Egyptian forces in 4.6, or the monstrous aboriginal cattle-thief Cacus in 4.9), the line between Roman and non-Roman becomes strangely porous and flexible, the grounds for defining either side slipperier and slipperier, until no clear, fixed, stable distinction can be drawn between one category and the other.

Indeed, an implied table of opposites similar to the Pythagorean categories whose internal contradictions we examined above organizes Propertius' poetry, a table broadly arranged along the twin axes "Man/Woman" and "Roman/non-Roman." Yet this taxonomy of contrasts appears precisely as an object of interrogation rather than obeisance, as Propertius' pattern of use shows. This emerges most clearly in the famous Tarpeia elegy (4.4): a series of images organized around water in its ritual and mundane associations with women subsumes the contrasts of the elegy's drama—Roman/Sabine, chastity/sexuality, loyalty/betrayal, truth/deceit—beneath the elemental oppositions solid/liquid and male/female. Yet Propertius' schema (in a far more principled fashion than is displayed in the Pythagorean table) reveals the putative "superior" term to be dependent on principles embodied by the subordinate, contingent, "inferior" term, which is thereby transformed; understanding of the marginal or deviant term becomes a condition of understanding the supposedly prior term. For example, the Vestal Virgin Tarpeia's trip to fetch water from a fateful spring produces an encounter with the Sabine commander Tatius and a passion for which she "betrays" Rome and her vows—but it also (albeit indirectly) begets Rome as Propertius' contemporaries know it, a city expanded and enriched via intermarriage by a dual Sabine-Roman heritage, as Tarpeia herself had proposed. Moreover, Tatius murderously deceives Tarpeia because she is a "traitor"; the poem ironically construes his deception as the benchmark of his masculine honor ("neque enim sceleri dedit hostis honorem"—"for not even as an enemy did he give honor to crime," 4.4.89). The very duplicity that the poem's metaphors associate with women's "fluid" instability, and that Tatius abhors in Tarpeia, founds *his* honor. Propertius anticipates Lacan here, in demonstrating that the incoherence of the Symbolic's (systematically jaundiced) account of Woman exposes its own conceptual shortcomings.

WOMAN AND *ROMANITAS*

It remains for us to trace precisely how the perplexities of the two binaries under examination, Man/Woman and Roman/non-Roman, intertwine, and the consequences that unfold from their functional failure. Žižek's definition of Woman as "a certain bar in the Symbolic universe" follows logically from the account given above of Her function as the deadlock that reveals the Symbolic's deficiencies; the gloss also, and importantly, makes this bar a function of signification, rather than of anatomy, or even of individual subjects per se. As we have seen, the Gallus poems of the Monobiblos unfold the problem of subjectivity—the impossibility of smoothly integrating, as an identity, the various parts of being in relation to a signifier—so as to illustrate paradigmatically the gaps and omissions in symbolization that Lacan gathers beneath the term "Woman." Though Cynthia initially appears as a disordering principle about to leap from harrowing Propertius to unmanning Gallus, the chaos of which she is the avatar extends far beyond her appearances in this puzzling series of elegies. Woman, as a concept, exceeds any particular representations of women, and enters the Gallus poems less as a namable female (Cynthia or whoever) than as conceptual deadlock.

The central conceptual deadlock that organizes the Gallus poems turns on the (re)definition of the citizen-subject within the Symbolic universe of Rome, especially as radically changed by the Republic's yielding to a de facto monarchy under Augustus. Focused as these poems are on defining the citizen-subject, they raise the questions, What is *Romanitas?* How is it constituted? How do subjects align (or fail or refuse to align) themselves with it? Under the pressure of these questions, the dyad Roman/non-Roman begins to slip and slide in Propertius' elegies in the same vertiginous ways as Man/Woman, a slippage comprehended by Lacan's magisterial pronouncement, "there is no sexual relation."[43] His dictum points to the fact that no complementary relationship exists between the two elements of *any* signifying dyad that could guarantee national, sexual, racial, or any other identity. The external boundary that divides Roman from non-Roman, Man from Woman, is thus reflected inward as an internal limit: the set of qualitative conditions that defines an object as itself become its own unattainable—because ungrounded—Ideal, the ever-receding vision of what it *ought to* (but never actually *can*) become. The key concepts of nationality and gender consequently always "go wrong" with respect to themselves. Searching for the true embodiment of "Roman" or of "Man" ultimately reveals that *no one* is Roman enough or man enough; every empirical Roman male contains something "unRoman" and "unmanly."[44] Book IV illuminates this impasse—the logical extrapolation of premises laid out in the Monobiblos, that the subject can never truly "heal" his perceived internal lack—by constructing various versions of Roman masculinity that curiously dissolve into asthenic parodies of themselves. The dedicated soldier Lycotas who fights on the empire's frontiers (4.3), the suavely successful rival who "cuts out" Propertius with Cynthia (4.8), and Hercules who "civilizes" the world (4.9) end as battlefield sensualist, aging pathic, and boastful transvestite respectively. Book IV's elaboration of *Romanitas,* like that of the Monobiblos, is rooted in the signifying relations that govern the subject, but it aligns the intractability of defining nationality even more intimately with that of defining gender. Tracing the origins of Roman cultural observances plots the *longue durée* of doomed efforts to find Being sustaining either sex or polity.

LAW

As the conceptual foundation of the state, Law expresses with particular pertinence the desire central to the efforts described above to extract stable meaning from pure difference, and to miscarriages of that desire.[45] Law—both as formal legal code and, more generally, as social constraint—runs aground upon the same conceptual impasse as the conceptualization of Man and *Romanitas:* it lacks an anchor for thought outside its own signifying system. The Propertian corpus summarizes this lack in the figure of Woman, who marks where Law's "objectivity" betrays its own narrow vision.

That putative objectivity has its roots in a particular phase of Roman history: Bruce Frier has documented a shift during the late Republic toward the notion of autonomous Law, toward Law envisioned as a cross-referenced and mutually defining set of rules.[46] Law so conceived is at base a system of signification: the meaning of each of its elements depends ultimately and solely upon that element's relation to all others in the system. Any statute or principle cited to legitimate another requires in its turn reference to yet another rule behind it, and so on, in an infinite regress. Ultimately juridical reasoning comes to rest in the logical opacity of desire: such-and-such is prescribed or proscribed because "it is the will of . . . [the gods, Nature, the emperor, the people, the senate]"—a will from which there is no appeal and for which there is no justification. Law turns forever upon its own axis, with nothing outside itself to found its demands.

Propertius dramatizes the ways in which Law fails by recording its particular inability to grapple with the lives of the women who appear on his pages: Tarpeia, the traitor for love who is herself cruelly betrayed (4.4); Acanthis, the realist *lena* touched by unexpectedly eloquent romantic visions (4.5); Cynthia, the revenant who in death exposes her lover's martyred history of their affair as a self-serving lie (4.7); Cornelia, the exemplary wife and mother embittered by how little she has to show for her virtuous life (4.11). Each of these women demonstrates the truth of Lacan's maxim that Law is instinct with "enjoyment" (*jouissance*)—that is, with non-meaning as such, being ungrounded in any transcendent reality.[47] When practiced at its purest—failing, in its magisterial indifference, to grapple with significant particulars—Law evinces an impossible cruelty and sadism that falls hardest upon those who, like women, constitute its blindspot.

SUBVERSION

Yet even as the scrutiny of Law finds Woman lacking—mentally, morally, or biologically "deficient"—Propertius elucidates the subversive power of Her presumed defects. When, for example, Cynthia returns unexpectedly from an excursion with a wealthy admirer to find Propertius dallying with other women (4.8), she not only turns her anger on him (ignoring her own betrayal), but blames his innocent slave, Lygdamus. The elegy seemingly assigns stereotypically feminine "hysteria" and "overreaction" to Cynthia; yet that misogynistic reading ill explains her lover's unbounded admiration for her imperiousness. He describes her, in fact, as if she were a conquering general; how can that pinnacle of the Roman military ethos, the ideal citizen-subject, sort with her "hysteria"?[48] It can if we consider that the subject emerges precisely insofar as the relation between cause and effect becomes unaccountable: we can never ascertain in advance the way the causes that determine us will exert their power over us, and to that extent we escape pure determinism (without which even the general's most virtuously disciplined actions mean nothing, because they lack the ethical dimension that deliberate action—involving choice or assent—grants).[49] The "irrational" Cynthia fascinates Propertius as an ironic version of that highest of Roman values, *libertas:* her feminine "unreason" constitutes a gesture of refusal, a refusal to be inserted in the "proper" nexus of causes and effects, and points to Woman, not Man, as the (Roman) subject par excellence.[50]

Feminine resistance also figures in more delicate structural elements, such as the suspense of an ending. We never learn, for example, the results of Cornelia's Underworld "trial" of her life that would determine her place in Hades (4.11); that silence indicts the very tribunal that presumes to judge her as unworthy to do so. But Propertius also works with broader and subtler patterns, sowing arresting, sensuous, counter-logical, and non-narrative details in many of Book IV's elegies; these details resist the linear pull of narrative to get to the conclusion's determination of meaning, with all its moral and normative implications. These elegies exploit every opportunity their stories' traditions offer for shock and dilatory pleasure in color, odor, sound at the expense of logically and efficiently unfolding a narrative focused on the glories of *Romanitas*. Sensual pleasure and pain emerge here on the side of the feminine in seductive and gruesome vignettes of ornament, flowers, slavery, and torture, concentrating on what the elegiac tradition too often distorts or dismisses. In 4.7, for example, Cynthia's badly-charred ghost appears to Propertius, reproaching him for her cheap and hasty obsequies, and for enduring his new mistress Chloris' appropriation of Cynthia's goods along with the torture of her faithful female slaves. Nonetheless, Cynthia's own tawdry end affords some unarticulated empathy with Chloris, who clearly sees Propertius' fickleness and provides against it, albeit with theft and cruelty: significantly, the ghostly Cynthia terrorizes Propertius, but not her successor. Cynthia describes a Hades that never truly resolves any woman's fate: the apparent necessity for judgment dissolves in a wealth of colorful details and in repetition without resolution. Her Underworld—a netherworld East full of exotic music, dance, and worship as well as beautiful condemned queens who circle, but never meet, their fates—refuses the tendentious burden of judging women. Its imaginative setting subverts the laws of the masculinist "real" world of Rome.

Such anarchic pleasure also shows up in the poetry's often extravagant verbal effects. Homophony, outrageous puns, seemingly meaningful sound patterns that lead to nothing but resist linear construction of the text register the workings of what Lacan calls *lalangue* ("llanguage"), the extra-linguistic effects of language that accrue to sound, rhythm, and repetition. In 4.9, for example, an elaborate rhyme scheme threads through the story of Hercules' encounter with Cacus, linking the pentameter endings; another repeated sound pattern weaves its way through the initial syllables of the words included in the final two distichs (a hymn to Hercules). At the level of form, the poem escapes linearity, with the Cacus episode's rhyme scheme referring to the final hymn's similar formalization, and vice versa. The elaborate sound patterns suggest a circular reading that opposes the narrative's straightforward advancement. By setting up a meaning effect counter to the linear narrative, *lalangue* resists the end of the poem's being taken as closure and thereby forever suspends the "moral of the story"—appropriate to the fact that Hercules' hypermasculine heroism in the first half of the poem yields, in the second half, to his boasting of his transvestite past when he dressed in women's clothing and performed women's tasks as Queen Omphale's slave. The hymn's concluding praise for the "Hallowed Father's" macho subjugation of a wicked world, coming hard upon the heels of this boast, oddly jars; it sends the reader back to search—vainly—for the chain of logic whereby this model for Roman masculinity and heroism strayed into such strange territory.

Thus far, I have detailed the conceptual impasses that accrue to subjects-in-language; the elegant ways such aporia is beguiled must also be scrutinized. After all, despite all the inherent impossibilities I have elucidated above, political and social systems and the subjects within those systems do function somehow. How do they manage? With stratagems that veil the terrifying groundlessness of subjectivity. For example, fantasies that implicitly allege the existence of a sexual relation that is forbidden rather than impossible figure prominently in Propertius' poetry (though deftly exposed *as* fantasies). Lacan labels such fantasies "courtly love," which he explains as "a highly refined way of making up for the absence of the sexual relationship, by feigning that we are the ones who erect an obstacle thereto."[51] The Propertian lover regularly and elegantly defers or abjures the encounter with his Lady, fostering the illusion that, if only this or that barrier did not exist, perfect bliss would be within his grasp; his way "just happens" to be barred by greedy *lenae* (Acanthis in 4.5), untimely death (Cynthia's in 4.7), wealthy rivals (a dandified *fainéant* with fast wheels in 4.8). Even the fortunate rival himself, invidious figure though he is, helps to represent enjoyment as forbidden rather than impossible, insofar as he constitutes a seeming exception to the rule that enjoyment is forever deferred: he *does* appear to attain the heaven of bliss that is the mistress, as the poor poet-lover never can. Cynthia sports the rival's lovebites (4.5), she writes him letters (4.5), she leaves town with him (4.8). The poet-lover leaves her comparatively unmarked and unmoved.

PAPERING OVER THE GAPS: *OBJET A*

All of the preceding stratagems cover over a break in a causal chain by implicitly alleging that the sexual relation *does* exist and *is* possible (though barred), as against Lacan's formulae of sexuation.[52] These formulae emphasize non-complementarity between the sexes, essentially saying that no relationship exists between what the loved one possesses and the lover lacks: desired object and desire can *not* be assimilated to cause and effect. Yet love flourishes somehow: what bridges the gap between what the lover wants from the beloved and what the latter has to give? Lacan answers, "*objet a*" (short for *objet autre*, "object-other")—the mysterious object that is "in the beloved more than the beloved." The lover loves something in the beloved of which the latter is unaware and cannot name (I can never articulate the exact cause of someone else's love for me). This mysterious "x" factor that is "in you more than you" putatively explains love—and hate—as a function of something other than, more than, the sum of the beloved's (or the enemy's) immanent properties.

Propertius evokes *objet a* early in the corpus—most clearly in a poem such as 2.3, where he finds himself at a loss to name exactly what about Cynthia sparks his love—but he develops its implications fully for both love and hate in Book IV. For example, he now provides his mistress with a *lena* (4.5), whose voice, like Cynthia's, speaks in his poetry after the bawd's death—a retrospective rewriting of himself, given that Cynthia never had a procuress before. Yet while his puzzling association of mistress and bawd through their post-mortem poems jars with his previous history of the affair, it elucidates the degree to which fantasy founds the lover's emotions. Even with her famous beauty eroded into grotesquerie by the funeral pyre, Cynthia continues to fascinate Propertius (4.7)—and, as an exact logical corollary, her *lena* Acanthis inspires his virulent hatred, though her social slide from Cynthia's privileged confidante to impoverished and dying beggar has changed all her attributes and rendered her powerless to harm him. What he loved and hated never lived in the objects of his passions, and so does not die with them.

Book IV takes *objet a*'s root function—to cover over a gap in causality—to its logical conclusions so that it ultimately transcends relations between couples. In 4.11, for example, Cornelia repeatedly links her chastity to the exemplary *Romanitas* of her ancestors and to the integrity of Rome itself under her husband's term as censor, as if her body's integrity (as *objet a*) were a "cause" that could homeopathically guarantee the desired "effect" of social integrity by spinning the fantasy of a perfectly harmonious, integrated polity.

On a lighter note, the operation of *objet a* also helps explain why Propertius prefaces a story of his groveling humiliation before Cynthia's wrath (4.8) with an apparently unconnected description of religious rites at Lanuvium. Juno's sacred snake eats food ritually offered by the Lanuvians and guarantees a fertile agricultural year, if the young women who make the offering truly are virgins. The religious portent fits the subject into the harmony of the divine universe; through the ritual, the devotee addresses the divine and the divine responds. A contingent effect (the year's fertility) is reconstrued as an "effect" indexed to the "cause's" (the ritual offering's) perfection, thereby offering the comforting illusion that an order beyond human control nonetheless—on occasion and if the exactly appropriate way can be devised to circumvent the intervening barriers—answers the petitioner. Propertius thus shapes Heaven as the divine hypostasis of courtly love's inscrutable Lady, with the religious devotee as anxiously petitioning lover—a sacred reflection, albeit ironic, of the mechanism behind his own "woman trouble," based as it is on steadfastly denying that "there is no sexual relation."

THE PLAN OF THIS BOOK

My juxtaposition of end and beginning of Propertius' artistic career has its roots in the critical tradition: seeing Books I and IV as a significant pair emerges as a slender but persistent thread within Propertius studies. W. A. Camps implicitly recognized the books' correspondence by the order in which he published his four-volume commentary: he began with Book I in 1961, but then skipped directly to Book IV (1965).[53] He remarks of his anomalous approach to the series of Propertius' works that his "edition of Book IV of Propertius was conceived as a complement to my edition of Book I (C.U.P. 1961)," intimating that the two books, each representing such "a distinct and interesting phase of the poet's activity," are more like one another than like the comparatively homogeneous Books II and III.[54] Paolo Fedeli duplicated Camps' anomalous transit in the opposite direction, first publishing an edition and commentary on Book IV in 1965, then turning his attention to the Monobiblos in 1980. Fedeli offers even less explanation than Camps for this oscillation between last and first, but W. R. Nethercut compensates for both scholars' taciturnity by elucidating the structural and thematic correspondences—centered on sharply juxtaposed vignettes of passion, mortality, and history—that mutually refer the one elegiac book to the other.[55] He particularly concentrates on the symmetries between the poet's significantly positioned "last words" on these subjects in both books:

> We ... come to the last poems [of Book IV] and find in their position and mood a counterpart to the ending of Book One, a review of Rome's contacts with her neighbors in the peninsula (1.21–22 and 4.10), an exhortation from one who is lost to one who is to carry on (1.21, Gallus to the passerby; 4.11, Cornelia to Paullus), and, amid death, the solitude of the bereaved (Propertius in 1.22, Paullus in 4.11) though others remain. Both the end of Book One (1.22) and the final elegy of Book Four look to the earth for compensation: in 1.22, Umbria's rich hills cover the bones of those who died at Perusia; in 4.11.100, Cornelia entrusts restoration for her life to the "kindly earth" (*grata rependit humus*). In this way Book Four appears most truly the work of Propertius himself, a new rendering, on the larger canvass appropriate to his years as a craftsman, of the achievement of his first book.[56]

In all fairness, it must be pointed out that where scholars see Book IV as a return to Book I, they merely follow a direction of reading that Propertius himself explicitly signposted. In Book IV, the *lena* Acanthis returns to the Monobiblos as exegete, quoting the opening lines of the book: "quid iuvat ornato procedere, vita, capillo / et tenuis Coa veste movere sinus?" ("what avails it, my life, to appear in public with carefully dressed hair, and to create gauzy billows in Coan dress?") 4.5.55–56 =

1.2.1–2, the first distich from the first non-programmatic poem in Book I). She reinterprets the distich not as a fine indifference to materialism, but as an impoverished lover's attempt to get something (his mistress' favors) for nothing (no gifts of costly adornment). Acanthis' quote means nothing unless read against its original appearance in the Monobiblos—her whole "hetaira-catechism" advising Cynthia how to provide for herself from wealthier lovers' gifts lacks point unless set against the tug-of-war between Cynthia's interests and Propertius' that is first and most sharply engaged in Book I.[57] The direct quote and thematic repetitions cast 4.5 as a "feminine" rereading of Book I, in the Lacanian, epistemological sense of "feminine": a persistent skepticism that calls into doubt masculine certitude and "reason."[58] Acanthis questions the lover's arrogant assumption that his mistress should count her financial security well lost for love. Yet the agenda Acanthis adumbrates exceeds the bounds of elegy 4.5: as Camps and Fedeli sensed, and Nethercut articulates, Book IV consistently calls upon us as readers to return and sift Book I again—chiefly to reevaluate (as I shall argue in succeeding chapters) the assumptions *behind* the Monobiblos' poetry, as the most energetic of Propertius' previous engagements with the sexual (non)relation and its unsettling implications, and to bring to the task a more disenchanted perspective. The following chapters strive to answer that call.

AN OUTLINE OF THE CHAPTERS THAT FOLLOW

I append the following brief summaries of the various chapters, so that the broad sequence of ideas, and the directions in which it develops, will be apparent at a glance.

Chapter 2, as described above, focuses on the Gallus poems of the Monobiblos and their curiously inconsistent protagonist(s); it examines Lacan's model of divided subjectivity and the way in which the model aligns apparently antithetical spheres—such as the erotic and the political—along a single conceptual axis. This preliminary foray lays the groundwork for examining Book IV's even more elaborate apparent disjunctions, and for seeing how they unfold nonetheless according to a logical pattern. The chapter scrutinizes ideology's appeals to the fractured subject's desire to be "healed" of division and lack, appeals based on offering illusory wholeness via commitment to culturally freighted icons of identity. Chapter 2 also surveys the unsettling historical conditions that obtained during the transition from Roman Republic to Empire and that strengthened the appeal of such ideological lures, while they rendered the goal of "wholeness" even more manifestly impossible.

Chapter 3 scrutinizes the Arethusa poem (4.3), discovering a paradox in the Roman matron's descriptions of her own lonely, industrious life and her soldier-husband's martial campaigns: the Roman ideal of the disciplined life to which they both hew contains the seeds of its very opposites—decadence and luxury. The attempts to unify and pacify the empire (attempts that both husband and wife serve) lead to contact with external *and* internal forces of decadence, luxury, "evil," that undermine the ethical consensus on which the empire is based. Similarly, trying to unite the world under a single empire paradoxically scatters Roman citizens as they defend and colonize the four corners of the earth; each must accordingly be represented by documents rather than being present in the flesh. Arethusa's marriage, for example, is reduced to letters exchanged over great distances between herself and her husband on his tours of duty. By contrast, the map over which she pores nightly in order to trace his movements optimistically displays the world as unified beneath the conquering gaze of Rome as the world's center and master—a vision of the world markedly at odds with Arethusa's experience of her long-distance marriage. The letter and the map thus embody the historical specificity of some of the divisions that Augustan ideology offered to heal, and underline the impossibility of that healing.

Chapter 4 expands on the idea of an invisible but ineluctable commerce between apparent antitheses (such as the Roman ideas of "good" and "evil") in examining the Tarpeia poem (4.4). Tarpeia's "betraying" Rome to the Sabines, for example, turns out to be a *felix culpa* responsible for the hybrid strengths of contemporary Rome, while her "honorable" judge and executioner Tatius reveals his own duplicity when he accepts her traitorous gift of Rome but punishes her for giving it to him. The poem demonstrates the epistemological falsity of the Symbolic's habit of dividing the world into paired, mutually exclusive opposites. Such pairs are shown to be, in the final analysis, conceptually untenable: the very distinctions that make up the case against the "traitress" Tarpeia—loyalty/betrayal, Roman/non-Roman, enemy/friend—collapse under the weight of their own instability.

Chapter 5, by analyzing the Acanthis poem (4.5), carries forward the idea of the Symbolic's inadequacy in order to focus specifically on its representation of Woman. In this poem, the extremes of Woman's representation (as beloved or hated, beautiful or ugly, innocent or intriguing) prove to be surprisingly interchangeable, because each extreme rests equally on fantasy. Propertius cannot logically articulate why he hates the bawd Acanthis, even when she has ceased to influence Cynthia against him; neither can he can explain rationally why Cynthia fascinates him (a fascination that persists—as 4.7 shows—even when she returns from the grave, burnt and horrific). Bawd and mistress are represented as revolving around a mysterious "x" factor at the core of each woman's being, a fantasy object that draws his undying hatred and undying love respectively, and that promises (falsely) to bridge the gaps in the Symbolic's reason by magically (and quite illogically) "explaining" either his hatred or his love.

Chapter 6 examines Cynthia's return from the dead (4.7), as chronicled in the poem that forms the thematic and numerical "epicenter" of Book IV. Weaving together and expanding upon several thematic threads prominent in the "feminine" perspectives of Book IV's other elegies, elegy 4.7 refocuses the idea of the Symbolic's inadequate representation of Woman specifically upon the deficiencies of elegiac poetry—its inability to render justice either to the representation of Woman or of Her desire. Cynthia reveals a demimondaine world of economic necessity far grittier and more precarious than elegiac feminine ideals disclose. Her tawdry, impoverished death confirms the idea that elegy's ideals of feminine self-abnegation, that would have the mistress place love and loyalty before economic survival, are hopelessly unrealistic; her end and her speech challenge the reader to review not only Propertius' own work but the whole elegiac genre with greater skepticism.

Chapter 7, by contemplating the Lanuvium poem (4.8), expands examination of the unreason behind elegiac expectations of the mistress and her behavior into a general analysis of the asymmetry and illogic that characterize relations between the sexes. In this poem, Propertius' inability logically to match cause and effect mirrors Cynthia's capricious behavior. He miscalculates when she will return from visiting Lanuvium's annual fertility rite and so allows her to catch him philandering with two female rivals; she waxes furious upon discovering his betrayal, even though her out-of-town foray was itself the pretext for dalliance with another man. Each lover's illogic unfolds in a way that illustrates not so much his or her own personal fecklessness, but how sex is (in Lacan's thinking) "the stumbling block of sense." Lacan redefines Man and Woman as neither biological nor anatomical entities, but rather as two different modes of logical impasse. *Ab origine,* these impasses map onto relations between the sexes the limits where reason fails, a failure captured in ancient as well as modern folklore about lovers' irrationality (which 4.8's slapstick conundrums compellingly exemplify). The poem also aligns love's roots in the realm beyond reason with religion's extra-rationality, so that Lanuvium's fertility ritual, and its faith in a realm outside human calculation (albeit a faith curiously touched with cynicism), provides an appropriate backdrop for the Cynthia-Propertius affair.

Chapter 8 looks at the Hercules poem (4.9), broadening the idea of asymmetry and illogic at work between seemingly "natural" pairs to include the conceptualization of gender and nationality, a conceptualization essentially dependent on the defining dyads Man/Woman and Roman/non-Roman. Here again Roman ideals' hidden commerce with their opposites comes into play: the poem regularly blurs gender boundaries and "rational" distinctions, each as a function of deconstructing dichotomies found to be untenable. For example, almost as soon as Hercules appears in the poem as hypermasculine proto-Roman hero who fells the aboriginal cattle-thief Caucus, he tries to wheedle his way into a women-only shrine on the strength of his transvestite servitude to an Eastern queen. This startling *volte-face* shows the boundaries between masculinity and femininity, Roman heroism and non-Roman barbarism, to be unstable—an instability based on the fundamental workings of language. The Symbolic, understood as the total set of signifiers, cannot be circumscribed; another signifier will always appear and change the meaning of every other signifier in the set. Accordingly, no stable context exists within which the meaning of "Man," "Woman," "Roman," "non-Roman," indeed, *any* signifier, can be ascertained with certainty; the very terms most freighted with cultural significance, most crucial to Roman culture, always fail of a fixed identity.

Chapter 9 examines the Cornelia poem (4.11), which refocuses the theme of the Symbolic's failures onto the failures of Law as its specific subset. Cornelia's post-mortem defense of her life reveals her terror of being assigned to oblivion in Hades despite having led an exemplary life. Her fear illustrates a central emptiness in the Symbolic: it has no conceptual niche for Woman as ideal (though it has for her male heroic ancestors). Just as other poems in Book IV have shown how the Symbolic fails to conceive of Woman adequately, because it can only define Her as "not-Man," so the Symbolic cannot adequately conceptualize heroism as applied to a woman. That deficiency exacerbates the subject's perception of internal division and lack. As the fear in Cornelia's speech reveals, the deficiency revealed in Rome's conceptualization of Woman burdens the dead young matron with amorphous, unanswerable guilt.

Chapter 10, the conclusion, summarizes how I hope this book has expanded the analysis of Propertius Books I and IV specifically, and anticipates what may be gained by the application of its methodology not only to other parts of the Propertian oeuvre, but to Latin literature in general.

CHAPTER TWO

"Shadow of a Doubt": Framing the Subject in the Gallus Poems

The evening and night winds here were, to Pierston's mind, charged with a something that did not burden them elsewhere. They brought it up from that sinister Bay to the west, whose movement she and he were hearing now. It was a presence—an imaginary shape or essence from the human multitude lying below: those who had gone down in vessels of war, East Indiamen, barges, brigs, and ships of the Armada—select people, common, and debased, whose interests and hopes had been as wide asunder as the poles, but who had rolled each other to oneness on that restless sea-bed. There could almost be felt the brush of their huge composite ghost as it ran a shapeless figure over the isle, shrieking for some good god who would disunite it again.

THOMAS HARDY

As mentioned in the introductory chapter, the obscure logic that governs Propertius' poetry has often been the despair of his critics. I perceive a method in his madness, one that revolves around divided subjectivity evidenced in the ways in which language subverts authority. This chapter situates a certain politics in the very foundation of psychoanalysis' approach to literature in order to forge a subtler instrument with which to analyze Propertius' famously disjunctive and famously iconoclastic poetry. Propertius has long been read as an "anti-Augustan" whose poetry—especially his early work—embodies political apostasy from Octavian's regime; yet in truth his poetry not only criticizes the particular politics of his day, but also scrutinizes its psychic foundation—the way politics makes its claims upon us through appeals to dimensions other than consciousness.

The Gallus poems of his very first publication, the Monobiblos, (1.5, 1.10, 1.13, 1.20, 1.21, and 1.22) are a particularly rich field in which to examine Propertius' elliptical poetics. This series of poems has troubled scholars because it refuses either to "hang together or hang separately" as a narrative, despite the fact that all its poems revolve around the same name. Each is linked to a "Gallus" either as its addressee or subject. Yet the same name designates both an infamously callous womanizer (1.5, 1.13.5–6)[1] and one woman's devoted slave (1.10, 1.13); also, for good measure, a pederast on the point of foundering in his affair (1.20); also a high-ranking officer of Octavian (if one accepts the identification of Propertius' Gallus

---

Thomas Hardy, *The Well-Beloved: A Sketch of a Temperament* (London, 1975 [1st ed. 1897]), 35.

with Cornelius Gallus, Egyptian prefect; I shall discuss the reasons for doing so below) and a dying anti-Octavian soldier of indeterminate rank (1.21, and likely also 1.22, Propertius' lament for a kinsman killed resisting Octavian's siege of Perusia).[2] Any logical relation between these widely various images of "Gallus" remains unarticulated. The sexual details of these poems might be reconciled with the erotic history of a man with catholic tastes and varying fortunes in love. Some ingenuity has been expended on this, but the very need to explain underlines the subtle strain such reconciliation places on the reader: too much has been omitted to make these erotic *volte-face* anything but startling.[3] And no one has attempted thus far to reconcile the diametrically opposed politics of the Augustan and anti-Augustan Gallus. Propertius offers his readers no help. He leaves the logical relations between images tantalizingly obscure; the connecting narrative must be supplied by the reader.

In short, these poems' details resist summation under the history of a coherent "Gallus."[4] Equally, they resist clean separation one from another, so as to produce discrete "Galli." A secondary, formal detail of the series urges us not to regard this unraveling as coincidence or the poet's carelessness. The series' final poems trouble the book's generic frame as well as its characterological frame(s). Two poems (1.21 and 1.22) graphically depicting civil-war deaths end a book devoted to love poems—an inconcinnity some see either as the manuscript tradition's, or the poet's own, failure, rather than artful design.[5] I argue, by contrast, that Propertius' multiple, discordant use of the name "Gallus," and the Monobiblos' concluding abrupt change in subject matter, designedly coincide in their impact on the reader. They are principled textual strategies that disrupt the way any conventional mode of reading constructs relations of cause and effect and produces at their conjunction deceptively integrated *dramatis personae*, both purely as effects of ideology.[6]

(NOT) KEEPING UP APPEARANCES

To be sure, "Gallus" is not the only name within the Monobiblos to which such anomalies accrue, nor is his (theirs) the only problematic voice: comparable strategies attached to some of the book's other dramatic presences generate comparable disjunctive tensions. For example, though Propertius regularly stages his poetry as if narrated *in propria persona*, a strange voice displaces his in 1.16, a poem implausibly presented as the meditations *à haute voix* of a house door.[7] That displacement parallels the supersession of narrators in 1.21 of the Gallus series, the entire elegy being the anti-Augustan soldier Gallus' dying words spoken to a friend fleeing the battle of Perusia. In both poems, the subject whom readers have come to expect the narrating "I" to represent shifts without warning, so that we struggle momentarily to grasp exactly who is speaking.

Characteristics of the Monobiblos' other portraits at times also hinder both the smooth reconciliation of, and clean distinction between, one sketch and another, just as in the Gallus poems (these confusions happen most often, interestingly, where these other portrayals converge upon the Gallus poems). Ellen Oliensis, for example, points out that Propertius depicts Gallus besieged by lovesickness almost as though he were the younger poet's doppelgänger (of which I shall have more to say below, once the poems upon which she bases her analysis have been unfolded in greater detail). But apart from Gallus, Cynthia suffers the most egregiously inconsistent portraiture: her image varies from dedicated quasi-marital partner (1.3) to grand courtesan (1.2, 1.11) to camp follower (1.8) to possessively jealous hysteric (1.6).[8] Yet when Cynthia's enigma, too, intertwines with that of the Gallus series, the doubt attached to her identity thickens in its turn the mystery behind the woman who erotically enslaves Gallus (1.10, 1.13). The astonishingly intimate knowledge Propertius records of his friend's mistress' nature (not to mention his nervous discouragement of Gallus' too-keen interest in Cynthia, noted in 1.5) suggests that Gallus has filched Propertius' beloved. Both 1.10 and 1.13 suppress the name of Gallus' inamorata, but Propertius' account of her extraordinary ability to change Gallus from dilettante of love to her obsessed slave matches Propertius' estimation of Cynthia's powers in 1.5. (A comparable ploy in 1.22 of the Gallus series—which dispenses with the name "Gallus" but supplies particulars of Propertius' kinsman's death that ineluctably align him with 1.21's dying civil warrior Gallus—urges a comparable conflation of identities.) If this enchantress is Cynthia, Gallus' grand passion grandly betrays his friend. Yet the poems' friendly and congratulatory tone pushes us simultaneously *not* to read the beloved as Cynthia: how could Propertius banter so jauntily with Gallus were the latter an intimate traitor?

The details that prompt these dilemmas, however, have not prevented readers from construing either poet-narrator or Cynthia as reasonably unified dramatic presences within the Monobiblos (no one has suggested, for example, that the enigmas of Cynthia's depiction or of Propertius' self-portrait force us to assume two or more different *dramatis personae* behind each of these names). Other faces sketched within Book I present even fewer problems: the histories and characteristics of Bassus, Tullus, and Ponticus all fundamentally cohere. Only Gallus presents insuperable difficulties, both to the reader who wishes to assimilate all instances of that name to a single individual, and to her who tries to apportion the name rationally among discrete individuals. Even so, the Gallus series differs from the other portraits of the Monobiblos only in the extremity of its centrifugal tensions: precisely insofar as its radically disjunctive portraits fail of unity, they dramatize by opposition the ways in which other portraits achieve the illusion of coherence. The Gallus poems' extreme disjunction casts suspicion upon the management of other textual portrayals whose cohesion would otherwise pass unquestioned;[9] yet it also presses us to inquire into how the illusion of unity is conferred on human subjects per se (given that identity is quite as much a matter of discursive construction outside texts as inside them). These poems are the ideal "lever" by which the management of unity can be pried apart; for this reason, I focus on the Gallus series exclusively within the Monobiblos, as representative par excellence of the disjunctive strategies I wish to elucidate.

Specifically, Propertius' deployment of conflicting representations of "Gallus" lays bare the process Lacan called *capitonnage*, or "quilting," by disrupting it. *Capitonnage* allows the divided subject to dissimulate his inherent fragmentation by identifying with some master signifier that guarantees his place in the interconnected symbols and meanings generated by his culture's institutions. He can thus function as a coherent whole (as "I") via ideological commitments that make the various parts of being (anatomy, intellect, desire, cultural ideals) cohere in an apparently natural fashion. Culturally freighted signifiers (Man, Woman, Citizen, Roman) constitute the quilting points (*points de capiton*) that promise to locate the subject and make him whole.

Yet the Gallus poems thwart such smooth coherence: details of these poems, no matter how apportioned among semiotic histories, cannot conjure up any coherent, discrete subject (or subjects). A minority of Propertius' critics, but a persuasive minority, identifies the "Gallus" of poems 5, 10, 13, and 20 as Cornelius Gallus, Octavian's Egyptian prefect and "Lycoris'" elegiac poet-lover, on strongly suggestive textual evidence.[10] I agree with this identification, but it creates more problems for coherence than it solves—designedly so, as I shall argue. For the moment, though, I defer elucidating my reasons for so believing until I can unfold the evidence for identifying Cornelius Gallus' presence in and behind the Monobiblos. Only the strongest arguments for the case are detailed here; two depend upon the appropriateness of Cornelius Gallus as Propertius' historical referent *hors de texte*, three focus on textual echoes between Propertius' poetry and other Gallan *loci classici*.

GALLUS THE POET?

The two situational arguments for identifying "Gallus" as Cornelius Gallus are the following:

First, the addressees of the Monobiblos are identifiable as real personages contemporary with Propertius (all except for Cynthia). "Bassus," to whom the poet directs 1.4, is universally agreed to be Bassus the iambographer mentioned by Ovid in *Tristia* 4.10.47 and "Ponticus," the recipient of 1.7 and 1.9, to be the epic poet mentioned in the same Ovidian passage ("Ponticus heroo, Bassus quoque clarus iambis"—"Ponticus famous for his epic verse, and Bassus for his iambic").[11] "Tullus," to whose ears poems 1, 6, 14, and 22 are directed, is identified as the nephew of L. Volcacius Tullus, the uncle being proconsul of Asia in 30–29 B.C.E.[12] On these grounds, we are at least incautious if *a priori* we assume "Gallus" to be a mere fiction unconnected to his famous namesake. Moreover, two of Propertius' addressees are identifiable as literary men, one as a military man; Francis Cairns has argued that "Gallus" neatly completes the pattern if and only if he combines in himself soldier and poet—that is, if he is Cornelius Gallus, the Augustan elegist and *vir militaris*. In support of his argument, Cairns deftly illustrates the numerous symmetries that govern the deployment and phrasing of the poems addressed to Bassus, Ponticus, and Gallus, showing that all are to be read as an interlocking set, with the attributes of their various addressees carefully balanced one with another.[13]

Second, in an argument that rests upon the same premise Cairns develops in 1.4 and 1.5, Richard Thomas argues for Cornelius Gallus' image as the only one that makes sense of 1.10.[14] Thomas develops a suggestion first made by Franz Skutsch[15] and later seconded by Anna S. Benjamin:[16] Propertius 1.10, which seems to confess to a voyeuristic evening of spying on Gallus making love to a woman, instead records allegorically Propertius' reading of Gallus' poetry. Drawing upon magical texts, erotic poetry, and New Comedy, Thomas argues that 1.10's motif of *agrupnia* ("sleeplessness") can be traced to a significant double root. On the one hand, Greek and Roman literati describe themselves and their friends spending "sleepless nights" trying to perfect their poetry in accordance with Callimachean aesthetic standards. On the other, the Graeco-Roman erotic tradition regularly has the lover wakefully pursue, or suffer from, his love. Catullus first combines these disparate traditions by virtue of their shared sleeplessness-motif: in c.50 he writes a poem to Licinius Calvus that portrays him (Catullus) as a lover inflamed to sleeplessness, but made thus wakeful by the seductive charm of Calvus' poetry. When Propertius revives the theme of wakefulness in 1.10, addressed to Gallus, the poem makes best sense if addressed to a literary man. Rather than confessing himself a crude voyeur, Propertius compliments Gallus as a poet by saying that reading his (Gallus') poetry about a love affair inspired *agrupnia* in Propertius—that is, it passed muster as excellent love-poetry. And if the Gallus of 1.10 is a poet, then he is unlikely to be other than Cornelius Gallus the Augustan elegist, whom Propertius himself mentions elsewhere as his own great predecessor (2.34.87–94).

Regarding arguments based on intertextuality: echoes of Cornelius Gallus' image as constructed in the sixth and tenth *Eclogues* punctuate the Monobiblos (many, though not all, in the poems addressed to a "Gallus"). Such references to Cornelius Gallus' vivid conjuration by Vergil that reverberate throughout Propertius' book compel the reader to surmise that the "Gallus" of these poems is Cornelius Gallus.

To support this interpretation, the evidence that Propertius invokes Gallan elegy must be unfolded, but I do so with circumspection. Some critics are prepared to see Cornelius Gallus' poetry directly behind the textual echoes between Propertius and the *Eclogues*. I, on the other hand, accept as my operating premise James Zetzel's suggested revision of ingenious, but perhaps overbold, reconstructions of Gallus' poetry from its suspected reflections in Augustan poetry: if for "Gallus" we read instead "Vergil's Gallus," then much of this speculation is not only brilliant, but irrefutably correct.[17]

We cannot know what Gallus' poetry was like in its totality; at best, we have some eleven chiefly fragmentary lines by which to judge him. Yet the fragment from Qaṣr Ibrîm has disappointed nearly all readers who accepted Vergil's panegyric of the man's verse.[18] If genuine, these fragments may explain history's near-total indifference to preserving Gallus' poetry. Perhaps our image of Gallus is only Vergil's invention of him. But whether or not that is true, Zetzel acutely observes that both the felicities of the sixth and tenth Eclogues, and their effect on later generations of Augustan poets, are best attributed to Vergil rather than to a phantom Gallus of whose oeuvre we are profoundly ignorant. As he says, applying Ockham's Razor to good effect: "ingenia non sunt multiplicanda praeter necessitatem." The Augustans read in Gallus what Vergil had taught them to see.[19] I confine myself, therefore, chiefly to correspondences demonstrable between Propertius' poems and the Eclogues, convinced that this is both our clearest and our most important evidence of Cornelius Gallus' image in Propertius' eyes; I shall venture only a few cautious speculations beyond this delimited territory.

The details noted by readers who have labored to find Gallan elegy in these poems are various, their significance argued by a wide variety of methodologies. The following three seem to me the best-established correspondences.

1. Propertius 1.8.7–8 strongly resembles *Eclogue* 10.46–49, especially the last three lines of the passage.[20]

> tu procul a patria (nec sit mihi credere tantum)
> Alpinas, a! dura nives et frigora Rheni
> me sine sola vides. a, te ne frigora laedant!
> a, tibi ne teneras glacies secet aspera plantas!
>   (*Ecl.* 10.46–49)[21]

You, far from your native country (let it not be mine to believe such an enormity!) see the Alps—ah! unyielding woman!—the frozen snow and cold of the Rhine, without me. Ah, may the cold not harm you! Ah, may the sharp ice not cut the delicate soles of your feet!

> tu pedibus teneris positas fulcire pruinas,
>   tu potes insolitas, Cynthia, ferre nives?
>   (Prop. 1.8.7–8)

Can your delicate feet press the hoarfrost layers, can you endure, Cynthia, the unaccustomed snows?

Servius tells us that *Eclogue* 10.46–49 are *translati* ("adapted") from Gallus' own work.[22] Propertius' own adaptation of the lines then conjures up all the more vividly Gallus' presence in the Monobiblos, by doubly referring to Gallus and to Vergil's homage to Gallus.

2. The Milanion episode in Propertius 1.1 suddenly shifts from the clear elegiac language of 1.1–8 into archaisms of diction and grammar, and obscure syntax. Further, as David Ross notes, Propertius 1.1.11 ("nam modo Partheniis amens errabat in antris"—"for now he wandered in the groves of Parthenius") echoes *Eclogue* 10.56–57 ("non me ulla vetabunt / frigora Parthenios canibus circumdare saltus"— "Not any cold shall prevent me from besieging the coverts on Parthenius with my hounds"). These are, in fact, the only two instances of Mt. Parthenius extant in

Augustan poetry, and we know that the Greek poet Parthenius dedicated his *Erotika Pathemata* to Gallus, for use in Gallus' poetry. The mountain's mention both in Vergil and Propertius likely nods to Cornelius Gallus by referring in learned and obscure fashion to his chief supplier of literary material. There are, in addition, situational similarities, elucidated by Ross and Joy King: Gallus is in Arcadia, sick with love, proposing to hunt (*Ecl.* 10.56–60); Milanion is in Arcadia, sick with love, actually hunting (1.11–14). Gallus is without *medicina* ("medical aid"), an unusual word, in *Eclogue* 10 (60), just as there is no medical aid for Propertius' love in 1.1 (25–28), nor any *medicina* for either the "Propertius" or the "Gallus" of Propertius 1.5 (27–28).[23] Vergil is a friend vainly offering help in *Eclogue* 10, as Propertius vainly appeals for help from his friends in 1.1 (25–26), and will not be able give help if his own "Gallus" falls in love with Cynthia in 1.5 (27–28).[24] Propertius' Milanion exemplum must point to a Gallan referent in *Eclogue* 10, if not to a passage from Gallus' own poetry.

3. Propertius' description of Pege's spring in 1.20 reminds us of Vergil's ecstatic references to Gallus' ekphrasis on the Grynean grove in *Eclogue* 6, and may even point to Gallus' ekphrasis itself. Ross notes that Servius Auctus, commenting upon the phrase "Grynei nemoris origo" ("origin of the Grynean grove," *Ecl.* 6.72) adds to an otherwise dry observation a curiously rich description of Gryneus as abundantly gifted with trees, flowers, and springs—exactly the elements that Propertius deploys in his description of his *fons*, whose rapacious inhabitants threaten to steal Gallus' beloved as they did Hylas.[25] Gallus' own ekphrasis on the Grynean grove very likely stands behind the coincidence between Servius Auctus' comment and Propertius' description of a place to which he draws his own "Gallus'" attention (as Ross skillfully argues).[26]

CRACKS IN THE PORTRAIT(S)

These textual echoes, and the broad hints that Propertius' "Gallus" is himself a poet, evoke Cornelius Gallus the elegist as the organizing figure behind these poems; yet that same figure subtly fractures among various erotic *types:* Propertius taxes Gallus' inveterate and maddeningly successful philandering in poem 5, presenting himself, by contrast, as faithfully devoted to one woman. Yet by poems 10 and 13, Gallus has become one woman's hopeless slave—possibly Cynthia's, as Propertius implies with a combination of smugness and bitterness. Cynthia or no, the woman disappears somewhere between 13 and 20, where Gallus now loves a beautiful boy, but seems to have lost his erotic touch: he constantly risks losing the boy to a rival. All this, as I have said, could be the downward spiral in an erratic sexual history; its curve retraces some of the *via dolorosa* Gallus trod in his own poetry, judging by the evidence of Qaṣr Ibrîm and the tenth *Eclogue*—but it is troubling that none of the ancient evidence mentions pederastic interests in Gallus' poetry or his life. If we have not lost some significant part of Gallus' poetry or *testamenta* that touched on his boy-love, then yet another detail works against a clean alignment with Cornelius Gallus; yet this very poem, 1.20, probably imitates what Vergil regarded as Gallus' masterpiece, his poem on the Grynean grove. Propertius' carefully sown clues point in opposite directions.

Still, this is a minor point: had the Juventius or Marathus poems been lost from Catullus' or Tibullus' work, no other ancient evidence would inform us of their pederastic verses.[27] But in the Gallus poems, class confusion seconds erotic confusion when Propertius stresses "Gallus'" *nobilitas* ("high birth/excellence") and aristocratic *priscae imagines* ("ancient deathmasks of the ancestors") in verses either quoted from, or modeled on, Cornelius Gallus' own poetry: "nescit Amor priscis cedere imaginibus"—"nor does Love know how to yield before ancient ancestral deathmasks" (1.5.24). Tränkle, noting the uncharacteristic repetition between this line and 1.14.8 ("nescit Amor magnis cedere divitiis"), suspects that Propertius is not quoting himself and cites Gallus as the source.[28] Tränkle bases his argument on structural details of the verse, but I would add that content seconds his opinion: Propertius' allusion unmistakably looks to elements of the tenth *Eclogue*. Vergil has Gallus yield to Love's cruel intransigence:[29] "omnia vincit Amor: et nos cedamus Amori"—"Love conquers all things; let us, too, surrender to love" (10.69, Gallus' final line). Propertius' repeated collocation of *Amor* and *cedere* echoes Gallus' portrait in the tenth Eclogue, and both his and Vergil's poem may well look to a passage or line from Gallus' poetry itself. Yet Cornelius Gallus was merely a provincial knight (*eques*); though a man who had risen to such power and influence as Gallus had achieved by the Monobiblos' likely publication date (29/28 B.C.E.) could conceivably have been called *nobilis* in a non-technical sense, the *priscae imagines* are quite specific. They are the exclusive perquisite of curule families; Cornelius Gallus does not qualify. Why would Propertius construct a poem so elaborately dependent on the portrait of Gallus drawn in the tenth *Eclogue*, not only in content but in phrasing and diction, so as to underline strongly his source and the allusion—and then direct that poem to a Gallus ennobled above any conceivable alignment with the Gallus who inspired that eclogue?

If the impossible upward mobility of 1.5's Gallus stumps the reader, she only encounters a greater blow in 1.21 and 1.22. Here is Gallus again—or rather, here is *a* Gallus, impossible to equate simply with the previous Gallus, and yet bearing marked resemblances to the earlier one, difficult to ignore. In 1.21, a Gallus who has fled the long, bloody, and cruel siege of Perusia that Octavian began in 41 addresses a terrified comrade who has stumbled across him in his death agonies. Though this Gallus escaped Octavian's troops, "unknown hands" ("ignotas manus," 1.21.8) have dealt him a mortal blow. The dying Gallus enjoins his addressee to keep the exact circumstances of his death a secret. He especially fears that detailed knowledge will upset his comrade's sister, to whom Gallus is tenderly devoted (persuasive opinion considers the woman Gallus' own beloved).[30] If she should come looking for his bones, Gallus says, "whatever bones she shall find scattered in these Etruscan mountains, let her know that they are mine" (1.22.10).

The Gallus of 1.21 fought *against* Octavian, while if the other Gallus poems allude to Cornelius Gallus (as I have been arguing), the Monobiblos' earliest audience knew well how the latter prospered as Octavian's loyal instrument. Yet on the other hand, several details curiously align even this anti-Octavian Gallus with Cornelius Gallus, poet and soldier. The Gallus of 1.21 is of Cornelius Gallus' generation, that is, several years Propertius' elder; he, too, is a soldier; his dying devotion is to a woman, as Vergil (in a lighter vein) painted Gallus as "perishing" in unshakable love of Lycoris ("indigno cum Gallus amore peribat"—"when Gallus was dying from unrequited love," *Ecl.* 10.10). Propertius teases and frustrates us by evoking, then denying, the numinous biography of his principal elegiac predecessor.[31]

What, then, is the effect of constructing these overlapping, but not quite alignable, "Galli" within a series of key poems in the Monobiblos? Why trouble one's poetry with these nagging but ungraspable ghosts? True enough that (as noted in chapter 1) they obviate the possibility of drawing *any* coherent subject out of these poems; yet just as important is their deployment within a field defined by one of the chief political figures of the day (Cornelius Gallus) and one of his master's worst excesses (Octavian's siege of Perusia). These are political poems from beginning to end of the series, not merely where they touch upon Perusia's fall in the Civil War (1.21, 1.22). Whatever else these poems concern, they touch on love as well as politics, and do not oppose the one to the other, as commonly argued in Propertius studies.[32] Rather, they pose love and the political as two sides of the same coin, bound together by common functional roots in desire. These poems revolve essentially around the operation of ideological quilting (*capitonnage*) and its illusory promise of "wholeness," a promise that conceptually links the erotic and political poems of the Monobiblos.

QUILTING

Though a modern term, *quilting* names a process already sketched in ancient philosophical texts. The most compelling of these models evolves in Plato's *Symposium* and *Phaedrus*. The *Symposium* imagines lovers to be remnants of an original separation who seek to be reunited, like two halves of a token (*symbolon*, 191d4).[33] The *Phaedrus* amplifies and refines this model by linking desire to the operation of the signifier. Lovers seek their complements by recognizing the "sign" of their tutelary god in their beloveds; both lover and beloved perfect themselves by becoming like the god, aligning themselves ever more closely with the divine signifier that conditions their desire (*Phaedrus* 252c3–253c2).

The import of these dialogues evidently appealed to Propertius, even if he knew of them only summarily and not by direct knowledge: his poetic ideal of love uncannily resembles Plato's. Plato attaches his philosophical project of self-perfection to passionate love, while other ancient philosophers (Aristotle, Epicurus, and the Stoics, to name only the most prominent examples) preferred the calmer joys of friendship as a vehicle of virtue. Propertius reflects Platonic values throughout his poetry insofar as he views loving Cynthia as a means of self-perfection. Because he loves her, he can write inspired poetry;[34] because he loves her exclusively, he lays claim to a lover's *askesis* of virtue;³⁵ because he loves her deeply, he expects the reward that entices lovers in the *Phaedrus* (256a8-e2) and the *Symposium* (192c7-e9)—not to be separated from the beloved after death.³⁶ But just as lovers seek "their other halves" in their beloveds, so ideology, too, promises completion. The Propertian subject attempts to fill out his constitutive lack by means of identification, by identifying with some master signifier guaranteeing his place in the symbolic network (i.e., in the interconnected social significations generated by his culture's institutions).³⁷

The rhetorical form of Propertius' Cynthia-poems (in addition to their idealist romantic content) links his beloved closely to the divine master signifier that confers upon Propertius his perfected identity. Cynthia's name derives from one of the god of poetry's (Apollo's) cult titles, a gesture virtually *de rigeur* among the Augustan elegists; but Propertius delights more than most in embroidering the conceit of the divinely inspiring *puella*.³⁸ Propertius perfects himself as poet and as faithful lover by singing of his mistress, and consequently gains Apollo's approval; his mistress thus embodies the divine "sign" that guides Propertius towards an aesthetics and an ethics of self-perfection.³⁹

My description of Propertius' erotic path reveals it as a subset of the process of quilting that constitutes ideology's appeal (including the ideology of love). Plato's further analysis of desire in the *Phaedrus* can help us see this; in that dialogue, Socrates discusses love in the context of rhetoric and its power to persuade. The lover's desire to regain an aboriginal self-perfection—his state of pre-corporal "wholeness" in which he glimpsed the Forms and his particular tutelary god—mirrors rhetoric's operation on its audience.⁴⁰ Rhetoric has the power to pin desire to objects (though, unlike philosophy, it does not interest itself in whether these objects are worth desiring). Rhetoric succeeds for precisely the same reasons Plato's *erôs*-driven philosophy succeeds—because it promises satisfaction to desire—but without the substance to fulfill its promises.⁴¹

Important to our purposes is the way Plato's model offers to align, rather than separate, the operation of love and politics upon the subject. Plato unfolds the workings of a force common to love and politics, that is, *peitho*, "persuasion"; he reveals its operation as identical in both realms. Whatever the nature of the signifier that promises to locate the subject, and thus fulfill him—be it Woman, *Romanitas*, Octavian/Augustus' "return to our ancestors' ways (*mos maiorum*)"⁴²—the relationship of desire is the same. The desired redemptive relationship is impossible—the subject can never be "whole," nor the amorous couple "one flesh"; the state can neither be perfectly coherent, nor perfect the subject. But this frustration, far from exhausting desire, guarantees its continual renewal in hope. The persistent delusion that desire *can* be fulfilled fuels the ardor of lovers, political zealots—and Propertius' own readers, who must keep seeking "the whole story" behind the "Galli" who flicker in and out of his verses.⁴³

However, in contrast to Propertius' sketch of his own perfection of identity under the influence of love for Cynthia, the first four poems of the Gallus series (1.5, 10,

13, 20) unfold the quilting point's operation in the erotic field from a rather darker perspective. They describe the *bon vivant* Gallus' amorous life from a decidedly disenchanted perspective by emphasizing quilting's *failures*—the way that it cheats or distorts the desire for wholeness and unity—and allying these failures to Woman in the form of Cynthia, the proximate object of desire common to Propertius and Gallus. In a subtly argued essay, Ellen Oliensis has shown that these four poems not only raise suspicion that a bevy of doppelgängers huddles under the common name "Gallus," but also imply that Gallus and Propertius are themselves doubles, with Woman mediating their mirroring relationship.[44]

In 1.5, for example, Propertius advises Gallus against pursuing his interest in Cynthia: Propertius paints a picture of himself and Gallus swapping tears and sighs over the (missing) body of Cynthia, as if they were amorous twins—or lovers: the two men's tears anticipate the mutual tears Gallus and his new girlfriend will soon exchange in amorous embraces ("vestris . . . lacrimis," 1.10.2). Like Catullus c.50—the obvious model for a literary, but also highly eroticized, encounter between men—Propertius 1.5 further confuses the question of Gallus' sexuality (and therefore of his identity) with teasing suggestions that the *amicitia* ("friendship") between Gallus and Propertius encroaches upon the territory of *amor* ("erotic love").

In elegies 1.10 and 1.13, Propertius pushes this suggestion of homosocial affinity toward a further extreme: describing the night of love Propertius witnessed between Gallus and his new girlfriend and offering his help as *praeceptor amoris* (10.15–28), Propertius declares himself to have been a *testis* ("witness") to the couple's embraces. As Oliensis points out, the sexual context shades *testis* with a trace of its anatomical meaning ("testicle"), as though Propertius had become part of Gallus' own sexual equipment. Lest that seem to overread, she notes that in 1.13 Propertius supplies a mythological precedent for the fusion of male bodies. He compares the couple's close embraces to Neptune's lovemaking with Tyro; but that required Neptune to "mix" with the rivergod Enipeus ("Haemonio . . . mixtus Enipeo," 1.13.21)—that is, two *male* bodies to fuse, catalyzed by a *woman*'s body. Moreover, the fact that (as remarked above) Gallus makes love to a woman rather too well known by Propertius and remarkably like Cynthia implies that both men occupy interchangeably (albeit uneasily) the role of Cynthia's lover.

Oliensis presents us with questions to accompany our earlier dilemma: now, in addition to, Who is Gallus, that is, how do we distinguish between one Gallus and another, or do we amalgamate all into one Gallus, we must ask, Who is Gallus, that is, how do we distinguish between one lover and another (Gallus and Propertius), or do we (*mirabile dictu!*) amalgamate them both into one? Propertius sharpens these questions by fashioning the amorous Gallus as a pale, thin, and tongue-tied mirror-image of his lovelorn self, ridiculous and shorn of resourcefulness, an equal companion ("pariter miseri," 1.5.29) to replace the equal companionship of Propertius' formidable mistress ("ire pares," 1.5.2).

Elegy 1.20 renders the erotic mirroring relationship between Gallus and Propertius most sharply, and yet with the greatest literary allusiveness. The elegy adduces the story of Hercules' companion Hylas, beguiled by his own reflection in a spring and ravished away by its rapacious nymphs, to warn Gallus that he must watch over his new boy-love with particular care.[45] Oliensis builds a complex but persuasive argument that links Propertius' allusion to Ascanius—a river near where Hylas stops to draw water and disappears—to Propertius himself and to dangerous allure. Propertius makes Ascanius both a corroborative witness to Gallus, seconding his own admonition of the beloved's vulnerability (4), and—as *indomitus Ascanius* refusing to yield before Hercules' grief—an image of the archetypal beloved inflexible before the pleading lover (16). Ascanius thus corresponds to Propertius as represented in the Gallus poems in the poet's dual capacity of advisor (*praeceptor amoris*) and quasi-beloved to Gallus. Moreover, from the many echoes of Cornelius Gallus' poetry concentrated in 1.20, Oliensis not only agrees with the scholars who conclude that the Gallus addressed must evoke Gallus the elegist, but argues in addition that the river Ascanius represents a lure to the elder poet. Ascanius figures the glittering surface of the Propertian text as a danger to which Gallus the elegist will be attracted and by which he will be seduced—perhaps, like Hylas, by the reflection of himself (his own poetry) therein. Oliensis outlines yet another way that the Gallus series confuses the question of identity: Gallus sees himself (his poetry) in Propertius (Propertius' poetry) and, like Hylas, when he reaches out to grasp what fascinates him, finds himself absorbed instead.

Oliensis' analysis of these four Gallus poems usefully outlines the operation of a quilting point in the erotic field—a radically troubled operation, whose failures Woman (in the guise of Cynthia) clearly reveals. Once Cynthia bisects the relation between Gallus and Propertius, the seemingly unambiguous quilting point "Lover" renders neither man whole, but rather troubles their discrete identities: their egalitarian misery over Cynthia's aloofness (1.5) makes them the quintessential elegiac lovers—but lovers of whom, given that commiseration over Cynthia eroticizes the bond with each other and yet makes her essential to this eroticization? The next permutation of the triangle—Gallus captivated by the woman likely to be Cynthia (1.10, 13)—fuses the two discrete male lovers into an oddly uneasy whole, with Propertius' edgy jealousy written over images of amalgamated bodies. Elegy 1.20 finally assimilates the amorous Gallus to an image (Hylas) that makes him a new Narcissus, a mythological figure who inextricably confuses the roles of Lover and Beloved; but Propertius raises this confusion to the second power when the entity that offers Gallus an image of himself is Propertius (Propertius' poetry). These paradoxes that Oliensis traces in the "tumbling triangles" she detects in 1.5, 10, 13, and 20 outline Propertius' critique of the apparently discrete identity (Lover) offered by social institutions in general, and by elegy in particular, as a subset of those institutions. Not by accident does Cynthia catalyze this collapse of the quilting point's operation: insofar as she figures Woman, she takes on Woman's characteristic function—to mark the point of logical breakdown within a system, the system here in question being the speciously secure sense of erotic identity and integrity conferred upon the subject.

Elegies 1.5, 10, 13, and 20 may be seen as Propertius' critique of how the desire for wholeness (mal)functions in the realm of *amor*. The final two poems of the Gallus series, 1.21 and 1.22, focus principally (though not exclusively) on the corollary realm, the realm of the political and of *Roma*. The present chapter has, to this point, outlined my theory as to why this entire series of six poems unfolds the way it does, analyzing the mechanism of quilting that animates the series and that mechanism's intellectual provenance (as well as its specific effects visible within the first four poems of the series, the more obviously erotic poems). But this bare speculation raises another question—a threefold question that seeks to contextualize Propertius' Gallus poems historically. In sketching the concept of quilting, I have drawn it ahistorically—justly so, because it grapples with an impasse that repeats itself throughout the (individual and collective) history of the subject.[46] But the configurations deployed to grapple with this impasse do differ historically. Even so, I do not view history as a straightforward explanation for these poems (as if historical event *x* "explained" the presence of detail *y* in the poems). The debt is rather the other way: the poems themselves are among the best primary evidence we have for the way the Romans construed contemporary historical events.

But which events? More specifically, why just at *this* particular historical juncture do *these* images of fragmentation appear in a Roman elegist's work? And why do they invoke the name of Cornelius Gallus—why does *this man* in particular become Propertius' icon of how quilting fails us?

DISPLACEMENT

Let me begin with the first part of my question, and with a premise that will surprise no one. I summarize the images that we have examined in the Gallus poems under the rubric "displacement," both in a literal and a metaphorical sense. Even if we bracket the doppelgänger relation between Propertius and Gallus implied in the first four poems, Gallus is *still* insufficiently anchored to his identity—or, more accurately, the signifier "Gallus" has two ultimately dissonant but nonetheless overlapping semiotic histories competing to secure it. The name floats unattached between (at least) two signifying chains, and cannot securely be anchored to either one without the other exercising claims upon it. These images of displacement correspond to the general chaos of the late Republic and early Empire, with its large-scale, profound shifts in social institutions and practices.

More specifically, these images of "losing one's place" correlate with the land confiscations and redistributions regularly enforced in the late Republic, but accelerated under the Second Triumvirate, with its pressing need to provide material rewards to its veterans.[47] The land distributions displaced Romans and Italians not just from property, but from a social identity. Vergil, who himself may have suffered the loss of his family property, equates literal displacement from the land with the unhinging of one's social identity in *Eclogue* 1. Meliboeus, whose property has been ceded to a veteran, contrasts his landless state with that of Tityrus; Tityrus will keep the land that, in his absence, called out for its master ("ipsae te, Tityre, pinus, / ipsi te fontes, ipsa haec arbusta vocabant"—"The pines themselves, Tityrus, the very water sources, even these trees were calling you," 1.38–39). Tityrus' land thus bestows an identity upon Tityrus, it "interpellates" him—and by implication the loss of Meliboeus' land partially unravels his subjectivity.[48] Propertius (another sufferer in the confiscations) confirms this suspicion that property confers social identity when he frames Tullus' question to himself in 1.22. Tullus asks the question that constructs the poem as a *sphragis* ("seal"), a way of identifying the work's author. This poem answers the question, Who are you?, but not quite along the generic lines established by similar *sphragis*-poems. Tullus asks "who are you?" as a function of "what does your family own? where are you from? what is your social status?"; he sees Propertius' identity solely as a function of property.[49] I shall return to this moment for a fuller analysis of it shortly, but I note it now as evidence that property ownership metaphorically distills social identity.

With the fact of vast shifts in property ownership I juxtapose the gradual changes in the definition of "citizen" that took place from the late Republic all the way through the imperial period. A long history of conquest meant that the Roman Empire was now a vast place, encompassing diverse races and cultures. Citizenship gradually became available to a broader and broader range of people within the Empire's borders, necessitating a profound shift in the conceptualization of "citizen."[50] Rights are now vested in the person conceived as an abstract individual, rather than as an "organic" member of a family, a tribe, a race. Yet the notion of citizenship never quite loses its "organic" roots: the literature of this period frequently reflects upon the question "who is a Roman?"—and thus upon quilting.[51] Alongside "constructivist" answers to the question that would organize citizenship criteria around the individual's achievements (the argument of, say, Cicero's *Pro Archia*) circulate "essentialist" answers based on some notion of an "organic" relationship to the soil, to ancient customs, to the ancestors. To name but a few examples of the latter (not as exhaustive, but exemplary): in *Eclogue* 1, Meliboeus scorns the absurdity of himself, a Roman citizen, farming in Africa, while some "barbarian" will harvest his (Meliboeus') crops. The outrage is as absurd as Tityrus' list of impossible conditions (stags feeding in the sky, fish consigned to land) that would precede his own ingratitude for the gift of continued tenure on his land.[52] Horace records that putting oneself up for public office immediately sparks inquiries into one's ancestry; un-Roman bloodlines disqualify the would-be candidate from legislating to "real" Romans (*S.* 1.6.34–39). Cicero and Octavian both tax Mark Antony with being too "foreign" in his ways: he emulates alien dress and habits of luxury, and treats Cleopatra as his Egyptian wife.[53] As these and other instances reflect, the increasing permeability of the category "Roman" ironically sparks anxious vigilance around its borders.[54]

At the same time that these social moorings are being transformed or destroyed, other avenues for achieving a social identity—a "place" in a metaphorical sense, a place in the symbolic network—effectively close to all except the extremely wealthy and powerful, or the Triumvirs' favorites. The ladder of advancement through the Roman magistracies known as the *cursus honorum* operates only for these latter, if it operates at all; it shuts out many of the *nobiles*, and the would-be *novi homines*[55] who might (like Cicero) have made their mark with peacetime accomplishments such as rhetoric. *Novi homines* under the Triumvirs are generally experienced men of war (*viri militares*) who have fought under the powerful; by contrast, many talented and educated individuals who could have advanced similarly in a gentler era now opt out of the *cursus* entirely. Catullus, for example, chronicled his disgust with politics in an earlier era; the next generation witnesses a veritable cataract of (admittedly more tactful) refusals from Vergil, Horace, Propertius himself, and Ovid—and these most visible of defections epitomized widespread voluntary withdrawal from an arena both too costly and too uncertain for all but a few to sustain.[56]

Thus far the strands of history I have elucidated distinguish a fairly broad swathe of time: the conditions to which I point obtain to varying degrees of intensity from the time of Marius and Sulla on up to Propertius' day and beyond. There is, however, a development more specific to Propertius' day that must condition our reading of the Monobiblos—specifically, of the Gallus poems threaded through it. That is the fact of Octavian's growing power and his rapid transformation from mere human being to emperor and god, constructed thus as *the* center of power in the Roman Empire.

MONARCHY AND THE QUILTING POINT

The details of Octavian's real or putative power both as Triumvir and as *princeps* continue to be hotly debated, but I follow the lead of such scholars as Fergus Millar in noting that Octavian is perceived as being the source of power in Rome, whatever the formal structure of government and law may have said otherwise. As Triumvir, he had the advantage of being highly visible and present at Rome, while Antony busied himself in the East; after the battle of Actium removed the latter from the political scene, the fine points of what did and did not legally fall within Octavian's purview frequently drop from sight, as petitioners, proconsuls, senators, and the like seek his favor and his commands.[57]

I specifically interest myself in the formal logic of Octavian's rule, because there particularly resides the key to the images of displacement and disintegration that clutter the Gallus poems. The language of hereditary right framed as a biological and natural claim to power appears early in Octavian's career. Octavian regularly styles himself "Gaius Caesar, son of the god" ("Gaius Caesar *divi filius*") after the Senate voted his adoptive father, Julius Caesar, divine status (1 January 42 B.C.E.). As Syme notes, speaking of the youthful Octavian shortly after the pact of Brundisium (40 B.C.E.):

> Private gratitude had already hailed the young Caesar with the name or epithet of divinity. His statue was now placed in temples by loyal or obedient Italian munici-

palities. At Rome the homage due to a military leader and guarantor of peace was enhanced by official act and religious sanction. Caesar's heir was granted sacrosanctity such as tribunes of the plebs enjoyed.[58]

Early in his principate, extravagant cults of Octavian/Augustus spring up and are more than tolerated by the new regime.[59] The symbolic claim is clear. Octavian's "father" was a god; he himself is worshipped as a god, and addressed in terms of divinity even by sophisticated Romans such as Vergil and Horace.[60] Octavian is *by nature* distinguished from his subjects, naturally suited to his place as *the* point at which power is concentrated (and perceived to be concentrated) in the Roman Empire.

What does it mean for Rome to pass thus into the hands of a de facto "divine" monarchy? The monarch (as Hegel, that ever-perspicacious political analyst, clearly saw) is the quilting point of an entire society, the point at which it assumes subjectivity. In him alone are nature and social position supposed to coincide: he is biologically suited to rule (as indicated by the fact that monarchy is a hereditary position)[61] and he does in fact rule (that is his social position).[62] But concentration on the monarch as the "unifying" head of society obscures the impassable gap between himself and his subjects: by the very fact that he is the *one* point in society where nature and culture coincide, then by definition nature and culture do *not* coincide at any other place. The monarch's subjects must therefore forever scramble, as if in some brutal Looking Glass world, to "stay in the same place," to prove themselves worthy of whatever place they attain in society.[63]

This interpretation of monarchy was available to the Romans themselves, as evidenced by Livy's history of early Rome—specifically, by his treatment of kingship. I do not draw attention to Livy because I see his books as representing the only possible Roman attitude toward monarchy—no such monolithic concept of historical consciousness could possibly be accurate. But he is closely contemporary with Propertius; he positioned himself as a writer of moral history from a disenchanted standpoint, one that views with alarm contemporary developments in Roman society; his account of Rome's early history bears the stamp of contemporary events in the late Republic and early Principate. All these reasons support reading his history as not only a critique of monarchy as a historical archaic institution, but an account of its perceived effects that reflects upon its de facto re-establishment with the principate.

Livy's account of the Roman "kings" describes men who do not inherit power but have it bestowed upon them by election. They approach, but never quite reach, Hegel's model of sovereignty until the advent of Tarquinius Superbus—precisely where, non-coincidentally, trouble with Roman monarchy begins. Tarquin, the supreme "bogeyman" of Roman kings, is the first to claim his throne as a hereditary right. Initially, Tarquin objects that the present occupant of the throne, Servius Tullius, was not duly elected (1.47.10). But when Servius reproves Tarquin for his pretensions to the throne, Tarquin loses control and exclaims, quite counter to his previous logic of "proper electoral procedure," "se patris sui tenere sedem; multo quam servum potiorem filium regis regni heredem; satis illum diu per licentiam eludentem insultasse dominis"—"The chair is my father's; a king's son is better heir to the throne than a slave. We have let you mock and insult your masters long enough," 1.48.2. The subsequent expectation of Tarquin's sons that one of them will inherit the throne (1.56.10–11) confirms that Tarquin, unlike his predecessors, thinks dynastically: kingship to him is an affair properly determined naturally, not electorally.

During Tarquin's reign, the identities of his subjects slip and slide curiously in a fashion that accords with Hegel's model of the hereditary king as the ultimate unraveler of identity: "suppliant fugitives" turn out to be *agents provocateurs*;[64] free Romans are set to servile tasks;[65] "traitors" are discovered among honest men, courtesy of manufactured evidence.[66] Even Brutus, the king's nephew, assumes the pose of a dullard to avoid arousing the king's jealousy (1.56.7–9). Tarquin's overthrow reverses all these slippages of identity, a peripeteia dramatically heralded by Brutus' apocalyptic transformation into eloquent and impassioned liberator ("ibi oratio habita nequaquam eius pectoris ingeniique quod simulatum ad eam diem fuerat"—"Here a speech was delivered by no means of the character and intelligence he had feigned up to that day," 1.59.8). Brutus facilitates Tarquin's overthrow by calling attention to the displacement from accustomed social identities the Romans have suffered under Tarquin: "'Romanos homines, victores omnium circa populorum, opifices ac lapicidas pro bellatoribus factos!'"—"'the Roman people, victors over all the nations around them, [have been] made artisans and stonecutters instead of warriors!'" 1.59.9.

Livy is at some pains to align the details of Tarquin's monarchy with more recent events. Brutus the liberator shouts Republican slogans, while Tarquin emulates, *avant la lettre*, the excesses of various Roman warlords such as Marius, Sulla, and Octavian himself.[67] He makes decisions on his sole authority and dispenses with consulting the Senate; he decimates the Senate and confiscates the property of his political enemies; he promotes Latins friendly to his interests at the expense of the Roman nobility (1.49.2–7). But of all Tarquin's spiritual descendants, only Octavian actually held that to which Tarquin laid claim: a throne that belonged to him and his heirs by biological and natural right. Livy's picture of the last days of the archaic Roman monarchy thus also speaks to the fresh emergence of its contemporary equivalent.

Under the new monarchy, as under the old, all but one Roman lose their familiar moorings of social identity, an unease whose roots Hegel traces to the failure of ideological quilting and whose symptoms we have seen reflected in contemporary sources. Octavian's subjects have not only been precipitated into a world that structurally dictates that they scramble for their places within a new symbolic social network; in this world, the old avenues for doing so—cultivation of one's patrimony, the *cursus honorum*—no longer exist, or no longer exist with anything like the same potential to offer a *place* that confers subjectivity upon its occupant.

Yet I do not point to these facts and these constructions of the social upheaval of the late Republic–early Principate as new—they are news to no one, nor do they fully explain the phenomena of the Gallus poems. Rather, these poems sketch more than a dissatisfaction with the way property rights or upward mobility works under Octavian. They reveal a disenchanted view of social placement, of quilting—a deep suspicion of the "official" explanation of its origins, purposes, and efficacies. These poems do not imply that certain well-conceived mechanisms for interpellating the individual have broken down and need to be fixed. Rather, they view the whole mechanism of social placement, of having subjectivity conferred on one by property, place, or the favor of those in power, as a sham and refuse it entirely. Elegies 1.21 and 1.22 indicate as much when they eschew the easy and obvious construction of Propertius' dead kinsman Gallus as soldier "fallen on the field of honor." That would accord better with the typical interpretation of Propertius as simply and unilaterally anti-Augustan: his kinsman would be positioned as the opposition's hero in the *Schlussgedicht* to Propertius' first publication. But Gallus dies rather as an anonymous pile of bones, killed by a purely contingent meeting with "unknown hands" (*ignotae manus*)—bandits, not enemy soldiers. If, as he himself says, "all the bones" found in Perusia's mountains must be considered his, that amounts to saying that he has himself no particular place or identity as the result of the carnage at Perusia. He is no one and he lies nowhere.

LETTING GO OF ONE'S PLACE

Propertius repeats this gesture of displacement when answering—or rather, not answering—Tullus' questions about his family's status and birthplace in 1.22.

> Qualis et unde genus, qui sint mihi, Tulle, Penates,
>   quaeris pro nostra semper amicitia.
> si Perusina tibi patriae sunt nota sepulcra,
>   Italiae duris funera temporibus,
> cum Romana suos egit discordia civis,
>   (sic mihi praecipue, pulvis Etrusca, dolor,
> tu proiecta mei perpessa es membra propinqui,
>   tu nullo miseri contegis ossa solo),
> proxima supposito contingens Umbria campo
>   me genuit terris fertilis uberibus.
>
> (1.22)

What kind of man I am as far as my family is concerned, where my family is from, who are my household gods, Tullus, you're always asking me in the name of our friendship. If the Perusine graves of our country are known to you, Italy's dead in her grim times, when Rome's own division ruled her citizens (for this reason are you especially a source of sorrow to me, dust of Etruria, because you suffered my kinsman's limbs to be scattered abroad, you cover the poor man's bones with no soil), the land that borders upon [Perusia] with its low-lying fields, fertile Umbria with her rich fields, gave birth to me.

I have previously remarked upon the oddity of Tullus' opening interrogative: Propertius quotes his first word not as *qui* but *qualis*—not "who are you?" but "what kind of a person are you with respect to your family's wealth and social standing?"—and Tullus continues in this vein by asking about the family's geographical origins (*unde*) and present location (*penates*).[68] Tullus' question offers Propertius in a most striking fashion the opportunity to locate himself (Propertius) within the symbolic network—and is refused. Propertius replies vaguely, evasively, with contingent and unspecific images such as mark his kinsman's death. He never really answers two of Tullus' questions (regarding his family and their material standing) and only hints obscurely at an answer to the third.

Note the halting, circuitous, and interrupted movement of Propertius' answer: we reach his birthplace—no, we almost reach it—through an oblique trajectory of contiguity. He begins in Perusia and lingers on its bloody history. An anacoluthon then interrupts that vignette, as he apostrophizes the "Etruscan dust" that refused to cover his kinsman's dead body.[69] The poem's leisurely course then turns toward Umbria, but only through a back-reference to Perusia's low-lying fields. Finally, the poet says "Umbria's rich fields gave birth to me"—vague help at best, since he provides no hint as to where in this extensive region his hometown might be. Propertius' unspecific geographic survey rejects a place in the symbolic network—a network defined, at least in part, by property, especially as property assumes the metaphorical power of defining one's organic relation to citizenship, to social identity. The movement of this poem skirts the borderlines of all pertinent territory, insofar as Propertius will not locate himself in a way that ratifies a center—a point of unification and reference—to the social and geographic territory his poem maps.

So much for the first two parts of my initial question, why these images of fragmentation, and why at this time? Now for the third part: why this man? Why should these poems about displacement revolve around a strongly suggested identification with Cornelius Gallus, the Egyptian prefect? To begin with, Gallus epitomizes the geographic and social displacements that Italy suffered in the years just before the principate. A *novus homo* from Gallia Narbonensis, he nonetheless secures his own advancement by becoming a *vir militaris* useful to Octavian the Triumvir. One of Gallus' early magistracies (41 B.C.E.) involved a role in the confiscation of lands and redistribution to veterans. He apparently did not divide land himself, but only exacted money from towns whose lands remained intact; nonetheless, he participated in a process that (as discussed above) unsettled the geographic bases of Roman identity.[70] Later (30 B.C.E. Octavian appoints him Egyptian prefect, whereupon Gallus unabashedly records his achievements in Africa in terms that invite comparison with the divine pharaohs.[71] While none of these facts make Gallus unique among Octavian's friends and aides-de-camp, combining them with his status as poet does. Gallus' erotic poetry earns him a place in the pantheon of elegists alongside Catullus, and others just as great, in Propertius' eyes; Propertius aspires to that status himself (Prop. 2.34.87–94). Yet Gallus paradoxically combines formidable artistic status (based, ironically, on a genre that rehearses the poet's abasement before a cruel, dominant mistress) with an actual social position of power and prominence. A more naïve Propertius might have been expected to covet that intoxicating combination, holding as it did the promise of direct intervention into history. The Propertius who wrote these poems, however, weighed the allure and found it wanting.[72]

Ultimately Gallus gains prominence in these poems because Propertius could have chosen no better way to deconstruct the concept of ideological quilting than to address Octavian's satellite at the zenith of his power and show the emperor's favored friend to be as unstable in his coherence as all the rest. Not the emperor's favor, nor even Cornelius Gallus' achievements as lover-elegist, can reliably secure him against disintegration—and Propertius makes such dissolution of the subject a problem from the very beginning of the Gallus series, in its moments of ironic bantering. Gallus will be incapacitated and disoriented if he loves Cynthia, Propertius threatens, just as Propertius himself has been: "nec poteris, qui sis aut ubi, nosse miser!" ("you won't be able to know, poor man, who or where you are!" 1.5.18); "nec iam pallorem totiens mirabere nostrum, / aut cur *sim toto corpore nullus ego*" ("and now you won't so often marvel at my pallor, nor wonder why I am wasted to nothing," 1.5.21–22). By the time we pass through the Gallus series and arrive at the sudden shock of seeing Gallus—*a* Gallus—a corpse in the Perusine mountains, the message is clear: Cornelius Gallus has no innate status such as his master claims as de facto monarch; he can easily be the other Gallus, Propertius' kinsman, an indistinguishable corpse lying in some mountain around Perusia; he could even be Propertius himself, divested of substance at Octavian's whim. Ironically, history proved Propertius right.

CHAPTER THREE

The Ethics of Evil: Arethusa to Lycotas (4.3)

Let me powre forth
My teares before thy face, whil'st I stay here,
For thy face coines them, and thy stampe they beare,
And by this Mintage they are something worth,
For thus they bee
Pregnant of thee;
Fruits of much griefe they are, emblemes of more,
When a teare falls, that thou falls which it bore,
So thou and I are nothing then, when on a divers shore.

On a round ball
A workeman that hath copies by, can lay
An Europe, Afrique, and an Asia,
And quickly make that, which was nothing, All;
So doth each teare
Which thee doth weare,
A globe, yea world by that impression grow,
Till thy teares mixt with mine doe overflow
This world, by waters sent from thee, my heaven dissolvéd so.
DONNE, "A VALEDICTION: OF WEEPING"

Propertius 4.3 has rarely caught the attention of scholars on its own merits: Harrauer's exhaustive bibliography of Propertius scholarship from the fifteenth century up to the early 1970s and the chronicle of subsequent years recorded in *L'Année Philologique*—though the elegy has garnered its fair share of textual criticism—list only four interpretive essays devoted exclusively to this epistle from a loving but lonely Augustan matron to her husband away on prolonged military duty; two of these circumscribe their aims to the explication of a single line or phrase within the poem.[1] Many of the books published on Propertius ignore the elegy entirely, or note it only in passing with a paragraph or two.[2] Within thematic discussions of Propertius' poetry, 4.3 typically earns a place as exegetical handmaiden, corroborating evidence to support interpretations of Book IV's more dramatic vignettes.[3] Both readers who seek proof of Propertius' sympathy with Augustan values (the

---

John Donne, *The Elegies and the Songs and Sonnets*, ed. Helen Gardner (Oxford, 1965), 69.

emperor's attempts to shore up traditional Roman marriage through propaganda and legislation, his efforts to legitimize and perpetuate militarily Rome's place at the center of a vast empire), and those more interested in clues to the poet's antipathy, generally pass lightly over 4.3 in favor of grander statements in these veins: Cornelia's review of her life as a virtuous matron of the Roman nobility (4.11), or the quasi-epic narrative of Augustus' naval triumph at Actium (4.6).

Propertius 4.3 has garnered only perfunctory attention even from readers who eschew political interpretation because it has been accepted at face value, as Propertius' portrait of a wife—virtuous and loving, but neither terribly bright nor interesting—writing to her husband away on military duty.[4] At best Arethusa receives patronizing praise for her muddle-headed affection. Margaret Hubbard's comments are among the earliest, but also the most eloquent, observations in this vein:

> The immense procession of relentlessly self-aware and persuasive heroes and heroines [in Roman poetry] can tax the mind, and this intellectualism certainly imposed a limitation rarely overstepped. It is part of the singular charm of Arethusa that by denying her efficient use of the rhetoric of persuasion, by showing her concentrated on the effort to make Lycotas see what she sees, never mind inference or connexion, Propertius has produced one of the few portraits antiquity offers of a good and beautiful noodle, loving, tender, and not in the least clever or formidable.[5]

The "noodle" gallantly supports her husband's military campaigning with supplies of homespun clothing and assiduous sacrifices. Also (as nearly all scholars note) the poem's sympathetic portrayal of a legitimate wife departs markedly from Propertius' steadfast preference for "irregular unions"—such as that between himself and his lover Cynthia—expressed in his previous three books. Little here to interest enthusiasts of Propertius the iconoclast.

There are exceptions to these rules: Judith Hallett and Maria Wyke, for example, both offer provocative and thoughtful readings of 4.3 that turn upon seeing the poem as a condemnation of Augustan military campaigning, a record of the injury wrought by a soldier-husband's enforced absence.[6] I agree that the poem views Rome's militarism with skepticism;[7] I shall show, however, that the problem inheres not in a particular historical moment, but in a profound contradiction at the heart of Roman mores.

The attention the elegy has earned heretofore passes too lightly over some of its quietly odd details. Why, for example, did Propertius choose once, and only once, to frame a love elegy in the form of a letter—what is the significance of this dramatic fiction unique within the Propertian corpus? And what of Arethusa's intriguingly various portrait? She is learned and intellectually curious enough to study a map of the territory covered by her husband's campaigns, at a time when neither maps nor a mastery of cartographic knowledge were common possessions (35–40); she shrewdly fathoms that greed, more than piety, lies behind official enthusiasm for her religious observances (62),[8] and that her nurse's comforting blandishments about winter weather forbidding travel are lies (41–42). Yet Hubbard and other critics have justly noted that Arethusa's letter rarely articulates clear and logical connections between her thoughts.[9] Why does Propertius draw his heroine as such an odd mixture of "noodle" and *docta puella*?[10] And why does *this* poem introduce Book IV's surprising experiments in female subjectivity, unprecedented in Propertius' work—what qualifies Arethusa to introduce the last book's female narrators? These and other questions merit deeper examination if we are fully to understand the poem's importance both in itself and within the context of Book IV.

CORRESPONDENCE

Arethusa begins her plaint by drawing attention to the physical evidence carried by her letter that testifies to her distress:

> si qua tamen tibi lecturo pars oblita derit,
>   haec erit e lacrimis facta litura meis:
> aut si qua incerto fallet te littera tractu,
>   signa meae dextrae iam morientis erunt.
>
> (4.3.3–6)
>
> If you miss any part as you read because it is smeared, my tears erased it. Or if any character puzzles you because of its uncertain formation, that's because I languish as my hand writes these words.

A letter is the only common instrument of communication that could relay such marks of the body between lovers at a distance. Arethusa's letter draws attention to her body as witness to knowledge rejected and suppressed by Rome's prevailing "wisdom." Love forms so small a part of the empire's calculations that it flatly forbids enlisted men to marry, while officers like Lycotas answer state demands that reduce their marriages to little more than exchanges of correspondence.[11] 4.3's attention to the body as the icon of another truth sounds a theme central to Book IV's concentration on the feminine, and thus appropriately introduces Propertius' meditation on Woman. In 4.4, for example, Tarpeia offers betrothal rather than armed opposition to the Sabine chief; proffering herself as pledge foreshadows the fact that intermarriage, not weapons, will ultimately secure Rome's ascendancy over its Sabine neighbors. Elegies 4.5 and 4.7 belie elegy's idyllic visions of lifelong fidelity by highlighting the gruesome, solitary ends of faded and forsaken beauties who bear the physical marks of poverty and neglect. Their ends are oddly mirrored at the other end of the social and matrimonial scale, when Cornelia sees the impossible demands of the Roman ethic as so many tortures inflicted on her own and others' flesh. Elegies 4.8 and 4.9 contrast the body's culturally inscribed exterior and its extra-symbolic interior as parallel, respectively, to sanctioned "official wisdom" and to the chaotic, disruptive truth it covers over. Everywhere, the flesh insists on what Rome does not want to know.

As Arethusa writes this letter marked with physical tokens of her loneliness, she surveys her husband's campaigns so as to place him at every corner of the empire, sometimes more than once (rather implausibly, as often noted—his activities exceed any known military endeavors undertaken in the Augustan period).[12] The terms of this geographical catalogue are nonetheless strangely familiar, though they echo literary rather than military history; specifically, they look to Catullus 11, another poem on erotic alienation.[13]

> te modo viderunt iteratos *Bactra* per ortus,
>   te modo munito Sericus hostis equo,
> hibernique Getae, pictoque *Britannia* curru,
>   *ustus* et *Eoa* decolor *Indus aqua*.
>
> (7-10)

Just now Bactra has seen you, because the eastern lands are revisited, just now the Chinese foe on his armored horse, and the wintry Getae, and Britain on her painted chariot, and the sunburned Indian, stained with the waters of the East.

> Furi et Aureli, comites Catulli,
> sive in extremos penetrabit *Indos,*
> litus ut longe resonante *Eoa*
>   tunditur *unda,*
>
> sive in Hyrcanos Arabasve molles,
> seu Sagas sagittiferosve *Parthos,*
> sive quae septemgeminus *colorat*
>   aequora Nilus,
>
> sive trans altas gradietur Alpes,
> Caesaris visens monimenta magni,
> Gallicum Rhenum horribile aequor ulti-
>   mosque *Britannos*
>
> (Catullus 11.1-12)

Furius and Aurelius, comrades of Catullus, whether he shall penetrate the far-off inhabitants of India, where the shore is struck by the far-resounding dawn-wave; or among the Hyrcani or the effeminate Arabs, or the Sagae, or the arrow-bearing Parthians, or the seven-mouthed Nile that dyes the sea; or if he shall cross the lofty Alps, gazing upon the monuments of great Caesar, and the Gallic Rhine (troubled water!) and those who come last, the Britons.

The italicized words mark geographical or ethnographic details repeated between the two poems, such as:

1. Indians (*Indos,* 11.2; *Indus,* 10)
2. Eastern water (*Eoa . . . unda,* 11.3-4; *Eoa . . . aqua,* 10)
3. Parthia (*sagittiferosve Parthos,* 11.6; *Bactra,* 7)
4. Britain (*Britannos,* 11.12; *pictoque Britannia curru,* 9)
5. discoloration by water (*septemgeminus colorat / aequora Nilus,* 11.7-8; *ustus et Eoa decolor Indus aqua,* 4.3.10; if we accept Housman's emendation of *ustus* to

tu(n)sus, then the resemblance to Catullus 11 strengthens, picking up *tunditur* from 11.4).[14]

Propertius 4.3 echoes Catullus 11, and never more obviously so than when Propertius' elegy unexpectedly veers northwest, to Britain, in the midst of a list of Eastern sites. Propertius thus reproduces the gesture that interrupted the direction of Catullus' geographical catalogue as it marched from the East towards Rome, only to skip over Rome and jump northwest suddenly over the Alps to Germany and Britain.[15]

Why would Propertius take such pains to recall Catullus' farewell to Lesbia? Surely the bitterness of the earlier poet's poem jars as a background invoked for Arethusa's plaintive but affectionate letter to her husband. Yet Catullus 11 shares with 4.3 an unexpected alignment of relations between the sexes with military-political relations between nations as the defining moments of *Romanitas*. Representative of Rome in Catullus 11 are her citizens' egregious accomplishments in these two arenas: Julius Caesar's expansion of the empire (9–12) and Lesbia's expansion of sexual possibilities, her embracing three hundred lovers at once (17–20). Moreover, Lesbia's sexual voracity figures Roman expansionism, which Catullus elsewhere (e.g., c.29) associates directly with insane extravagance.[16] The desire for conquest—indiscriminate, greedy, and wasteful—unites both sexual and political spheres.[17]

SPINNING MAN

Propertius 4.3 accepts Catullus' suggestion that Rome's military engagement with other nations mirrors her citizens' sexuality, structurally and functionally, but paints this mirroring relationship as more than an historical contingency, part of the evils that accompanied the Republic's demise and the Principate's birth. Rather, the relationship revolves around a fundamental conceptual deadlock in Roman identity, particularly Roman male identity—a deadlock founded in part on the impossibility of defining "Man" and "Woman," "Roman" and "non-Roman," as stable essences rather than as mere terms in a differential relationship (as established in chapter 1, "Citizens and Lovers"). The impossibility either of evading or solving this deadlock paradoxically motivates repeated futile attempts to do so. Hence the implausibly comprehensive design of Lycotas' campaigns: they represent frenetic activity as a concept, rather than as historical fact,[18] with Lycotas' assignments forming an icon of repetition.[19] Hence also the curious conceptual thread Arethusa spins between ceaseless military campaigns at the extremes of the empire and the familiar narrow confines of domesticity:

> occidat, immerita qui carpsit ab arbore vallum
> et struxit querulas rauca per ossa tubas,
> dignior obliquo funem qui torqueat Ocno,
> aeternusque tuam pascat, aselle, famem!
> (19–22)

May he die, the one who snatched a palisade stake from an innocent tree and fashioned mournful trumpets from harsh-voiced bones; he deserves to twist rope more than Ocnus (who sits sideways to his work) and eternally to feed your hunger, little ass!

Ocnus twisted rope in Hell for the bottomless hunger of an ass as punishment for failing all his life to control his wife's extravagance; her squandering made all his hard work futile. Arethusa's allusion reverses the sexual and spatial relations of the fable: Ocnus as husband catered to his wife, but Arethusa as wife industriously and ceaselessly supplies her rapacious husband (with warm home-woven cloaks, for example); Lycotas' rapacity finds its scope in the extremes of the world, while the greed of Ocnus' wife expressed itself close to home. Yet Arethusa's allusion to a parable of domestic squabbling summarizes national tensions so shrewdly that details of scale and gender fade to insignificance. Propertius 4.3 shows sexual and national relations revolving about a common axis, their tensions founded on the impossibility of conceiving these relations essentially. Masculinity and the dominion over Woman that it implies are for Ocnus not a fact or birthright consubstantial with male anatomy, but an achievement—and an achievement he signally misses. Similarly, defining Rome through defense of her geographical, political, and conceptual boundaries is a battle always to be fought again—with such as Lycotas to fight it—rather than a secure possession, an identity. Filling out the empty frame of *Romanitas*, especially for Rome's men, is a Sisyphean task.

Propertius' elegy shares with Catullus 11 a disturbing contiguity that traces the expansive extremes of Rome's empire within a narrowly circumscribed domestic economy at her center; also like Catullus' poem, 4.3 depicts the empire's edges as strangely intense arenas for the negotiation of sexuality as well as sovereignty. Catullus imagined his path across the world both as an itinerary of implied sexual conquest (he will "penetrate" the Indians, 2) and an ethnography based on sexual stereotypes (the Arabs are "effeminate," the Parthians characterized by their phallic-shaped arrows, 5–6). Arethusa's letter repeats this gesture of alignment between the sexual and political spheres as she imagines Lycotas' military activities. His army life takes place in a strangely hypersexual hinterland, where amid the rigors of army life, erotic lures abound:

> dic mihi, num teneros urit lorica lacertos?
> num gravis imbellis atterit hasta manus?
> haec noceant potius, quam dentibus ulla puella
> det mihi plorandas per tua colla notas!
> (23–26)

> tell me, can it be that the shield-strap chafes your arms? can it be that the heavy spear blisters your unwarlike hands? Better that these things hurt you, than that any girl give your neck marks that must make me weep!

Here and elsewhere the elegy portrays sexuality in the contested borderlands as a shifting and unstable field. Arethusa characterizes Lycotas as having "unwarlike hands" (*imbellis manus*) and "delicate arms" (*teneros lacertos*), oddly portraying him as a soft and rather effeminate boy—implausible of a man who has negotiated the campaigns she attributes to him, even if their scope is exaggerated. Some have dismissed these details by saying that they indicate her alternately jealous and romantic imagination of the man she loves; but that would not explain why this creeping eroticism and effeminacy also affects Lycotas' enemies:[20]

> ne, precor, ascensis tanti sit gloria Bactris,
>   raptave odorato carbasa lina duci,
> plumbea cum tortae sparguntur pondera fundae,
>   subdolus et versis increpat arcus equis!
> (63–66)
>
> Let not, I beg you, the glory of the ascent of Bactra be worth so much, nor the fine linen snatched from a perfumed lord, when lead weights are scattered from the twisted sling, and the crafty archer lets fly his whistling arrows, though his horse is turned in retreat!

This scented nobleman, clad in exquisite linen, resembles less a dour foe than an attractive *puella* (elegy's ubiquitous alluring young woman). *Odoratus* ("fragrant") in Propertius often denotes perfume associated with feminine or androgynous charm; *carbasa* occurs only here in Propertius, but *carbasus* ("fine white linen") he associates with women's garments.[21] Moreover, the elegy concentrates on Lycotas denuding his enemy, rather than more pragmatic possibilities (killing the opponent, for example, or plundering his more marketable assets—gold, jewels, coins, fine weapons—instead of cloth that has seen the worst of battle). Lycotas' encounter with the enemy oddly resembles the amorous tussles between Propertius and Cynthia, which also focus on struggles over clothing.[22] Yet Arethusa's imaginative vignette eerily reverses Propertius' representations of his erotic bouts with Cynthia as "battles" worthy to replace epic subject matter: now battle itself appears in the guise of erotic contest, between a Roman soldier and his curiously seductive enemy.[23]

"EVIL, BE THOU MY GOOD"

The seductiveness of this enemy merits attention, because it bears upon the exact nature of the conceptual deadlock at the heart of Roman identity. Catharine Edwards' recent comprehensive study of Roman morality has shown that Romans saw their nation's identity as founded upon superior moral qualities.[24] To her observation must be added the fact that these virtues revolve around the harsh disciplines necessary to military life: self-denial, hard work, endurance. For example, Sallust and Livy both link the empire won by the Roman ancestors' military successes to those ancestors' circumspect, spare mode of life, seeing a causal link between the two: the ancestors built the empire on the foundation of *labores* ("toil"), *disciplina* ("discipline"), *paupertas* ("poverty"), *parsimonia* ("frugality").[25] Yet though war forges these virtues, it also destroys them. Sallust remarks bitterly that once Rome vanquished her last serious rival, Carthage, the chief motivation for strict adherence to military discipline disappeared, and Rome deteriorated into greed and luxury (*Cat.* 10). Sallust does not suggest, however, that this moral deterioration followed a cessation in military activity—to the contrary, luxury becomes inextricably entwined with army life, its natural consequence:

> L. Sulla exercitum quem in Asia ductaverat, quo sibi fidum faceret, contra morem maiorum luxuriose nimisque liberaliter habuerat. Loca amoena, voluptaria, facile in otio ferocis animos molliverant. (Sall. *Cat.* 11.5)
>
> So that he might make the army that he had often led in Asia loyal to himself, Sulla maintained it contrary to the customs of the ancestors, in luxurious living and excessive freedom. Pleasant places, indulgences, had in leisure easily softened their warrior's courage.

Propertius' seductive enemy commander, as an image of war's potential to corrupt, summarizes a felt contradiction at the heart of Rome's defining commitment to a martial ethic. Livy and Polybius second Sallust's uneasiness about the effect of war on morality, as Jasper Griffin notes:

> Livy laments, of Marcellus' triumph over Syracuse in 211: "That was the beginning of the vogue for Greek works of art and of the modern rage for looting sacred and profane objects on a universal scale" (25.40.1). Of Vulso's triumph over Asia in 187 he laments: "The source of Eastern luxuriousness was brought to Rome by the army on this occasion" (39.6.7–9). With art goes *luxuria*, debauchery: Polybius says the triumph of Aemilius Paullus in 168 turned young men's minds to "catamites, courtesans, music and drinking."[26]

When late Republican and Imperial historians speak thus of war and soldiering as introducing luxurious appetites both to the soldiers and to the populace at large, they articulate a curious paradox: the very qualities deemed antithetical to luxury—self-denial, hard work, endurance—themselves elicit that vice. Sallust appears uneasily aware of this, insofar as his description of the deterioration of Roman moral and political life traces a trajectory that begins not with Roman virtues atrophied, but rather magnified: being exaggerated, virtue reveals the structure it shares with vice.

> Sed primo magis ambitio quam avaritia animos hominum exercebat, quod tamen vitium propius virtutem erat. Nam gloriam, honorem, imperium bonus et ignavos aeque sibi exoptant; sed ille vera via nititur, huic, quia bonae artes desunt, dolis atque fallaciis contendit. (*Cat.* 11.1–2)
>
> But at first ambition more than greed goaded people's hearts—which after all was a vice rather close to virtue. For glory, honor, power, the good man and the villain equally desire for themselves; but the former attempts it by an honest path, while the latter, because he lacks honest skills, strives with trickery and deceit.

The good man and the ignoble man share the same structure, differing only in content, in the specific means by which they seek their common goal. The flaw here elucidated—the hidden commerce between virtue and vice, that assimilates the one to the other—indicates that Rome's identity, founded on her primordial virtues, contains within itself its own inversion. What curious equation is at work here, that the very characteristics that constitute Roman identity themselves undermine it?

THE VANISHING MEDIATOR

Slavoj Žižek's ruminations on the logical mechanisms behind the erection of mores can help us here. Žižek draws upon a concept elucidated by Fredric Jameson in analyzing the work of Max Weber, a concept Jameson calls the "vanishing mediator." Jameson applies the concept to Weber's analysis of Protestantism as the mediator between medieval feudalism and bourgeois capitalism.[27] Weber had observed that medieval Catholicism limited the sphere of asceticism to particular strata within the church—to the saints, for example, or to the religious orders; but Protestantism conceived of religion as pandemically relevant to the life of all believers and articulated an ideal of Christian life as intrinsically ascetic, even for the laity and even in mundane, everyday practices. Hence the emergence of the Protestant "work ethic" that enjoined the Christian to live in temperance and modesty, renouncing consumption. The Protestant accordingly accumulated wealth rather than spending it. The concept of the "vanishing mediator" devolves from the fact that this high-minded ethic led to its very opposite—to secular accumulation as an end in itself—and that this apparent transformation was inevitable, because it was not, in fact, a transformation at all. The ascetic Protestant worker already is the acquisitive secular capitalist in *form*, insofar as Protestantism has articulated economic activity as the domain of the manifestation of God's grace; the Protestant lacks only the capitalist's specific content. Once acquisition is legitimated as an end in itself, the further step to secular acquisitiveness requires only that the very religion that enabled such a shift gradually dwindle in importance as sanction. Religion's work having been accomplished, it can drop away.

Žižek refines this analysis by aligning it with the Lacanian concept of *méconnaissance*, "misrecognition," whereby the subject fails to recognize in the Other his own inverted image. Similarly, the utopian vision that controls any ethical system *is* in fact the very fundamental structure of the subject's present existence: the "vulgar" activities that appear to betray his high ideals already realize the ideal after which he strives.[28] From this perspective, *Romanitas* bears within itself the seeds of its own contradiction: the virtues that prove Rome's moral excellence, support her conquest of foreign territory, and define Roman identity are a constellation of traits that, like Protestantism, catalyze an exchange of energies between otherwise mutually exclusive terms. Self-denial, compulsive effort, and tolerance of adverse circumstances can be harnessed to any ambition, beneficent or malicious, without fundamentally changing the *structure* of the good. The ease with which principled virtue can shift into principled vice raises the spectre of an ethics of evil not fundamentally distinguishable from an ethics of good. Precisely this horrifies Cicero and Sallust about the ne'er-do-well and suspected revolutionary Catiline: he endures cold, hunger, sleeplessness, ceaseless work, and self-denial as stoically in the service of libertinism as any Cato or Regulus in pursuit of honor; Catiline cheerfully harnesses Roman ideals to anathema.[29]

Moreover, a shared structure between vice and virtue implies the inevitable conversion of one to the other: compulsive work and parsimony lead to the accumulation of material wealth; military success based on strict discipline leads to contact with foreign cultures and their "decadent," "luxurious" customs; expanding the empire's bounds makes it all the more difficult to maintain Rome's political and conceptual centrality. Catharine Edwards draws attention to Ovid's remark upon the Roman state, "gentibus est aliis tellus data limite certo: / Romanae spatium est urbis et orbis idem"—"to other nations, territory with a fixed boundary has been given; the expanse of the city of Rome and of the world are the same" (*Fasti* 2.683–84). Of this she shrewdly observes: "a state that shared its boundaries with those of the entire world effectively had none. The city was full of people whose families had not long lived in Rome; Roman citizens dwelt all over the known world. To be Roman no longer meant to be an inhabitant of the city of Rome. What then could it mean?"[30] On the evidence of Propertius 4.3, it means nothing fundamentally different from the Other and his "decadence."

JUST WOMAN

The contours of this contradictory rapprochement between "virtue" and "vice," "Roman" and "Other," shape Arethusa's portrait of herself spinning wool at home for her husband's needs in camp—yet not all of its oddity is Propertius' invention. Arethusa's self-portrait borrows heavily from that secular saint of Roman mythology, Lucretia, especially as portrayed in Livy's definitive version of her rape by the Etruscan-Roman prince Sextus Tarquinius. Livy's portrait of the early Roman noblewoman is nearly as complicated as Propertius' sketch of her latter-day counterpart, being traversed by the same tensions: as a portrait of the exemplary *men's* lives and mores Livy announced he would lay forth in his book, the men who "inaugurate and increase Rome's dominion," the tale is curiously cynical.[31] The Roman noblemen-soldiers who ride back to Rome with Collatinus to find his wife Lucretia chastely spinning wool with her maids do so in an idle moment during a national project of robbery. They have besieged Ardea desiring to plunder the city's riches rather than responding to any legitimate offense or soldierly ambition, as Livy clearly says (1.57.1–2). They have already idled away the protracted siege in drinking and dining; the contest of wifely virtues but diverts them afresh from boredom. Lucretia's hard work and self-denial contrasts not only with the carousing of the other princes' brides, but with that of her husband's military companions as well (1.57.4–11). Livy's picture reveals no great difference between the vices he laments among modern Romans and the idolized past, except in Lucretia: the integrity of Roman identity, the assumed *mos maiorum*, rests entirely on an exemplary *woman*.

Contemporary history furnished an egregious model of this same trope: Augustus supported his austere public image by having the women of his household spin clothes for him—an absurd, but apparently effective, symbolic contrast to his fabulous wealth and rumored private excesses.[32] While Roman writers frequently play upon the etymological connection between *vir* ("man") and *virtus* ("moral excellence") portraying rectitude as an exclusively male province, Livy's portrait of the "good old days" divides ethical labor as his emperor did: his tale shows the entire weight of virtue resting on Lucretia, as though her saintliness absolved the men from the burden of Roman identity.[33]

Propertius expands upon the interlocking contrasts Livy sketched—between Roman soldiers and one exemplary wife; between two economies, one of self-denial and the other of luxurious consumption—by having Arethusa reproduce the picture of Lucretia as chaste spinner for her soldier-husband. Arethusa lives in the midst of *both* economies' contradiction: surrounded by wealth, a spirit of asceticism nonetheless makes her indifferent to these luxuries, as she thriftily spins wool for her husband (4.3.33–34, 51–53). Livy's mythology of the roots of the Roman "character" located a contradiction *ab origine* at that mythology's heart, in the contrast between Lucretia and the officers assailing Ardea; Propertius simply pushes that contradiction to its logical conclusion. The elegist depicts luxury at the edges of the empire, corrupting Roman masculinity—Lycotas' soldiering, as imagined in this poem, appears little more than an essay in debauchery and pillage—while virtue finds a feminine champion, determined but harried, locked in a losing battle at Rome's heart. Arethusa, the modern Lucretia, spins as an exercise in absurd necessity. The wealth surrounding her renders her labor materially superfluous at the same time that it necessitates her spinning as a symbolic effort. She (as Woman) must bear the weight of Man's identity as compulsively working ascetic; as in the Lucretia story, the contradiction at the heart of Roman virtue finds expression in a contrast between men aligned with the pursuit of wealth and the "good woman" aligned with the renunciation of wealth.[34]

Like Livy's tale of Lucretia, Arethusa's self-portrait intertwines the spheres of sexuality (relations between husband and wife, Man and Woman) and nationalism (relations between Rome and other nations, Rome and Roman citizen); unlike Livy, she sketches sexuality and national identity as pivoting upon repetition inspired by futility. Lycotas' campaigns *for* Rome prevent him from residing *at* Rome—his *Romanitas* depends upon cyclical exile from the city. Arethusa spins constantly, an icon of a good Roman wife's duty to oversee the domestic economy—except no Roman household commands her Lucretian industry, but the bottomless need of her husband's military encampments abroad. She assiduously offers sacrifice for her husband's return to married life, yet his safe return makes his departure inevitable. The logical contradiction structuring these examples indicates that the repetitions originate in a structural flaw, a flaw that motivates endless, and endlessly frustrated, attempts to overcome it. Arethusa's vignettes describe a common revolution around the axis of identity—around *Romanitas*, particularly the "Romanness" of men, as the paradigmatic citizens. Arethusa's marriage fits Lacan's observation on the sexual non-relation, that its ever-repeated frustrations stem from the impossibility of a truly complementary relationship between the positions Man and Woman, a relationship that would anchor Man's identity in being, rather than in mere opposition to the other term, Woman.

The same logic governs the frustrations of nationalism: the longing for an essential "Romanness," an ethos and ethics of Rome, inspires repeated attempts to transcend the merely differential relationship that distinguishes Roman from non-Roman, "virtue" from "decadence"—and consequently, inspires blindness to the way that one term merely inverts the other without essentially changing its structure. Lycotas' eerie plasticity and exotic setting point to an intertwining of all these logical patterns: he wavers, in Arethusa's imagination, between hardened, manly campaigner and soft, effeminate *puer*, loyal citizen and thrall of the enemy's material and sexual lures (25–26, 51–52, 64, 69–70).

THE FATHER OF ENJOYMENT

Lycotas' ambiguous confrontations with the Other also juxtapose sexuality and nationalism insofar as they illustrate Lacan's conceptualization of the masculine: a universality based on a single, subverting exception. In Lycotas' confrontation with the perfumed enemy general at the edge of the world, Roman masculinity meets its despised mirror image in the decadent Eastern prince, who nonetheless symbolizes what structurally informs Roman identity: Rome's ascetic discipline bent to luxurious acquisition. But the hostile commander represents more than a foil or even *frère enemi* to Rome's soldier. Lycotas, disciplined Roman subject who submits to Law, discovers a doppelgänger at the edges of the world who paradoxically summarizes both the contradiction and foundation of Law's universality.

Lycotas' confrontation with the Other rests on the logic of Freud's *Totem and Taboo*. Freud's essay unsurprisingly traces Law to the (primordial) Father as agent of prohibition, a role familiar from Freud's earlier writings on the Oedipus complex. His mythical history sketches a tribe's powerful leader and father who, by keeping all the women of the tribe to himself, inspires resentment in his followers-sons. The sons eventually rebel and murder him, but remorse leads them to renounce the reward their deed has gained—the women; hence the inception of Law as the incest taboo.[35] Yet, as Slavoj Žižek has pointed out, the Father who anchors prohibition as the basis of Law is, paradoxically, the voracious, uninhibited, cruel tyrant—the "Father of Enjoyment," Žižek christens him; 4.3's sketch of Roman confronting the decadent Other reflects just that logical relationship.[36] The scented enemy commander only inverts the Roman ethos, without changing it structurally—which emerges in Lycotas' imagined libertinage at the borders of the empire. Arethusa sees him as growing thin from the rigors of army life, his hands and arms chafed by heavy weapons, while at the same time he succumbs to women mysteriously abundant and available on the frontier (4.3.23–27). She even (as remarked above) assimilates his combats to erotic contests, imagining him unclothing his oddly seductive enemy in battle (64). The poem thus sketches wars of foreign conquest as sources of "enjoyment," both in the common and in the Lacanian sense of that word. They pour forth corrupting pleasure, and so expose a fundamental non-sense, a contradiction (the Lacanian meaning of "enjoyment") in Roman identity: *Romanitas* is literally unthinkable without the decadent, despised Other. The Other "opens up the space for" Roman virtue to be conceived; paradoxically, the Other's vice is therefore logically prior to, more fundamental than, *Romanitas*.[37] Little wonder, then, that the spectre of decadence haunts Lycotas in the execution of his central Roman duty, vigilantly (and futilely) to police the geographical and conceptual boundaries of *Romanitas*.

GENDERED LOGIC

Roman masculinity viewed thus through a Lacanian lens emerges as a logical relation rather than a matter either of anatomy or geography. The implications of this formulation emerge fully if we consider the way Lacan, in his twentieth Seminar (*Encore*), defines masculine and feminine via symbolic logic as antinomies of conceptualization. Žižek, aligning Lacan's elaboration with one of the psychoanalyst's chief sources, Kant's *Critique of Pure Reason*, summarizes gender opposition as follows:

> Both feminine and masculine positions are therefore defined by a fundamental antinomy: the masculine universe involves the universal network of causes and effects founded in an exception (the "free" subject which theoretically grasps its object, the causal universe of the Newtonian physics); the feminine universe is the universe of boundless dispersion and divisibility which, for that very reason, can never be rounded off into a universal Whole.[38]

The subject who assumes the masculine position believes that he sees all, and can grasp the pattern that unites disparate phenomena into a whole "freely," that is, without himself affecting, or being implicated in, his calculations; the subject who assumes the feminine position shies away from such hubris, doubting that the world can be understood so easily and aloofly. The images surrounding Lycotas' military activities and Arethusa's view of them repeatedly reproduce this contrast between masculine and feminine as universality versus heterogeneity, (false) confidence versus skepticism. Chief among these is her map, wondrous and unusual instrument for a Roman household.[39]

> et disco, qua parte fluat vincendus Araxes,
>   quot sine aqua Parthus milia currat equus;
> cogor et e tabula pictos ediscere mundos,
>   qualis et haec docti sit positura dei,
> quae tellus sit lenta gelu, quae putris ab aestu,
>   ventus in Italiam qui bene vela ferat.
> (35–40)

And I learn, in what part the Araxes that must be conquered flows, how many miles the Parthian horse runs without water; and I am compelled to learn these painted worlds from a wooden plaque, and of what nature is this arrangement of the clever god: what land is stiff with cold, which is crumbling from heat, what wind bears your sails into Italy.

Arethusa's map surprises simply because our information about Augustan-era maps points to grand and public affairs, august expressions of Rome's supremacy as "mistress of the world" (*domina orbis terrarum*), rather than to private possessions. The huge *mappa mundi* executed by Agrippa at Augustus' command comes first to mind: Claude Nicolet's skillful analysis shows how these Roman representations of the world were used ideologically, as instruments designed to demonstrate Rome's centrality both geographically and politically.[40] Arethusa's map nonetheless reflects these grander maps insofar as it perfectly expresses the masculine epistemological position. Her cartographic overview depicts the world as a universal network of causes and effects founded in an exception—the "free" (Roman) subject assumed as the observer of the map, who masters the object of his contemplation both epistemologically and militarily. Arethusa's map renders the world graphically as a Whole, and appends "causal" explanations of its order: "this land is stiff because it is cold; that land is rotten because it is hot; in Parthia, horses can go without water for long distances" (36, 39). Natural history and geography are made to support Rome's superiority over the rest of the world,[41] while offering a graceful excuse (in the form of Parthian horses' toughness) for Rome's inability to control Parthia, an annoying exception to her self-image as the world's conqueror.[42]

Yet the map's observations on Parthian toughness also introduce a shadow of doubt to Rome seen as the world's overlord—a feminine skepticism strengthened in Arethusa's own description of her map. She names part of the landscape portrayed as "the Araxes that must be conquered" (4.3.35), a double-edged comment. Dee observes: "*vincendus Araxes* (35) may carry some mild sarcasm—one thinks of Darius and Xerxes."[43] While neither monarch had any particularly memorable contact with the Araxes, both were persistently troubled by bodies of water in their military campaigns, all through their own overweening self-confidence. Darius unthinkingly placed the fate of the Persian empire in the hands of one man by appointing Histiaios of Miletus to guard the bridge the Persian king had thrown over the Bosphorus and the Danube in Scythia (Herodotus 7.10 γ-δ. Darius was lucky—Histiaios proved loyal, despite the enemy's efforts to persuade him to destroy the bridge—but the Persian king risked much. Xerxes, on the other hand, raged infamously when his bridge over the Hellespont smashed in a storm, ordering the strait flogged, branded, and chained (7.34–35). The Araxes, as a similar expanse of water that "must be conquered," ironically shades Arethusa's description of its creator as *doctus*: ("cogor et e tabula pictos ediscere mundos, / qualis et haec *docti* sit positura dei," 37–38): laid out on a map, the world seems knowable, able to be mastered both epistemologically and physically. Sufficient knowledge, coupled with sufficient might, should ensure the observant and calculating conqueror's success. But the god's "arrangement" (*positura*) is not so easily grasped. *Positura* implies an organizing rationale and a sophisticated divine mind, just as the map of the arrangement is comprehensive and rendered a rational whole. Yet the word "doctus" subtly fractures that perspective: Richardson notes that *doctus* is "the word P. reserves for what is elegant and clever"[44]—not a word to imply wisdom, as one might expect from a god, but cleverness, drollery, wit at someone else's expense.[45] *Doctus*, in Propertius' vocabulary, hinges on irony, and thus on the principle that someone will miss the jest: such wit aims at the select few, rather than the vulgar many.[46] How, then, can the perceiver ever be sure that she or he sees as one of the cognoscenti?

Doctus introduces a crack into the epistemological premise of the map, that posits an object (the world, and the chain of causality supposed to shape it) to be understood and therefore mastered by an autonomous, objective subject. Arethusa's choice of words subtly implies that that subject is a fool, who thinks he masters the world (both in the epistemological and in the political sense) merely because he thinks; the *doctus* god's-eye view, on the other hand, assumes the ironic, feminine epistemological position. The map's promise to render the world available for immediate apprehension is therefore illusory, the witty god's joke on humanity. Xerxes received just this object lesson in how little certain geographical elements adhere to an obvious, predictable chain of causality (though he characteristically refused the lesson); Darius arrogantly assumed that he knew how to conquer a river, failing to see how thin he stretched the thread on which hung his campaign's success, because he depended on one geographical weak link. These princes summarize the logical conundrum that something must *always* escape calculation in order logically to produce the "free" subject posited as grasping the chain of causality: the subject assumes that his own calculations do not implicate him (as Darius and Xerxes assume that *they* can act freely, but nothing and no one else can—no contingency, therefore, need be taken into account). Similarly, the knowledge available from Arethusa's map plays its observer false, insofar as it purports to offer a comprehensive and transparent representation of its object; it corresponds to "masculine" knowledge.

The faint "cracks" traced in the map's view of the world as Rome's dominion hint at a feminine epistemological position, suspicious of any attempt to round a collection off into a Whole. Arethusa's viewpoint deepens and emphasizes this feminine epistemology of "not-all," of comprehensiveness without universality; she sees the world as "boundless and dispersed," fractured by exceptions to Roman domination. Her letter describes a series of loosely connected vignettes (her troubled nights, her spinning, the rounds of worship services, her puppy Craugis' barking). Even Lycotas appears to her as a fetishized set of disembodied limbs—hands and arms rubbed raw by his weapons, neck marked with women's teeth, face thinned by hunger. Her skeptical and fragmentary view yields a more comprehensive picture that takes into account such embarrassing details as the Parthians' and the Araxes' tough intransigence, the dull absurdities of Roman matronal life, the fragility of her husband's body-discipline. By contrast, scientific, "objective" knowledge she takes *cum grano salis,* seeing the interested subject-position behind it. She knows, for example, that her solicitous nurse's meteorological explanations for Lycotas' absence are lies fashioned to soothe her ("curis et pallida nutrix / peierat hiberni temporis esse moras"—"And my nurse, pale with worry, lies that these are the winter season's delays," 41–42). Arethusa's letter dramatizes the irreconcilable deadlock between "feminine" and "masculine" ways of organizing phenomena as the central tension that shapes *Romanitas.*

THE LETTER AND THE MAP

Arethusa's map and her letter, as symbols both of dispersion and integration, together summarize the specific tensions that traverse the notion of *Romanitas* in the late Republic and early Empire. As Claude Nicolet has pointed out, the empire's expansion during the Republican period presented unprecedented problems in administering the territory obtained. The exigencies of administration forced a broad reconceptualization of the parameters of citizenship and political office: timocratic, familial, and personal structures gradually gave way to topography as the basis of administration. Organization by tribes or centuries no longer served in the face of the citizen body's dispersion on the one hand and Augustus' reaffirmation of Rome as the geographical, political, and spiritual center of the empire on the other. As Nicolet puts it, the circulation of documents had to replace the circulation of people if administration were to continue to be centered at Rome; topography offered the easiest principle by which to organize these tokens of the far-flung and heterogeneous body of Roman citizens (hence Augustus' division of Italy into the twelve *regiones*).[47]

Arethusa sketches a melancholy picture of the citizenry's dispersion: all the world may see Lycotas in the flesh, but husband and wife can only exchange letters. Her letter thus represents the fact that most of the population of the empire whose borders Lycotas defends are citizens only to the degree that they have been replaced by symbols in the empire's administrative network. Her map, on the other hand, guides the circulation of such symbols, in, say, the transport of the documents necessary to the census from the corners of the empire to Rome, where they are recorded and analyzed. The letter and the map between them summarize *both* masculine and feminine epistemological perspectives on *Romanitas:* the letter's mobility metonymically represents the citizenry's increasing heterogeneity and geographic dispersion, that requires its representation by documents; the map, on the other hand, guides efforts to weave this heterogeneity into a Whole, both by directing the documents to Rome, and representing as a unity the territory Rome anchors. The poem records tensions in this symbolic organization of space, in large and small arenas: Rome may be the center of the world, but Arethusa sketches it as a desert, its people replaced by mere tokens of themselves—she kisses Lycotas' arms in lieu of himself (30); in the middle of the city, her house is so silent and deserted she welcomes her puppy's barking (55). Yet (as noted at the beginning of this chapter) intractable traces of physical being that refuse symbolization—her tear-smudges—mar her letter, the representation of herself (3–4). There is "something in Rome that is more than Rome," and it struggles, constantly, to emerge.

CHAPTER FOUR

"Beyond Good and Evil": Tarpeia and Philosophy in the Feminine (4.4)

> *Past and past the waters glide,*
> *And I bathe my hands and hair.*
> *Lo, my hands stain not the stream.*
> *Did I not say this was a dream?*
> *Face nor hands are hard and red,*
> *And soft leaves drop all round my head,*
> *And soft weeds round my dipping feet*
> *Stir and change and gleam.*
> *I rest! My rest is very sweet.*
> SWINBURNE,
> "THE DREAM BY THE RIVER"

Propertius 4.4 retells as a love story how the Vestal Virgin Tarpeia betrayed Rome to the Sabines. As in other versions of the tale, she bargains with Rome's enemy and leads them into the Capitoline citadel by an unsuspecting path; the Sabine king, Tatius, rewards her by having his soldiers crush her to death beneath their shields. But Propertius uniquely attributes her treason to passionate love for Tatius: she bargained to be his queen, not for gold, as more cynical authors have it.[1] How to interpret this elegy's revision of a founding Roman myth has puzzled numerous commentators, who commonly throw all questions onto the axis of Augustan politics. Some see the poem as evidence of the poet's tardy sympathy with Augustus' program: Propertius allegedly repudiates pure love-elegy as inimical to Augustus' moral and political reforms and condemns Tarpeia to prove he has rejected his old elegiac sympathies.[2] Others detect irony beneath his patriotism, proclaiming his "Augustan" moral severity but a thin veneer, donned for protection from an increasingly intolerant regime: Propertius reveals his still-warm elegiac loyalty, they say,

---

Algernon Swinburne, *The Complete Works of Algernon Charles Swinburne*, ed. Edmund Gosse and Thomas James Wise (London, 1925), 1:99.

when he converts a tale of Tarpeia's greed into a chronicle of her star-crossed love for the Sabine king.[3]

Yet this poem's ambiguities, which lend themselves to such divergent interpretations, exceed the frame of Augustan politics alone. This chapter argues that elegy 4.4 interrogates the very binary logic implied in framing its loyalties as either "pro-Augustan" or "anti-Augustan."[4] One of Lacan's most inspired and unorthodox disciples, Luce Irigaray, can help us here by extending the trajectory of Lacan's thought on the feminine far beyond where it stood at the time of his death in 1981.[5] Her work confronts contemporary thought with the problematic elements of a consistently unacknowledged symbolization system that does *not* cleanly divide into binary oppositions—a system she calls "feminine" insofar as culture has (as we have already noted often in this book) traditionally assigned the messier ambiguities of thought to Woman as a force of disruption and disorder.[6] Guided principally by Irigaray's critique of conventional epistemology, I shall show that the Tarpeia poem abounds in details that cannot be captured in "either/or" logic—details linked (non-coincidentally) to feminine desire.

Take, for example, the fatal body of water that initially brings together Tarpeia and Tatius. The paths of Sabine king and Vestal Virgin cross at a shepherd's spring that Tatius palisades for his military camp; Tarpeia sees him when she draws water from the spring, and falls passionately in love. But how she *can* draw water despite Tatius' barricade has baffled commentators. Emendations and line transpositions have been freely offered to try to bring these puzzling verses into sensible coordination. Some scholars make two springs from one,[7] or banish one of the irreconcilable allusions to it;[8] others poke holes in the barrier;[9] still others try a combination of approaches.[10] Yet each suggested change to the text garners trenchant objections and small assent.

The spring's inconvenience to smooth explanation is striking: both carefully guarded and easily available to an unarmed enemy girl, it cuts across the very conceptual categories that seek to define it. The spring deconstructs such oppositions as enemy territory/native territory; inside/outside; martial/pastoral; closed/open. Tarpeia's act of daily devotion to Vesta marks this mysterious fount as intractable to conventional logic; we can neither locate it entirely within, nor entirely without, Tatius' barricade.

Moreover, as the work of Harry Rutledge, John Warden, and F. E. Brenk makes clear, water is throughout the poem's central point of reference.[11] Stunned by Tatius' good looks, Tarpeia drops her ritual water-jar when she first sees him (21–22); she invents ritual excuses to visit the sacred spring, so that she can spy on her beloved (22–23); she worries that her tears of amorous frustration may have quenched the perpetual flame on Vesta's altar (45–46). The elegy's liquid imagery measures Tarpeia's desire for Tatius as a passion that exceeds all "proper" bounds. But *why* water—why does *that* element in particular govern this poem (rather than, say, the commoner erotic metaphors of fire or heat)?[12]

THE MECHANICS OF FLUIDS

Luce Irigaray's essay "The Mechanics of Fluids" can illuminate the water imagery that organizes this poem's resistant ambiguities; her thought also sheds light on why the heart of the elegy takes shape in Tarpeia's own words, a long soliloquy that mimes desire articulated from a "feminine" vantage point. Irigaray assesses conventional epistemology as (mis)informed by an exclusionary model of understanding—a model that grapples with the welter of phenomena by calling upon binary opposition to establish distinctive classes. Such a model takes "black" to be the opposite and exclusion of "white," for example, as "male" of "female," "rational" of "irrational," "good" of "bad." Each term is logically impenetrable to the other, as if founded upon a metaphorical "mechanics of solids." Moreover, the meaning produced by such binarisms is never neutral: one term is always posited as inferior and supplementary to the other, as "female" commonly is to "male." Various types of post-structuralism have demonstrated the falsity of this construction, by showing the putative "superior" term to operate according to principles embodied in the "inferior, supplementary" term, which is thus transformed.

Yet Irigaray goes beyond demonstrating "bad faith" to show the putative knowledge produced by these binarisms to be implicitly gendered male. Her assumption should be familiar territory to classicists; Genevieve Lloyd has shown that the Pythagoreans offered an early example of it. Their famous table of opposites construes the "bounded"—that is, that which can be grasped by the rational subject as precise and clearly determined—as male and good. The female and bad aligns with the "unbounded"—the unlimited, irregular, and disorderly.[13] In contrast to this tradition, Irigaray seeks out a "feminine" logic that escapes the conceptual tyranny of stable forms, and that offers a new metaphorical basis for thinking—a logic analogous to the "mechanics of fluids." Fluids "resist" in that they refuse to be reduced to mathematical formulae, like the more biddable nature of solids. Fluids challenge the idea that dividing the world into clean oppositions ("either x or not-x") adequately expresses some underlying truth.[14]

The metaphoric logic behind Irigaray's quest would have been familiar not only to the Pythagoreans, but to Romans near Propertius' own time. Sandra Joshel and Catharine Edwards have recently documented the extent to which Rome characterized the rejected, inferior, and untrue as liquid and feminine, while ascribing hardness, dryness, fixity, and masculinity to "the good." Sallust, Horace, Seneca, and others speak of vice in images of insidious flood that wash away both personal virtue and the social order, softening and effeminizing Roman moral rigor.[15] Joshel and Edwards concern themselves chiefly with ethical discourse, but set in the wider context of Roman moral philosophy, the trajectory of their thought intersects epistemology itself. Cicero, for example, treats "the good" as virtually synonymous with "the real," with "being" as opposed to "seeming," as in the Platonic and Stoic traditions he inherits. The truth the vicious person fails to see resembles the Platonic Forms—solid, stable, measurable.[16] Cicero also plays upon the etymological connection between *virtus* and *vir*, depicting moral truth as something solid and masculine in the midst of feminine flux; his philosophy can justly be described as a masculinist "mechanics of solids."[17]

These associative links among untruth-as-vice, the feminine, and liquidity—as opposed to truth-as-virtue, the masculine, and solidity—clarify some of the recalcitrant details of the Tarpeia elegy. Yet the poem does not simply reproduce Roman conceptions of "masculine" versus "feminine" properties. Rather, Propertius questions Rome's cultural prejudices by revealing the hasty sutures in logic that support them. When he unfolds Tarpeia's story and grants her a voice, he sketches an epistemology much closer to the beliefs of Heraclitus, for example, or the Skeptic philosopher Carneades (whose visit to Rome so deeply impressed its citizens in the century before Propertius' own).[18] Both these thinkers deny that philosophy elucidates a truth conceived as the fixed substrate beneath phenomena in flux. Both challenge the idea that the universe naturally divides into fixed and stable binarisms; for neither is philosophy the grasping of stable forms.[19] Taken to its logical conclusion, this alternate frame of reference not only undermines the hierarchy that raises Man over Woman, but denies that such dichotomies order existence in any meaningful way.

IN A STRANGE LAND

With this philosophical background in mind, let us turn to the poem's opening and consider the uneasy montage of disjunctive images that shuffles before the reader's eyes:

> Tarpeium nemus et Tarpeiae turpe sepulcrum
>   fabor et antiqui limina capta Iovis.
> lucus erat felix hederoso conditus antro,
>   multaque nativis obstrepit arbor aquis,
> Silvani ramosa domus, quo dulcis ab aestu
>   fistula poturas ire iubebat ovis.
> hunc Tatius fontem vallo praecingit acerno,
>   fidaque suggesta castra coronat humo.
>
> (1–8)

I shall speak of the Tarpeian grove and the sordid tomb of Tarpeia and the captured threshold of ancient Jove. There was a fertile grove enclosed in an ivy-covered dell, and many a tree murmurs in reply to nature's waters—the branchy home of Silvanus, to which the sweet shepherd's pipe bade the sheep withdraw from the heat and drink. This spring Tatius bounds with a maple palisade, and encircles his loyal camp with piled-up earth.

We are offered the queer juxtaposition of a grove, a tomb, and a hostage god's threshold—a completely imaginary triad, to boot. Tarquin destroyed Tarpeia's burial place when he built the temple of *Iuppiter Capitolinus*;[20] the two monuments never shared the hill.[21] As for the "Tarpeian grove" (*Tarpeium nemus*): many reasonably find this element disturbing, insofar as Propertius introduces and drops it with equally little ceremony, even though his aetiological program should compel him to trace its history; moreover, no other source attests its existence. Accordingly, some adopt Kraffert's emendation to *scelus* ("curse; crime") while others assimilate the *nemus* to the *lucus* in line 3—though that helps little, given that the *lucus* also fails to inspire an aetion, it just colorfully shades the background.[22] The question of what these and the other prominently placed elements of the ekphrasis have to do with one another—how we might reconcile the elements of a peaceful pastoral scene (grove, spring, sheep, shepherd's pipe) with a tomb, or, more strangely still, with the martial elements picked out by "Jove's captured threshold," Tatius palisading the spring and arraying his army around it—Propertius leaves unanswered.[23] But the obscurity of the opening ekphrasis dramatizes the role interpretation plays in what passes for perception. Ancient as well as modern analyses of perception recognize the way that convention inscribes and naturalizes interpretation in the visual artifact, so as to make a legible whole out of disparate objects.[24] Stripped of such subtle framing, the opening lines, in their obstinate opacity, baffle any claim to the "pure" perception of truth, truth unmediated by representation: their apparent heterogeny demands a new way of seeing the (previously) unimaginable. The rest of the poem elaborates upon that need for a different vantage.

In the next moment after this serenely pastoral opening strangely stained with martial and morbid elements, Tarpeia sees Tatius for the first time and the water-jar slips from her nerveless fingers.[25] Graeco-Roman art and legend lend her gesture sinister significance. Giulia Sissa has discussed the ways in which the ancients associated vessels, especially water vessels, with female sexuality.[26] A woman's sexuality is a container for the precious resource of fertility, a container properly unbreached. That metaphorical thinking shapes Roman folk-legend when, for example, Tuccia the Vestal disproves the rumors of her unchastity by miraculously carrying water in a sieve.[27] Being chaste, she can magically seal a container that should leak—but the Vestal Tarpeia, whose love has made her ritual chastity impossible to her, makes even an unperforated container spill its contents. Moreover, as Tarpeia drew this water to clean Vesta's temple, the poet remarks that the jar "hurt her head" ("at illi / *urgebat* medium fictilis *urna* caput," 4.4.15–16). That phrase eerily echoes another Propertian heroine (whose story I shall scrutinize further in chapter 9): when his idealized Roman matron Cornelia swears to her own chastity under threat of the Danaids' suffering, she says "if I lie, may that fruitless water jar, the punishment of the sisters, hurt my shoulders" ("si fallo, poena sororum / infelix umeros *urgeat urna* meos," 4.11.27–28). Sissa has shown that the Danaids' unfillable sieves represent their flawed sexuality, failed as maidens and failed as brides.[28] Propertius' elaborate cross-referencing between his two elegies casts the shadow of those sieves upon Tarpeia's oozy, burdensome water-jar.

Yet the symbol of these murderous brides does not unambiguously condemn Tarpeia: Propertius writes her story as both the same and significantly different. True that Tarpeia expects to wed Tatius. She says, for example, "Rome betrayed comes to you as no insignificant *dowry*" ("*dos* tibi non humilis prodita Roma venit," 4.4.56). Tatius' last words to her echo this expectation when he says "*Marry*, and ascend the bed of my kingdom!" ("'*nube*' ait 'et regni scande cubile mei!'" 4.4.90). But in contrast to the Danaid myth, this bridegroom kills the bride: the Capitoline that Tatius mockingly calls his "marriage bed" sees *his* murderous duplicity, not Tarpeia's. And though scrupulous to punish her, Tatius happily keeps the fruit of her treachery, Rome. Tatius lies and deceives—the very acts supposed to define women, especially in sexual affairs.[29] The poem proffers this, *à l'air naïf*, as the benchmark of his honor: he dupes Tarpeia and thus "not even as an enemy gave honor to crime" ("neque enim sceleri dedit hostis honorem," 4.4.89). Yet this articulation ironically makes the "superior" term depend upon principles defined by the rejected, subordinate term: "masculine honor" becomes a subset of "feminine wiles."

A BEND IN THE WALL

Even without the hypocrite Tatius as her foil, Tarpeia-as-flawed-vessel embodies a principle strangely necessary to Rome's welfare, if little acknowledged: the breach she opens in Rome's walls gives them a necessary elasticity. David Konstan has elucidated the way Roman historiography grapples with the contradictory effects of boundaries: boundaries define the city-state, but they also limit its growth and expansion.[30] Sandra Joshel and Patricia Joplin have, in turn, demonstrated the metaphorical alignment between physical and conceptual boundaries of the state, and female sexuality; sexual unions, whether rapes, marriages, or seductions, regularly "breach" the polity's defining limits so that it may move on to a new phase. Livy, for example, dramatically connects the ultimately fatal sexual assaults upon Lucretia and Verginia to the downfall of the Roman monarchy and of the *decemviri*'s tyranny respectively.[31] Similarly, Tarpeia makes possible Rome as Propertius and his contemporaries know it. Pierre Grimal notes that the Caesars proudly traced their ancestry all the way back to the Sabine king, Tatius; the Sabines in general figure importantly in Roman history. Their stealthy entry into Rome sets the stage for eventually reconciling the two warring factions and, gradually, for Rome to absorb her former enemies completely.[32] Tarpeia's action is both abhorred and utterly necessary—the type of *felix culpa* that Roman legend regularly stages and that just as regularly demands the sacrifice of a woman.[33]

Tarpeia thus bears the unhappy burden of history: the resolution she proposes to Rome's conflict with the Sabines foreshadows the principles of their eventual reconciliation.[34] Tarpeia says that her marriage will "dissolve" ("solvere," 59) the two established battle lines and "soften" ("molliet," 62) their arms (her metaphors of liquescence and plasticity are telling). Marriage does do so, but not hers to Tatius; rather, the Sabine women's to Roman men.[35] Yet her ironically prophetic scheme again shows the "dominant" term to depend upon principles established by the "subordinate, contingent" term: Rome's integrity as a polity—what it means to *be* Rome—depends on the city's infiltration by foreigners because of women. By this process, the poem not only transforms the subordinate term, so that Tarpeia's betrayal becomes a blessing, but questions the very logic that sees "integrity" and "infiltration" as antitheses.

Water images plot the progression of Tarpeia's passion: she invents ritual needs to wash her hair in the river so that she can gaze upon Tatius more often (4.4.23–24); she laments Vesta's extinguished sacred flame, "spattered by my tears" (4.4.45–46); her plan to betray the city revolves equally around guiding the Sabines along a hidden Capitoline path slippery with invisible springs (47–50), and taking advantage of Rome's holiday drunkenness, its watches "dissolved" at Romulus' command ("Romulus excubias decrevit in otia *solvi* / atque intermissa castra silere tuba"— "Romulus decreed that the watches be dissolved for the holiday, and also that the camps fall silent, with the martial trumpets temporarily discontinued," 79–80). Mere plot exigencies cannot explain this strange concatenation of liquidity: for example, though three whole lines are devoted to describing the oozy path to the Capitoline, no one slips under Tarpeia's guidance, and the expansive detail seems otiose.[36] Yet all these passages feature liquid creeping out of its "proper" place to create minor or major instances of upheaval, a chaos chiefly defined by law or ritual. Tarpeia's hair-washing, while not culpable per se, falsifies ritual, in that she invents bad omens as her pretext. Her tears extinguish Vesta's flame, the religious sign that corroborates Rome's own integrity and continuity as a state. The hidden waters on the Capitoline threaten not only those who tread the path, but the Romans, too, by giving them a false sense of security (they do not bother to guard this slippery "back door" to the city). And the city's drunkenness relaxes discipline under siege, very nearly to its inhabitants' destruction.

BACCHANT OR AMAZON?

Most of these images are intriguing but minor stitches in a complex tapestry—save one: as Tarpeia rushes to find Tatius and offer him Rome, Propertius compares her to a woman running alongside a river. The Vestal "rushes headlong, just as a woman from Strymon, her breast bared by the torn fold of her dress, alongside the swift Thermodon" ("illa ruit, qualis celerem prope Thermodonta / Strymonis abscisso pectus aperta sinu," 4.4.71–72). The cunning oddity of this image sketches a woman "out of place," for whom no clear context can be found. John Warden elucidates the picture's duplicity: mentioning the Thermodon suggests an Amazon and the woman's nude breast corroborates this, given Graeco-Roman sculpture's tradition of Amazons with one breast bared.[37] But, as Warden points out, Amazons belted back their garments to expose the breast, rather than tearing them. Torn garment and headlong haste imply a Bacchant, especially since erotic passion drives Tarpeia; Latin literature often represents women's love as inspiring maenad-like behavior.[38]

Warden principally elucidates the parallels between Propertius' Tarpeia and Vergil's Dido, reading the Vestal as a response to the Sidonian queen. His fine exposition renders his point inescapable, yet some observations he prematurely subordinates to Dido's image, and these deserve consideration in a fuller context.

For example, although Warden initially finds tension in the juxtaposition of Bacchant, so often a convenient figure for a woman passionately in love, and a traditionally "manhating" Amazon, he later observes: "As one gazes more steadily at the two figures, one begins to suspect that they are not as diametrically opposed as might appear at first sight. The pack of wild women who tore apart Orpheus and Pentheus might seem, at least to the threatened male, all too reminiscent of the women warriors of the Thermodon."[39] He marshalls this duplicity to support reading Dido, the chaste warrior-queen turned impassioned lover, behind Tarpeia; yet, when seen in the context of Propertius' other references to Maenads and Amazons, the implications of 4.4's composite *sauvagesse* open out onto the intertwined problems of the feminine within and without the state, and the inadequacy of thought to frame her.

Propertius' own sketches of Bacchants are few, but richly suggestive: in 3.22, Bacchants figure as fierce manhunters, who define Greek "barbarity" as opposed to Roman decorum (however ironic the comparison may be). Italy may congratulate itself, he says, that here "savage Bacchants do not hunt Pentheus in the woods" ("Penthea non saevae venantur in arbore Bacchae," 3.22.33). In 1.3, Propertius compares his lover, insensibly slumbering and thus unresponsive to his attentions, to an exhausted maenad wrapped in a sleep indifferent to man after communion with her god ("nec minus assiduis Edonis fessa choreis / qualis in herboso concidit Apidano," 1.3.5–8). Cynthia is the sleeping maenad of Greek vase paintings, and Propertius the satyr who spies upon her—but as on those vases, always in vain, the object of the maenad's sleeping inattention or waking rejection.[40] Propertius represents Amazons with like ambiguity: Warden notes that the poet's women-warriors disquietingly juxtapose the eroticism of female nudity with weapons and belligerence.[41]

When brought to bear upon the Tarpeia poem, these vignettes attest aspects of Woman's desire that escape Man's calculation: beside blind hatred or blind love for his sex arises a mystifying passion for war or for god, passion that places Man nearer margin than center of any epistemology—*if* he figures at all. In the light of these images, as well as of their wider cultural context, the Bacchant and Amazon evoked by Tarpeia in flight together sketch the extremes of Woman's figuration, but extremes that keep eerily collapsing into one another. Bacchant and Amazon share a passion for the divine, whether Ares, Artemis, or Dionysos;[42] they share a penchant for violence and a capacity to exceed the place marked out for Woman within the polity.[43] They can be construed as opposites, given their reversed—though oddly symmetrical—relations to Man and the state. Love-mad women behave like maenads, and so inscribe the Bacchant as "manlover," while the Amazon is "manhater" par excellence;[44] the Bacchant originates within the city-state and is drawn outside its confines, while the Amazon dwells at civilization's borders, but is drawn into war with those at its heart.[45] Yet Propertius' juxtaposition emphasizes all the elements that overlap in their respective mythologies. This disturbing tendency of one figuration of Woman to collapse into another suggests some fundamental miscalculation: if "manhater" and "manlover" are fundamentally so indistinguishable, if feminine margin and center of the state exchange places so readily, are "Man" and "state" meaningful reference points? Something incalculable by these yardsticks flashes in Woman's desire, something that collapses categories previously seen as mutually exclusive and stable.

That "something" erupts at the very heart of the city, in the figure of its stability and continuity—the goddess Vesta. The virgin goddess paradoxically fans the flame of Tarpeia's love as she sleeps:

> dixit, et incerto permisit bracchia somno,
>   nescia se furiis accubuisse novis.
> nam Vesta, Iliacae felix tutela favillae
>   culpam alit et plures condit in ossa faces.
>   (4.4.67–70)

[Tarpeia] spoke, and stretched out her arms/surrendered her embrace[46] to uncertain sleep, not knowing that she slept with fresh furies. For Vesta, happy guardian of the flame of Troy, nurtured her [Tarpeia's] guilt and buried more torches in her bones.

This witchlike Vesta answers to the twin images of Bacchant and Amazon she inspires Tarpeia to emulate, in their broadly overlapping contradictions. Vesta here feeds passion, though herself ritually its enemy; she overturns Rome, her own city, from its very heart, stretching its extremes to include the Sabines; she modulates erotic passion into war and violence.[47] Her flame itself embodies irresolvable contradiction. The flame came from the ruins of Troy; as evidence of Rome's continuity and stability, it nonetheless bears the trace of transience and destruction, especially since that flame now incites Tarpeia's betrayal of Rome.[48] Vesta's weird image points to aspects of the very heart and origins of Rome—aspects characterized as feminine—whose conceptual intractability Rome dissimulates.[49] The poem marks feminine desire as a different economy of thought, wherein traditional categories of thought are exceeded and binary opposition, as the foundation of meaning, collapses under the weight of its own conceptual inadequacy.

Vesta also inspires images that elaborate the spatial contradictions she embodies, as the foreign transient at Rome's heart who nonetheless "protects" its boundaries (after her fashion). Let us return for a moment to the Bacchant-Amazon whom Tarpeia imitates under Vesta's goading: this woman in mad career cannot easily be located in anything like recognizable space. If she is a woman from Strymon, why does she run alongside the Thermodon a thousand miles from her home?[50] Like the mysterious spring that opened this poem, we are offered yet another surreal geography of water; it, too, suggests eerie mobility in apparently stable categories (such as Cappadocia versus Thrace), and it marks that mobility as feminine. Always, before thought can overtake it in this poem, the feminine is already elsewhere.

WANTING IT ALL

Not surprisingly, just this aspect of Woman's desire—its mobility and collapsing of conceptual categories—marks Tarpeia's passion. As we have seen, this poem's imagery hospitably embraces categories Roman culture generally construes as polar opposites, antitheses upon which "reason" and "truth" putatively rest. The poem disturbs, displaces, and recombines classification in dizzyingly fluid formations that undermine the easy familiarity of the original categories themselves. Consider how the following passages describe Tarpeia's bewitched fascination with Tatius.

> vidit harenosis Tatium proludere campis
>   pictaque per flavas arma levare iubas:
> obstipuit regis facie et regalibus armis,
>   interque oblitas excidit urna manus.
>
> (4.4.19–22)

She saw Tatius practicing on the sandy fields and raising his ornamented weapons above his tawny crest;[51] she was struck dumb by his face and his kingly weapons, and the urn fell from her oblivious hands.

> "Ignes castrorum et Tatiae praetoria turmae
>   et formosa oculis arma Sabina meis,
> o utinam ad vestros sedeam captiva Penatis,
>   dum captiva mei conspicer ora Tati!"
>
> (4.4.31–34)

"O fires of the camps and headquarters of Tatius' bodyguard and Sabine arms, beautiful to my eyes!" [I shall discuss the translation of the second distich below.]

> "ille equus, ille meos in castra reponet amores,
>   cui Tatius dextras collocat ipse iubas!
> quid mirum in patrios Scyllam saevisse capillos,
>   candidaque in saevos inguina versa canis?
> prodita quid mirum fraterni cornua monstri,
>   cum patuit lecto stamine torta via?"
>
> (4.4.37–42)

That horse, that's the one who will take my love back into camp, whose mane Tatius himself will arrange to fall to the right! What wonder that Scylla attacked her father's hair, and that her fair limbs were turned to savage dogs? What wonder that the horns of the monstrous brother were betrayed, when the twisted way lay open as [Ariadne's guiding] thread was reeled in?

> "te toga picta decet, non quem sine matris honore
>   nutrit inhumanae dura papilla lupae."
>
> (4.4.53–54)

"You the toga with its insignia suits, not him whom the hard pap of a she-wolf nursed, without the honor of a mother!"

Tarpeia's admiration for Tatius' appearance curiously revolves as much or more around what is *not* Tatius as what is: his horse, his weapons, the weapons of his soldiers, his imagined beauty in an ornamented toga. True, erotic poetry sometimes praises the beloved's dress alongside the elegance of her or his features (though more often in describing women than men), but such descriptions usually subordinate dress to person. By contrast, 4.4 sets Tatius' arms ("regalibus armis") paratactically side by side with his face ("regis facie") as if both excited Tarpeia's wonder equally. Moreover, nothing affords a precedent to the way her desire spreads so as to encompass his horse (37–38) and even his entire army and their arms (31).[52] Stahl rightly perceives the embarrassment of these lines and strives to explain it away: "Although her affection now seems to widen from Tatius (19, 21) and his arms (*arma*, 20, *armis*, 21) to Tatius' soldiers and their arms (31/32), this plural is rather to be seen psychologically as a multiplication of beloved Tatius himself...."[53] Yet saying that she "multiplies Tatius himself" hardly lessens the oddity: she thus makes of Tatius Hobbes' Leviathan in military dress. As for her queer fixation on her beloved's horse (37–38), it moves Stahl, like Rothstein before him, to rationalize it as her envy of the attention horse receives from rider.

> She identifies the horse as the one she now sees every day from her rock and which enjoys the privilege of Tatius' personal care (how much she herself would like to receive his attention!).[54]

> Statt des einfachen, "das Roß, das Tatius reitet," hebt Tarpeia das beneidenswerte Glück des Rosses hervor, das von Tatius selbst gepflegt wird; eine Art des Empfindens, die der antike wie der modernen Erotik geläufig ist.[55]

Yet Stahl cites no textual support for thus translating Tarpeia's thoughts, and Rothstein's attempts to find parallels in Greek poetry are inexact at best: his citations all *explicitly* articulate the wish to be some object that offers proximity to the beloved, an element crucially missing here. The poem offers no gloss on Tarpeia's fascination with the steed; rather, like the passions of Bacchant and Amazon, Tarpeia's love for Tatius encompasses also the beasts of the field and the implements of war, while—again like these wild women—her ardor displaces Man and state as central, unified points of reference, gliding indifferently between singular and plural, animate and inanimate, beast and human and monster.

Tarpeia's gaze, that restlessly creates new "wholes" for its delight out of a list-like collection of objects (arms, man, horse, toga), takes to its logical extremes an operation inherent in the cultural construction of desire. Culture writes conventional readings of what is desirable (or not), organically united (or not), onto the object, offering interpretation as "perception"; Tarpeia's novel fetishism throws this bad faith into relief.[56] Her eclecticism steps just far enough outside the bounds of quotidian expectation to undermine the notion that the content of passion defines natural complementarities or natural objects. Her gaze thus repeats and reverses an effect of the poem's montage-like opening, where we were baffled of constructing a sensible whole out of the disparate symbolic resonances grove, spring, sheep, shepherd's pipe, tomb, and army brought to the picture. Divested of any obvious guidelines, her visions of the beloved render uncanny and unreadable the homely furniture of human desire.

Fittingly, Tarpeia expatiates on her ardor by likening it to mythical passions that wrought monsters.

"quid mirum in patrios Scyllam saevisse capillos,
    candidaque in saevos inguina vera canis?
prodita quid mirum fraterni cornua monstri,
    cum patuit lecto stamine torta via?"
                    (4.4.39–42)

"What wonder that Scylla attacked her father's hair, and that her fair limbs were turned to savage dogs? What wonder that the horns of the monstrous brother were betrayed, when the twisted way lay open as [Ariadne's guiding] thread was reeled in?"

It does not puzzle her that, for love, Scylla would suffer herself to be metamorphosed into half-maiden, half-monster; no longer wonderful to her are the histories of the house of Minos, whose wife Pasiphaë loved a bull and disguised herself as a cow to enjoy him. Tarpeia lays claim to annals of passion that make nonsense out of any notion of what is "natural"; love's assumed objects, its expected effects, turn topsy-turvy. She claims instead a history of desire, marked as feminine, that exceeds any notion of Man and Woman as natural complementaries, or the state as the lodestone of human loyalties. The icons of Tarpeia's love stand perforce outside human sexual relations: Scylla's genitals become dogs; Minos' daughter, Ariadne, eventually becomes a god's (Dionysus') consort rather than Theseus'. Such longing shapes grotesques of in-difference, confusing the realms of beast and god, erasing assumed touchstones of human identity, unraveling existing social order without regret.

FEMININE SYNTAX

Tarpeia's strange amalgamations that sketch the shifting amorous subject and object parallel her mobile position in articulating her love. Tarpeia assumes, Amazonlike, the role of autonomous subject of desire and diplomacy in making her own marriage pact and treaty ("hoc Tarpeia suum tempus rata convenit hostem / pacta ligat, pactis ipsa futura comes"—"Tarpeia, having decided that this was her time, met with her enemy; she concludes a pact, with herself as companion according to the terms of the pact" [or, "with herself as companion to those with whom she had concluded the pact"], 4.4.81–82).[57] Even were she not a Roman woman and a Vestal consecrated to chastity, these prerogatives would be her father's and Romulus' respectively rather than hers; her independent marriage brokering and her treason are set paratactically side by side as virtually equivalent acts ("prodiderat portaeque fidem patriamque iacentem / nubendique petit, quem velit, ipsa diem"—"she had betrayed both the entrusted responsibility of the gate and her fatherland lying helpless, and she herself seeks what she wants, the day of her marriage," 4.4.87–88). Yet, even as she fantasizes offering herself to Tatius, her terms play curiously and paradoxically between subject and object, active and passive positions:

"o utinam ad vestros sedeam captiva Penatis,
    dum captiva mei conspicer ora Tati!"
                (4.4.33–34)

I shall discuss the translation of these lines below.

"o utinam magicae nossem cantamina Musae!
    haec quoque formoso lingua tulisset opem.
te toga picta decet, non quem sine matris honore
    nutrit inhumanae dura papilla lupae.
hic, hospes, patria metuar regina sub aula?
    dos tibi non humilis prodita Roma venit.
si minus, at raptae ne sint impune Sabinae,
    me rape et alterna lege repende vices!"
                (4.4.51–58)

"O would that I knew the songs of the sorceress-Muse! Even this tongue would help my handsome man! You the toga with its insignia suits, not him whom the hard pap of a she-wolf nursed, without the honor of a mother! Shall I thus, my foe, be feared as queen in my father's hall?[58] Rome comes to you as no humble dowry! Or at least, lest the Sabines' ravishment go unpunished, rape *me* and pay back in turn with the law of 'an eye for an eye.'"

Take, for example, the difficulties of 4.33–34: is Barber correct in printing Gronovius' suggestion *ora* or should the major manuscripts' *esse* be preferred—a reading that dictates *conspicer* be read as truly passive rather than deponent? And what about the ambiguity of the second *captiva* in 34: does it modify the implied subject of *conspicer* or the emendation *ora*? Between the emended and unemended versions of these lines, we have as possible translations "would that I, a captive, might see the face of my Tatius"; "would that I might be seen to be the captive of my Tatius"; "would that I might see the captive face of my Tatius"—the last imagining a reciprocal love-match in which each would be the captive of the other. But, as Paul Allen Miller and Charles Platter have pointed out, "there is no way to decide between these competing readings on grammatical bases alone.... Each of these readings is defensible and the attempt to promote one over the other reveals more about the reader than the poem. Rather the very inability to assign absolute agency to either party is consonant with the structure of the poem as a whole."[59] The rest of Tarpeia's soliloquy elaborates upon just that indeterminacy: she imagines herself actively offering herself, as passive object, to Tatius, sees herself as war-captive, strangely pliant witch, bride, rape-victim. The oddity of saying "she offers herself as rape victim"—how can she be raped when she longs for the embrace of her addressee?—underlines, by its very logical contradiction, the slippery duplicity of fantasy, the way in which it deconstructs the notion of unified subjects and objects that underwrite normative conceptions of desire. Tarpeia's soliloquy anticipates the logical moves in Freud's key essay on fantasy, wherein he analyzes the phenomenon as a series of syntactical permutations on the sentence "a child is being beaten" that shift the fantasizer back and forth between observer and participant, active and passive, subject and object, even female and male.[60] Irigaray lays claim to psychoanalysis' instructive elucidation of that language-based instability in conceptual divisions when she imagines "feminine" syntax:

> What a feminine syntax might be is not simple or easy to state, because in that "syntax" there would no longer be either subject or object, "oneness" would no longer be privileged, there would no longer be proper meanings, proper names, "proper" attributes . . . Instead, that "syntax" would involve nearness, proximity, but in such an extreme form that it would preclude any distinction of identities, any establishment of ownership, thus any form of appropriation.[61]

The form and content of Tarpeia's fantasies trace that syntax exactly: "I wish that I were your captive/your sorceress/your bride/your rape victim" scatters Tarpeia among vagaries of will, consent, and power. On the one hand, if Tatius captures or rapes her, her consent to the action ceases to be at issue and (as Livy argued for Lucretia) she cannot be held responsible.[62] The infractions against Vesta and Rome she so wants would then be freed of moral consequences—in theory. Yet Tarpeia complicates her will when she herself constructs herself as passive victim within the fantasy: her daydream oxymoronically reads as "I desire not to desire the thing I desire: I wish to have it forced upon me."

But in addition to object of rape or capture, Tarpeia also wishes herself Tatius' bride, or powerful witch. I have already noted the oddity of Tarpeia's arranging her own marriage with Tatius: while the formalities of Roman marriage pact and ceremony construct a bride as passive party, the object of exchange between two men, Tarpeia imagines herself as marriage broker.[63] But she does not thus unambiguously usurp power: she becomes both subject and object in this exchange, giving herself away. Similarly, while the witch she wants to be represents a feared pinnacle of female power, Tarpeia's wish to be only Tatius' instrument also complicates this image: her incantations would forward her *lover*'s agenda, not her own ("haec quoque formoso lingua tulisset opem," 52).

Within this complex picture of Woman's desire, we cannot settle upon a simple answer to the question "what does Tarpeia want?" nor, therefore, to "what is she—traitor, victim, or benefactor? what is her degree of culpability?" Rather, we revolve dizzyingly among imponderables, among fractions of subjects organized around epicenters of will, power, and desire. The entire congeries of volition and submission grows even more complex because Vesta renders inevitable what Tarpeia had only debated.[64] Who, then, is culpable for Tarpeia's actions? I have argued against reading Tarpeia solely as a response to Vergil's Dido, but here she does conjure up the same unresolvable problem of agency hinged upon a woman's fatal and fated "offense" (*culpa*) that *Aeneid* 4 broaches.[65] Yet Propertius has replayed the enigma in such a way that the characterization of Tarpeia's desire shifts into the field of its conceptualization, and stages the impossibility of its being conceived. Tarpeia dramatizes an impasse in "reason" that, without making the questions of guilt and innocence, betrayal and benefit, offender and victim any less importunate, renders them not only unanswerable, but unaskable, in the terms laid down by received thought.

Given the uneasy conceptual fluidity Tarpeia embodies within Roman myth, Tatius' response reads as a particularly brutal concrete metaphor: crushing her beneath Sabine shields "puts the lid on" the vertiginous questions her brief history poses.[66] Or almost so: the poem closes with the lines "the name of the mountain was got from Tarpeia as leader; watcher, you have the reward of an unjust lot!" ("a duce Tarpeia mons est cognomen adeptus: / o vigil, iniustae praemia sortis habes," 4.4.93–94). The Capitoline is hers, finally, as *mons Tarpeius*—but whose is the injustice? The perfectly ambiguous *vigil*, "watcher," glances both toward Tarpeia and Jupiter, the Capitoline's god: Propertius has told us that she watched to open up Rome and the god watched to punish her for it.[67] Was it unjust to kill her, or to make the god's invaded home her monument? The poem ends in a studied refusal to sort out who is offender and who offended. The final distich's irreducible ambiguity insists that any choice would be based on the same false conceptual distinctions the elegy as a whole has exploded; the Tarpeia poem refuses that choice as its ultimate ethical gesture.

CHAPTER FIVE

The Return of the Dead: The Acanthis Elegy (4.5)

> *I found that ivory image there*
> *Dancing with her chosen youth,*
> *But when he wound her coal-black hair*
> *As though to strangle her, no scream*
> *Or bodily movement did I dare,*
> *Eyes under eyelids did so gleam;*
> *Love is like the lion's tooth.*
>   YEATS, "CRAZY JANE GROWN OLD
>   LOOKS AT THE DANCERS"

Propertius' elegy on the lately deceased *lena* (procuress) Acanthis (4.5) records her cynical catechism of his mistress Cynthia on the ways to inspire desperate ardor and lavish generosity in one's lovers. Despite the questions this eccentric poem inspires (how, for example, has Cynthia suddenly obtained a *lena*, when she never had one before?), Acanthis has sparked surprisingly modest and hermeneutically restricted attention.[1] Debate over 4.5 generally focuses on questions of dating, language, and genre: scholars argue over whether the poem belongs to Propertius' early or late years of composition, what debts its complex diction owes to epic, comedy and mime, and precisely where it leans upon other literary descriptions of *lenae*. While these exchanges have accomplished much important work, they leave untouched the poem's overall interpretation, regarding it as unproblematic. Propertius exposes the venality of an old procuress in all its ugliness (so the common reading runs) and asks but simple justice when he wishes on her the miserable death and afterlife that he has the good fortune to see fulfilled.

This is all the more surprising given 4.5's structural and thematic similarity to 4.7 (Cynthia's return from the dead) and 4.11 (Cornelia's speech from the Underworld), to which scholars readily grant complexities of conception that demand close attention to nuances.[2] Like Cynthia and Cornelia, Acanthis enters and exits her poem as one of the dead: the lover curses the *lena*'s sepulchre and shade, wishing upon her eternal thirst, the insults and missiles of other lovers, a fig tree to des-

---

William Butler Yeats, *The Collected Poems of W. B. Yeats* (New York, 1951), 255. Reprinted by the kind permission of Anne Yeats.

ecrate her tomb (4.5.1–4, 75–78). Yet between these two moments, 4.5 wavers between past and present tenses in speaking of the old woman, as if unsure that she has really died; most strikingly, it describes her putative magical powers in the present tense, as though she still lived to wield them (9–10, discussed further below). These lines' sudden shift in temporal perspective implies that Acanthis lives on in some form after her physical death (an idea more fully developed when Cynthia and Cornelia return as voices from Hades). She still possesses power from beyond the grave, at least in her hold on the lover's imagination—his vivid record of her advice to Cynthia, and his reaction to it, attest this. As the prelude to 4.7's reproachful courtesan and 4.11's embittered matron, the "revenant" Acanthis offers a disenchanted view of the mores governing Roman women's behavior, and she foreshadows Cynthia's and Cornelia's fierce intransigence when she argues her case. Propertius allots that candor and fury exclusively to women claimed by death's domain: the "return of the dead" in Book IV marks the uncanny appearance of truths about women that challenge received wisdom. The ghosts of 4.5, 4.7, and 4.11 figure crucially in the interpretation of a book focused (as I have argued in chapter 1) on Woman as *the* icon that locates the failings of cultural symbolization systems. Given that Acanthis' cool impeachment establishes the fundamental terms for Cynthia's and Cornelia's plaints, she deserves equally meticulous attention.

Kathryn Gutzwiller's sensitive examination of the poem already takes welcome exception to overhasty acceptance of Acanthis' condemnation.[3] Gutzwiller, like her predecessors, places the elegy in the context of its antecedents in comedy, mime, and epigram—but rather than assimilating Propertius' individual vignette to the generalized lineaments of a genre picture, she notes the poem's distinctive differences from these sources as well as its similarities. Acanthis has virtues the stereotypical madam lacks, such as sustained poetic eloquence and a selfless concern for her protégée. Gutzwiller forcefully argues that Propertius has modified the standard portrait of the *lena:* unlike depictions common to other genres, he shows Acanthis to have some justice on her side, reason to her argument, even romantic sensibility in her soul—while by contrast he paints himself (as elegiac lover) a cruel and bloodthirsty hypocrite.

However, certain questions remain unanswered even after Gutzwiller's stimulating and thoughtful treatment of the poem. First: she has rightly observed that Book IV regularly challenges the lover's point of view in a way unprecedented within the corpus. But if 4.5 grants us "a more objective, distanced perspective on the lover,"[4] how exactly does it differ from, say, 4.7, in which Cynthia also sketches a mean, selfish, and dishonest Propertius? What does *each* poem accomplish such that *both* are necessary to Book IV's agenda?

A second question arises parallel to the first: quite apart from how or why Acanthis may supplement 4.7, why is she brought onstage at all? She ill fits the record of Propertius' affair with Cynthia set down in the previous three books (as scholars have frequently noted): however Cynthia's always-ambiguous status may be conceived, as *matrona* gone wrong or demimondaine, she has no connection with any *lena* outside this poem, but transacts her business with her lover(s) quite independently.[5] Acanthis' anomalous appearance in 4.5 has made some hesitate to identify the woman she addresses as Cynthia[6]— though such caution raises the difficulty of explaining why the elegy would repeat lines famously addressed to Cynthia to convince *another* woman that her lover's gifts are worthless (as noted at the end of chapter 1, Acanthis quotes from elegy 1.2 the very first words Propertius spoke to Cynthia).[7] Moreover, as K.-W. Weeber argues, the carefully managed strategies detailed in Acanthis' hetaira-catechism (tantrums, jealousies, excuses for postponing assignations) correspond too closely to Propertius' history of his affair with Cynthia to suggest plausibly that the old woman's advisee is anyone but Cynthia.[8] Acanthis' appearance as a factor in the Cynthia affair assigns implausibly belated blame for the liaison's difficulties to a third party, and urges us to ask: Why "remember" the old woman only now, *après coup?*

Gutzwiller demonstrates that 4.5 invites a rereading of Propertius' earlier books of elegies; this chapter expands the scope of her thesis by arguing that the rereading extends beyond Propertius' reevaluating his avowed erotic creed through Acanthis' mouth.[9] Rather, 4.5 comprehensively interrogates the desperately flawed structure of relations between the sexes; Acanthis' anomaly and unpunctuality are central to the disquieting investigation.

A PORTRAIT IN PERSUASION

The poem opens with Propertius cursing Acanthis' grave (1–4) and cataloguing her powers as a witch; his description implies his rage, but 4.5 nonetheless courts belief.[10] The catalogue of Acanthis' abilities and practices falls within generic lines mapped out by other Roman poets' descriptions of witches' powers, such as the sorceress whom Dido claims will rid her of unrequited love, and the one Tibullus employs to cozen a too-vigilant husband.[11] Indeed, Acanthis rather pales next to the horrors Horace imagines of Canidia: she certainly does not practice human sacrifice.[12] Propertius unsettles the reader's expectations, not when he describes Acanthis, but when she herself speaks. Gutzwiller compares the elegy to *Amores* 1.8, Ovid's portrait of the *lena* Dipsas, and notes that, surprisingly, Acanthis' counsel evidences neither venality nor self-interest—as Dipsas' advice clearly does.[13] Acanthis speaks eloquently and learnedly, ornamenting her argument with mythological allusions and intricate rhetorical figures, and rising to pathos when she evocatively describes the rose gardens at Paestum suddenly blighted by a summer scirocco (61–62). She can be accused, at worst, of hardheaded realism in her advice to Cynthia, advising the younger woman to put long-term economic self-interest ahead of the *beau geste* her lover urges upon her, fidelity to a gifted pauper. The details of Acanthis' speech, Gutzwiller concludes, reveal the old woman's unexpected depth and humanity.[14] I propose, though, to examine Acanthis not so much to show that the old woman has a case—Gutzwiller clearly proves that she does—but to ask why *Acanthis* must be the one to urge it. The elegy draws her portrait so finely, from her variegated mannerisms of speech to her disenchanted perspectives on youth and love, as to argue that this wealth of detail figures crucially not only in the interpretation of her message, but in the poem's overall meaning.

How exactly has Propertius painted Acanthis? As surprisingly dogged, for one thing.[15] She returns again and again, both in eloquent and vulgar turns of phrase, to the chief gravamen of her advice: "look to the cash!" ("aurum spectato," 4.5.53).[16] But why need she repeat herself so insistently? Admittedly her advisee, on the evidence of Propertius' other three books, is no simple mercenary: Cynthia displays altruism alongside venality in her long career as mistress, and might at moments be inclined to fall in with her lover's idealism.[17] Still, after assimilating the other books, the reader can hardly imagine a Cynthia who would need this much persuasion, even as a novice, ultimately to favor her own interests. The old woman observes that Cynthia already has expensive tastes (21–26) and presumably also the will to fulfill them. Where Ovid's Corinna blushes modestly at Dipsas' suggestion that a man might wish to purchase her favors (*Am.* 1.8.35), Cynthia evidences no such demur at Acanthis' advice. Why, then, does Propertius represent Acanthis as reiterating her message so persistently when her own shrewd analysis of Cynthia's predilections indicates that the old woman preaches, if not exactly to the converted, then to the easily convertible? Is Acanthis simply plagued by an old woman's garrulity, or is her repetitiveness significant?

REREADING THE PAST

Structural and thematic redoubling throughout the poem—an "eternal return" that shapes Acanthis' death and afterlife as well as her speech—argues for repetition's being no simple character stroke, but a concept crucial to 4.5's interpretation both in itself and in the light it casts upon the previous corpus. Propertius' curses ask that Acanthis reproduce in death the forces that (according to his testimony) governed her life. He describes an "interfering" old woman who works tirelessly when the world sleeps to foil the plans of watchful husbands or impoverished lovers (14, 73), a type whose sedulousness ancient literature classically linked to love of drink.[18] Accordingly, Propertius prays that her shade repeat both facets of her life as he represents it: may she thirst unappeasably and find no rest (2–3). He gets his wish—almost: his philippic implies the actual return of such a shade when (as mentioned above) he suddenly imagines the dead Acanthis as if still alive and wielding her powers:

> illa velit, poterit magnes non ducere ferrum,
>   et volucris nidis esse noverca suis.
>   (9–10)

> Should she wish it, the magnet will not draw iron, and the bird will be a stepmother to her own nest.

Yet this Acanthis neither thirsts nor wanders unquietly; rather, she practices an uncanny ability to sunder bonds of attraction, even in animals or inanimate objects. The abrupt tense shift from past to present in speaking of Acanthis figuratively grants Propertius a restless, repetitive *Nachleben* for his enemy, but not the one for which he asked: she "returns" to life in his imagination, not in an aimless frenzy, but vividly animated by the same will to control attraction that sought to shield Cynthia from unprofitable liaisons, and that opposed him at every turn.

Other passages further elaborate Acanthis' career as imagined revenant, with Propertius strewing evidence for the posthumous repetition of her will throughout her speech. The old woman's various devices for cajoling money out of the lover and increasing the mistress' hold over him can, as remarked above, be matched by scenes from Propertius' other three books: Cynthia pleading the rites of Isis as a reason for sexual abstinence, or exploding with anger at his peccadilloes, or arousing his suspicion and jealousy because her crowded house reminds him of the courtesan Thais' establishment.[19] Poem 4.5 rereads Propertius' "woman trouble" as Acanthis' "eternal return"; the elegy gathers together the disparate threads of Cynthia's recorded behavior and reduces them to order as the posthumous unfolding of the *lena*'s demand that economic self-interest come first, well before altruism. But why insist on this reinterpretation, when, as noted, it jars with the previous record of Cynthia conducting her sexual affairs *sans* mediator? Because it ultimately exonerates Cynthia: though Acanthis infuriates Propertius, the elegy offers her advice to the younger woman as the source that conveniently "explains" his mistress' irritating actions. According to this revision, the dead Acanthis poisoned the affair between Propertius and Cynthia implicitly from the beginning of its history in the Monobiblos. He thus retrospectively reconstrues the previous corpus as a record of failure for which Acanthis, rather than Cynthia, bears the blame; the love affair's vicissitudes evidence a "return of the dead" in the form of Acanthis' continuing influence over his mistress. Yet second thoughts do not accrue entirely to the credit of the lover's case: where 4.5 urges rereading upon us most insistently, with Acanthis' own citation of the Monobiblos (4.5.55–56 = 1.2.1–2), she glosses the lines as swindling rather than asceticism (54).[20] Given the mistress' (*amica*'s) general economic vulnerability, depending as she does on the generosity of her lover(s), Acanthis' point tells; rereading cuts both ways in this poem.

Given the weakness of his case against her, precisely what *is* it about Acanthis that so inflames the lover's ire? Scholars usually point to her counsel of economic self-interest before all other considerations as the reason,[21] especially given that her tenets directly oppose his doctrine of placing love above all material, social, or political considerations.[22] The logical consequences of Acanthis' beliefs lead her to balk the lovers' affair, allegedly by magic as well as dissuasion. Yet the old woman's money worries are not for herself: she frets for Cynthia, acknowledging her protégée's taste for luxury and advising the younger woman how to satisfy her own predilection, without any expectation that Acanthis herself will benefit. Predictably, Propertius sophistically twists her concern for another's welfare into an accusation of "greed."

Examining the logical contradictions that mark the lover's bitter sketch of Acanthis' "interference" proves generally revealing, highlighting as it does more than one aspect of his "bad faith"—the unsuspected coincidences between his interests and his alleged enemy's actions. For example, Propertius lists hippomanes among the magical means deployed against him ("in me / hippomanes fetae semina legit equae"—"against me she gathers hippomanes, the seed of a pregnant mare," 17–18)—a curious weapon for Acanthis to use, given its power as an aphrodisiac.[23] Why should someone who has tried repeatedly to separate Propertius and Cynthia so work at cross-purposes with herself? Most commentators take the lines to indicate that she attempted to poison Propertius, though with slender lexical evidence to support this interpretation of hippomanes as poison.[24] Shackleton-Bailey and Richardson, on firmer ground, retain the idea of hippomanes as aphrodisiac, but run into difficulties explaining the purpose of her potion. Shackleton-Bailey speculates that she wished to divert Propertius' attention to another woman; Richardson, that she strove to reduce him to his mistress' helpless slave. However, having him fall in love with another woman where the poem mentions none strains sense; as for reducing him to Cynthia's slave, his abject obedience would not repair his relative poverty, the one flaw Acanthis finds irremediable and no less objectionable in a milquetoast than a roaring boy.

The apparent *lapsus calami* that lists hippomanes among Acanthis' weapons reflects in miniature the non sequitur of calling concern for another's economic welfare "greed": in both instances, Propertius attributes malice, intent, and responsibility to Acanthis that his own testimony subtly gainsays. Moreover—like slips of the tongue, convenient lapses of memory, and other parapraxes—the incongruity reveals a deeper truth. Acanthis' alleged vices, such as covetousness, reflect and magnify aspects of Cynthia's self-assertion that rile her lover (on the evidence of other poems).[25] We have already examined how the dead old woman provides a convenient whipping post onto which responsibility for his mistress' "faults" may be transferred, sparing Cynthia's ideality. The *lena*'s tardy arrival in the corpus as *esprit d'escalier* usefully supports Propertius' love to the degree that she redeems Cynthia's character. Acanthis' opposition to the liaison thus operates as a hippomanes of fantasy, allowing Propertius effectively to allege that "if only Acanthis had *not* existed, there would have been no unhappiness between myself and Cynthia; the object of my desire, in herself, was ideal and fully deserved my devotion."

THE OBSCURE OBJECT OF DESPITE . . .

Notwithstanding Acanthis' usefulness to his rewriting the history of the affair, Propertius' hatred of her verges on unreason in its dogged single-mindedness. He traces a path from the apex of her alleged power (puissant magic) to its nadir (solitary and impoverished death). Yet the "fall" he so records raises fewer questions about the old woman than about himself. According to his own testimony the *lena*, as object of his hatred, changes completely within the course of the poem. Once powerful even over the elements of nature, she becomes physically weak and socially downtrodden; once Cynthia's confidante and mentor, she later wastes away as an isolated outcast; once able to borrow the shape and vigor of animals, she deteriorates into mortal illness. Whatever erstwhile opposition she presented to Propertius has vanished, *and yet he continues to hate her.* A puzzle: when every one of Acanthis' objective properties has changed to its opposite, what remains to hate in her?

Propertius' illogically persistent thirst for vengeance, continuing even after her death, points to an irreducible kernel round which his aversion to the *lena* coalesces, something that cannot be articulated as a logical proposition along the lines of "I hate her because she is (terrifyingly powerful, a jinx to love relationships, a threat to my vitality, an interfering busybody . . .)." His antagonism operates as if above and beyond all Acanthis' putative loathsome properties existed some mysterious "x" factor that inspired hatred even when all such features have vanished. He fastens upon the paltry details of her squalor to justify his malice when Acanthis lies sick and dying, gleefully pointing to a foul, stolen headband (71–72) as evidence of the old woman's avarice. Yet the absurdity of his proofs shows that he cannot in fact pinpoint exactly what he despises about her; no matter the intellectual resources mustered for the problem, the ultimate object of his animosity remains ineffable. The fact that this mysterious "x" cannot find expression, and yet forms the putative core of Acanthis' personality so strongly sketched within the elegy, indicates an encounter with that which ineluctably evades symbolization, the category of phenomena Lacan labeled the Real.

The Lacanian Real differs from "reality" insofar as it includes phenomena that most of us would consider unreal (dreams and hallucinations, for example); these phenomena nonetheless impinge on our lives, often with dramatic results. Face to face with the Real, "the mind makes contact with the limits of its power, with that which its structure cannot structure."[26] The Real evidences itself in, for example, the clumsy paradoxes of racial hatred. Racists formulate a plethora of logically contradictory accusations about the Other to justify their hatred (that other races are, for example, shiftless and lazy, but at the same time compulsive workers who steal employment from "legitimate citizens"—i.e., members of the dominant group).[27] These self-contradicting reproaches indicate that a fantasized "kernel of being" organizes the racist's conception of the Other, something over and above any nameable, immanent, symbolizable properties the despised group possesses (such as being hardworking or indolent). This kernel *makes* a member of the group the Other (in the eyes of the dominant group), and hence makes him objectionable. As mentioned in chapter 1, Lacan calls this "x" factor enfolded by fantasies of identity *objet a*. *Objet a* is a little piece of the Real that eludes all attempts to reduce it to symbolization and that persists as an inert remainder. In the Acanthis poem, Propertius has once again stumbled upon the "little piece of the Real" that organizes subjectivity.

. . . AND DESIRE

I say "once again" because his sketch of Acanthis and his hatred for her structurally reiterate, point for point, his portrayal of, and passionate love for, Cynthia: he molds his mistress around an equally inarticulable core. In 2.3, for example, Propertius considers a number of possible objective catalysts for his love (Cynthia's beautiful face, her lovely voice, her skillful lyre-playing); yet he discards each one by saying, "no, it cannot be that, either."[28] He finally despairs of putting his finger on the exact feature that inspires his love, contenting himself with general hyperbolic praise of her power to fascinate. Nonetheless, he returns to this puzzle from a different angle when he bitterly dismisses Cynthia at last in 3.24, telling her that his praises for her beauty were all false:

> mixtam te varia laudavi saepe figura,
>   ut, quod non esses, esse putaret amor;
> et color est totiens roseo collatus Eoo,
>   cum tibi quaesitus candor in ore foret.
>   (3.24.5–8)

> I have often praised you as a composite of various kinds of beauty so that love might think you what you were not. And your complexion, how often it was compared to the rosy Dawn, when the alabaster in your cheeks was makeup!

His dismissal does not imply that Cynthia was actually plain: *candor* (8), "shining fairness," simply denotes a different kind of beauty from the rosy blush he attributed to her. He substituted what he wished her to be for the way she represented herself, without ever being able to grasp the essence of her attraction for him. Even the moment of disillusionment reveals nothing essential about her: when he finally observes Cynthia's pallor, he still only sees makeup ("*quaesitus* candor," 8), another version of "what she is not." From the peak of his fascination to the nadir of his disgust, the core object of his passions ultimately eludes him.

Something about Acanthis and Cynthia escapes Propertius' grasp and constitutes a source of fascination for him even after the objective properties of these women have either changed or been dismissed as the object-causes of his reactions. Not by accident, then, does 4.5 link the careers of *lena* and mistress, though the connection jars with his previous history of the affair. Propertius' indignation at Acanthis' stolen headband is symptomatic: he reacts to this petty larceny as though it epitomized all Acanthis' wrong to him—and so it does. Acanthis, the thief of baubles, appears more damningly in this poem as a "thief of enjoyment," having "stolen" Propertius' enjoyment of Cynthia the "way it might have been" without the old woman's intervention.

Yet his rage at her "theft" conceals the embarrassing secret that he never possessed what was allegedly taken from him: Cynthia-as-object lies forever beyond his—or anyone else's—grasp. Jacques-Alain Miller has expressed this inescapable human impasse as follows:

> We know, of course, that the fundamental status of the object is to be always already snatched away by the Other. It is precisely this theft of enjoyment that we write down

in shorthand as minus phi, the matheme of castration. The problem is apparently unsolvable as the Other is the Other in my interior.[29]

Miller's statement that the theft precedes any (external) thief turns upon Lacan's model of the subject as constructed around a fundamental lack imposed by language, by the ineluctable gap between the "I" who speaks and the "I" represented in speech.[30] Lacan illustrates this gap with his ingenious dismissal of the famous Liar's Paradox: the statement "I am lying" is only a paradox, he remarks, if one does not realize that two "I's" are involved—the one who speaks, and the one represented by that speech—and only one of these is lying.[31] This gap or lack inevitably returns in human symbolization systems represented as some essential part of the subject, his most precious possession, alienated from him, rendering him metaphorically "castrated." Desire resulting from this aboriginal lack motivates a futile search for the object as if it were a missing part of the subject: desire turns ultimately upon a search for identity, for "what is missing from *me*." In particular, Man's commerce with Woman as object of desire seeks to ground the identity "Man" by construing Woman as His complement, His "other half," as if the positions Man and Woman were interlocking identities founded on essence rather than mere signifiers defined only by difference.

This search for complementarity ultimately bears upon the production of meaning per se, insofar as the signifiers Man and Woman represent in exemplary fashion the way language, like all symbolization systems—which Lacan collectively designates "the Symbolic"—produces meaning through binary opposition. The way that the conceptualization of gender slips and slides, unable to ground the primary dyad "Man/Woman" in any pre-symbolic reality, epitomizes the inadequacy of the Symbolic as a whole: the Symbolic lacks the capacity to ground itself in a signifier *not* defined purely through difference but possessed of an unassailable ontological status. Lacan's infamous aphorism "the sexual relation does not exist" summarizes just this lack of any complementarity that would support essential identities, not only for Man and Woman, but for *any* signifier. Commerce between the sexes in particular rests, in Lacan's view, on dissimulating the lack of an essence to gender; hence he punningly equates the term *jouissance* ("enjoyment," but also "orgasm") with "non-meaning as such."[32]

Lacan's model of the subject of desire fits Propertius' self-construction as the perpetually frustrated lover-poet, who has always lost something essential to another—his woman, his patrimony, his chance to be an epic poet.[33] More particularly, though, Lacan's sketch of the sexual non-relation as a grappling with non-meaning illuminates Propertius' repeated moments of impasse. Wherever he strives to grasp the nature of his relation to Cynthia, whether he stalks the source of its enchantment (2.3) or its disappointment (3.24), he grapples in vain to articulate something upon which signification cannot find a foothold, that "falls outside of" the Symbolic. The impasse reduces him to saying, "it is not that, nor yet that, nor that either. . . ."[34]

THINGS FALL APART

Nonetheless, Propertius avails himself of the only graceful way out of the dilemma created by the sexual non-relation when he reconfigures the impossibility of enjoyment—an impossibility founded on the fundamental status of the subject—as a *prohibition*. A third party (Acanthis) blocks his access to Cynthia: she sets the watchdog on him (73–74), advises his mistress against unprofitable liaisons (47–48, 54, 57–58), and urges the young woman to find wealthy lovers in order to coin her beauty into gain (49–53). Yet his portrait of the *lena* symptomatically conjures up the very essence of the impasse Acanthis glosses: the Symbolic can find no purchase on her as a phenomenon. We have already seen how Propertius' description of her wavers between extremes of power and weakness; he even seems uncertain whether she lives or has died. His record of her speech, too, sways giddily between high-style poetic expression, learned allusions to mythology, and pungent vulgarities borrowed from comedy, mime, and everyday idiom (as commentators at least since Tränkle have remarked).[35] Representations of Acanthis slide as if unanchored between the antitheses that found meaning (weakness/power; death/life; high style/low style), attesting that another logic impossible to capture in binary opposition governs her portrait: she exceeds the Symbolic as governed by "reason" and its stepchild, "common sense." Around Acanthis, all attempts at symbolization fail; she figures the intrusion of another order into the Symbolic—the intrusion of the Real as that for which the Symbolic cannot account.

Propertius sketches the effects of this intrusion on quotidian expectations of cause and effect, the laws assumed to underpin the Symbolic, when he describes Acanthis' powers as a witch. For the most part his material touches upon generic commonplaces—drawing down the moon, shape-changing, deceiving the wary—but includes a power puzzling in its vagueness, and precisely as such, appropriate to the Real-as-ineffable. "Quippe et, Collinas ad fossam moverit herbas, / stantia currenti diluerentur aqua" ("in fact, if she should toss herbs collected near the Colline gate into a ditch, things solidly fixed would dissolve in running water," 11–12). Camps and Richardson find this expression so enigmatic that they gloss it as power over green crops ("herbas") and crops standing in the fields ("stantia"). However—as Camps scrupulously notes even while defending his reading—such a use of *stantia* has no parallel in extant Latin literature. The unease of two such sensitive readers should give us pause; it indicates the disturbing implications of the distich's imprecision. *Stantia* embraces any solid upright object at all, a term all the more menacing for its lack of specificity. Propertius sketches a moment in which all the world's organization as conferred by the Symbolic melts away, leaving only the chaos of the Real. Matter forgets itself and the laws that govern it, as the permanent foundation of the world we know trickles through our fingers.[36]

Acanthis' "hetaira-catechism" reproduces this fundamental derailment, insofar as it destroys any sense that Woman possesses a substantial core, something irreducible to be loved (or hated) *behind* all the observable features. Acanthis teaches her disciple various poses to grieve the lover, and a few gestures to enchant him as well; her counsel implies that neither coldness nor amiability from the beloved has any intrinsic basis whatsoever—the mistress merely performs whatever role momentarily advantages her. Acanthis thus reduces Woman to a series of strategically devised veils ultimately hiding . . . nothing. The old woman radically undermines the lover's fantasy of an inexpressibly precious substance hidden within the beloved that fascinates him, but that escapes causal explanation—the fantasy Propertius pursues so energetically in elegy 2.3 and that underwrites *objet a*'s power. Insofar as Acanthis shows the beloved to be devoid of substance, an image strategically composed to irritate or please, she threatens the *lover's* stable sense of self, too. His mistress can hardly be his complement if composed of airy nothings;[37] she cannot ground his identity either as lover or as poet of her charms and irritations.[38] No wonder, then, that Propertius depicts Acanthis as a witch able to subvert nature and undo matter itself, so that the world dissolves in the face of her power. His extravagant claims have a personal application: the old woman undermines *the* crucial *objet a*—the enchanting quiddity he imagines at the center of his mistress' being—that justifies his poems and confirms his identity as poet, lover, and Man.

Acanthis' implied portrait of the "ideal" hetaira has other unsettling implications that also draw a significant response from Propertius. Woman seen as a series of masks donned to complement Man reveals Her inadequate definition within the Symbolic: She emerges only through antithesis, as merely "not-Man." *Objet a* springs from this conceptual deficiency within the Symbolic, both marking and dissimulating whatever cannot be thought or spoken within the limits defined by the binary "Man/Not-Man." (This excess gives rise, for example, to the question, What is Cynthia apart from her lover's constructions of her?—an enigma that 3.24's petulant retraction of his flatteries engages, but signally fails to solve.) *Objet a* provides a "screen" for fantasy that sets symbolization in motion, as when the lover justifies his attachment by imagining an ineffable siren's core to his beloved. But while Acanthis insists on Woman as insubstantial fantasy, Propertius' tenacious hatred of the *lena* denies the dilemma in which her revelation places him. He disavows her construction of Cynthia as cipher by attributing to Acanthis *herself* an *objet a:* his hatred insists that there *is* "something" in Woman, an essential kernel that can provoke his loathing even when (as we have seen) every one of Her objective properties that irritated him has disappeared.

Yet the structure of the poem itself reveals the logical weakness of this attempt to find a tangible enemy. Even Acanthis cannot bear the entire burden of Propertius' resentment; he must construct a further despoiler, in the form of the putative "rich rival lover." Though proffered as the principal thief of enjoyment within the poem, Acanthis has remarkably ascetic tastes. Even in her heyday as Cynthia's welcome confidante, Acanthis' tepid attitude toward riches reveals her *contemptus mundi*. While haranguing Cynthia to secure all possible luxuries, she herself scorns antique paintings as mere "rotting pictures" ("putria signa," 24). By contrast, the rich rival to Propertius she urges Cynthia to cultivate fully embodies the blissful enjoyment the old woman supposedly bars; the rival supplements Acanthis' role as prohibiter. As in previous poems devoted to the subject of Cynthia's wealthy admirers, 4.5 erects the rival as a figure of excess. He, unique among subjects, really *does* have access to bliss: his money will buy him anything, most particularly the heaven that Cynthia's favors constitute in Propertius' eyes. In 4.5, the rival's excess even manifests itself in marks of violence his mistress bears. Acanthis advises:

> "semper habe morsus circa tua colla recentis
>   litibus alterius [alternis *Barber*] quos putet esse datos."
>   (39–40)

"always have fresh lovebites around your neck; let him think these inflicted by disputes with another man!"

Yet notwithstanding these physical signs of the rival's existence, the *lena* speaks of him chiefly as an effect of perspective. Propertius' three earlier books treated Cynthia's other admirers as solid facts discovered through his jealous watchfulness. By contrast, Acanthis emphasizes playing up to erotic jealousy with bruises that may be thought (*putet*) to be from a rival's violent attentions. The old woman's advice reduces the rival to a clever stratagem; she forces a rereading of his assumed presence in the previous books. Now the rival appears to be a mere sign, an *objet a* in his own right whose features the fantasies of others will fill out. Not only will Propertius as jealous suitor obligingly lend the rival materiality, but so shall we, the readers who have eavesdropped on the imagined affair between Propertius and Cynthia during the course of three books.

LOVE BEFORE THE BAR

Yet Acanthis' curious terminology in sketching the rival as putative source of the mistress' bruises emphasizes his status as a schematically necessary, but empty, placeholder in an erotic triangle. Acanthis describes a quarrel with such a lover as a *lis* ("dispute") where one would expect the more usual term *rixa* ("brawl"). As Camps and Richardson both note, *lis* does not point to physical struggle, so would be unlikely to cause the bruises that must appear about Cynthia's neck.[39] *Lis* at root means "lawsuit"; it differs from *rixa* not only in abjuring physical violence, but in being a contention enacted for the eyes of a third party—the judge or jury appointed to hear the trial. A *lis* deduced from the marks of the putative wealthy rival sketches the triangular frame assumed by the sexual non-relation even in the absence of a tangible other.

Invoking the idea of a lawsuit in this context points to Law's surprising imbrication with the realm of erotic license the rival figures. Law springs from construing enjoyment not as impossible, but as laid under prohibition: Freud outlined as much in *Totem and Taboo*'s story of the greedy tribal leader-father sketched above in chapter 3.[40] The dubious historicity of Freud's account does not concern us, only its structure as a necessary supplement to his earlier formulation of the Oedipus complex.

Freud's essay shows how Law summarizes the sexual non-relation as Man's and Woman's relation, not to each other (that would be the "sexual relation" that does not exist), but of each to a third term, to the murdered "Father of Enjoyment," the *one* being imagined as "having had everything." The Father's murder conveniently relegates him to the realm of absence, while the sons' renunciation of the women their patricide won them reconstrues enjoyment—the fantasized, impossible excess the greedy tyrant embodied—as something voluntarily renounced. Killing the Father thereby conveniently transforms impossibility into prohibition. Read according to the same logic, the rival's punctual, self-satisfied appearance signals hope for Propertius, as the obverse of the poet-lover's fantasy. The other man's wildly passionate enjoyment of Cynthia, fierce enough to leave her bruised, paints that bliss as only circumstantially beyond Propertius' reach—just a matter of finances and luck, really—not as intrinsically unobtainable. The rival's imagined transports also beguile Propertius with fantasies of Cynthia as the nonpareil mistress and Muse, the woman who will underwrite his identity as lover and poet—as if Woman really *did* exist as something solider than just "not-Man."

Rewriting relations between the sexes as a lawsuit instead of a brawl underlines the degree to which the assumed binary, complementary relationship between Man and Woman is aboriginally sundered by a third term. The party occupying that third place can be wealthy rival, hostile procuress, or whoever. He or she only marks the place of the Other in the affair—ultimately, the place of the Symbolic and the limitations it imposes on relations between subjects. Like the formalities of some interminable trial, the Other promises but prevents a "resolution" of the impasse between Man and Woman. Such a resolution is impossible, because it would depend upon abolishing the lack that produces the alternately poisonous and beguiling fantasies that frustrate relations between the sexes; that very lack defines the subject, so resolution would mean destroying the subject. The Acanthis elegy records some of the feints and stratagems organized about this impasse.

OWED TO WOMAN

To step back for a moment and place 4.5 in the context of the elegies it conditions within Book IV: on the one hand, 4.5 foreshadows 4.7—Cynthia's diatribe against Propertius' elegies as false and exploitative tales of *her* faithlessness that dissimulate his own—insofar as it, too, offers a disenchanted second look at Propertius' poetry conditioned by a dead woman's tale. On the other, the Acanthis-elegy's interrogation of the high-minded mores prescribed for the mistress' behavior prefigures Cornelia's defense of her life before the Underworld court, in which the Roman matronal ethos is subtly but no less bitterly weighed and found wanting. Taken together, these three elegies all show that when the dead return in Book IV, they carry joyless truth to the living: they bear witness to the sexual relation's absolute failure.

That general observation in turn offers us a clue to gauging 4.5's specific office within Book IV. We have seen that, like 4.7 and 4.11, 4.5 broadly interrogates the construction of Woman, and by implication, her relation to Man; yet unlike the other two poems, the mutual scorn between Acanthis and Propertius fully *stages* the tension between the sexes, rather than just reporting it. Where Cornelia's husband, Paullus, receives her speech in silence, and Propertius merely sets the scene for Cynthia's dramatic entrance and exit as ghost, 4.5, by contrast, takes shape as Propertius' malediction and indictment of Acanthis, minutely detailing the hell he wishes upon her after death and recording all the reasons she deserves it; she in turn lays bare the self-interest behind his erotic asceticism. His irrationally persistent hatred of Acanthis parallels the degree to which she undermines his position *qua* lover and *qua* Man, and constitutes the fulcrum on which the elegy's interpretation turns. Elegy 4.5 engages Woman's demonization in a way that (more starkly than either 4.7 or 4.11) foregrounds Man's role and interests in painting Her thus black.

The other, intimately related theme that structures these three pivotal poems in Book IV is the Return of the Dead, a repeated motif that compels us to ask a simple, even naïve, question of this, the foundational revenant elegy: why *do* the dead return? Lacan has posed this query to ancient texts (such as the *Antigone*) and extracted a deceptively simple answer: because they were not properly buried—something went wrong with their obsequies.[41] Žižek aptly summarizes Lacan's meditations on the phenomenon: "the return of the dead is a sign of a disturbance in the symbolic rite, in the process of symbolization; the dead return as collectors of some unpaid symbolic debt."[42] Propertius wishes just such a symbolic omission on Acanthis when he hopes that her grave will be adorned with a broken-necked wine-jar ("sit tumulus lenae curto vetus amphora collo," 75)—a vessel incompletely destroyed, as opposed to the more thoroughgoing breakage required by funeral rites. Breaking a vessel associated with the dead person symbolically releases her or his spirit from its earthly abode, by getting rid of familiar objects that might otherwise entice the shade to linger among the living; by contrast, the wine-jar Acanthis' grave will sport still retains its essential integrity and usefulness—its symbolic efficacy is reversed.[43] Marked by this sign, her posthumous existence winds around a repetitive, futile attachment to a world Acanthis cannot leave behind: the wine-jar incompletely broken summarizes the sins of omission Acanthis' advice to Cynthia unveils. The conceptual lacunae she counters, that would rarefy the elegiac mistress into pure self-denial, all ultimately revolve around the lack of any signifier for Woman's desire in a system implicitly centered on the signifier "Man"; that omission returns as "unpaid debt," haunting elegy with its shadowy, but persistent, complaint.

This fundamental omission in Woman's representation renders legible the fact that 4.5, like 4.7 and 4.11, turns upon Law, support and subset of the Symbolic, in its specific manifestation as the ethical judgment of Woman. While Cynthia in 4.7 brands Propertius' poetry about her as unfaithful whore pure slander, and paints an Underworld that eschews any simplistic distinction between so-called Good and Evil women, Cornelia in 4.11 justifies her life in a way that calls into question the very ethical codes imposed upon her as legitimate wife (*matrona*). Acanthis in 4.5

anticipates both skepticisms, casting doubt equally on the criteria that putatively condemn and ennoble Woman, when she rejects as naught but a poor man's scam the *beau ideal* of impoverished fidelity Propertius manufactures for Cynthia; the *lena* shrewdly turns his own lines against him (4.5.55–56 = 1.2.1–2). Acanthis, like Cynthia and Cornelia, stages the place of the Law as radically empty and aligns herself instead with the Real: she refuses the customary graceful dissimulations of Woman's inadequate representation and insists instead upon the "inconvenient" ruptures in that fiction. If the Symbolic cannot adequately account for Woman, her poem implies, it can hardly judge Her. Acanthis "returns" from the dead to insist on the *whole* story.

CHAPTER SIX

"The Book of Revelation": Cynthia's Truth (4.7)

This living hand, now warm and capable
Of earnest grasping, would, if it were cold
And in the icy silence of the tomb,
So haunt thy days and chill thy dreaming nights
That thou wouldst wish thine own heart dry of blood
So in my veins red life might stream again,
And thou be conscience-calmed—see here it is—
I hold it towards you.

KEATS

As noted in the last chapter, the Acanthis poem (4.5) introduces the leitmotif of the "return of the dead" to Book IV, a theme that connects elegies 5, 7, and 11. The elegy on Cynthia's death (4.7) returns to the motif and paints it in even more scarifyingly vivid colors: Cynthia appears to Propertius in a vision with a score to settle. She presents a horrific sight: her body has been charred by the funeral pyre, her lips scoured by the river Lethe, and her bones rattle. She appears in a fury, accusing Propertius of being under a new woman's sway. But, more surprising by far than either her appearance or her accusation, her picture of their affair and its aftermath radically conflicts with the way Propertius has depicted their relations in his previous three-plus poetry books. She was the faithful one, not he, she says (53; cf. 13, 21, 49, 72, 93), she the one who ran risks to meet him secretly in the Subura (15–18). Now her rival, a jumped-up streetwalker named Chloris, vindictively torments Cynthia's old slaves, while Propertius acquiesces. But no matter: Cynthia resides blameless with the Virtuous Beautiful Women of myth in the Underworld (a neighborhood she describes as puzzlingly indistinct from that of the Evil Beauties of myth). Saying she will await his death, when they shall "grind bone on bone" eternally, she vanishes.

But why did she come? Why, that is, would Propertius raise the possibility that his sketches of their love affair, his life's work, are lies? And why, even more embarrassingly, does she appear precisely now in Book IV, right after the hymn (4.6) that celebrates the naval battle at Actium, and implicitly put the elegist's most patriotic gesture into question also? Can Propertius say nothing without contradicting him-

---

John Keats, *Selected Poems and Letters*, ed. Douglas Bush (Boston, 1959), 250.

self? Just prior to introducing the dead Cynthia in 4.7, he laid before the reader a paean to Augustus' victory at Actium, the central poem among Book IV's eleven elegies. The poet's reflection on the battle that decisively defeated Mark Antony and Cleopatra, and awarded Octavian undisputed supremacy in Rome, turns upon a long central speech: a grimly bellicose Apollo exhorts Augustus to victory as his and Rome's divine patron, a champion with the face of an avenger and monster-slayer (4.6.31–36). The god has, at least temporarily,[1] doffed any reminder of his divinity's tenderer side, the easygoing, bemused lyrist whom Propertius found so congenial a sponsor to erotic elegy.[2] Phoebus' changed image in 4.6 implies that his poet and devotee Propertius has himself determined to fulfill completely the patriotic promise of Book IV's opening elegy (4.1) and turn his back on erotic elegy in order to pursue more martial, nationalistic, and correspondingly loftier themes.

But then comes Cynthia in 4.7, with her startling and ennobling revelation of her own faithfulness, an abrupt *volte face* from the Actium elegy's programmatic implications. Poem 4.7 not only returns to erotic elegiac themes, but renders Cynthia as mythologically commanding a presence as Apollo. The poem lingers upon her appearance as 4.6 did upon the god's; the structural echo underlines the poignant familiarity and horror of each visage (dead beloved mistress, divine lyrist turned bloodthirsty).[3] Cynthia enters as a golden, terrible ghost to match the golden, terrible god in her unfaltering observance of *fides* ("'me servasse *fidem*,'" 4.7.53, an assertion of loyalty that rivals "vincit Roma *fide* Phoebi," 4.6.57).[4] By contrast, 4.7 rather tarnishes Propertius' image: he did not keep faith, and lied about it. His poetic record of the affair, outside this single elegy, consistently makes Cynthia the fickle offender, he the long-suffering victim—an account his mistress' post-mortem disclosure flatly contravenes.[5]

How do we broker the claims of elegy 4.7 against those, first, of Propertius' other Cynthia poems, and second, of 4.6's quasi-epic ambitions? Some previous interpreters of 4.7 have discussed the problem of Cynthia's sudden rehabilitation and her embarrassing revelation of Propertius' bad behavior in terms of "comic exaggeration," "satire," or "irony";[6] others consider the incident evidence of Cynthia's contradictory character, whether as a matter of historical record or of Propertius' noble tact and self-delusion.[7] Erich Burck numbers among the few who take Cynthia's assertions seriously, and the only scholar (to my knowledge) who has seen that 4.7's ghostly apocalypse begs comparison with 4.6's divine revelation: he perspicaciously emphasizes the fact that raising Cynthia to the imaginative plane of the Actium poem, the level of myth and of poetic immortality, seconds the appeal for careful comparison Book IV's physical juxtaposition of the two poems makes.[8] Burck, however, remarks upon the paired elegies' rhetorical trajectories that elevate Apollo and Cynthia to iconic status merely to conclude that these poems thematically mark nationalistic and amorous inspiration as the "two centers of the poet's life"—a reading unfortunately circumscribed by the biographical fallacy. It remains to account for the pair's structural significance within Book IV as a whole, as thematically and numerically the book's center and "epicenter" respectively.

DOUBLE VISION

The Actium elegy (4.6) forms not only the numerical center of Book IV, but also, in the eyes of many scholars, its thematic heart.[9] The general trend of interpretation sees 4.6 as a patriotic poem, whether the critic views Propertius' effort as wholehearted or not.[10] In line with the program broached in 4.1—to exalt Rome by drawing a connection between its contemporary observances and their venerable roots—the battle of Actium appears in 4.6 (it is said) as the inauguration of a new era under Augustus; the *princeps*, as divinely-aided leader, vanquishes the powers of disorder, unreason, and feminine tyranny emergent from the East. To be sure, the poem is not entirely unproblematic; a minority of scholars even sees it as intentionally parodic (whether comically or grimly so), marshalling many valid points to support their views. Yet their arguments fail to neutralize into insignificance the strong colors of 4.6's patriotic gestures: the vividness of these distinguishes 4.6 within Book IV, strongly marked as all its other elegies are by cool suspicion of prevailing Roman ideology.[11]

However, pronouncing upon 4.6's status as either "true" political panegyric or mere pretender does not engage us here, only its function as general antipode to themes articulated elsewhere in Book IV—most especially in 4.6's "diptych partner," Cynthia's return from the dead in 4.7. Elegy 4.6 contrasts with the rest of Book IV insofar as customary thematic "gem" and "foil" have exchanged places. The feminine suspicion that we have seen trained upon Roman nationalist and masculinist pretensions generally in Book IV recedes for the moment into the background (though it does not disappear entirely).[12] Contempt for the feminine, celebration of clear-cut hierarchies of dominance and power, and an absence of self-doubt, all exalting a self-assured Roman masculinity, constitute 4.6's foreground; they render the elegy an icon (albeit an imperfect icon) of the unquestioning nationalistic "masculinism" that we have seen articulated with particular clarity in, say, the Arethusa elegy's portrait of Roman imperialism (4.3). In discussing 4.3, the masculine position emerged as an (unjustified) assurance that one's knowledge was complete and sufficient; 4.6 extends this line of thought to the point that it embodies a masculinist poetics par excellence,[13] insofar as it declines to question the self-evident "verities" of *Romanitas*, lacking even the ray of skepticism the disillusioned Arethusa offers in 4.3.[14]

Elegy 4.6's close relation to 4.7, however, effectively creates two centers for Book IV, one patriotic, one erotic-elegiac, so that the masculinist and nationalist assumptions articulated in 4.6 do not ultimately rest unchallenged.[15] Burck points to the structural appropriateness of Book IV's double center as a reflection of the duplicity of its programmatic opening. In the second half of elegy 4.1, the astrologer Horos answers the poet-narrator's vision of a poetic monument to Rome and her glory articulated in the first half; Horos presents the case for elegy and for Cynthia as the principal source of the poet's inspiration, and rebukes Propertius' nationalist ambitions. The opening poem's two halves juxtapose a "masculine" and "feminine" poetics: faith in clean conceptual dichotomies, hierarchy, and epistemology confronts a thorough skepticism that undermines the elegist's projected aetiological program. Horos urges not only erotic elegy's worthiness to recapture Propertius' attention (4.1.71–74, 135–50), but the intricacy and challenge of what lies beneath its deceptively simple surface ("'eludit palmas una puella tuas'"—"'one girl still evades your conquest,'" 4.1.140; "'at tu finge elegos, fallax opus: haec tua castra!'"—"'but you fashion elegy (treacherous work!): this is your field,'" 4.1.135). Cynthia iconically represents a "feminine" truth that still eludes Propertius.

As Horos' vision for Book IV responds to Propertius', so elegies 4.7 and 4.6 respond to one another. Elegy 4.7, the "epicenter" of Book IV, not only criticizes specifically 4.6's masculinist pretensions to the true interpretation of history, but looks both backward and forward in Book IV to summarize generally the book's "feminine" themes of skepticism, of a truth told by those (especially, but not exclusively, women) whom history would prefer to silence and forget. Yet the battle is not engaged simply between a grand national vision and the humbler concerns of the demimonde: in its "conversation" with 4.6, elegy 4.7 discovers an uncanny collusion between the traditional values of *Romanitas* and the Young-Turk code of erotic elegy supposed to subvert them. Cynthia asks specifically that Propertius burn his own poems about her (4.7.77–78), repeatedly expressing disgust at the contrast between his poetry's praise of her (4.7.49–50, 78) and his hardhearted neglect she suffered after her death (4.7.23–34, 47–48, 70). That gap between promise and performance raises questions not only about the accuracy of Propertius' poems, but invites closer scrutiny of the beliefs that fundamentally animate love elegy *in toto*, and that shape the ethos Catullus, Tibullus, and Ovid, as well as Propertius, helped create. Book IV's consistent duplicity (in all senses of that word) in fact delivers a more accurate picture of the complexity of the world in general and of poetry in particular.

How different, in truth, is the elegiac ethos from the *mos maiorum*? Elegies 4.6 and 4.7 together imply a difference more apparent than real. The Actium poem—Book IV's most obvious and internally consistent gesture toward traditional Roman values—evinces open contempt for feminine dominance ("altera classis erat Teucro damnata Quirino, / pilaque feminea turpiter acta manu"—"the other fleet, and the spears thrown by a woman's hand, had been condemned by Trojan Romulus," 4.6.21–22), while erotic elegy in general nominally elevates women to a position of mastery, calling the mistress *domina*, the slave's term for his female master. Yet Propertius 4.7 sketches a relationship of power between lover and beloved that in fact accords the male his traditional place of dominance, insofar as the poem discloses the mistress' entire dependence on her lover for economic support and social status. Or again, while 4.6 lays claim to a self-assured knowledge of the truth (especially the truth of history) that centers on Rome, 4.7 finds (and disputes) an equally self-satisfied "received wisdom" in the versions of women's history commonly retailed by elegy, women condemned or exalted according to an entirely male-centered system of values.[16] Finally, the Actium poem's alignment of Rome and Roman history with divine moral order by styling the poet-narrator as priestly celebrant of Apollo, and the god as patron of Rome's victory, finds a response in the equally divine system of 4.7's Underworld. We shall see that 4.7's sketch of the next world—concentrated almost exclusively on the fate of myth's famous beauties—traces in Hell elegy's system of values that make unquestioning loyalty to one's man its fundamental (if often unrealized) ideal. The ideal is so conceptually inadequate, however, that even Hell cannot make good on its dubious condemnation of history's "Evil" Beauties.

Yet elegy 4.7 does more than respond to the grand gestures of 4.6; it serves, in fact, a pivotal summarizing function for all of Book IV. The chronicle of Cynthia's ghostly return matters less as an elegy that unfolds a particular concept than as a comprehensive (if summary) articulation of themes developed at greater length elsewhere in Book IV; 4.7 functions as midway conspectus and coign of vantage. Accordingly, I delegate fuller exploration of the psychoanalytic principles that govern 4.7 to other chapters of this book, wherein I discuss Book IV's elegies that sound these depths more completely; here, I content myself largely with cross-references to those chapters when evoking a psychoanalytic concept. Yet my discussion of 4.7 will trace the poem's articulation and development of the remaining elegies' several themes into a pattern at once uncannily familiar and provocatively strange.

THE PROMISE OF *JOUISSANCE*

Take, for example, 4.7's engagement with *jouissance* ("enjoyment"), that is, with the conceptual impasses inherent to any logical system and what these reveal; we first examined *jouissance* in the context of the Acanthis elegy (chapter 5), yet the reactions inspired by 4.7 point to a similar failure of sense crucial to understanding Cynthia's reappearance. The critical assessment of the ghostly Cynthia's revisionist history as pure comedy (of varying degrees of savagery) or pure mercurialism reproduces a rhetorical trope the poem itself unravels—that of constructing Woman as a set of irreconcilable contradictions. Like the other elegies that we have examined (and shall examine) in this book, 4.7 systematically elucidates the paradoxes inherent in the cultural construction of Woman, but goes beyond this to probe these logical breakdowns for an alternate order of thought, for *jouissance;* in so doing, it organizes the aporiae revealed by Book IV's elegies under either the grim, or the hopeful, side of *jouissance* (hope can be extracted from the chaos of *jouissance* insofar as, under repressive conditions, logical failure offers the possibility of relief or resistance).

The Acanthis elegy (4.5) introduced the dire side of *jouissance* by showing the basis both of love and despite for Woman to be pure fantasy, a mysterious "x" factor imagined to reside in the object of passion or hatred (though none the less powerful for being imaginary). *Jouissance*'s baleful aspect comes to light again in elegy 4.11 (chapter 9), wherein Law itself—in its specific instantiation as the code that governs Roman matrons' behavior—reveals itself to be predicated upon nothing inherent in nature, or divine will, or any other inalterable order, but in fact upon the very antitheses of Law itself, upon violence and transgression.[17] Elegy 4.7 acknowledges and deploys this aspect of *jouissance* when it interrogates the ethos elegy prescribes for *puellae* ("girlfriends/mistresses"), a code formally the same as that of Roman matrons, if different in content. In so doing, 4.7 weaves together the perspectives of 4.5 and 4.11 to produce an entirely new *tertium quid,* and the first glimmerings in Book IV of a hopeful side to *jouissance.* Elegy 4.7 particularly scrutinizes elegy's (mis)constructions of Woman (just as 4.5 did) and finds in them not only a basis in pure fantasy (as Cynthia's refuting Propertius' version of their affair implies), but grounds upon which to anticipate 4.11's indictment of divine order for the erroneous judgment of Woman. Like Cornelia in 4.11, Cynthia in 4.7 describes a Hades whose ethical authority comes to grief over its own internal contradictions.[18] In 4.7, however (unlike 4.11), Hell stymied over the judgment of Woman appears unable to enforce its judgments of Her, and effectively commutes its own sentences (of which I shall say more below).

Other details of 4.7 further elucidate the positive, hopeful side of *jouissance* instinct in the very logical breakdowns that make it visible. For example, a minor leitmotif within 4.7 tentatively examines the curious extra-linguistic effects of puns (chiefly in the "speaking names" of its *dramatis personae*) and so foreshadows the Hercules elegy's (4.9) more extended and audacious exploration of how *jouissance* manifests itself in the extra-linguistic effects of language at play (Lacan christened these effects *lalangue,* a concept I shall examine in detail when I analyze the Hercules poem in chapter 8). But 4.7's grander trajectory also recalls the irrational opulence with which Acanthis describes the rose gardens at Paestum; her exuberant portrait advances 4.5's plot not at all, and so constitutes a formal superfluity within the poem's narrative economy. Yet 4.7 develops Acanthis' luxuriant but truncated gesture into a lush alternate world, fashioning a utopian Hades organized around *jouissance,* around (narrative and ethical) non-sense and sensuality. The ghostly Cynthia's rambling tale of an oddly indiscriminate Hell refuses "common sense," refuses the conventional scale of ethical values that peremptorily divides women into "good" and "evil" on the basis of impossible demands.

FOILING EXPECTATIONS

Considered in its own right, though, aside from its references to other poems of Book IV, 4.7 seems at first blush a congeries of nonsensical disparities. Cynthia's combined jeremiad and travelogue of the Underworld offers the oddest mix of contraries, oscillating wildly between the aesthetic and the gruesome. Cynthia opens her harangue with a vivid picture of the pauper's funeral she received at Propertius' hands: no guard with his cane rattle to scare witches and evil spirits away from her body, nothing but a broken tile propping up her head. From the squalid miserliness of her funeral arrangements she passes on to the post-mortem torture of her slaves, dwelling both on the grisly torments she wishes on those who betrayed her and on the vindictive punishments Propertius' new mistress, Chloris, now metes out to the few Cynthia-loyalists. But this grim catalogue also blossoms unexpectedly with moments of pure aesthetic fascination: the color and odor of the hyacinths and nard she missed at her funeral (32–33); Chloris' costly finery, so laden with gold that it sweeps the ground (40); the molten ruin of Cynthia's golden image, melted down by Chloris to provide a dowry for herself (47–48). Moreover, a punning humor hovers just below the surface of Cynthia's diatribe: each slave's name fits her crime. Petale (roughly "petal," "flower," or "wreath") is punished for supplying garlands to Cynthia's tomb; Lalage (or "Babbler") suffers because her former mistress' name is too often on her tongue; and treacherous Nomas ("The Numidian") used poisons worthy of Numidia's infamously venomous snakes.[19] Examples of this wordplay could be multiplied.[20] Cynthia's harangue seems caught in a tug-of-war between contradictory elements: realism versus romanticism; the grisly versus the aesthetic; the serious versus the humorous.[21] How can we reconcile this hodgepodge collection of divergent elements so as to yield a sensible reading?

The problem of 4.7's disparity has not gone unnoticed, nor are proposed answers lacking; broadly speaking, critical solutions dictate that the reader choose up sides between the "serious" reading (which tends to pull the realistic and gruesome in its train) or the "humorous and ironic" reading (which chiefly subsumes romantic and aesthetic interpretations).[22] From either side of the divide, observations that undermine a tonally consistent reading are either minimized or dismissed. Occasionally, attempts have been made to preserve both aspects of the poem, but without any convincing explanation of their juxtaposition that extends beyond Propertius' supposed love for aesthetic *frisson* or lively characterization.[23] Yet the point of Cynthia's diatribe lies in its very incongruity, a point not exhausted by considerations of aesthetics. Its apparent incoherence has ethical import: it evokes the Tarpeia elegy's (4.4) meditation on the inadequate conceptualization of the feminine, insofar as 4.7, too, dramatizes insufficiencies in prevailing modes of thought about women, specifically the women of elegy and their demimonde counterparts. Yet 4.7 extends the trajectory of 4.4's thought to include reflection on the imaginative oppression not only of women, but of slaves, the lower classes, and the world that all such bodies inhabit.

That world is one that men of Propertius' class would know chiefly as tourists rather than as denizens—the world of the socially feminized.[24] By "socially feminized" I mean women, of course, particularly women of the lower classes—but not just women. The term comprehends slaves as well, of either sex—indeed, all those alienated from the sources of power in Rome and intimately interconnected in the Roman imaginative demimonde.[25] This extends to alienation from discursive power, too: it is a commonplace, as true of ancient Rome as anywhere else, that representation belongs to the dominant group, silence to the oppressed. Women, slaves, and the lower classes exist in Propertius' poetry constrained by limits of literary genre that are also conceptual limits. But while these limits speak to the preconceptions that typically color perceptions of the Other, Propertius does not just mindlessly reproduce such prejudices. Commentators have often noted, for example, that 4.7's representation of tortured slaves aligns it with Roman comedy, and they have concluded on that basis that we can dismiss these painful vignettes as humor, not to be taken seriously.[26] But as Holt Parker has argued in a recent essay on torture in Roman comedy, torture—even on the stage—is never quite that simple.[27] Parker notes that the threat of torture must at least be entertained as a horrific possibility in order for the relief of its being deferred or averted to be felt as comic. I would extend the trajectory of Parker's argument in applying it to Propertius: in 4.7, Roman comedy's delicate equipoise between horror and laughter spins dizzily out of balance—and for a reason. The history of responses to 4.7 shows that the humor does not smoothly accord with the rest of the poem's elements. Readers either perceive it as incongruous or doggedly insist upon its comic effect, seemingly to keep black humor from becoming a black hole that sucks up all the fun. This very incoherence whispers guilty knowledge of the elegist's representational and epistemological limits, and a desire not so much to transcend these limits (an impossible agenda) as to expose them, to jar the reader out of complacent credulity, to force him to interrogate his own comfortable suppositions about another, marginalized world (an example of *jouissance*'s hopeful side, where it disrupts "what we all know to be true" such that it awakens skeptical scrutiny of prevailing ideology). Bringing Cynthia's ghost back from the grave to depose her lover's faithlessness and attest to her own faithfulness, against Propertius' record of the affair, is but one way that elegy 4.7 ambushes the elegy-reading audience by revealing that "everything you know is wrong."

In previous poems, Cynthia herself has figured the conceptual limits that hem in Propertius' representation. Throughout his work, Propertius grants Cynthia opportunities to speak and fictively to represent herself such as no other elegiac woman enjoys. Cynthia talks often enough, at sufficient length and with contrary passion, to make elegiac mistresses like Lesbia, Delia, and Corinna seem taciturn, pliant ghosts by comparison. Cynthia's expression regularly and deliberately opposes her lover's proprietary fantasies about her. In poems 1.3 and 2.29a/b, for example, Propertius weaves around her sleeping form aestheticizing reveries about her as a dreaming naiad, or a Bacchant, or mistress of a gang of Cupids. She quickly dispels these conceits when she awakens and angrily berates him as faithless gadabout or jealous spy.

Propertius' portraits of Cynthia consistently make his representation of her a question negotiated between lover and beloved, between poet and his creation—and, consequently, between text and reader. But in 4.7, this problematic expands to include an entire underclass world disadvantaged in a struggle for accurate visibility. The conflict elucidates another perspective on the elegiac mistress, one that implies necessary connections to a material world that elsewhere the genre largely suppresses or glosses over; these connections draw the *domina* uncomfortably close to the slave. Though Propertius himself plays the lover-as-slave (*servus amator*), the dependence of women like Cynthia on their lovers radically undermines their construction as (female) masters. Their "dependence" is both economic and representational: Cynthia's real-world counterparts relied upon their lovers for economic survival, whether that meant basic subsistence (for the poor doxy) or a polish that allowed her access to aristocratic society (for the soignée courtesan).[28] To the extent that Cynthia dwells upon shabby details of her cheap funeral, for example, she echoes Acanthis' message in 4.5 that implicitly warns her charge to make provision for the day when her lover fails her. But elegy 4.7 expands the scope of Acanthis' *Hetärenkatechismus* beyond purely economic concerns, extending attention to women's reliance upon men for representation in art. Where Cynthia's sisters figure in literature, that picture too rests on the men who wrote, and thus on a male conceptualization of women; the tension in 4.7 between the aesthetic and the gruesome, the funny and the serious, is a function of this problematic.[29] The punning slave-names, the rival's glittering finery, belong to the register of aestheticizing poetic representations that form one pole in the tug-of-war straining previous poems. These stylistic "forepleasures" expedite the audience's absorption of the content, displacing scrutiny of that content in favor of the pleasure afforded by its package.[30] The slaves' tortured bodies, on the other hand, and the harsh economic realities that force Chloris to think already of a dowry to attract the next man, refer to material relations larger, grimmer, more complex than the elegiac Symbolic can accommodate; they bespeak a ticking bomb tucked inside the pretty package. A literary signifying system fetters Cynthia and her poetic sisters as much as the economic system of Rome enslaves their demimondaine counterparts.

INDICTING ELEGY

Cynthia's accusation that Propertius lied, her concentration on the pain hidden beneath elegy's pleasure, and her demand that he burn his poetry, raise the question whether men can write truthfully about women: can knowledge transcend gender-position? Both Cynthia's accusation and the poem's other recalcitrant details dramatize two gender-specific systems of truth: on the one hand, public, "official" truth, promulgated by Man's written word (like elegiac poems); on the other, private, experiential truth, felt in the (female) body and inscribed upon (women's) flesh. Public truth accords with the complacently willing blindness most dramatically mounted on display in, say, the Actium elegy (4.6) and its seemingly unreflective patriotic gestures (though, as we have seen above, erotic elegy enjoys its own share of such blindness); private truth aligns with intimate knowledge that disrupts the smooth functioning of the Symbolic, waylaying "common sense" and "what everybody knows" with its rude intrusions of what must be spoken as opposed to what is allowed to be said—in short, with *jouissance*. Provocative irruptions of what appears nonsense from the dominant ideology's point of view characterize most of the poems in Book IV; particularly dramatic examples appear in, say, Arethusa's vision of defending the Roman empire as an essentially erotic enterprise (4.3), or Tarpeia's unsettling of apparently fixed conceptual categories such as "inside/

outside," "enemy/native," "benefit/betrayal." Poem 4.7, however, expands upon these subtle suggestions to interrogate the world its own elegiac genre has imagined.

Cynthia's own oddly gruesome appearance points to a private, feminine truth; when Propertius has Protesilaus return from the dead to visit his wife in poem 1.19, no such grisly details embellish the hero's corpse. But Cynthia's much-abused body figures experience excluded from relations as conventionally portrayed between elegiac lover and *domina*. The Propertian lover, like his fellows, worries about his lady's fidelity, and sees all relations with other men as motivated by pure greed.[31] Cynthia's accusation that such poetry is all lies finds support in her focus on demimonde economics and the vicissitudes of dependence. As noted, Cynthia refers in passing to Chloris smelting her predecessor's image to get a dowry; Cynthia chiefly directs her anger over that at Propertius and his acquiescence ("te patiente," 47). The details of her own funeral supply a rationale for why she terrorizes the poet, while letting his mistress off the hook. The shabbiness of Cynthia's obsequies align it, ironically, with the funeral of her *lena*, Acanthis, whom Propertius reviled in poem 4.5; he denounced as meretricious greed Acanthis' advice to the younger woman not to put all her eggs in one basket with men. But Cynthia's poor funeral argues that Acanthis' advice made good economic sense. As Kathryn Gutzwiller has pointed out in her insightful essay on 4.5, there is no retirement plan for the elegiac mistress: we never see one grow old, comfortably supported by her lover's affection and money. Outside elegy's picture frame, the mistress ages, and is cast aside. Elegy translates as "female greed" the simple realization that a prudent woman must provide for her own future, by maximizing her material gain while she is young—and unless she has the good luck to have an exceptionally rich and generous lover, that means having more than one lover.[32] In a gesture unparalleled in elegiac poetry, Propertius candidly places in his mistress' mouth a description of the squalid end to which elegy's romantic expectations of a mistress would lead her.

This focus on elegy's truncated truth does much to account for Cynthia's portrait of the Underworld, puzzling for its lack of demonstrable moral eschatology. The elegiac expectation that the *domina* be altruistically loyal to the lover ostensibly divides 4.7's Underworld. Yet significantly, the poem articulates a topography and a logic of feminine virtue shown to be untenable. The river Lethe supposedly divides "Good Women" like Andromeda and Hypermnestra from "Evil Beauties" such as Pasiphaë and Clytaemnestra. It rewards virtue with permanent residence in Elysium:

> nam gemina est sedes turpem sortita per amnem,
>   turbaque diversa remigat omnis aqua.
> unda Clytaemnestrae stuprum vehit, altera Cressae
>   portat mentitae lignea monstra bovis.
> ecce coronato pars altera rapta phaselo,
>   mulcet ubi Elysias aura beata rosas,
> qua numerosa fides, quaque aera rotunda Cybebes
>   mitratisque sonant Lydia plectra choris.

Andromedeque et Hypermestre sine fraude maritae
    narrant historiae tempora [pectora *O*] nota suae:
haec sua maternis queritur livere catenis
    bracchia nec meritas frigida saxa manus;
narrat Hypermestre magnum ausas esse sorores,
    in scelus hoc animum non valuisse suum.
sic mortis lacrimis vitae sanamus [sancimus *Barber*] amores:
    celo ego perfidiae crimina multa tuae.

(4.7.55–70)

For there are two places allotted alongside the unlovely stream, and a different crowd rows on divergent water. A wave bears the adultery of Clytaemnestra, another carries the wooden monstrosity of the Cretan woman's pretended cow. Look, here comes another group in a garlanded skiff, where a happy breeze softly brushes the roses of Elysium, where the rhythmical lyre and the bronze cymbals of Cybele and the Lydian plectra make music for the mitre-wearing choruses! Andromeda and Hypermnestra, wives without deceit, tell the well-known perils of their lives. The one complains that her arms are bruised by her mother's chains and that her hands had not deserved the cold stones; Hypermnestra tells of the enormity her sisters dared and that her courage was not up to the crime. Thus with the tears of death we heal the loves of our lives: but I conceal the many transgressions owed to your faithlessness.

Yet if some process of ethical division and collection does prevail in the Underworld, how are we to account for the fact that Cynthia describes its workings on two prehistoric queens in the present tense? If the Underworld truly divides Elysium from Tartarus, should not Clytaemnestra and Pasiphaë have reached their appropriate neighborhoods by now? Why are they still floating aimlessly on the Lethe?[33] This splendid tableau implies that the river does not in fact accomplish any moral purpose, but leaves both good and evil beauties suspended in a repetitive limbo—an impression seconded by the fact that, though Propertius describes the Underworld as divided into two places ("gemina est sedes . . . sortita," 55), he uses no plurals to describe it.[34] An accumulation of further anomalies suggests another logic at work here, one that undermines the moral program ostensibly governing the Underworld. For example, Andromeda and Hypermnestra, defined as "brides without deceit" ("sine fraude maritae," 63), typify the "Good Women"; yet as examples, they strain even this minimal definition. Andromeda chooses spouse over parents (unremarkably enough). But Hypermnestra's choice raises an uncomfortable ethical problem: being "without deceit" ("sine fraude") to her husband entailed deceiving her sisters. The poem tacitly undermines her decision by phrasing it as a mere loss of nerve: "in scelus hoc animum non valuisse suum" ("her courage was not up to the crime," 68). Moreover, just as with the tableau of Evil Women, all verbs describing the activities of Good Women are in the present tense. Cynthia implies not only that Andromeda and Hypermnestra go on reciting their harrowing lives after death, but that they still wear the effects, as if frozen in time; their wounds are always healing, but never healed. Andromeda's arms, for example, are still bruised from the chains in which she awaited the sea-monster her mother's boasting aroused (note the present tense infinitive in "haec sua maternis queritur *livere* catenis / bracchia"—"she complains that her arms *are bruised* from her mother's chains," 65–66).[35] Such details undermine any sense that these "blameless brides" have earned a fitting reward. Rather, they seem obsessed with the pain imposed by their conventionally virtuous lives and baffled of any permanent relief; Clytaemnestra and Pasiphaë are by comparison serene.

The poem accumulates these strange moments in which virtue's reward and evil's punishment dizzyingly exchange attributes, eventually collapsing all distinction between "Good" and "Evil" Women. By so doing, 4.7 enlarges upon a line of thought that began in the Tarpeia elegy (4.4) and ends in the Cornelia elegy (4.11), rising in Cynthia's portrait of Hell (*mirabile dictu!*) to its most hopeful moment. Propertius 4.4 and Propertius 4.11 dwell upon the inadequate conceptualization of the feminine and its implications for condemnation or salvation. On the one hand, Tarpeia's betrayal of Rome nonetheless accounts for contemporary Rome's hybrid strengths; on the other, Cornelia's exemplary adherence to matronal mores guarantees her no share in her male ancestors' honors. Rome cannot properly assess the one woman's *felix culpa* or the other's impeccable virtue, much less offer either woman redemption. Here in 4.7, though, the impossibility of cleanly separating feminine good from evil appears to have stymied the whole system of judgment and given every *condamnée* an eternally suspended sentence.

Yet scholars have often ignored or discounted the awkward details I have cited, wanting to see in the Underworld a coherent eschatology that efficiently separates feminine sheep from feminine goats, or they point to the anomalies as evidence that Propertius was not really "serious" about constructing a moral universe, being rather more taken with the idea of a beauty pageant of the dead.[36] But the details must be taken seriously, precisely *because* they undermine any possibility of the Underworld's moral coherence in this poem: that fact aligns conceptually with 4.7's prominent focus on the feminine body and the body in pain, on slavery, economics, and degradation. Cynthia's portrait of Hades sketches a moral universe much more finely nuanced than the official "truth" of elegiac myth will allow, by deploying elegy's favorite representations of Woman, drawn from the mythic repertory, against itself. Insofar as these representations are constructed solely around the support of Man, even at the cost of all other relationships, they totter under the weight of their own illogic as emblems of virtue. Little wonder that Cynthia's diatribe also punningly describes the instruments of women's constraint as literary figures and terms. She complains that a *codex* painfully burdens her grave-decorating slave Petale; the word means "wooden block," but also "book-roll," and the second meaning is hard to escape when that slave's name, "Ms. Wreath," is itself a learned literary pun on the cause of her punishment.[37] Such details not only anticipate the Hercules' elegy's (4.9) use of puns' extra-linguistic effects to make a point, they combine with visual double-entendre to underline the message: Cynthia feels with horror the ivy of Bacchus strangling her bones and insists that it be removed, thereby rejecting the icon of the very god Propertius styles "patron saint" of his own verse.[38] The poet, out of his mistress' mouth, subtly lays bare the degree to which his own medium is implicated in perpetuating an unsustainable "truth" about women.

TARRYING IN THE REALM OF THE SENSES

But does Propertius have an alternative, aside from ironizing these portraits of Good and Evil Beauties such that one can hardly be distinguished from the other? If the problem stems from the historical narrative that separates these women on false premises, then the solution cannot rest on an appeal to the very same premises that found that narrative. In constructing his portrait of the Underworld, Propertius sabotages the tendentious histories that divide these women by ironizing not only the tradition's content, but its structure, too. Various critics have remarked upon the repetitive quality of Propertius' Underworld. Whereas other models stipulate that the dead, if properly buried, are ferried across Lethe only once, Propertius' dead return nightly to the upper world.[39] As remarked above, the Good Beauties narrate the perils of their lives, apparently without ceasing, despite the promise of progress in "sic mortis lacrimis vitae sanamus amores" ("thus we heal the loves of our life with the tears of death," 69): they are still regaling each other with these tales upon Cynthia's (comparatively recent) arrival.[40] Moreover, the content of their tales and Cynthia's gloss upon them are curiously skewed to imply that their apotheosis as Good Beauties has nonetheless left a bitter taste in their mouths: P. J. Enk says more than he realizes when he observes "quomodo poeta dicere potest feminas illas de amoribus suis loqui, cum queratur Andromeda de catenis, Hypermestra scelera sororum, suam innocentiam narret?" ("Wherefore can the poet say that those women speak of their loves, when Andromeda complains about her chains while Hypermestra describes the crimes of her sisters and her own innocence?").[41] Their concentration on complaints rather than passion imply that the game was not worth the candle, if what they remember of their amours consists of the fear, blood, and pain from which the latter arose.

And what of their bower of not-so-perfect bliss, this abundantly sensual and exotic place? It abounds with the scents of roses (60), the noise of brass cymbals and the riotous Eastern worship of Cybele's elect (61–62); why? Cynthia exploits every opportunity her ekphrasis offers for sensual pleasure in color and sound, at the expense of advancing the narrative towards the end, in all senses of that word, the conclusion and the purpose of these women and of their stories. She makes the Underworld revolve around repetition and dilation in sensuous details—an elegant form of foot-dragging that subtly resists, on principled grounds, Hades' heavy hegemonic burden of judging women. Hell, as articulated in her vision, embodies *jouissance*, insofar as it infinitely defers the end of each woman's story. It forever holds in abeyance the perspective from which each mythic beauty's history might be viewed as a whole and measured against masculinist ethics in order to be judged definitively as good or bad. Hell prefers voluptuous elaboration, for the Evil Beauties as well as for the Good: the former float forever upon waves distinguished by the eye-catching image of a wooden cow that yet has not, apparently, sealed anyone's fate. The setting for all this is, appropriately enough, an ersatz, netherworld East, populated by celebrants of Cybele and Lydian choruses (61–62) as well as dead beauties sprung from Greece and Egypt (57, 63). This imaginative setting takes advantage of the conventional interpretation of the East as the inversion of Rome to represent the laws of the "real world," the masculinist world of Rome, in a mirror-reversal perpetual Saturnalia.[42]

In sum, 4.7 dramatizes with deadly irony the bitter obverse of elegy's received wisdom and its unsuspected attachments to the masculinist *mos maiorum* portrayed in the Actium elegy; it unravels elegy's half-truth that promulgates women both too good and too evil to be believed, that promulgates the religion of their exclusive loyalty and of their sublime indifference to economics. Propertius indicts the elegiac tradition as representing only Woman, a masculine fantasy. The bravura diatribe he gives Cynthia passionately contrasts with that fantasy women's (lived, experienced) reality, in all its pain and all its attachments to the concrete and material, as figured by the female body.

CHAPTER SEVEN

Cynthia Returns from Lanuvium (4.8)

Maud Gonne at Howth station waiting a train,
Pallas Athene in that straight back and arrogant head.
YEATS, "BEAUTIFUL LOFTY THINGS"

DISORDER

Elegy 4.8 is often called Propertius' one attempt at pure comedy—by general consensus, a successful effort.[1] The elegy tells, in humorously self-deprecatory fashion, how Propertius came to grief trying to revenge himself on Cynthia. She had gone on an excursion outside Rome with a foppish wastrel; stung by her desertion, he invites two somewhat disreputable women, Phyllis and Teia, over for an evening's revel. The party falls flat: the women cannot divert his mind from thoughts of his lover. Cynthia's unexpected arrival on his doorstep in the midst of the festivities brings the evening to a chaotic end, as she drives out her rivals and punishes her lover severely. A wary reconciliation closes the poem.

The elegy has been the subject of unobtrusive but steady attention over the last several decades, culminating in the generous scope of Marion Komp's 1988 monograph that grants half its pages to the poem's careful analysis.[2] Komp's book, like the majority of scholarship, treats 4.7 and 4.8 as a meaningful diptych, with good reason: only these elegies in Book IV unequivocally revisit the love affair that occupied Propertius' first three books, since only they refer to Cynthia by name.[3] The poems' position, side by side in the collection as we now have it, reinforces their singular *déjà vu*.[4] These facts alone invite readings that deliberately pair the two, and scholarship has diligently elucidated numerous less obvious correspondences of vocabulary and theme that unite them.[5] Yet the poems' conspicuous interrelation underlines, rather than softens, the embarrassment of their order: why portray Cynthia's death in such gruesome detail in one and in the next spring her vigorously alive upon the poet's shocked audience?[6] The jarring effect has been

---

William Butler Yeats, *The Collected Poems of W. B. Yeats* (New York, 1951), 300. Reprinted by the kind permission of Anne Yeats.

deemed less worthy of the first century B.C.E. than of nineteenth C.E., a *fin-de-siècle* that had more obviously "learnt to finger the secret springs of the horrible."[7] At one time, the poems' hysteron-proteron order was considered evidence for the fourth book's posthumous editing by a clumsy hand; of late, majority opinion sees too many structural niceties of correspondence among all the book's elegies to credit such a theory.[8] Yet to banish the posthumous editor to outer darkness cannot erase the sense of abrupt and unsettling transition that haunts 4.7 and 4.8, internally as well as in their relation to one another. Rather, their collective incoherence makes better sense viewed as a principled textual strategy, consistent with the fact that disjunction within each poem dramatizes the nuances of their respective subject matters.

Of the two, 4.8's structural logic is the most obscure, and for that reason, will occupy our attention in this chapter, as the more vivid example of how disjunct form shades interpretation of content. For example, after the first distich tantalizingly hints of scandal in Rome ("disce, quid Esquilias hac nocte fugarit aquosas, / cum vicina novis turba cucurrit agris"—"learn what panicked the watery Esquiline last night, when the neighborhood crowd ran through the new fields"), Propertius abruptly jumps twenty miles southeast to Lanuvium and begins a long excursus on that city's snake-cult associated with the worship of Juno Sospita. Each year, selected young women from Lanuvium descend a long dark cave, carrying food for Juno's sacred serpent; it rejects the offering if any girl is not virgin, and such iniquity calls down punishment (capital punishment, Propertius implies) on the offending young woman. However, if all goes well, the maidens return to their parents and the farmers shout, "it will be a fertile year!"[9] Propertius leaves us to conjecture how the provincial ritual constitutes an appropriate proem to the Esquiline riot, and in fact, the problem is never adequately solved. Eventually he tells us that Cynthia and her companion went to Lanuvium ostensibly to witness the ritual (15–16), but also denies that the journey had any real connection to Juno's cult: "causa fuit Iuno, sed mage causa Venus" ("the pretext was Juno, but the *real* cause was Venus!" 16).[10] Nonetheless, Propertius expends elaborate strokes describing the mere pretext of his lover's visit, then unceremoniously precipitates his reader into the scandalous details of her journey to Lanuvium (15–26), only to switch venues and apparent rationale once more by plunging back into the equally disreputable facts of his debauch in her absence (29–48). His aetiological gesture of describing the Lanuvium snake-cult trails away into nothing: the poet ultimately offers no explanation of the cult's origins or significant nomenclature, still less of its significance to his story.[11] Rothstein attempts to explain the divagation as inspired by the fourth Book's avowed aetiological program, a program waylaid in this poem by Propertius' greater interest in Cynthia's hoydenish behavior en route, while Pasoli detects in the detour a more mischievous "autoparodia" of the book's avowed intentions.[12] Camps and Richardson abandon the struggle and classify the poem unequivocally as a love-poem, not an exercise in aetiology;[13] most other commentators delicately skirt the question of how exactly the excursus on the Lanuvium cult fulfills any larger structural scheme.[14]

Yet two recent studies—by José Turpin and J. D. Noonan—surmise that the relevance of Lanuvium's celebration of maidenhood lies, paradoxically, with sex. Both scholars argue that the ritual functions as an oblique sexual allegory, a fitting background to the poem's more explicit sexual content.[15] They unfold a plausible allegory: the cave at Lanuvium (like the city's gates, the object of Propertius' yearning reverie at 48) suggests the female genitalia, while the snake represents the male. The rite at Lanuvium explicitly sacralizes virginity in the service of (agricultural) fertility, but Propertius' concern with his mistress' "unchastity" when she deserts him for an elegant *flâneur* implicitly colors his description of the town and its ritual site. The excursus thus spoofs his own anxiety.

Turpin's and Noonan's explanations draw Lanuvium into plausible relation with the rest of the poem, yet their insight—that the sexual relation usefully glosses the poem's specific content—can be expanded to encompass more than just the poet's disquiet over Cynthia. The idea of sexuality-as-ordeal summarized by the Lanuvium snake-rite fits the dismally failed eroticism most everyone in the poem suffers. Erotic relations appear in this poem as a series of impasses: Propertius' embarrassing impotence in the midst of his infidelity (47–48), Phyllis' and Teia's tainted and undependable sexual charms (29–32), Cynthia's curiously truncated tryst with the "plucked ne'er-do-well" ("vulsus nepos") that brings her back to Rome too soon (implying that her dalliance was unsatisfactory) (15–26), the lovers' uneasy reconciliation whose ambiguous quasi-military jargon hints of continued hostility (88). In ironic contrast to these antipathetic venues, sexual innuendo shades a remarkable percentage of the poem (quite apart from the Lanuvium cult's description). Propertius uses the word *concubitus*, for example—which usually means "sexual intercourse"—to describe his merely reclining with his guests Phyllis and Teia, anticipating what he hopes from them. Scholars have seen only slightly subtler references in Cynthia's deliberately driving through the "foul spots" ("impuros locos," 22) on her way to Lanuvium—supposed to glance obliquely at her lack of (sexual) discrimination[16]—and in Propertius unsuccessfully "seeking Venus" ("Venerem quaerente") as he dices, blind to his guests' charms (45–46). The elegy even closes with *double entendre:* the final distich, "atque ita mutato per singula pallia lecto / respondi, et toto solvimus arma toro," reads as "and so, once the bed's sheets had been changed one by one / I rose to the occasion and we unsheathed our weapons," (87–88).[17] Why is sex everywhere in this poem (even spread allegorically over a ritual celebrating chastity) and successful nowhere?

THE SEXUAL NON-RELATION

Lacan—or more precisely, the elaboration of his thought in the work of his followers—can help us here. For example, applying Slavoj Žižek's work on sexuality to Propertius 4.8 reveals that the wide reach of sexual implications in the poem proceeds from (rather than contradicts) its pandemic sexual failure. In analyzing how sex can become the universal signified of every activity and object, Žižek argues that the phenomenon points to an inherent impasse.

> This universal surplus—this capacity of sexuality to overflow the entire field of human experience so that everything, from eating to excretion, from beating up our fellow-man (or getting beaten up by him) to the exercise of power, can acquire a sexual connotation—is not the sign of its preponderance. Rather, it is the sign of a certain structural faultiness: sexuality strives outwards and overflows the adjoining domains precisely because it cannot find satisfaction in itself, because it never attains its goal.[18]

Failing of the goal in one sense or another can be amply documented from Propertius' whole chronicle of his affair with Cynthia, not just this poem; his verses schematically mirror a *via dolorosa* of sexual antagonism that anticipates the elegant sorrows of courtly love. However, 4.8 intensifies the sense of impasse by reducing him to impotence and his mistress to violence, degradations that the fragile congeniality of the poem's conclusion does more to underline than to erase (as we shall see). The elegy may be read—in this as in other respects—as a conspectus on their entire relationship, especially since it is his collection's very last word on the subject. Beneath the joyful comedy of this elegy lurks an unresolved tension, rendered all the more insistent by the uneasy proximity of Cynthia's ghost in 4.7 and her embittered retrospect on their romance. Why should Propertius' final word on the affair be so fraught with doubt and subterranean despair?

The poem, read as a conspectus, subtly shifts our perspective in a way that is simultaneously an exoneration and the counsel of despair. That nothing, not even a determined attempt at lightheartedness and comedy, can quite banish the sense of failure from Propertius' and Cynthia's liaison indicates a flaw inherent rather than contingent, endemic to sexuality per se rather than to the lovers' peculiar shortcomings. Certainly the dismal history of antagonistic relations between the sexes (quite apart from Cynthia's and Propertius' part in it) argues that sexuality cannot realize a relationship of true complementarity between Man and Woman; Lacan begins his explanation of this defeat (in *Encore*, his twentieth seminar) with the pitiless pronouncement that "there is no sexual relation." Joan Copjec's illuminating reading of *Encore* aligns Lacan's failure of sex with a failure of language, or better, of signification (thus showing Žižek's observation—that sexual language stems from the failure of sex—to be the converse of *Encore*'s central point).[19] Copjec renders the seminar's chief innovations clear by beginning with the same basic question Lacan inherited from Freud in contemplating sexuality: What *is* sex? Psychoanalysis, she observes, elucidates human sexuality as a product of signification—more precisely, as the effect of signification's *deadlock*. Sexual difference is not unambiguously marked anatomically, chromosomally, or hormonally, yet neither can convention alone account for it; sex is neither simply a natural fact, nor reducible to any discursive construction. Sex cannot, finally, be reduced to sense; to the contrary (as Copjec sums up the problem), "sex is the stumbling block of sense."[20]

In chapter 3, I mentioned Lacan's conceiving sexual difference in terms of a logical relation in his twentieth seminar. *Encore* opposes masculine to feminine as two different ways of apprehending phenomena: the masculine, from a position of (false) confidence, sees the world in terms of universality; the feminine, from a position of skepticism, sees it as ungraspable heterogeneity. But Seminar XX also rethinks sexual difference from a different (though complementary) angle as two different modes of logical impasse—a perspective more relevant to our purposes in grappling with the apparent illogic of 4.8. *Encore* assigns two formulae of sexuation to Woman: "there is not one x that is not submitted to the phallic function/not all x is submitted to the phallic function."

A word is in order here on Lacan's terminology, especially the phrase "phallic function," which has not appeared previously in our discussion of Propertius. Lacan's formulae express ideas of gender and subjectivity already set out in this book; they appear here translated into a strict formal logic. We have, in fact, unfolded the phallic function's work before, albeit not under that name. The phallus, in Lacan's system of thought, is the universal signifier of desire, in both subjective and objective senses: it abstractly designates desiring (the fundamental status of the divided subject), and the object desired. Yet as a signifier, it is devoid of substance and corresponds to no actual subject or object whatsoever. Rather, the phallus stands behind all other signifiers of desire, such as the culturally freighted icons discussed in chapter 2 ("good citizen," "good lover," "good man," etc.) that promised to heal the subject of his division and lack; it grants these signifiers value, as if it were the (radically empty) Platonic Ideal in which they all participated, though reducible to none of them. When, therefore, the divided subject submits himself to limits placed upon his desire—when he submits to the social constraints imposed by these cultural signifiers, for example, in the hope of assuaging his perceived internal lack[21]—he ultimately submits to the phallic function as, essentially, the principle of setting limits to desire.

The broad pattern of the phallic function setting limits in order to assuage desire and to achieve (an illusory) "wholeness" can be assimilated to the masculine perspective discussed in chapter 3. The subject who assumes the masculine position believes that he can intellectually grasp disparate phenomena; motivated by the desire for meaning, he strives to master their heterogeny and mold it into a conceptual Whole. This exercise necessarily entails delimitation, since in order to wrest a comprehensible pattern (however specious) from his observations, he must exclude *something* against which his data may be defined. Only thus do his data become an exclusive set whose members' inclusion is ordered by a principle, rather than an indiscriminate congeries ordered by none. Fundamentally, of course, he must, by presuming his own objectivity, exclude from his calculations himself as observing subject, and his desire (the very factors that preclude objectivity).

The phallic function's role in delimiting in order to achieve meaning—or rather, the failure of that role—impinges upon Seminar XX's "feminine" formulae of sexuation insofar as they proceed from a contradiction internal to a fundamental rule of language. This rule prescribes the way we determine the value of a signifier—appropriately enough, since to ask, What is sex? is ultimately to ask, What do the signifiers "Man" and "Woman" mean? The rule demands our belief in the inexhaustibility of the process of meaning—in the fact that there will always be another signifier to determine retroactively the meaning of all that have come before—at the same time that we must presuppose "all the other signifiers," the total milieu necessary for the meaning of one. The same rule of language requires, and precludes, the completeness of the system of signifiers. Without the totality of the system there can be no determination of meaning, and yet this very totality would prevent the successive consideration of signifiers that the rule demands. Lacan's formulae essentially say that Woman emerges where no limit (no phallic function) intervenes to inhibit the progressive unfolding of signifiers.[22] Hence the endless and internally contradictory predicates that culture regularly asserts of Woman. These cannot be organized into a sensible Whole: she is Whore and Madonna, deceiving and naïve, greedy and self-sacrificing, divinely wise and the nadir of unreason.

This sheds a different light on the heterogeny of predicates Propertius' corpus assigns to Cynthia; Lawrence Richardson remarks on her bewilderingly kaleidoscopic guises in the *Monobiblos*:

> The picture of Cynthia that must be put together is of a woman who is shown us by turns as a *casta puella* who spurns the poet's desperate love and devotion (1.1), a frivolous and vain creature of fashion entirely preoccupied with her own appearance (1.2), a devoted mate who can berate the poet for his desertion of her for an evening while he has gone off carousing (1.3), a doxy willing to threaten to follow a rich suitor to wintry Illyria (1.8), yet tearfully insistent that P. give up thought of a career and the chances of lining his pockets in Asia to dance constant attendance on her in Rome (1.6), a vindictive little trollop ensconced in the society of the demimonde of Rome (1.5), and a courtesan accustomed to spend her holidays grandly among the pleasures and temptations of Baiae (1.11)—to name only some of the guises in which we meet her in the first half of the first book.[23]

Elegies 4.7 and 4.8 together simply telescope the inconsistency that organizes the figure of Cynthia into the span of some two hundred lines. As Richardson observes:

> The extremes of Cynthia could hardly be more sharply drawn, the vindictive, brooding woman of the ghost poem who can demand that the poet destroy his poems and yet claim that she had always loved him and the fine, spirited girl of the present poem [4.8] who will engage happily in a wild donnybrook with her rivals, exact outrageous terms of peace from her unfaithful lover, and then go to bed with him contented and serene, and without ever explaining her own behavior.[24]

Other poems of the corpus often point irritably to Cynthia's quixotism as contributing to the affair's failure, but 4.8 frames her tergiversations as symptom rather than cause: her contradictions point to a logical impasse at the heart of the sexual relation in which both partners participate, but that burdens them differently (as we shall see).[25]

Propertius also participates in contradiction (both in this poem and throughout the corpus), but a contradiction oppositely structured. Lacan says of Man that "there is at least one *x* that is not submitted to the phallic function/all *x*'s are submitted to the phallic function." As Copjec remarks, these formulae *do* draw a limit to the unfolding of signifiers—the "at least one" exception—but an internally contradictory limit: what does "all" mean when "one" is excepted? Much of Propertius' corpus dramatizes this paradoxical limit in the form of his envious construction of his rivals. He regularly depicts himself as a lover woefully handicapped by poverty in his pursuit of his mistress (subject, that is, to the "lack" that informs the phallic function) while the wealthy, fortunate rival is the necessary, but impossible, exception to this rule. The rival "always gets the girl"—but his final appearances in the corpus reduce him to an effect of perspective. In elegy 4.5, for example (as we have already seen in chapter 5) the mistress' cunning attempts to foster jealousy conjure up a competitor who circumvents the phallic function, but more as phantom than substantial fact. Here, in elegy 4.8, the figure of the wealthy rival arises again, this time as the *vulsus nepos* who accompanies Cynthia to Lanuvium; this prodigal comes garishly fraught with contradiction between his status as fortune's favorite in the Propertius-Cynthia affair, and his objective properties. Dee points out that when Propertius describes his enemy as "depilated" ("vulsi," 23), he sketches a pathic whose wealth derives from rich male lovers; the spendthrift blanches at a beard ("barba pudenda," 26) because it interferes with his role as epicene love object.[26] Moreover, the wastrel's need artificially to make himself smooth implies that he is rapidly losing the youth that makes him desirable to men.[27] Propertius' jibe that his rival must soon sell himself as a gladiator speaks to the other man's spendthrift habits, but also to the imminent disappearance of his wealth's source. Propertius depicts his rival less as Cynthia's complement than her mirror: the *nepos*, too, depends precariously upon his sexuality for his daily bread. Cynthia's sudden return from her tryst with him hints that this rather pathetic figure, youth and finances dwindling, cannot in truth bear the weight of Propertius' grand jealousy: Propertius is surprised *in flagrante delicto* because he expected the *nepos* to keep her happily occupied rather longer than the poor man could manage.

Seen in the whole context of the sexual relation's failure, though, the *nepos'* shabby manhood is simply inevitable: masculinity and femininity are both logically impossible, as Lacan's formulae on the sexual (non)relation make clear, deriving as they do from a conceptually crucial limit either forsworn (by the feminine side) or speciously imposed (by the masculine side). Accordingly, no man or woman may say that he or she embodies this thing, "masculinity" or "femininity." Sexuality is thus rendered imposture and masquerade—more to the point, a radically *asymmetrical* charade that can discover no fitting union between its two masks. Sex becomes a signifier empty of content, without a signified, making its rude takeover of "innocent" language logically apt: it achieves a universal dimension precisely because a specific sense has been evacuated from it. Sex is always a potential co-sense (anything can be seen as "alluding to *that*") because it always fails to find its "proper" sense, the signified content proper to itself.[28] The wild proliferation of sexual innuendo in elegy 4.8 perfectly suits the poem's amorous frustrations and enmities insofar as they constitute a comic distillation of the sexual relation's failure.

THE BREAK IN THE CAUSAL CHAIN

A failure of logic akin to the sexual relation's central stumbling block transforms Propertius' one comedy into unabashed slapstick: elegy 4.8 reflects and amplifies a certain illogic that has always plagued Propertius' recorded relations with Cynthia, but never quite so riotously.[29] We have already seen that Propertius not only grossly overestimates the *vulsus nepos*' fascination, he also ignores his own knowledge of Cynthia when he invites Phyllis and Teia for the evening. His description of Cynthia's journey to Lanuvium implies intimate knowledge of her jehu's driving habits; knowing also that she travels fast and light in a two-wheeled *carpentum* (23), why does he court destruction by arranging this ill-timed *fête intime*?[30] Similarly, when Cynthia returns and discovers his unfaithfulness, she rather overreacts, given that she herself went to Lanuvium precisely to betray *him* (51–52, 55–57, 61–67, 73–86). The lovers apparently cannot put together cause and effect properly.

Of course the ancients did not (any more than the moderns) consider lovers the most reasonable of creatures, and Propertius often openly, though defiantly, declares his own folly.[31] Yet in this poem, Propertius simultaneously amplifies the effect and shifts the heavier burden of illogic to Cynthia when he spirits away even the flimsiest pretext for her anger at his slave. She outdoes her own unreason in judging her lover's offense when she turns from strictures on Propertius to peevish vengeance on the innocent Lygdamus: "Lygdamus in primis, omnis mihi causa querelae, / veneat et pedibus vincula bina trahat"—"Lygdamus especially—the whole cause of my complaint!—let him be sold and drag double chains upon his feet" (79–80). More than one commentator has puzzled over how Lygdamus can be blamed for an adventure that stemmed entirely from Propertius' own initiative; only the dead Cynthia demanding her "poisoner's" torture (but not being able to decide, or care, who among Propertius' slaves this should be) can match this outburst for illogic (4.7.35–38).[32]

This is not the first time that Propertius has grappled with the fact that his mistress does not act with strict predictability. The obscure relation between cause and effect in Cynthia's heart baffles Propertius repeatedly in the first three books: scorn does and does not make her heart grow fonder,[33] a rich rival's money does and does not tempt her,[34] poetry makes her now kind, now cruel to the poet.[35] Yet previously Cynthia's quixotism only puzzled and frustrated Propertius; even here, Cynthia's peremptory judgments of servant *and* master seem at first glance to fit the stereotype of women as always exasperatingly "blowing things out of proportion, overreacting." That notwithstanding, Propertius admires her arbitrary imperiousness ("furibunda decens"—"insane rage becomes her," 52) and describes it in heroic terms (55–56, 63, 82).[36]

Jon Elster's meditations on human whim are of use to us here, as an entry (though no more than that) into the problem of Cynthia's mercurial behavior; he has attempted to reduce such phenomena to order with the concept of the *mechanism*. "A mechanism is a specific causal pattern that can be recognized after the event but rarely foreseen. . . . it is less than a theory, but a great deal more than a description." For example, if denied what they want, humans will sometimes be satisfied with what they have (the "sour grapes syndrome")—or may crave the prohibited more precisely because they cannot have it (as "forbidden fruit"). If people pursue a certain habit in one sphere, they may sometimes also pursue it in another (the "spillover" effect); they may also act oppositely (the "compensation" effect).[37]

Yet Žižek, commenting on Elster, points out that mechanisms cannot be conceived as simply occupying a middle position on a common scale whose extremes are universal theory (with predictive power) and mere description. Rather, mechanisms constitute a separate domain of causality whose efficiency obeys radically different laws: the specificity of mechanisms turns on the way in which the same cause can trigger opposite effects. Different subjects, in a self-reflective way, determine which causes will determine themselves.[38] The mechanism—that quixotic gesture of freedom—defines the subject.

Inspired by Propertius' ill-fated dalliance with Phyllis and Teia, Cynthia beats and humiliates him one moment, then happily makes love to him the next (64–67, 73–88); her unpredictability models the gap between cause and effect that *is* subjectivity. The subject emerges precisely insofar as the relationship between cause and effect becomes "unaccountable": we can never ascertain in advance the way the causes that determine us will exert their power over us. Cynthia's "fickleness" becomes an index of, not a degeneration from, humanity; from indeterminacy, she culls the shadow of freedom, if not the pure substance.[39]

Of particular interest to us is the fact that, here as elsewhere, scholars often read her radically different reactions to the same cause as specifically feminine.[40] They do not exactly err in so doing, but "female fickleness" bears deeper scrutiny in the light of Elster's and Žižek's elucidation of unpredictable subjective determination: Cynthia's "feminine" suspension of the causal chain points to Woman, not Man, as the subject par excellence. Cynthia fascinates Propertius as a spectre of freedom; her feminine "unreason" constitutes a gesture of refusal, a refusal to be inserted in the "proper" nexus of causes and effects.[41]

COURTLY LOVE

Yet even a fascination for defiance does not fully explain Propertius' almost embarrassing enthusiasm for his mistress' display of high temper and for his own humiliation. Cynthia's sudden intrusion upon Propertius' private debauch comes as an unexpected (and strangely welcome) surprise: impotent and unhappy despite Phyllis' and Teia's best efforts, he had imagined himself before the gates of Lanuvium, the city of the divine ritual that (he thought) held Cynthia (47–48). She bursts in the door at that very moment and his relief is palpable, nor much diminished by high-handed punishment for his sins. Propertius admires her imperiousness and her outrageously one-sided prohibitions (she forbids him even casual contact with women in future); he neither sulks nor rebels, though her double standard earlier *had* driven him to revolt ("cum fieret nostro totiens iniuria lecto / mutato volui castra movere toro"—"since her offense against my bed happened so often, I decided to move *my* camp to another bed," 27–28). He finds her beautiful in her anger (52), her look and actions evoking an epic conqueror (55–56, 63, 70–82). Even the conventions of *servitium amoris* do not necessarily demand that the lover enthuse over his mistress' tyranny, only that he comply. Why should Propertius be such a happy idiot?

His joy subtly draws attention to who really benefits from amorous "slavery": the Lady's demands, however inscrutable, capricious, even cruel, effectively dissimulate the sexual relation's failure. By elevating Woman to the place of the Lady, courtly love posits her as locating desire's fulfillment and ratifying the lover's supposed knowledge of his own identity as Man. Yet at the same time, her demands insure that he can only approach such fulfillment via the elaborate detours she specifies. These detours infinitely defer the encounter with her, and thereby put off the moment when the lover would be forced to acknowledge that attaining such a heaven of bliss is not prohibited, but rather impossible, because "there is no sexual relation": no symmetry exists between the positions Man and Woman, lover and beloved, that confirms the identity of either, or makes up one harmonious Whole. Cynthia magnificently relieves Propertius of the embarrassment of re-experiencing sexuality's failure (of which his impotence has already given him a taste) by driving out Phyllis and Teia and prescribing a monk's life for him in future (75–78). As *belle dame sans merci*, Cynthia is (to borrow Lacan's words) "a highly refined way of making up for the absence of sexual relationship, by feigning that we are the ones who erect an obstacle thereto."[42]

OBJET A: IN YOU MORE THAN YOU

One could be forgiven for wondering, though, whether Cynthia's physical violence to her lover does not strain even the wide tolerance of courtly love, and push us closer to something like sadism. When Cynthia returns to Propertius' house after routing her rivals, she assumes the hauteur appropriate to a triumphant general and dictates terms of "surrender" to her lover ("accipe, quae nostrae formula legis erit"—"hear what my terms are," 74)—but she also bites him until she draws blood, scratches his eyes, and beats him cruelly (65–67). The corpus as a whole has not prepared us for this—though elegy 3.8 had elaborated, at a purely theoretical level, the idea that violent behavior signals true love. In that elegy, Propertius had invited Cynthia to "prove" the depth of her affection by wounding his face, threatening his eyes, marking his neck (3.8.6–7, 21–22). Yet his invitation can only be sarcastic hyperbole in Book III: Cynthia may have raged at him verbally, but her worst physical gesture in the whole of the corpus thus far has been to push (dramatically, but harmlessly) a small, light food table at him as he reclined on a dining couch (3.8.3–4).[43] In 4.8, by contrast, Cynthia does in fact wound her lover's face, eyes and neck, waxing physically violent for the first and only time in the corpus (64–66). She even exceeds his ironic invitation to violence extended in 3.8: there he had asked merely for a bruise on his neck to display to his envious peers as a sign of her love ("livor," 3.8.22), but in 4.8 her "lovebite" draws blood ("imponitque notam collo morsuque *cruentat*"—"she made her mark upon my neck and her bite drew blood," 65).[44] What has this savagery to do with love?

Everything: Cynthia bites and wounds the surface of her lover's body as yet another effect of the necessary asymmetry that founds the sexual (non)relation. Lacan's formulae of sexuation, with their emphasis on non-complementarity, essentially say that no relationship exists between what the loved one possesses and the lover lacks. Yet love and desire flourish somehow: what fills in the gap between what the lover wants from the beloved and what the latter has to give? Lacan answers "*objet a*"—the mysterious object that is "in the beloved more than the beloved." The lover loves something in the beloved of which the latter is unaware and cannot name (I can never articulate the exact cause of someone else's love for me).

Žižek draws our attention to the lover's experience of the beloved's body in order to dramatize the disjunction between the two positions. I can regard my lover's body as an object of aesthetic pleasure, or of sexual desire, or of biological study (the effect of flesh, blood, glands, and the like); yet I cannot translate one domain into the other (cannot, for example, see sexual attraction as entirely a matter of blood or muscles or pheromones, of biological determinism) because they belong to heterogeneous orders. Even if biochemistry successfully isolated the hormones that governed the rise, intensity, and duration of love, the actual experience of love *qua* event would still maintain its autonomy, its radical heterogeneity to its bodily cause. The body's depth can be read as extra-symbolic "cause" of the surface "effect"—but an effect already incommensurate with its cause, because surface and depth belong to heterogeneous orders.[45] In this context, it makes sense to call Cynthia's laceration a "lovebite" (*nota*), even though the term is usually reserved for mere bruises. Her gesture sketches a desire to break the barrier between symbolized surface and depth; she breaks into her lover's body as if to draw out from it the fantasized *objet a*, the presumed object-cause of desire.[46] She acts out Lacan's cryptic summary of love: "I love you, but because inexplicably I love in you something more than you—the *objet petit a*—I mutilate you."[47]

RELIGION

Objet a's particular usefulness lies in denying a break in the causal chain, proffering itself as putative cause (of sexual desire, for example). This conversion of contingency into causality conceptually grounds in yet another way the apparent whimsy of including religious cult in an erotic poem. We have spoken of the Lanuvium snake-cult as allegorically reflecting Propertius' desire for Cynthia, but the cult also mirrors the structure of Cynthia's desire for Propertius. Like Cynthia's vicious probing of her lover's body, the snake-cult at Lanuvium scours causelessness for a (projected) cause. Žižek notes that divinatory rituals (like Lanuvium's) search for *objet a*, for the "little piece of the Real" that manifests itself in the Symbolic as the ultimate support of symbolization's network. Contingent natural events—comets, thunder, the flight of birds—become prophetic signs, indicating that the abyss separating the Real and Symbolic has been bridged momentarily: the Real answers the signifier's appeal.[48] When Juno's snake eats the maidens' ritual offering, for example, her devotees consider this not a biological relation of cause and effect ("the snake was hungry and therefore ate"), but a breakthrough between the divine and human realms. The event assures participants that they (or, more particularly, the Lanuvian debutantes) are in harmony with the divine order; accordingly, the agricultural year will be fertile. An arbitrary effect thus becomes a necessary "answer" from the Real to a human demand. The fantasy sketched in this religious inquiry posits an order beyond human control (and regularly beyond symbolization) that nonetheless, on occasion, answers the petitioner if the proper way can be devised to circumvent the intervening barriers. Receiving an answer fulfills the petitioners' desire, insofar as it apparently confirms a relation between the Symbolic network of the prediction and the events of "real life": suddenly "it all makes sense," the *facta bruta* of existence have meaning and conform (reassuringly) to an order. (The idea of petitioning an inscrutable power for the fulfillment of one's wish also obviously resembles courtly love and the Lady's quasi-divine position within it; the Lanuvium ritual thus reflects the structure of *Propertius*' longing as well as Cynthia's.)

But what of Cynthia's desire for a "fling" that propels her to Lanuvium? Does that not put her at variance with the ritual? After all, the cult's implicit claims to coordinate the human community with the divine rest on assaying female virtue: chastity (among the young girls it sends down to feed the snake) assures agricultural fertility. Currie may be ungallant to remark that "there would have been no point in sending Cynthia down with the basket to the serpent," but he expresses plainly an uneasiness other commentators only insinuate.[49] Propertius ostensibly makes her presence anomalous to the ritual when he insists that she went to pursue chastity's opposite (16)—and yet his elaborate description of her pilgrimage becomes an awkwardly disproportionate effort if read as nothing more than a mean-spirited joke at Cynthia's expense.

Those who argue for a purely sarcastic interpretation of her pilgrimage seem not to have noticed that her subordination of the ritual's universal, communal claims (community survival as a function of Woman's chastity) to particular human desires (the pursuit of a love affair) perfectly reflects a stratum of motivation implicit in the ritual itself. Propertius himself represents the rite as a tourist attraction rather than an august solemnity ("hic ubi tam rarae non perit hora morae"—"here, if anywhere, the hour spent for so unusual a stop is not wasted," 4),[50] and archaeological evidence indicates that his interpretation was not entirely strange—perhaps not even unwelcome—to the Lanuvians.[51] The ample temple grounds of Juno

Sospita, where the ceremony was enacted, include such features as a large *temenos* ("sacred precinct") and a lengthy portico designed to shelter shops; these concessions look to the accommodation and comfort of a "tourist" crowd in addition to dedicated votaries.[52] Such provisions indicate a tolerance of dilettantes, that is, potentially "disenchanted" viewers of the ritual. Moreover (though it is risky to argue *ex silentio*) the rite's apparent unfailing perfection suggests theatrical management and a certain generous interpretation of the ritual's divine protocols. No embarrassing incidents of unchastity betrayed have come down to us, in contrast to many horror stories recorded of erring Vestal Virgins detected and punished; A. E. Gordon, who does not hesitate to speak of "priestly fraud," suspects that someone trained the snake to insure the ritual's favorable outcome.[53] However that may be, the cult emerges in elegy 4.8 from particular, mundane human desires: the Romans' for sightseeing, the town's for tourists, everyone's for a cheerful sign. Cynthia's role as "bad girl," as "inconsistent woman" who subordinates public observance and community weal to private ends, thus captures the particularity and inconsistency masquerading as universality and community in the religious ritual. Arriving with her ostentatiously irregular lover, she even parodies Juno Sospita as she careers recklessly down the Appian Way, assuming the goddess' posture as Lanuvian coins record it. Cynthia's hoydenish tourism takes the form (but not the fantasized content) of "pious" pilgrimage in an ironic, "feminine" mimesis.[54] Though antithetical to Lanuvium's explicit purposes (testing virginity), her pilgrimage yet accords with its implicit purposes (tourism); the queer ease with which Lanuvium can accommodate her liaison attests to the accuracy with which she has captured its internal contradictions. Her presence ironizes the claims of the community to evaluate Woman ethically.

"Woman," says Hegel, "is the eternal irony of the community"—a phrase that captures Cynthia's performance perfectly, as well as foreshadowing Lacan's meditations on sexuality's internal contradictions. Žižek points out that, while Hegel may seem to ascribe to Woman the narrowness of a private perspective, it would be odd if one who so eloquently championed Antigone thought of such resistance as a mere gender-specific failing. Rather, Woman is the cynic capable of discerning behind the portentous forms that allegedly govern public welfare the private motives of those who propagate these forms; Cynthia exposes the inherent limitation of the social totality's standpoint.[55]

A fundamental contradiction analogous to that which Cynthia elucidates at Lanuvium emerges willy-nilly in the poem's final scene, though it closes on the lovers' "reconciliation." Propertius and Cynthia compose their differences at last through the elaborate divagations of a ritual focused on purity (83–87) that nonetheless concludes in an equivocal light. The description of their detente—"toto solvimus arma toro" (88)—glances toward reconciliation and continued discord simultaneously; by analogy, the phrase Propertius has coined could mean "we downed arms" or "we unsheathed our weapons." Given that he locates the force of his phrase "toto . . . toro," he inevitably evokes loveplay, but loveplay troubled by the suggestion of insurmountable obstacles: we cannot unambiguously interpret the poem's closing either as "peace" or "renewed hostilities."[56] This ambiguous closing phrase perfectly captures the essence of sex as a failure of signification, since it proffers alternatives—menace or promise, end or beginning, union or division—between which we cannot choose: we can exclude neither term as untrue (i.e., we cannot draw a limit, the dilemma of Woman's side of sexuation) even though the phrase is offered to us as decisively and sublimely ending the poem's general discord (i.e., as the "one" exception to desire balked for "all," the contradiction of Man's side of sexuation). As a backward glance on the affair, the poem's final phrase maintains a perfect double vision.

CHAPTER EIGHT

Hercules in Rome (4.9)

*Like amnesiacs
in a ward on fire, we must
find words
or burn.*
OLGA BROUMAS,
"ARTEMIS"

Propertius 4.9 is the poet's most extended poem on Hercules. It narrates several events in the Greek hero's Roman career: his defeat of the monstrous cattle-rustler, Cacus, a victory the Ara Maxima commemorates; the tired hero's unsuccessful appeal for hospitality from the women of the Bona Dea shrine and his subsequent enraged assault upon the shrine; his prohibition of women worshippers at his Ara Maxima. After a flurry of interest in the late seventies and early eighties, the poem has received little attention from scholars. Prior to Francis Cairns' recent (1992) erudite analysis of 4.9's generic antecedents, *L'Année Philologique* records 1982 as the publication date of the last essay devoted solely to the elegy's exegesis.[1] The poem has given rise to a startling divergence of opinion on a variety of points: its "tone," its coherence, its political import (if any). Scholars see the poem both as serious, even mournful, a portrait of Hercules as long-suffering victim[2] and (more recently) as farce, Hercules as a paraklausithyron's comically unsuccessful "lover," caught up in a pastiche of Vergilian epic.[3] Both the comic and the tragic interpretations must strain to explain why Propertius would include two such different stories within one poem: Hercules' violent battle with the monster Cacus on the one hand, and his bombastic, but virtually harmless, revenge upon the Bona Dea's shrine. Either the battle with Cacus must be read as farce (despite its epic gestures) to match the Bona Dea story, or the Bona Dea story is pathetic and heroic (notwithstanding its comic elements) to sort with Cacus' destruction. Generally speaking, the efforts to unify this poem under the banner of tragedy or comedy accord with attempts to see it as a pro- or anti-Augustan poem, respectively. Propertius' humor pokes fun at Octavian's pretensions to align himself and his regime with the myth of Hercules at

---

Olga Broumas, *Beginning with O* (New Haven, 1977). Reprinted by the kind permission of Yale University Press.

Rome, or, alternatively, Propertius' solemnity intends a handsome poetic compliment to these aspirations.

Such unifying, monotonal readings of 4.9 do it little justice: its divergences and disjunctions are basic data produced by the poem that cannot and should not be ignored.[4] The Hercules poem's apparent inconsistencies problematize its status as an aetiology and impede the smooth functioning of the very program that ostensibly motivates Book IV. "I shall sing of ancient rites and their appointed days, and the ancient names of places" ("sacra diesque canam et cognomina prisca locorum," 4.1.69) announces a search for what is originary ("prisca") in present-day Roman observances and in the names that dot the contemporary landscape. Elegy 4.9's thoughtful impediments force a scrupulous examination of the conceptual premises, ideological implications, and hegemonic force of the search for origins—seen as a desperate and doomed search for essence—in two particular realms: the Hercules–Cacus episode broadly focuses the implied interrogation on nationalism, while the Bona Dea episode moves it into the realm of gender.

THE BEGINNING OF THE END

Propertius' aetiological program for his fourth book reflects in microcosm a long tradition of Rome forging a sense of its identity as a nation by writing its own history; histories locate points of origin that purport to explain contemporary cultural configurations.[5] Historiographers seek to explain a culture's end (in both senses of that word) by finding the mirror of its present-day culmination, and of its putative purpose, in its origin. The origin demonstrates destiny insofar as it contains the end *en germe;* on the other hand, insofar as the origin differs from the end, it registers "progress" (or "deterioration," depending on the historiographer's relative optimism). Propertius' chief source for his version of the Hercules–Cacus battle, *Aeneid* 8.184–305,[6] has often been read as assuming the triumphalist mandate of finding the present in the past. R. D. Williams, for example, sees the *Aeneid*'s Cacus episode as parallel to "the task of Aeneas (and Augustus) of ridding the world of barbaric and archaic violence," and other scholars have elucidated in detail the correspondences among Vergil's portraits of Hercules, Aeneas, and Augustus.[7] Vergil's reconstruction of Rome's prehistoric past foreshadows the destiny of Rome as moral arbiter and *force majeure.*[8]

To this it may be answered—correctly—that other, far more cynical interpretations of the *Aeneid* in general, and the Hercules' episode in particular, are possible.[9] David Quint, for example, notes that the *Aeneid* itself "devotes a considerable part of its energy to criticizing and complicating what it holds up as the official party line."[10] Vergil sows suspicion of his own Hercules, savior of the Arcadians from Cacus, by putting the tale of the hero's exploits in the mouth of Evander, king of an Arcadia that once more needs allies against a formidable enemy, Mezentius. Evander's simple morality-play account has an implicit agenda—to persuade Aeneas to emulate Hercules by opposing the "barbarian" Mezentius and placing

Trojan troops at the service of Arcadia's national interests. (The shortcomings of Evander's parable are later thrown into relief when Mezentius—the obvious allegorical match to Cacus—makes a surprisingly noble end to his life.) Yet it was Vergil's fortune (or misfortune) to pen the most influential summations of Rome's dominant ideologies of nation and gender in his epic, his own reservations notwithstanding; little wonder, then, that Propertius chooses to address his response to Vergil's crystallizations of those ideologies. Propertius appears to have read—and rejected—the *Aeneid*'s mandate as imperial panegyric rooted in a genealogy that amounts to prophetic typology: "nec mea conveniunt duro praecordia versu / Caesaris in Phrygios condere nomen avos" ("nor is my breast suited to establish Caesar's name among his Trojan ancestors with austere poetry," Prop. 2.1.41–42).[11]

By contrast to the account in *Aeneid* 8, the recalcitrant oddities of Propertius' Hercules saga frustrate any attempt to see either destiny or change registered in his backward glance at the origins. Though 4.9's aetiological explanations derive from the hero's Roman adventures, none adequately motivates the poem or draws the elegy's elements together in a coherent pattern. The poem mentions the Ara Maxima (whose building and rites set the seal on Vergil's Hercules narrative), but only glancingly (67–68). As Warden and Richardson point out, Propertius never describes the altar's actual construction, only registers the accomplished fact in a throwaway participial phrase.[12] The poet grants more attention to a fantastical etymology of the area along the Tiber known as the Forum Boarium, supposed to be so christened by Hercules' recovery of his cows (16–20); he perversely bypasses the more plausible (if no more correct) etymology recorded by Varro that traced the name to the existence of an ancient cattle market on the site, to correspond to the nearby sections called Forum Holitorium and Forum Piscarium.[13] Propertius then lavishes attention on Hercules' prohibition against women worshippers at the Ara Maxima, a consequence of the hero's pique at being refused entry to the Bona Dea shrine (21–70). Hercules' edict falls legitimately within the poet's stated intent to analyze the origins of contemporary ritual observations, but an abrupt transition to a hymn in praise of the hero as "Sanctus" ("the holy one") skews the episode's relevance (71–74).[14] Hercules' violent assault on the Bona Dea shrine cuts the ground from under the hymn's epithet: how can he be "holy" if he violates a shrine prohibited to men?[15] The closing hymn to Hercules offers an end that is not an end: its surprising content throws all 4.9's loosely aligned components out of joint, exchanging closure for circular repetition. The codicil's disaccord sends us, the readers, back to the beginning to reread the poem, searching in vain for the overlooked detail that would motivate this final address to "Hercules the Holy."

The hymn's two couplets themselves reflect in miniature the sense of an ending elided that bends the poem's narrative trajectory into a circle. I have mentioned that the lines resist clear relation to the poem, and thus cannot grant it closure such as would draw a coherent pattern out of its divergent threads. In addition, though, most editors find both the content and the order of the last four lines themselves puzzling: given that (as Butler and Barber observe) the elegy lauds Hercules for purifying the world ("manibus purgatum *sanxerat* orbem," 73), we could expect a title that played upon that praise, in accordance with the fourth book's aetiological program. For that reason, Heinsius and Richmond emended the manuscripts' lamely passive "Sanctus" ("Hallowed") to "Sancus" ("Hallower").[16] But whatever the title, why would Propertius hail Hercules by a name whose origin he has yet to explain, and then slip in the etymology as an afterthought? Schneidewin's broadly accepted transposition of the manuscript order attempts to address this problem by making lines 73–74 precede 71–72 (while Richmond is so impatient of 71–72 in their present position that he banishes them to precede line 1, making the poem open with a prayer).[17] Still, Rothstein and Richardson—a formidable minority— dissent; to Richardson, the transposition amounts to a counsel of despair, since the transposition hardly improves the logic of the passage's progression. Yet even these two editors differ widely in their interpretation of the manuscript order: Rothstein accepts order and content without reservation, but Richardson (reading *Sance* in 72) brackets 73–74, "in the conviction that [the distich] is a gloss to explain the name *Sance* that has crept into the text."[18]

What does this widespread dissent as to the order and content of these final lines mean? The range of scholarly opinion allows either couplet to succeed the other— or be banished to the poem's proem—or be excised from the text entirely. The finale of Propertius' poem resembles the epitaph of Midas the Phrygian that Socrates cites with contempt in the *Phaedrus* because any line may succeed any other; Midas' epitaph serves as counterexample to Socrates' ideal "organic" rhetoric, in which part fits part like the limbs of a body (*Phaedrus* 264). The very coherence of that body constitutes a claim to its truth value. The best rhetorician is the philosopher, Socrates argues, because her supreme command of the truth enables her to forge conceptual connections closely based on it, and correspondingly plausible to her audience (*Phaedrus* 261e-262b, 273d-274a). Socrates' "organic" aesthetic shepherds us toward only one "logical, natural" end, via a persuasive force that makes its chain of ideas seem elucidated from the very fabric of the universe.[19]

Elsewhere in his poetry, Propertius gratefully exploits this Socratic metaphor that sees artfully shaped language as equivalent to a body: he repeatedly equates Cynthia's body with (the nature of) his poetry.[20] But 4.9's organization around explicit and implicit images of the body's disintegration—Cacus smashed by Hercules' club, the Bona Dea's "putrefied shack" ("putris . . . casa," 4.9.28), her priestess' fillets colored like clotted blood ("puniceae . . . vittae," 4.9.27)—indicates a counter-aesthetic at work here. The interchangeable order of 4.9's finale refuses "organic" coherence and its implicit claim to truth value; as such, it problematizes the interpretation not only of the hymn itself, but of the entire poem to which the hymn ostensibly provides closure. Elegy 4.9 points to the chaotic mess beneath language's speciously smooth surface that Socrates' metaphor of biological organicity covers over in silence. The poem evades a decisive pattern, its interchangeable disintegration drawing attention to its own artful—and artificial—status.

The poem's other oddities, major and minor, can also be broadly organized as anomalies of ordering—in particular, of temporal ordering. For example, Camps and Richardson both note that Propertius has Hercules' recovered cattle "consecrating" the Forum Boarium in a spot that was, when the hero arrived shortly before, under Tiber's waters.[21] The narrative thus wavers in its description of the low saddle between the Forum Romanum and the Forum Boarium, oscillating between a time when the Velabra was, and when it was not, flooded by the Tiber; it juxtaposes the two in easy indifference to temporal logic. I have also noted the discomfort critics feel over the poem's juxtaposing Hercules' vengeance on Cacus with his assault on the goddess' shrine; Propertius' contemporaries apparently shared such unease, since he alone of the Augustans joins the two events in a single time frame. With both these gestures, Propertius refuses the tendency of his contemporaries to make time an instrument of history: in retelling Hercules' defeat of Cacus, Livy, Ovid, and Vergil link earlier and later events in meaningful relation. Hercules' victory variously parallels Romulus' "taming" of his people's wild spirit (Livy), or Aeneas' championing of Arcadia against the new "monster" Mezentius (Vergil), or Augustus' and Tiberius' protection of Rome, and their deification (Ovid). In the *Aeneid* in particular, Evander's narrative accomplishes its own implicit prophecy by tracing over the ethical and political complexities of Aeneas' entry into Latium the clear outlines of a morality play. While Evander's narrative does not banish all ambiguity from the picture, he offers Aeneas a pretext for concentrating on the bold strokes rather than the fine details. By contrast, Propertius' anomalous juxtapositions sever time as silken thread of significance. The elegy's time contradicts rather than seconds itself, by drawing water over the Velabrum and banishing it in the space of fourteen lines: time in this poem becomes a contingent and nomadic frame to events that emphasizes the randomness of Rome's mythic past, like a camera snapped haphazardly. The egregious "misapplication" of this frame, that indifferently captures the sublime and ridiculous elements of Hercules' career, works against the tendentious ordering of events into prophetic history. The poem's calculated ineptitude foregrounds the need artificially to impose a frame in order to make such a history.

THE VICISSITUDES OF LANGUAGE

The patterns traced above, usually put down to 4.9's "playfulness" (at best) or poetic failure (at worst), instead evidence resistance to, and an investigation of, the ways we construct narratives about the world and its events. Fundamentally, these patterns examine "how things mean" and are thus caught up in questions of signification. In the next part of this chapter, I shall show that Propertius' investigation unfolds in a principled fashion the conceptual limits of signification, traced in the separate but intertwined registers of nationality and gender.

The complex patterns of 4.9's narrative proceed from a few words, familiar names within Propertius' contemporary landscape, for which the poet seeks an explanation. The poem begins with the humble fact of language and with a language that has slipped its moorings: the need to proffer an aetiology assumes that the rationale behind the contemporary name is no longer transparent to its audience. In the absence of any such explanation, the name—the signifier—is purely arbitrary: why should the words "Forum Boarium" call this patch of ground to mind, why should "Velabrum" bring another particular piece of Rome's geography before the mental eye, why should "Ara Maxima" conjure up this specific cult center and no other? If the relation between the components of the sign (signifier and signified) is arbitrary, then there is no defining property that, say, the concept "Forum Boarium" must retain in order to count as the signified of the signifier "Forum Boarium." But if this linkage is arbitrary, how do we know what the signifier means? Only from its differential relations with other signifiers: "Forum Boarium" acquires meaning in distinction from "Forum Holitorium," "Forum Piscarium," "Circus Maximus," and the like. This fact has some dizzying consequences: because the signifier has no natural relation to the signified, and *a fortiori* the sign none to the referent (the object in the "real world"), the relation between language and any external realm to which it may be posited as reference ("reality," "pure thought," "immediate sense-data") is severed. Words ultimately relate only to themselves.

Lest I be accused of imposing an anachronistic view of language upon Propertius' elegy, note that Plato comes to fundamentally these same conclusions in the *Theatetus*, though he views them with alarm rather than Saussure's complacency; David Bostock sums up the dialogue's *aporia* as follows:

> The theory of "Socrates' dream" (201c-202d) brings out the fact that a definition of one thing will explain it in terms of *others*, and these other things will have to be *known* if mastery of the definition is to manifest knowledge of the thing defined. But if this means that these other things in turn have to be defined, a vicious regress apparently follows. In short: definitions must eventually end in indefinables.[22]

Nor does Plato find a way out of this dilemma—the *Theatetus*' conclusion (206c-210a) simply undermines the rest of the dialogue's apparent progress toward a rigorous answer to the fundamental question, "What is *x*?"[23] Language, as a search for meaning, turns forever in a vicious circle.

All this notwithstanding, the very form Propertius uses to launch his meditations on Rome's landscape—the aetiology—embodies a desire to extract essence from the relationship of pure difference that founds language. Etymology, a significant prop in his survey of Rome, forges a linguistic version of the meaningful relation between historical origin and end that we traced earlier in this chapter. Etymology posits that in the word and its meaning can be traced *en germe* a capsule summary of the circumstances that forged a causal link between signifier and signified (as in the "naturalist" theory of language pursued by the Stoics and Epicureans).[24]

Book IV repeatedly stages that causal link in its investigation of the origins of "ancient names" (4.1.69); 4.9 in particular abounds in both etymological explanations and the abbreviated nods toward putative etymologies known as *figurae etymologicae*. Besides explaining the title (along with the ritual observances) of the Ara Maxima, Propertius alludes in passing to the putative derivation of *Velabra* from *velificabat*, "sails" (5–6), because the Tiber's flood was supposed originally to have made the region navigable (as it indeed appears near the beginning of 4.9, though not thereafter).[25] The phrase *pecorosa Palatia* (3) similarly refers to Varro's derivation of *Palatia* from *balare*, "to bleat"; examples of such allusions could be multiplied.[26] These etymological links offer to bridge the gap between the purely arbitrary nature of names and a rational connection to the nature of the thing named.

Yet at the same time, clues sown throughout the poem work against the assumption that it forges a naturalist theory of language. I have already remarked that, among a number of plausible etymologies, Propertius flaunts the egregiously "bad" and absurd theory that founds the name of the *Forum Bo(v)arium* upon Hercules' cows (*boves*) recovered from Cacus. Further, sprinkled in among the plausible *figurae etymologicae* are outrageous puns that point to no rational or historical link between similar sounds: *incolumes/incola* ("safe/denizen"), 4.9.8–9; *furem/furis/fores* ("thief/of the thief/doors"), 4.9.13–14 (about these I shall have more to say presently). In the midst of etymologizing familiar place-names, Propertius sows beguiling false trails built on specious homophonies. The prominent collocation of these words that teasingly suggest, and frustrate, meaningful relation, builds a case for the arbitrary nature of language. Propertius' absurd puns oddly resemble serious demonstrations of Saussure's theory that meaning in language emerges from pure difference—in this case, phonic difference: a thief (gen. *furis*) is not a door (gen. *foris*) merely by the difference of one vowel.[27]

DEFINING *ROMANITAS*

Propertius' meditation on language intersects his programmatic concern with aetiology precisely where the latter seeks to define *Romanitas* by tracing its origins. Book IV's patriotic celebration in verse (4.1.67) promises to array Rome as the city has arisen from its primordial beginnings.

> optima nutricum nostris lupa Martia rebus,
>   qualia creverunt moenia lacte tuo!
> moenia namque pio coner disponere versu
>   (4.1.55–57)

> She-wolf of Mars, you were the best of nurses for our country; what walls have grown from your milk! I shall try, then, to arrange those walls in reverent verse.

That project implies some thought for what constitutes Rome. The search for national identity structurally and functionally duplicates the search for "ancient names," in that each quest exemplifies the principle of differentiality by which language functions. National identity emerges as a relationship of pure difference within a system of signifiers: if I define myself as Roman, I distinguish myself from a Parthian, a Chinese, or Briton—precisely the series of contrasts Arethusa graphically traces upon her map as she follows her husband Lycotas' military movements through foreign territory (4.3.7–10; cf. chapter 3 above). To the degree that Arethusa depicts Lycotas as "out of place" fighting foreigners—contrasting, for example, his plain, rough accoutrements with their gaudy and prodigious war implements—to that degree does she sketch the contours of a Roman identity.[28] But that conceptual boundary between Roman and non-Roman is also—perversely—reflected inward, to constitute a search within Rome itself for "what is truly Roman," what corresponds fully to the notion of *Romanitas*. The programmatic first poem of Book IV sets this up as a problematic of tracing the origins, so that searching for the sources of contemporary cultural configurations implies searching for *Romanitas* as destiny: what quintessence of "Romanness" found expression in the path traced between Rome's origin and the Rome of Propertius' day?

Book IV's investigation does not, however, evade the arbitrariness of language that ultimately severs *Romanitas* from any external support. Elegy 4.1's description of the overall program imagistically captures this transformation of an external boundary that circumscribes an autonomous system based on pure differentiality into an internal limit. In the search for "true Romanness," this limit prevents *anyone* from being "really Roman": no empirical Roman can ever match the ideal standard of "Romanness." Propertius 4.1.55–57 promises to raise Rome's defensive walls (*moenia*) in his verse; these walls are the boundary that divides "us" from "them." But the particular walls that "grew from the milk of Mars' she-wolf" were used *ab origine* to distinguish degrees of *Romanitas* before they ever marked off Roman from foreigner. One popular account, recorded by Livy, sketches Romulus' and Remus' rivalrous attempts to found the new settlement that will be Rome; Remus inadvertently settles the dispute by leaping over his brother's newly-built walls, inspiring Romulus to kill him (Livy 1.7.2–3). The walls divide not (proto) Roman from foreigners, but the "true Roman"—the one destined to found the city of Rome—from his identical rival. Moreover, Propertius' telegraphic allusion to the feral twins' fabled rivalry itself draws a distinction, measuring the impassable gap between present-day empirical Romans and the ancestors who defined *Romanitas*.[29] Propertius quietly snaps any connection to a meaningful origin when he remarks "nil patrium nisi nomen habet Romanus alumnus/ sanguinis altricem non putet esse lupam" ("the Roman shares nothing with his ancestors except his name; he would not be able to suppose that a wolf was foster-mother to his blood," 4.1.37–38). Romulus and Remus locate the point with respect to which the contemporary Roman always "goes wrong" relative to himself: his civilization can never shake this legacy, nor its bloodshed ever be redeemed by similarly fortuitous results. To that degree, the twins' paradigm—albeit bloody, violent, and internecine—is an "ideal" unattainable by the *Nachgeborene*. "Romanness" thus becomes an internal limit, an unattainable point that prevents empirical Romans from ever achieving full identity-with-themselves.[30]

Variations on this theme of trying vainly to locate essential *Romanitas* are repeated throughout Book IV. In 4.6, for example, Romulus himself comes back at the battle of Actium to condemn Antony's fleet, thereby separating "real Romans" from those whose Romanness has been vitiated by their submission to eastern, foreign, and female command under Cleopatra ("altera classis erat Teucro damnata Quirino, / pilaque feminea turpiter acta manu"—"the other fleet, and the spears hurled by a woman's hand, had been condemned by Trojan Romulus," 4.6.21–22). However, since he comes back as "*Trojan* Romulus" ("Teucro Quirino," 4.6.21), that is, in a guise hardly less foreign or eastern than Antony's Egyptian allies, the apparently firm distinction he represents slips and slides vertiginously. Even Romulus cannot recover his Romanness at Actium.[31]

ROMAN VERSUS OTHER

"Romanness" constructed as internal limit is the logical corollary of "Romanness" as external boundary; not surprisingly, therefore, 4.9 interrogates the logical limitations to conceiving Rome both as a function of "Roman versus Other" and of "Roman versus Roman." Ethnography, as a subset of history and often intertwined with geography, interested the Romans, even if principally as consumers rather than producers.[32] Ethnography in the Republic and early Empire chiefly stages the confrontation between Rome and Greece, as exemplified in comparative biographies like Plutarch's *Vitae Parallelae* and Cornelius Nepos' *De viris illustribus;* Greece enjoys special status as the paradigm of culture, but some account is taken of other cultures.[33]

Propertius' most obvious model for the Hercules–Cacus episode, *Aeneid* 8.184–305, sketches in miniature the complex eddies of ancient ethnography laid under contribution to shape Rome's identity; 4.9's Hercules saga can be seen as, in part, a response both to the *Aeneid* and to its larger cultural context. The *Aeneid*'s account of the battle between Hercules and Cacus chiefly follows the "parallel-lives" organization of ethnography; Evander aligns (proto) Roman Aeneas with the Greek hero Hercules—the latter a model for emulation, as against the subhuman aborigine, Cacus.[34] Propertius unfolds a significantly complicated palimpsest over the *Aeneid*'s stark account. The details of 4.9 play upon the inherited theme of elucidating *Romanitas* by having Hercules define Rome topographically, as he founds the Forum Boarium and the Ara Maxima to celebrate his victory. Exactly how does Propertius reshape Hercules' conflict with Cacus—so strongly formed by Vergil— as a moment in the definition of national identity?

Among other modifications, Propertius makes the story a dyad rather than a triangle: Propertius does not even mention Evander. His omission eliminates one thread of the account (noted by Servius in his commentary on *Aeneid* 8) that makes it a battle between "The Good Man" (*eu-andros*) and "The Evil Man" (*kakos*).[35] Propertius goes behind Vergil's epic to a broader range of historiographic sources: he refers, for example, to Cacus as Hercules' host. Though the treacherous host offends

Jove, the guest-god, the very fact that Cacus can be evaluated according to the criterion of hospitality evokes the account of Diodorus Siculus, who records that "Cacios and Pinarios" received Hercules with all due honors.[36] On the other hand, Propertius makes Cacus triple-headed, a being more monstrous in his person than the miscreant sketched in *any* of the principal Augustan accounts (including those by Livy and Ovid):[37]

> sed non infido manserunt hospite Caco
>   incolumes: furto polluit ille Iovem.
> incola Cacus erat, metuendo raptor ab antro,
>   per tria partitos qui dabat ora sonos.
>   (4.9.7–10)
>
> But they did not remain safe, Cacus proving an untrustworthy host: he fouled Jove with his theft. Cacus dwelt there, a robber from a fearsome cave, who uttered divided sounds through three mouths.

Even the stylistics of Propertius' description oddly undermine its burden: Warden remarks Propertius' "confusion" of Cacus with the three-bodied Geryon, the quaintly circumstantial detail of his description ("he uttered divided sounds through three mouths"), and the line's internal rhyme and careful organization that balances adjectives against (postponed) substantives each side the displaced relative at the line's center. From these details, he argues persuasively that Propertius has turned Cacus "into a very 'mannered' monster, something quite different from the incarnation of evil and unreason in Vergil's melodramatic morality play"[38] (about this, I shall have more to say presently). Taken in his totality, the Cacus of Propertius 4.9 curiously recollects mythic threads at odds with one another. Propertius reminds us of his thief's (lost) status as human, even a pillar of the community, while simultaneously sketching Cacus as both droll exaggeration and monster; the poet is thus truer to Cacus' function within the mythic tradition. Propertius draws upon versions of Cacus that Evander's account (like Livy's and Ovid's) quietly suppressed;[39] he aligns his aborigine with a varied tradition that makes Cacus everything from pastoral robber to Evander's slave to king and even ambassador from the east. J. G. Winter's analysis of the myth is worth quoting:

> Cacus is a constant, but constantly changing, feature of the myth. The Romans themselves appear to have known scarcely more about him than is known today, and hence a new characterization could easily be effected for him without disturbing popular tradition. In Livy and the first account of Dionysius [of Halicarnassus] we found him to be a pastoral robber; in the Origo [Gentis Romanae], a slave of Evander with thievish propensities; in the second account of Dionysius, a ruler over a wild race of men; in Strabo, wholly absent; and in Solinus, an ambassador, in bondage, from the east.[40]

Propertius grasps the fact that Cacus is but a structural convenience in the myth, able to be played off against his counterpart(s) to elucidate any dyad of ethical properties. His portrait of Cacus, in ranging broadly among these characterizations, confounds any *one* portrait of Cacus.

As if in response to his enemy's baffling complexity, Propertius' Hercules also blurs in outline as he trails strangely incongruous allusions: he enters bluff, brawny, and belligerent, matching the paradigm of *Romanitas* sketched in the *Aeneid*. Yet he unexpectedly softens upon his victory, thanks to another Vergilian echo. Addressing his recovered cattle, Hercules quotes the elegant rustics of the *Eclogues*. "Ite boves, Herculis ite boves," he croons ("get along, cattle, get along, you kine of Hercules," 4.9.16–17), echoing the cadence and carefully balanced structure of the *Eclogues*' closing line: "ite domum saturae, venit Hesperus, ite capellae" ("get along home, you well-fed nanny-goats, get along, evening is coming," *Ecl.* 10.77).[41] Propertius gradually reshapes Hercules from bellicose hero into mirror of a languorous shepherd touched by melancholy love (a *lèse majesté* appropriate to elegy rather than to epic).[42]

In Propertius' account of the encounter between Hercules and Cacus, the quest to extract an essential relation out of a purely differential system fails spectacularly. If the *Aeneid*'s Hercules exemplifies *Romanitas* as moral *force majeure*, and Cacus as barbaric Other, the appropriate object of such force, Propertius troubles this clean binary opposition such that neither party can fully achieve identity-with-himself. Different provenances compete to define each combatant, with the result that neither can attain *himself* as a fixed, stable identity with which he is fully coterminous. This destabilizes the clean conceptual antitheses the *Aeneid*'s narrative sketched—civilization versus barbarism, law versus lawlessness, control versus chaos—antitheses that molded Hercules into paradigmatic Roman hero, and suggested the existence and shape of a Roman Heroism (as well as a non-Roman Barbarism) above and beyond any empirical Romans or non-Romans. Propertius' account, by contrast, resists the smooth integration of either term into a Platonic ideal.

HERCULEAN LLANGUAGE

Thus far in examining the problematization of meaning in 4.9 I have traced the effects of arbitrariness and differentiality as principles governing the two halves of the sign, signifier and signified. I have, however, confined myself largely to elucidating these effects in the poem's larger narrative patterns; yet 4.9's language and stylistics *per se* are both so odd as to deserve special attention. I remarked earlier upon the outrageous puns dotting the narrative, and to these strange plays on similar sounds must be added the extended rhyme-patterns woven throughout the poem. Are these significant or not, given that they fall outside any purely linguistic model for producing meaning? I shall argue that they are meaningful, but in order to do so, I must expand the conceptual premises upon which I have so far based my analysis of the poem.

I spoke above of language's arbitrariness, its lack of any necessary or causal link to what it names. That principle (as Slavoj Žižek points out) constitutes language as a totality by drawing a boundary around it: one posits an external realm with reference to which language is "arbitrary" ("reality," "pure thought," "immediate sense-data"). Paradoxically—in a move that mirrors the erection of national identity—language is constituted as a whole not by adding something, but by taking it away: the "whole" is founded on a constitutive exception (as "Roman" initially rests on an opposition to "non-Roman"). But given that language is arbitrary and meaning depends upon pure difference—upon the sign's relation to other signs in the system—*and* given that the same holds true for all these other signs, the external boundary disappears. The signifying system, lacking any external support, relates only to itself. The entire system turns in vain, striving to attain *itself* as a totality, a consistent whole (just as "Roman" as external boundary is reflected into "Romanness" as internal limit, to become the ideal that all empirical Romans strive in vain to attain).[43]

What happens when the boundary disappears? We are left with what Lacan calls *lalangue* ("llanguage"), the inconsistent, "non-all" entity logically primordial to *la langue* as totality—that is to language viewed as the abstract ideal of grammatical and syntactical rules generalized from particular speech-acts, "how speech is supposed to mean."[44] Llanguage generates meaning effects that spill over the conventional rules for interpreting language, contingent effects manifest in puns, portmanteau words, rhyme, rhythm, and the like. The concept of llanguage can help us analyze the bizarre preciosities of the verses with which Propertius narrates the Hercules–Cacus saga.

John Warden has painstaking analyzed the saga to elucidate its peculiar sound patterns. However, Warden dismisses these effects as meaningless *sprezzatura* on Propertius' part; they merit more serious attention. Consider again, for example, the two couplets that introduce Cacus (4.9.7–10, quoted above in "Roman versus Other"). The chiastic sound pattern of the line endings and beginnings (*Caco/incolumes . . . incola/Cacus*) sketches a close, quasi-punning relationship between "denizen" (*incola*) and "safe" (*incolumes*); staying *incolumis* in fact proves to be more nearly the *incola* Cacus' concern than immigrant Hercules' or his cattle's. This *sotto voce* suggestion playfully foreshadows the battle's outcome, but it also draws upon a sinister pattern into which Vergil's Cacus-episode fits: the *Aeneid* consistently shows the realization of Roman destiny as injuring the inhabitants anywhere it intrudes, though in each case the Romans are formally "innocent," either because they are but indirect causes or because they "act in self defense."[45] In the *Aeneid*, this "curse" cuts down Dido in Carthage, Turnus and his followers in Latium, even Evander's son Pallas among the Arcadians. Propertius' wordplay edges Hercules' victory that much closer to bullying, because it shades his triumph with overdetermination. Poor nerveless Cacus *has* to steal the cattle as a formal necessity for constructing the myth of Roman heroism—he must become the oppositional term that allows Roman manifest destiny to be construed as strictly ethical. Cacus never had a chance against the exigencies of *Romanitas*.[46]

Another evocative sound pattern further underlines Cacus' purely formal role in the general pattern of destruction:

> nec sine teste deò: furem sonuere iuvenci,
>   furis et implacidas diruit ira fores.
> Maenalio iacuit pulsus tria tempora ramo
>   Cacus...
>
> (4.9.13–16)

Not without a god as witness: the cattle bellowed "thief!" and anger tore asunder the unappeasable doors of the thief. Cacus lay dead, his triple brow shattered by the club from Mt. Maenalus.

Warden notes the "near-pun" on *furem ... furis ... fores*, but makes nothing of it. The quasi-pun gains point, however, insofar as it emphasizes how little difference Hercules' destruction of the thief and his doors makes between them. Doors and thief fall in about a line apiece (as opposed to Evander's *grand guignol* depiction of Cacus' death). Once again true to Cacus' role as depicted in the polymorphous mythic tradition (and in contrast to the *Aeneid*'s richly detailed clash of determinate Good and Evil) Propertius reduces Hercules' enemy to the myth's "furniture," a prop on which the plot turns, but that need be no more filled out with details than the doors to the thief's cave.

The near-pun implies a shift in perspective, a stepping back from Cacus as *content* to make Cacus as pure *form* visible anew. The poem earlier evoked some of the mythic tradition's congeries of characterizations, in which Cacus appears as pastoral robber, thievish slave, ambassador in bondage, courteous host, and so on; here, though, the poem reverts to a severe reductionism that empties Cacus of positive content. Like the signifier "Roman," Cacus initially emerges from a field of pure differences without positive content; yet by that very fact he absorbs and organizes existing expectations of the Other within himself as capacious symbolic vehicle. Elegy 4.9 makes visible the process whereby Cacus not only pins down Roman heroism by opposition, but "gives body to" free-floating anxieties about the Other.[47]

Lalangue emerges in the Cacus episode as the source of contingent, fortuitous meanings; it also appears in the section's oddly consistent rhyme scheme, but with an impact less easy to pin down. Warden aptly summarizes the pattern:

> The final words of the pentameters are as follows: *tuis, boves, aquas, Iovem, sonos, boves, fores, boves, boves, forum*. This is almost a systematic rhyme, the recurrence of the *-o, boves* four times (with the rhyming *Iovem*) and the chiastic *fores, boves, boves, forum*. This degree of formalisation is highly unusual.[48]

The elaborate rhyme scheme is almost incantatory; it looks forward to a similar rhyme scheme based on word beginnings (also noted by Warden) in the closing hymn to Hercules:

> *Sanc ... pat. ... sal ... Sanc ... sanx ... sic ... Sanc ... Tat ... com ... Cur.*[49]

Here again, at the level of form in addition to content, the poem escapes linearity, with the Cacus episode's rhyme scheme referring to the final hymn's similar formalization, and vice versa. The elaborate sound patterns enforce a circular reading that opposes the narrative's straightforward advancement. In setting up a meaning effect counter to the linear narrative, *lalangue* works against the end of the poem being taken as closure; it thereby suspends the poem's end and any straightforward "moral of the story" that might otherwise be imputed to it. Through the hymn that celebrates Hercules' having subdued the world's barbarity threads a rhyme scheme that reminds us of his less-than-edifying triumph over an embodiment of "Evil," a triumph the jingly line endings and summary haste reduce to a cartoon.

THINKING THROUGH THE BODY

The Bona Dea episode, like the Cacus–Hercules episode, uses the concepts that inform *lalangue* to approach the problem of extracting meaning from a purely differential system, but transposes them into the register of gender, seen as the oppositional relation between the signifiers Man and Woman. Little wonder in that, given that *lalangue* turns upon the distinct, but related, concept of *jouissance* ("enjoyment"); the latter intimately shapes Lacan's analysis of gender. Whereas *lalangue* is the non-all, non-universal collection of meaning-effects that escape the ordered principles of *la langue*, *jouissance* locates the enjoyment of a non-all, non-universal knowledge that also escapes accounting according to any single, logical principle. Poem 4.9 figures this renegade knowledge and illicit pleasure/pain as bodily disintegration.

I mentioned above that the Bona Dea episode's diction oddly draws upon imagery of broken and rotting bodies; these references have a quite specific provenance. The portrayal of the Bona Dea's shrine (23–30) draws particularly upon the *Aeneid*'s grisly description of Cacus' cave (as Warden, following Richard Heinze's suggestion, has shown).[50] The putrefaction of the "putris casa" (28) and the color of clotted blood ("puniceae vittae," 27) correspond to the rotting bodies and gore-saturated earth around the Vergilian monster's home.[51] This correspondence forms part of the evidence that Warden tellingly summarizes as Propertius' "cannibalism" of the *Aeneid*:

> It is the Vergilian account that not only provides the main lines of the narrative—the description, the hearing of the telltale sound, the chase, the shattering of the obstacle, the struggle—but is also used as the main quarry for the diction. Propertius rummages through, picking up bits and pieces for use without much respect for the context. The effect of this cannibalising—this breaking down and redistributing of parts—is to sound false and beguiling echoes, to lead the mind to seek for correspondences which when found are delusory; to create an epic ambience which is denied and subverted by the narrative itself.[52]

Warden concludes, though, that leading the reader a merry chase is an end in itself: Propertius thus demonstrates his ability to transform meaningful epic into virtuosic, but merely playful, elegy.[53] Yet deployed in a poem demonstrably organized about the theme of dehiscence—tracing, in its structure and its motives, the places where order falls apart—these muted suggestions of the-body-in-pieces deserve fuller consideration. Propertius disturbingly links the different registers (epic and farce) of his poem's two stories by echoing the *Aeneid* in ways that break out of the proprieties that govern Vergil's epic. Elegy 4.9 thus fragments the moral and historical "knowledge" of Rome's prehistory deployed within the *Aeneid*—of Roman history as a fateful struggle between the powers of light and darkness—short-circuiting one level of the epic's governing logic. The parts of Vergil's poem so appropriated are deployed according to the same "inorganic" notion of the parts' relation to the whole that interchangeably orders distichs of the hymn to Hercules at 4.9's close. Warden compares Propertius' method of composition to violence wrought upon the body—to cannibalism—and aptly so. Beneath the poem floats an excess that threatens to tear apart our (the readers') illusions of unity, rational order, and coherence that "make sense" of everything, and that allow us to enjoy a place and identity within this sensible order. So might the skin that renders the body coherent and identifiable tear and spill its contents in nondescript red ruin.[54]

GENDER-BENDING

The Bona Dea's shrine is imagined beneath such an aegis of the body's radical transformation: Tiresias is its unsettling emblem, a terror to frighten away unwanted guests (4.9.57). Yet through this transformation comes another order of (feminine) knowledge that defies certainty or accounting; this knowledge breaks through the orderly organization of conventional wisdom ("what everybody knows," the "masculine" side of Lacan's gendered epistemology) and the latter's specious claim to totality. Propertius pursues the theme of the Other as unknowable, mysterious, and essentially ungraspable—because produced solely by a relationship of pure differentiality—into the realm of relations between the sexes when he stages Hercules' confrontation with the Bona Dea's devotees.

After his defeat of Cacus, Hercules finds himself tortured by thirst; he has heard the laughter of women inside the Bona Dea's shrine, however, and though in the well-watered Tiber valley, insists that he can find no source to slake his thirst other than their sacred fount. After appealing to the implacable gatekeeper on the basis of his dire need and the consideration due his heroic status, he urges her, astonishingly, to relax her prohibition against men because his fearsomely hypermasculine appearance merely conceals his experience with a feminine toilette:

"sin aliquem vultusque meus saetaeque leonis
    terrent et Libyco sole perusta coma,
idem ego Sidonia feci servilia palla
    officia et Lydo pensa diurna colo,
mollis et hirsutum cepit mihi fascia pectus,
    et manibus duris apta puella fui."
(4.9.45–50)

"If my face and these lionskin bristles and my hair frizzled by the Libyan sun frighten anybody, I'm nonetheless the same guy who performed a maidservant's duties and used a Lydian distaff to spin my daily allotment; I wore an imported red shawl, and a soft bra bound my hairy chest, and I made a pretty good woman, despite my callused hands."

Hercules' peculiar willingness to emphasize his transvestite career has (when noted at all) largely been interpreted as further evidence of Propertius' aiming for the humorous deflation of his epic hero.[55] But if the explanation were that trivial, why would Propertius have the priestess-gatekeeper reply by naming Tiresias, whose myth (in its wider repercussions) expands on the theme of transsexuality?

"magno Tiresias aspexit Pallada vates,
    fortia dum posita Gorgone membra lavat.
di tibi dent alios fontis: haec lympha puellis
    avia secreti limitis unda fluit."
                    (4.9.57–60)

"Tiresias the seer saw Pallas when she laid aside her aegis and bathed her strong limbs, and a great price was paid. May the gods grant you other springs: this water flows for women only, its wave off the beaten track and of channel set apart."

Other stories provide stronger warnings against profaning the secrets of goddesses—Actaeon, for one, violently gave up both life and human form, not just his gender, when he accidentally happened upon Artemis bathing. Tiresias, on the other hand, gains as much as he loses for having seen the goddess naked: a great price was paid, but by him or her? He forfeited his eyesight, but the goddess in turn had to compensate him with the gift of "second sight"—an ambivalence perfectly captured in the hexameter's progression from the ambiguity of "magno" to "vates." Why would the gatekeeper weaken the force of her warning by using this decidedly ambiguous example?

Francis Cairns has mused, *en passant*, that Tiresias' significance rests in the part of his myth that portrays him as a transsexual as well as a prophet.[56] I shall attempt to have the courage of Cairns' convictions and to show by detailed examination that the prophet's gender-crossing is indeed crucial to the poem's interpretation. The gatekeeper proffers one account of Tiresias' blindness, but held up in warning to a Hercules who has just drawn attention to his own transsexuality, the prophet's name inevitably recalls the variant accounts that sacrificed Tiresias' sight to Hera's wrath rather than Athena's. When Hera and Zeus quarreled over which sex derived the greater pleasure from intercourse, they called upon Tiresias to referee the dispute; he qualified as judge because he had been transformed into a woman as the consequence of having interfered with two snakes copulating (repeating his interference later restored his maleness). Tiresias sided with Zeus, claiming that women enjoyed greater pleasure than men; Hera, piqued at losing, blinded him, but Zeus compensated him with the gift of mantic skills.

Interestingly, the precise account Tiresias offered the gods is a mystery that joins gender-differentiation to a logical impasse much like the conceptual difficulties that plague Roman nationality. Timothy Gantz summarizes the evidence for the exact answer Zeus and Hera received:

> Something has gone afoul in the account, for Apollodoros first says that, reckoning such pleasure into nineteen parts, man enjoys nine and woman ten, then cites two hexameter lines in which man enjoys one of ten shares and woman all ten. Both confusion in the first version and interpolation of the second have been suspected. But the second version with its hexameter quote and one-to-ten ratio also appears in the scholia to *Odyssey* 10.494, and something very close to it in the scholia to Lykophron 683. This last, however, also brings in something about nine shares, and knows too a version in which the ratio is one to nine out of a total of ten. This slight difference probably reflects uncertainty over whether men and women could be rated separately on the same scale or had to share out the ten parts of it between them; the resulting ten parts for women in the first instance and nine parts in the second may then have led to the erroneous notion of nineteen parts, and Apollodoros' probable error.[57]

This garbled account of Woman's pleasure recurs to the central problem addressed by elegy 4.9: the conceptual inadequacies of a system of definition based on pure difference. The Tiresias-myth's varied account of Woman preserves the traces of different conceptual deadlocks derived from trying to seize the object of inquiry on the basis of a single principle. Ancient as well as modern constructions of gender relations conventionally make Woman the exclusion that constitutes Man as a totality—Aristotle, for example, describes Woman as a "deformed" Man, and similar thought controls the gynecological writings of the Hippocratic Corpus, of Celsus and Soranus.[58] Man regards Himself as the norm of "humanness" per se, measuring Himself against Woman as the deviation that defines the norm. This renders Man and Woman as "Man" and "not-Man," mere positions mutually cross-referenced within a signifying system, and as such unstable. Tiresias' own story points to this instability when he crosses so easily from one side of the gender-divide to the other. Yet the prophet cannot smuggle an account of Woman across that same divide; a definition as only "not-Man" cannot adequately express Her, so that she remains a persistent "blind spot" for Man.

Tiresias' myth thus rounds off the pattern that unites 4.9's seemingly disjointed collection of details: it demonstrates language's inability to name an essence in the objects it denominates, insofar as Man and Woman, like Roman and Other, or Roman and "real" Roman, emerge as positions of pure differentiality. The Bona Dea episode has merely transposed the problem into the register of gender rather than nationalism. Tiresias' example seconds the implications of Hercules' own transsexuality: a hero who can plead for himself as a "pretty good woman" with the change of a few surface details—on with *fascia* and *palla*, off with lionskin and sunburn—points to Man and Woman as the shifting effects of signification.

Yet the poem represents this instability as leading (just as in the case of nationalism) to the quest for something essential in gender positions that could fix and stabilize them—for the "Platonic ideal" of Woman that would guarantee Her identity (and, more to the point, Man's). The poem telegraphically captures Hercules' legendary womanizing in his insistence on enjoying the water guarded by and for women, when the Tiber valley abounds with water. His libertinage becomes legible as a search for the ideal feminine; his "thirst"—a trope for erotic desire—rejects all waters except that consecrated to Woman: the Bona Dea's fount is set aside for no less than a goddess' ritual observances.[59]

His legend, taken as a whole, supports this interpretation. Hercules uses and discards particular women throughout his career as if in a perpetual search for the feminine ideal; eventually he rejects each particular woman because she does not measure up to Woman. Nicole Loraux summarizes Hercules' erotic career by remarking that "the female body as an object of conquest and pleasure is continually new for him," but the obverse of this truth is that each body is also continually palling, revealing its empirical differences from a fantasized Universal and driving Hercules on to the next instantiation. In Sophocles' *Trachiniai*, for example, Deianeira plots Hercules' career as always reaching for the next beauty that is blossoming as his old love fades in his eyes (*Tr.* 543–49). His continual need to renew conquest and pleasure means that something always remains in abeyance, something he seeks in the next object of desire.

Hercules' own transsexuality (like Tiresias') indicates the futility of his quest, since it points to gender-categories as unanchored to any substratum of Being. His rather mean-spirited prohibition against women-worshippers at the Ara Maxima—oddly petty as the great hero's final word—desperately fends off the large questions raised by his own, and Tiresias', change of gender positions. Hercules falls back in the end upon a circular definition of the sexes, in default of any more substantial difference: women will be excluded from his shrine—therefore, women are those who will be excluded from his shrine. Gender difference re-emerges by fiat, conveniently covering over the initial dilemma by a *petitio principii* (how is the Ara Maxima's doorman supposed to treat a cross-dressing worshipper? As abomination, or purest devotee, the one who most closely emulates the god himself?). Hercules' prohibition parallels the extinction of his consuming desire for the mysterious fount (63–64): from now on, his ban says, "I (Man) don't want to know anything about it (Woman); I persuade myself that my knowledge is already self-sufficient." The inconvenient, riddling, renegade knowledge of Woman is refused and covered over, a fresh blinding of Tiresias.

CHAPTER NINE

The Phenomenology of the Spirits (4.11)

> *Pale, beyond porch and portal,*
>   *Crowned with calm leaves, she stands*
> *Who gathers all things mortal*
>   *With cold immortal hands;*
> *Her languid lips are sweeter*
> *Than love's who fears to greet her*
> *To men that mix and meet her*
>   *From many times and lands.*
>
> *She waits for each and other,*
>   *She waits for all men born;*
> *Forgets the earth her mother,*
>   *The life of fruits and corn;*
> *And spring and seed and swallow*
> *Take wing for her and follow*
> *Where summer song rings hollow*
>   *And flowers are put to scorn.*
>
>   SWINBURNE,
> "THE GARDEN OF PROSERPINE"

Propertius 4.11 is typically accorded exceptional status within his corpus, singled out for enthusiastic accord with, or equally passionate demur from, Scaliger's assessment of it as "the queen of elegies" ("regina elegiarum").[1] Its unusual aspects are readily apparent: composed to acknowledge the death of Cornelia, daughter of Augustus' ex-wife Scribonia, the elegy takes shape as the dead woman's own words from beyond the grave. She argues the merits of her life before a tribunal in Hades that is to judge her and assign her a place in the Underworld.[2] Aside from the novelty of such a legalistic setting, the conceit affords a woman the opportunity, for the first time in Propertius' poetry, to articulate the code that governs Roman matronal life; the poet's concentration on demimondaine women (princi-

---

Algernon Swinburne, *The Complete Works of Algernon Charles Swinburne*, ed. Edmund Gosse and Thomas James Wise (London, 1925), 1:300–301.

pally his lover Cynthia) largely eclipsed that possibility in his other poems. The grounds in all this for assessing the poem as a *volte-face* from Propertius' previous work are obvious, but no consensus has emerged regarding the precise significance of the poet's apostasy. Stahl and Wyke, for example, see the poem as reversing the oppositional stance articulated in Propertius' love poetry—specifically, as signaling his weary capitulation to Augustan ideals of marriage and family,[3] or setting aside "ideological unorthodoxy" in favor of traditional Roman gender protocols.[4] From this (somewhat disdainful) viewpoint, Cornelia emerges as an "anti-elegiac woman." Highet, Alfonsi, Grimal, Luck, and others concur in reading 4.11 as an apostasy, but they admire the poem precisely for that reason. They see it as a paean to married love, to a near-Christian attitude toward death, to the highest Roman virtues, to the virtues of maternal and wifely self-sacrifice.[5] On the other hand, a few see 4.11 as yet another poem of resistance, though disguised: Richardson reads it as a monument to the bleak selfishness of the code Roman aristocratic men imposed upon their women, while for Curran, a profound despair at the fact of mortality so colors the poem as to render all Cornelia's matronly virtues virtually meaningless.[6] La Penna, Hallett, Hubbard, and Sullivan—the least sympathetic of Cornelia's readers—find the dead woman's exemplary virtue cold and unengaging.[7]

Scholarly thought on this poem, as surveyed above, divides roughly upon the issue of 4.11's attitude toward adherence to a code: either the poem sincerely praises the virtues of a Roman matron (and by implication, the conventional Augustan Roman standards of social and sexual decorum by which Cornelia has molded her existence), or it reveals the emptiness and futility of a woman's life lived by such standards. The two principal axes of reading the poem are shaped by the concept of Law (meaning all social constraints, not just those embodied in formal legal codes), so that Cornelia's life embodies Law as honorable paradigm on the one hand or as meaningless horror on the other. My analysis of the poem will show that these are not, in fact, antithetical readings so much as *recto* and *verso* of a problematic that the poem dramatizes: the problem of Law itself and of its duplicity (in all senses of the word).

ASKING FOR JUSTICE IN HELL: *JOUISSANCE* AND THE LAW

A clue to this reading may be found in the puzzling horror of the setting for Cornelia's "trial." Most ancient portrayals of the Underworld are admittedly drear, but a strange sentience distinguishes Cornelia's vision. She addresses Hell as if it were alive and of evil intent:

"damnatae noctes et vos, vada lenta, paludes
    et quaecumque meos implicat unda pedes,
immatura licet, tamen huc non noxia veni . . ."
(4.11.15–17)

"Doomed darkness and you swamps, sluggish shallows, and whatever wave winds about my feet, you know I have come here untimely, but innocent . . ."

Gordon Williams and Leo Curran note that Propertius has modeled this passage on similar passages from Vergil's descriptions of the Underworld in *Aeneid* 6 and *Georgics* 4:[8]

> quos circum limus niger et deformis harundo
> Cocyti tardaque palus inamabilis unda
> alligat et novies Styx interfusa coercet.
> (*G.* 4.478–80)

[Those who died untimely deaths] the black slime and the misshapen reeds of Cocytus and the unlovely swamp, with its sluggish water, holds fast and Styx, nine times interposed, constrains.

> fas obstat, tristisque palus inamabilis undae
> alligat et novies Styx interfusa coercet.
> (*Aen.* 6.438–39)

It is forbidden, and the unlovely swamp of bitter water holds [the suicides] fast, and nine times Styx interposed constrains [them].

But Propertius has strengthened the implication of sentience in Vergil's *alligat* ("holds fast") by having Cornelia appeal to the dank waters and darkness directly as "you." Her address lends *implicat* ("winds about") a sense of purposiveness: the water entwines itself around her feet as if alive and vengeful, and she, terrified, protests her innocence.

The poem's lurid depiction of the place of the Law illustrates to perfection the Lacanian concept that Law is implicated with "enjoyment," where enjoyment bears the technical meaning of "the limit of interpretation; nonmeaning as such."[9] Lacan's startling marriage of conceptions suits a poem in which the significance of Cornelia's obedience to her caste protocols can be read so differently, as either sublime self-sacrifice or meaningless waste. In the debate over 4.11, his analysis of Law can help us shift attention from What does it mean for Cornelia to obey the Law? to How does that Law mean? What, ultimately, is the conceptual ground of the Law, and does anything found the Law, so as to give it coherence and "solidity"?[10] The answer, of course, is "no"; the Law, like any other system of signification, rests self-enclosed on difference. Each of its elements depends ultimately for its meaning upon that element's relation to all others in the system; no anchor or guarantee of the system's truth exists that transcends the differential system itself.

ROME AND THE DARK SIDE OF THE LAW: AN EXCURSUS

Lacan's concept of Law as ungrounded in any unshakable foundation would at first glance seem to be foreign to ancient thought—particularly to Roman thought, given Rome's pride and confidence in its juridical tradition—yet in fact, more than a few ancient sources anticipate Lacan's skepticism on this point. For that reason, I have thought it worthwhile in the immediately following pages to sketch ancient conceptualizations of the Law parallel to Lacan's that would have been part of Propertius' (and his audience's) cultural context. I have a double goal, to unfold the implications of Lacan's paradigm fully, clearly, and precisely, and to demonstrate its relevance to ancient thought. The exercise will provide an intellectual background that enables us to see the same principles at work in Propertius' poetry. What Propertius expresses sparely and subtly becomes more legible once we have traced the bolder etching of the motifs in other authors; I ask the reader's patience, then, for this short but useful excursus prior to analyzing the patterns of Law that specifically govern the Cornelia elegy.

Modern jurisprudence exemplifies par excellence the principle of interdependence upon which Lacan's analysis of Law depends: it explicates any particular law's validity through reference to another law or principle (written or unwritten) as its embodiment, refinement, or supplement. As Bruce Frier shows, however, the roots of that procedure reach back to Propertius' own century, in the profound changes jurists and jurisconsults like Cicero wrought in late Republican and early Imperial juridical thinking. Frier notes in Cicero's treatments of the subject a determined effort to wrest the implementation of justice away from prevalent rhetorical relativism (which favored persuasive advocacy over dependence on statute law) toward the concept of "autonomous law," legislation viewed as an independently existing and self-consistent set of rules to be applied in individual cases.[11] The shift is well-established by Propertius' own time, and evident, for example, in Livy's reverent reference to the Ten Tables (rather than, say, to offices or deliberative bodies or procedures) as ground and legitimation of all Roman justice:

> Centuriatis comitiis decem tabularum leges perlatae sunt, qui nunc quoque, in hoc immenso aliarum super alias acervatarum legum cumulo, fons omnis publici privatique est iuris. (Livy 3.34.6)
>
> A meeting of the Assembly by Centuries[12] was held and the laws of the Ten Tables were adopted, which even now are the fountainhead of public and private law, beneath the huge modern accumulation of laws piled on top of other laws.

Such a shift toward the notion of autonomous code envisions Law as a cross-referenced and mutually defining set of rules—that is, as exactly the system upon which Lacan bases his analysis. Any statute or principle cited to legitimate another, if called into question, requires in its turn reference to yet another rule behind it, and so on, in an infinite regress. Ultimately juridical reasoning comes to rest in the logical opacity of desire: such-and-such is law because "it is the will of [the gods, Nature, the emperor, the people, the senate]." To the question, "Why is it their will—why does that justify it?" no answer can be given beyond "it just is."

Cicero, of course, ultimately moors legal rules in the rather amorphous concept "natural law"; but other schools of thought remove that anchor from Law's referential chain and thus bring it closer to Lacan's picture. The Skeptics and Epicureans, for example, regarded Law as without grounding in any transcendent realm of truth or being. The Epicureans believed Law, or in their terms, "justice" (*to dikaion;* dikaiosunê), to be purely conventional, based upon human weakness and self-interest. The system of rules that brokered human fears rested fundamentally on agreement not to harm in exchange for not being harmed, but Epicurus annexed no "deeper truth" of benevolence in this formulation. As he said, "it [justice] is nothing in itself," merely a self-interested compact (as against Plato, who asserted the independent existence of virtues).[13] The Skeptics—insofar as Carneades memorably and persuasively formulated their doctrine—added to Epicurean conventionalism a vertiginous awareness of how restricted in its domain "neither to harm nor be harmed" may be. For example, in Carneades' famous 155 B.C.E. speeches at Rome (one praising justice, the other refuting that praise) he assesses "justice" as a purely local affair. He credits the Romans with having justice in the form of laws and constitutional practices, but observes that these work entirely in the interests of Rome and against those of non-Romans: "What are the advantages of one's native land save the disadvantages of another state or nation? That is, to increase one's territory by property violently seized from others."[14] This view of justice strips it down to self-interest entire, without even the comfortable sense that the compact, however artificial, benefits all parties concerned.

We need not refer only to the rarefied realms of philosophy, however, to locate suspicion of the Law as an ungrounded system of dicta. Among Propertius' contemporaries, Livy's story of Verginia and Appius Claudius the decemvir (3.44–58) portrays the Law as inherently vitiated by the impossibility of its own claims to transcendent, impartial truth, and thus an apt vehicle for particular desires—as Lacan would say, it reveals itself to be instinct with enjoyment (*jouissance*). *Ab Urbe Condita* sketches explicitly the pattern of Law's partiality and cruelty hidden beneath an appearance of magisterial objectivity that, I shall argue, controls Propertius 4.11 implicitly. No sooner are the Twelve Tables of laws in place as the first codified foundation of Roman justice than all the vices of the decemvirs (the ten men commissioned to distill customary law into the Tables) emerge as they use the legal code to their own ends. The crowning example is Appius' lust after the beautiful young Verginia, which ultimately brings about the decemvirs' downfall. Appius invokes the machinery of justice to represent Verginia as a "runaway slave" who must be restored to her "master," a client of Appius happy to serve as his patron's pimp.

Appius scrupulously observes both substantive and procedural codes in this story.[15] After staking his claim in the Forum, the client has Verginia summoned to court, over which Appius Claudius presides as judge; the young woman's advocates appeal to Appius to release her to the defendants' custody until her father Verginius (then on active military service) can be summoned to Rome. Her reputation can thus be protected while the case is mooted. Verginia, however, is a minor and not legally independent (*sui iuris*)—accordingly, only her absent father (as *paterfamilias*) can make a counterclaim regarding her freeborn status. Appius' client thereby claims her as his property (perfectly legitimately, if diabolically), the defense having gone by default—and Appius defends the judgment by saying that "ceterum ita in ea firmum libertati fore praesidium, si nec causis nec personis variet" ("the law will prove a sure defense of liberty only if its application varies neither according to persons or cases").[16] Appius succeeds in snaring his prey precisely by appealing to the principle of "autonomous law" that motivated the crafting and adoption of the Twelve Tables in the first place. Behind the rigorous insistence on the Law's universality and neutrality lies nothing but particular desire—Appius' for Verginia.[17]

Appius Claudius could be dismissed as a hypocrite who betrays the Law without impugning its validity—yet several details of the narrative resist that reading, among them Livy's emphasis on the strict legal protocol observed not only by Appius Claudius, but by all the decemvirs. They tyrannize not by breaking the Law, but by manipulating it to their own purposes, to which it is horrifyingly suited. The decemvirs gain power precisely because the Law must be articulated: during the period devoted to reducing customary legal precepts to a written code, the decemvirs are appointed as a government immune from appeal, that is, from the Law itself. Yet they are deemed just to the degree that they deviate from the Law. When, for example, strong evidence places the patrician Publius Sestus under nearly-irrefutable suspicion of murder, the decemvir Gaius Julius omits his own right, under the terms of his appointment, to pronounce summary justice, and allows Publius Sestus a trial. This is accounted ready and equitable justice, quasi-divine[18] in its purity; the same probity is seen in the decemvirs' readiness both to soften one another's pronouncements and to honor these palliations.[19] The decemvirs become "ten Tarquins" precisely when they begin to exercise the Law in all its rigor, refusing appeals and expanding their powers rapidly by observing its minute conventions.[20] For example, they thwart the Senate's move to break their power with adroit maneuvers that observe the letter of legal procedure, but defer all action and foil independent judgment. The question of the decemvirs' proper term in office is referred to future debate—ultimately to Appius Claudius himself (!) as president of the assembly that created the present decemvirs.[21] Appius' attempt to satisfy his sexual appetites by cleverly manipulating legal procedure to entrap Verginia merely epitomizes the implacable exercise of power that earns the Decemvirate the Romans' hatred. Appius and his fellows are the Law in all its sadistic unreason and cruel enjoyment.

R. M. Ogilvie also makes it clear that the whole episode of the Decemvirate comments obliquely upon Roman history closer to Propertius' time, clothed as Livy's narrative is in the observances of late Republican and early Imperial politics; Ogilvie traces distinct parallels to Sulla's and Julius Caesar's careers, as well as to the Second Triumvirate.[22] Livy's historiographic anatomy of the Law thus speaks to the series of regimes leading up to his (and Propertius') own day, and to their capacity for juridical rigor equally suffused with sadism and caprice.

Livy fills out in greater detail the sinister relationship between Law and inhuman cruelty that Propertius himself unfolds definitively in the Cornelia poem—but not only there. Propertius 3.15, for example, recounts how Dirce maltreated her husband's former wife Antiope; eventually, Zethus and Amphion—Antiope's sons by Jupiter—exact vengeance by having a wild bull dilacerate Dirce. Poem 3.15 dramatizes the bloody agony and horror of the *lex talionis* that makes victimizer into victim, punishment into repetition of the offense. Propertius dwells on Dirce's shattered body strewn across Zethus' fields—fields that "reek" with blood ("prata cruentantur")—and on Amphion's bloodthirsty paean of triumph; all this he credits, with bland irony, to Jove's "justice" (39–42), the very Jove who had refused to save his lover from Dirce's tortures (19–24). Jove emerges from 3.15 less as arbiter of justice than refined sadist, who crucifies the guilty without delivering the innocent. Elegy 3.19 also tells a story of justice fundamentally vitiated by cruelty: Scylla betrays her father Nisus because she has fallen passionately in love with his enemy, king Minos, and made a pact with him; Minos reneges after triumphing over Nisus and "rewards" his victory's engineer by lashing Scylla to the underside of his ship so that she drowns. For being thus "fair" in the case of his enemy ("aequus in hoste," 28), he deservedly rules in Hell; Minos' betrayal and murder of his lover, Scylla, throws the fine irony of Propertius' statement into relief. Minos' "justice" smugly accepts the rewards of his illicit pact while transferring all the consequences to his infatuate accomplice. Both 3.15 and 3.19 demonstrate that the idea Livy unfolds in his history of the Decemvirate—that Law, practiced in all its rigor, cannot be distinguished from crime—finds sparer but no less cogent expression in Propertius' elegies, even before its definitive flowering in the Cornelia poem; *Ab Urbe Condita*'s emphatic detail merely usefully illuminates the pattern that more subtly organizes Cornelia's plaint.

OBJET A: PATCHING THE (W)HOLE

If the Law, despite its mask of sober purity, is so giddily unanchored in any bedrock of truth and falls obviously short of its own claims to consistency and totality, how does it work at all? Lacan repeatedly considered how systems of signification generate meaning, the Law being but a special case of the problem; over time he developed the related concepts of the quilting point (*point de capiton*) and *objet a*, each envisioned as providing momentary fixity to chaos. The quilting point is already familiar to us from our examination of the Gallus poems, where we saw how culturally freighted signifiers could "quilt" the divided subject's perceived internal fragmentation into a putative whole (chapter 2). *Objet a*'s complementary function emerged in our analyses of Propertius' poems on Acanthis (4.5) and Lanuvium (4.8), where it could be seen to cover over gaps in the causal chain by providing a dazzling "cause" for love or hatred where none, in fact, can exist (chapters 5 and 7).

In order best to understand how the quilting point and *objet a* make Law mean something, however, we must step back for a moment and place them more firmly in the context of the failings fundamental to signification. The common function of wresting a (specious) whole out of fundamentally heterogeneous, chaotic, nonsensical phenomena links the quilting point and *objet a,* and crucially connects them to the production of meaning within a differential system of signification.

They are needed so desperately because, in a purely differential system, meaning inheres in no one of its elements. Rather than unfolding from some initial kernel, meaning is produced contingently and retroactively when "punctuation" of some kind grants provisional closure to a subset of signifiers (just as the meaning of a sentence only fully emerges when a period, interrogation mark, or exclamation point closes it). The quilting point represents this closure. Strictly speaking, no signifier has *any* signified until combined with other signifiers, as a numinous effect of the articulation as a whole—meaning has only shadowy and evanescent status as the effect of signification (rather than its substance or ground). Lacan's perspective on interpretation thus displaces any search for a mythical signified in favor of scrutinizing the quilting point that momentarily stabilizes the various floating signifiers. The quilting point makes the signifying chain a meaningful whole, at least provisionally.

However, something always escapes this quilting—in essence, the pure groundlessness of the system itself, the fact that its meaning depends upon pure difference rather than upon a privileged relation to truth. *Objet a* emerges from this failure, both to mark the place where meaning fails, and to cover it up; *objet a*'s duplicitous operation can be located where some object exerts a fascination far in excess of its apparently immanent properties, where it attains numinous status and thereby "explains" the system's failure in terms that allow it (the system) to come off gracefully. For example, between the corporatist vision of the polity as an organic whole, a social body in which the different classes are like members that each contribute harmoniously to the whole according to its function, and the actual society split by antagonistic struggles, *objet a* emerges to broker the difference between ideological fantasy and reality. In Livy's own record of the struggle between the orders—of which Appius' conniving at Verginia is but an episode—wealth and the class divisions it enforces fulfill this function in one phase of the narrative. Patrician government in Rome promises harmony—but when the promise remains unfulfilled and the commons (*plebs*) secede from Rome, Livy lays the blame not upon the concept of oligarchy itself, but upon blinkered factionalism and patrician greed[23] that have scourged Rome's many plebeian debtor-bondsmen.[24] However, the Senate's ambassador to the rebellious commons, Menenius Agrippa, magically restores harmony with a homely parable of the body politic: when one day the limbs refuse to feed the "idle" belly, they soon discover that it provides the blood that feeds them in turn (2.32.8–11).[25] Paradoxically, Menenius' tale achieves its end by consecrating the object of contention, not denying it: he refigures wealth as society's vital fluid rather than its gall (though circumstances hardly support the allegory). Wealth thus assumes the function of *objet a* as illusory "cause" and "cure" of the conflict.[26] Wealth, as a stimulant to greed, explains the failure of the body politic, but in such a way that the original premises behind the ideological fantasy (that social harmony depends upon the "proper" subordination of commons to the elite) remain unquestioned; by *objet a*'s timely intervention, "everything suddenly makes sense."[27]

If we return to our discussion of Law, we can see that *objet a* offers (falsely) to ground the Law's apparent "totality." Nothing founds the Law's claims to universality and impartiality, but *objet a* gives it the illusion of a self-consistency purified of desire. In the story of Appius and Verginia, we can locate *objet a* in Woman, or more specifically, in Woman's sexuality (as shall also prove the case in the speech Propertius gives Cornelia); Verginia, as the catalyst for action against the decemvirs, embodies *objet a* insofar as she provides both for the success and the failure of the quilting point *libertas* ("freedom").[28] Appius Claudius, consistently represented as a proud aristocrat, assuredly commits an illegal act when he pretends that a freeborn woman is a runaway slave and takes steps to have her given over to his confederate's custody—yet he and his colleagues had already done worse in regularly countenancing profitable murders under the guise of lawful punishment.[29] When extended to the body of Verginia, Appius' highhanded presumption takes on the power to galvanize action among the commons, to motivate concerted demands for democratic reforms; but the denouement of the case makes it less than clear that equitable access to the Law is at stake here. After killing his daughter to "save" her from Appius' violation, Verginius and his daughter's erstwhile betrothed, Icilius, manage to rouse popular feeling against the decemvirs, only to retrace their (the decemvirs') steps. First they establish analogues of the Decemvirate in the form of military tribunates, then they pursue the tribunate themselves and use its powers to pass ever more stringent laws against the decemvirs, as well as the senatorial class in general (3.51.1–13, 3.54.11–3.55.15). When at last Verginius can proceed against Appius with impunity, he proves himself a worthy student of the decemvir's manipulation of the Law. Appius' appeal to argue his case is denied until the former decemvir can prove that he did not hand over a free citizen to a man who claimed her as his slave (3.57.5); Verginius thus impossibly requires Appius to prove his innocence before Appius can prove his innocence.[30] Verginia emerges as *objet a* in this episode to the degree that she "explains" the failures of the system from either side. The Law's failed claim to universality and impartiality, to being grounded in something other than desire, is on the one hand reduced to Appius' particular desire and, on the other, to Verginius' "just" revenge. In this view, the Law does not fail because of its own inconsistency, but because its executors lust for a woman, or for her vengeance. Either perspective trivializes the horrifyingly cruel effects of the Law by seeing them as purely contingent rather than structural.

Feminine sexuality similarly emerges as an object of obsessive fascination in 4.11, though Propertius unfolds a subtler drama than Livy's high tragedy of lust and tyranny. Commentators note with some embarrassment Cornelia's obsessive, and at times near hysterical, insistence on her own chastity, by far the chief subject of her defense. More curious still are the witnesses she calls to attest to her virtue, drawn first from the military conquerors in her family and from their conquests:

"testor maiorum cineres tibi, Roma, colendos,
    sub quorum titulis, Africa, tunsa iaces,

† et Persen proavo stimulantem pectus Achille,
    quique tuas proavo fregit Achille domos, †
me neque censurae legem mollisse neque ulla
    labe mea vestros erubuisse focos."
                    (37–42)

"Witness the ashes of my ancestors rightly venerated by you, Rome, beneath whose titles you, Africa, lie beaten and bruised, and Perses, whetting his courage with the thought of his ancestor Achilles, and he who broke your house, though your ancestor *was* Achilles, that neither did I soften any law of the censorship nor did any stain from me make your hearths blush."

Commentators have greeted the daggered distich, 39–40, with consternation. Certainly the line is troubled, and to compound the problem, the page missing from our oldest manuscript, N, contained these lines, so that its testimony can only be conjectured from two copies, μ and υ. The vulgate reading is meaningless, as Butler and Barber note ("et Persen proavi stimulantem pectus Achilli / quique tuas proavo fregit Achille domos"), so Lipsius' emendation to "proavo . . . Achille" has been almost universally accepted. After that, however, no consensus emerges as to how to interpret or emend the hexameter; most editors demur at Cornelia's calling upon Perses—king of Macedonia defeated by her illustrious ancestor, Aemilius Paullus—to witness her virtue.

Without claiming that what we have precisely records what came from Propertius' hands, I nonetheless argue that Cornelia's naming her family's defeated enemy as a character witness does not in itself justify emendation; the matter requires further thought, especially for the line's context. In the previous distich, Cornelia has already coupled her ancestors, the Scipiones, with their object of conquest (Africa) personified as a bruised and beaten body.[31] The next distich, if we accept only Lipsius' minimal emendation, would similarly couple conqueror with objects of conquest, Aemilius Paullus (the "qui" of the pentameter, according to the most widely accepted interpretation) with his foe Perses.[32] Moreover, Cornelia has made a habit already of calling upon her family's traditional enemies—Aeacus, for example (19)—to take part in her trial, as likely to be the most stringent executors of justice: her gesture's bravado vividly asserts her innocence and defiance all at once.[33] Perses would thus fall logically into the category of those who have little reason to prevaricate for her sake, but who (she implies) must perforce do her justice because her life is beyond reproach. As for his personal knowledge of her chastity, he has as much or as little as her dead ancestors, the Scipiones and Aemilius Paullus.

But whether we accept the "strong" reading of 39–40, making Perses a direct witness to Cornelia's chastity, or one of the "weak" readings that render him the object of some illustrious ancestor's military conquest, Cornelia's summoning of witnesses for her defense inescapably constructs her chastity as continuous with, and structurally analogous to, the success of Roman imperialism.[34] Her ancestors credibly witness the successful vigilance Cornelia has mounted over her own body boundaries precisely to the degree that they themselves have defended the boundaries of the Roman empire. Her chastity, like Verginia's, figures the integrity of the body politic.[35] Propertius represents feminine sexuality as guarantor and model of Rome's national coherence and integrity—a pattern further elaborated when Cornelia addresses her daughter as "born the image of your father's censorship" ("specimen censurae nata paternae," 67). Her daughter guarantees the "consistency" of her father's oversight of the Law, presumably because she resembles him and thus testifies to his ability to enforce virtue at home as well as publicly. But the emptiness of this guarantee emerges from the fact that Paullus' censorship was far from distinguished, according to the evidence of Velleius Paterculus.[36] Cornelia's daughter occupies the position of *objet a*, an apparent guarantee of coherence that, upon closer examination, turns out to be the marker of *in*coherence—of the Law's falling short of its own claims to totality—embodied in an object of mysterious fascination.

Woman thus becomes the guarantor of the Law's consistency: successful control over her sexuality attests the Law's effectiveness and the coherence of the body politic underwritten by the Law (while failure can be gracefully blamed on *Her*, rather than on impotent justice or class conflict). Woman represented as of Lucretia-like chastity and probity summarizes the nation's "renunciation of enjoyment," in both the weak and the strong sense: the weak sense meaning "the refusal of pleasure," and the strong, "the denial of ultimate conceptual groundlessness in the social order." Cornelia supposedly embodies the "ways of the ancestors" (*mos maiorum*), but her mesmerizing epiphany conjures away scrutiny of the conceptual foundation of that standard's power to (re)shape Roman society; she buries doubt beneath the dazzling image of a dead paragon.

THE URNS OF THE DANAIDS

Or almost so: this poem repeatedly offers us loose threads to pick at, insisting upon its own interrogation. One of these places emerges where, true to the logic of *objet a*, Cornelia herself seems obsessed with an object in a way that its immanent properties cannot explain. Cornelia returns again and again in her speech to the image of an urn: she mentions it three times, in different contexts:

"aut si quis posita iudex sedet Aeacus *urna*,
    in mea sortita vindicet ossa pila"
        (4.11.19–20)

"or if some Aeacus as judge, with his urn beside him, should pass judgment on my shade once the lots are cast"

"ipsa loquor pro me: si fallo, poena sororum
    infelix umeros urgeat *urna* meos."
        (4.11.27–28)

"I speak on my own behalf: if I lie, let the punishment of the sisters, the unhappy urn, press my shoulders."

"quaelibet austeras de me ferat *urna* tabellas:
turpior assessu non erit ulla meo . . ."
(4.11.49–50)

"Let any urn you wish bear the severe judgments: none of my ancestresses shall be shamed because she stood by me in court."

The first urn holds the lots drawn to decide the order of cases to be heard in the Underworld court; the second continually leaks and so frustrates the Danaids' attempts to carry water in Hell, punishment for murdering their cousin-bridegrooms on the wedding night; into the third the jury casts votes to decide the fate of the accused. The repeated image of the urn brings together a judgment on female sexuality (Cornelia's chastity as the case on trial) and a myth fashioned around female sexuality (the Danaids)—but beyond that the fit seems, at first, rather loose. On the evidence of Aeschylus, the Danaids reject their cousins the Aigyptioi not simply because they honor their father Danaus' endless quarrel with his brother Aigyptos, but because their revulsion for their cousins extends to disdain for sexual relations as such.[37] Given that Cornelia strives to prove herself chaste in marriage, why would she call down upon herself (if proven false) a punishment meted out not to adultery, but to a chastity even more fiercely determined than her own?

Both the Danaid legend and Cornelia's strange Underworld trial sketch Woman as disruptive force: Her sexuality either veers toward licentiousness (the implied obverse of Cornelia's obsessive defense of her own chastity) or obstinate virginity (the Danaids). Either way offers the Law advance provision for its own ineffectiveness, as if to say: "the social body *would* cohere, were it not for Woman's errant sexuality." Insofar as Her sexuality is evoked as the Law's guarantor and its arena, the same vessel (the urn) metaphorically represents each. Yet, even so, the entry of the Danaids' urns into this poem cannot entirely be reduced to the Law's own excuse for itself: Cornelia's bitterness undermines any picture of her as apologist for the Law. The image requires further explanation.

The imagery in Cornelia's speech superimposes a figure for female sexuality (women as "vessels") upon the urns that constitute the Law's materiality.[38] These urns "give body to" Law as abstraction, but thereby reveal its particularity and partiality hidden beneath the guise of objectivity and universality. The urns' burdens—lots cast at random to decide the order of cases, and secret ballots cast to decide each case—give to the Law the semblance of impartiality and impersonality, whereas the infamous example of Appius and Verginia points to Law's articulation and execution as ultimately equivalent to the will of its executors. In this poem, too, Cornelia's alignment of the Danaids' vessels with those of the Law hints at its subjectivity. The Danaids' legend involves two crimes, their rape by the Aigyptioi and their murder of the rapists—yet punishment answers only one of these crimes: the Law, as articulated by men, reveals itself cruelly blind to crimes against women. Cornelia explicitly rejects the Danaids as exemplars of Woman, yet implicitly aligns herself with them in that she arrives in the Underworld as yet another victim of "rape": "nec mea de sterili facta *rapina* domo" ("nor was my ravishment made from a sterile house," 4.11.62); "vidimus et fratrem sellam geminasse curulem / consule quo, festo tempore, *rapta* soror" ("we saw my brother, too, hold the curule seat twice, being consul in that solemn time in which his sister was ravished away," 4.11.65–66).[39] Further, both *rapta* and *rapina* echo the Sabine tradition of marriage by abduction, as Leo Curran notes: Cornelia's image of herself as stolen reaches back to the foundation of Roman legal institutions upon a primal crime.[40] Moreover, F. O. Copley shows that the poem partially relies upon the conventions of the paraklausithyron; its opening passage casts Paullus, weeping and suppliant at the impassable barrier between himself and Cornelia, as the conventional elegiac "shut-out lover" (*exclusus amator*).[41] The logic of the opening points to death as Paullus' rival, Cornelia as death's abducted bride; she comes to Hell, then, as a new Persephone—an image that again involves her court of Law's venue in obscene enjoyment.[42]

Cornelia's speech depicts the Law as the locus of sadistic, impossible demands, as her counter-examples to the Danaids indicate. Cornelia names as witnesses to her virtue Claudia Quinta, who received superhuman strength to move the barge carrying the Magna Mater's image off a sandbar, and Aemilia the Vestal Virgin, granted wondrous power to rekindle Vesta's altar fire after her careless disciple had let it die. These "witnesses" imply that meeting the Law's demands requires a miracle, and that nothing less procures exculpation. Indeed, Cornelia's almost hysterically insistent claims of chastity insinuate that nothing in her power to produce can satisfy the court, that its demands are capricious and therefore by definition unsatisfiable. The other testimonies to the Law's efficacy in this poem indicate the same, founding virtue on tortured, broken, and burnt bodies: on Africa bruised beneath the Scipiones' titles; on Cornelia herself "branded" like a slave with her love for her children ("nunc tibi commendo communia pignora natos: / haec cura et cineri spirat *inusta* meo"—"now I entrust to you our common pledges, our children: this concern even now has life, *branded* upon my ashes," 4.11.73–74); on the vengeance visited on broken Ixion, exhausted Sisyphus, starving Tantalus.

THE SACRIFICE OF THE SACRIFICE

The Law, as we have been tracing its features thus far in this essay, appears as an external terror in Cornelia's speech, whose inscrutable iron demands she has nonetheless valiantly met to the best of her ability. More than one scholar has noted how the chronicle of her self-sacrifice aligns her with Alcestis, another bride dying young in the service of her husband and family.[43] Certain details of phrasing in Propertius' poem strongly suggest that the poet had Euripides' play about the Greek heroine specifically in mind; this makes the differences between the two versions of a young wife's death all the more striking.[44]

Commentators often focus, for example, on the fact that Cornelia (unlike Alcestis) does not demand that her husband honor her death by remaining celibate for the rest of his life. She might easily have argued that her life devoted to him justified the sacrifice, much as Alcestis insists her dying for Admetus obligates him. Moreover, the idea of making Paullus an *unifeminus* (married to only one woman in his lifetime)[45] to match Cornelia as *univira* (married only once) better fits the elegiac standard of male fidelity to one woman, even beyond death, that Propertius has championed.[46] As noted, he clearly represents Paullus as suffering elegiac lover in the poem's opening images. Why, then, after this elegiac topos has carefully built an alignment between the situation in 4.11 and the preoccupations of Propertius' amatory work that antedate the fourth book, while the phrasing alludes to the *Alcestis* in addition, does Propertius have Cornelia speak as if she expected Paullus to remarry?

Readers have taken Cornelia's apparent equanimity over being replaced by a new wife alternately as a measure of her selflessness or of her coldness: either she cares so much for Paullus that she wishes him to have every happiness after she dies (including a spouse) or she cares so little that his remarriage is a matter of indifference to her; the text will support neither reading smoothly. True enough, as Richardson remarks, Cornelia has not "a single word of love or affection, or even sympathy, for Paullus."[47] Yet she shows much concern for her children, and that, after all, founds her predecessor Alcestis' prohibition against Admetus' remarriage: Alcestis does not wish her children to suffer under a stepmother's jealousy.[48] However Cornelia felt about Paullus, her own conception of the stepmother, whose prickly caprice she subtly but deftly sketches, would with equal logic dictate that *Cornelia* insist on her husband's celibacy so that her children be saved from a new woman's inhibiting presence.[49]

If Cornelia's attitude toward her widower cannot explain her equanimity, what then is at stake in her departure from Alcestis' example? Cornelia's refusal of Alcestis' "bargain" removes her from the expected relationship of exchange with the Law, whereby the individual's sacrifice of his particular desires nets him social compensations in the form of prestige, wealth, even the more esoteric rewards of faith and religious community. Cornelia opened her speech by severing any connection between self-sacrifice and reward: not only does her social position not matter in the face of death, but neither does the virtue of having had three children—she has all the same come to be but a handful of ashes:[50]

> "quid mihi coniugium Paulli, quid currus avorum
>   profuit aut famae pignora tanta meae?
> non minus immitis habuit Cornelia Parcas:
>   et sum, quod digitis quinque legatur, onus."
>   (4.11.11–14)

"What use to me was my marriage to Paullus, my ancestors' triumphal chariots or so many pledges of my reputation? Not any less did Cornelia meet an unkind fate: even so am I a burden that may be gathered in five fingers."

The bitterness of her tone, though, suggests that some link between renunciation and compensation was to be expected—not surprisingly, given that her reference to her children points directly to Augustus' legislation on marriage (*lex Iulia de maritandis ordinibus*, 18 B.C.E.) and its proffered "right of three children" (*ius trium liberorum*). Augustus' statute aimed to increase both marriage and reproduction in the polity by (among other provisions) releasing freeborn mothers of three legitimate children from the irksome legal necessity of having a guardian, thus granting them many of the same privileges that adult freeborn men who were *sui iuris* enjoyed.[51] The *leges Iuliae*, however, were but one of Augustus' efforts to incorporate the familial, religious, and social activities of matrons into the larger political order.[52] Given the crucial roles such women had played in the patronage network[53] that dominated the ostensibly straightforward Republican political system,[54] the emperor stood to benefit from harnessing that feminine force in support of his new political order. Given Cornelia's membership in Augustus' extended family, her emphasis on her exemplary maternity speaks also to the visibility of the female members of the emperor's household; their maternal virtues—crucial to Augustus' dynastic ambitions—were regularly highlighted for Rome's edification.[55] However, the rewards promised to the cooperation of such matrons, in or out of the imperial family, Cornelia ultimately finds poisonously hollow.

Her speech's disillusioned progress toward the passage in which she pointedly sidesteps Alcestis' demand upon the living thus traces, *avant la lettre*, the dialectic of *Bildung* ("development/culture/education") in Hegel's *Phenomenology of Spirit*—a dialectic that can save us from the Hobson's choice of reading Cornelia as either sublime martyr or self-righteous prig.[56] Hegel's general importance to Lacan's thought is well documented,[57] but the philosopher's reflections on *Bildung* specifically anticipate Lacan's formulation of the divided subject's relation to the quilting point (as examined above in chapter 2). Hegel in essence unfolds the consequences of the quilting point's radical failure, when it can grant the subject no secure place in the Symbolic network nor any salve to the sense of his or her innate deficiency. The *Phenomenology of Spirit* traces the series of exchanges between subject (self-consciousness) and substance that reward the subject's increasing alienation (his yielding of all substantial content to the Other, the State) with the tangible and intangible social compensations of honor, wealth, religious faith, and the like (rewards chiefly important, in Lacan's view, for their power to paper over the subject's inherent division and displacement). Hegel follows the dialectic all the way up to its logical point of breakdown, where the subject "gets nothing in exchange for everything"—that is, in exchange for no compensation at all, he sacrifices individual desires for Absolute Will, which, being at its most abstract, can give nothing in exchange.

> In the world of culture itself it [self-consciousness] does not get as far as to behold its negation or alienation in this form of pure abstraction; on the contrary, its negation is filled with a content, either honour or wealth, which it gains in place of the self that it has alienated from itself; or the language of Spirit and insight that the disrupted consciousness acquires; or it is the heaven of faith, or the Utility of the Enlighten-

ment. All these determinations have vanished in the loss suffered by the self in absolute freedom; its negation is the death that is without meaning, the sheer terror of the negative that contains nothing positive, nothing that fills it with a content. At the same time, however, this negation in its real existence is not something alien; it is neither the universal inaccessible necessity, in which the ethical world perishes, nor the particular accident of private possession, nor the whim of the owner on which the disrupted consciousness sees itself dependent; on the contrary, it is the universal will which in this its ultimate abstraction has nothing positive and therefore can give nothing in return for the sacrifice. But for that very reason it is immediately one with self-consciousness, or it is the pure positive, because it is the pure negative; and the meaningless death, the unfilled negativity of the self, changes round in its inner Notion into absolute positivity.[58]

Getting nothing in exchange for everything, the "sacrifice of the sacrifice," describes Cornelia's trajectory precisely. Hegel's point, in sketching the dialectic of culture, is to trace the transformation of an external Terror (the irrational whims of the State, Hegel's specific reference being the Jacobin Reign of Terror—an historical moment whose capricious and violent judgments were not unlike those of the late Republic and early Empire in Rome) into an internal moral Law, that aligns the subject's "free will" with universal moral Law severed from reward, and thus from the particular motivations that enslave Will to the world of objects. But, as Žižek points out,[59] the point here is not to domesticate the Terror's traumatic impact—far from it: rather, the dialectic's logical outcome installs in the subject a malign kernel of dread, to terrorize him from within, something that subverts the very kernel of his identity in that he can never meet its demands and is forever guilty in its eyes.[60]

The reading of sacrifice Hegel offers us renders sensible several aspects of the text I have mentioned often, but most readings either ignore or "gentrify" out of their true horror, such as Cornelia's abject terror of the Law. I have already noted that her insistence on her chastity and her summoning of miraculous female ancestors to witness her purity renders Law a locus of demands she can never meet. But the *Phenomenology of Spirit* also predicts that this external Terror will ultimately reveal itself as implacable internal hindrance—as, by her own testimony, it does: "mi natura dedit leges a sanguine ductas / nec possis melior iudicis esse metu" ("my own nature gave me laws drawn from my blood, nor could you be more virtuous from fear of a judge," 47–48). The most impossible of all judges mounts his inquisition from within Cornelia herself.

Further, Hegel's analysis of the "nothing-for-everything" exchange traced in the subject's ultimate alienation also clarifies the demand Cornelia substitutes for Alcestis' demand of her husband's eternal celibacy. Cornelia asks Paullus to speak to her image with pauses in between, as if he were waiting for answers from his living wife: "atque ubi secreto nostra ad simulacra loqueris, / ut responsurae singula verba iace" ("and even when you speak to my image in private, speak your words at intervals, as if to one who shall answer," 83–84); the request has embarrassed one commentator as "close to bathos."[61] Yet Cornelia simply asks for a version of Alcestis' compensation: the soliloquizing Paullus, like the celibate Admetus, is to act as if his wife were still alive. The significant difference between Alcestis' and Cornelia's request lies in the fact that the Roman matron's is purely formal and empty of content. Her directions to Paullus erect the image of marriage as a harmonious Whole built from Man and Woman as complementaries, a unit that is (in the thought of such as Cicero and Lucretius[62]) the origin and microcosm of social unity as such, of the body politic. But in Cornelia's picture of marital fidelity, "Woman does not exist," even in the form of a tribute to Her sacrifice, such as Admetus' celibacy constitutes for Alcestis: pantomime conversation costs Paullus next to nothing. Cornelia's request subtracts Woman from the marital "conversation" as the illusory guarantor of the Other's consistency and cohesion, thereby exposing the insubstantiality of the principles to which she has subjected the whole of her life.[63]

Cornelia's somewhat macabre stipulation that their marital exchange continue as empty form is a "sacrifice of the sacrifice": insofar as she (unlike Alcestis) refuses to bar Paullus' remarrying, she ceases to exist as a prohibition and therefore as part of Law's structure. Her choice far more radically criticizes the principles that have structured Paullus' life (and her own): she sacrifices the exchange of his celibacy for her death in order to be absolutely nothing. Cornelia will exist in their "conversation" only as the pauses between his words—precisely as *nothing*, silence, non-meaning. She exists in the Law (insofar as matronage reflects Law's essential principles) not as its reflection, but as the place where it "gaps"—where the inadequacy of its own claims to transcendent meaning stands revealed, in that it could make no other place for her sacrifice beyond this silence.

Curiously, Cornelia asks of Paullus the very thing that Euripides' Admetus promised himself, an image of the lost wife treated as the living wife (*Alc.* 348–52); the silence that represents Cornelia in Paullus' conversation also calls to mind the determinedly silent Alcestis Herakles wrests from death and hands over to Admetus at the end of Euripides' play (*Alc.* 1119–46). These echoes of *Alcestis* underline the absence of any Herakles from Propertius' version of female sacrifice: no one and nothing redeems Cornelia's sacrifice. Her final words underline that omission when she obliquely and rather bitterly compares her fate to Hercules': "moribus et caelum patuit: sim digna merendo / cuius honoratis ossa vehantur avis" ("virtue has even opened heaven [to some]: may I be found worthy through my merit, let my bones be conveyed to my honored ancestors," 101–102). In contrast to Euripides' denouement, the poem ostentatiously refuses the idea of return to the world of the living: "cum semel infernas intrarunt funera leges / non exorato stant adamante viae" ("when once the dead enter upon the laws of Hell, the ways rise up in adamant," 3–4); Propertius even contravenes his own vision of the Underworld in 4.7 (whence the dead return nightly to the upper world) to raze deliverance from Cornelia's Hell.[64]

Equally, the poem suspends the idea of progress to some suitable *denouement* analogous to Hercules' divinization, an ending that would compensate or redeem Cornelia's sacrifice, and thus make sense of the Law that informed that surrender. She gets neither heaven nor heroism: Wyke points out that 4.11's Underworld exceeds even the gloom of *Aeneid* 6 in that Propertius allows no final parade of Roman heroes, though Cornelia's concentration on her illustrious ancestors, and her hope that she may join them, would make such an uplifting tableau logically apt. Not even a vision of the Blessed Fields graces Cornelia's Hades, as it does 4.7's. Indeed, we never hear judgment pronounced upon Cornelia's merits: we end the poem, not with her exoneration, but with a vision of her witnesses (including the emperor Augustus) eternally bathed in tears. Propertius forever defers the ending to Cornelia's trial, and thus suspends its meaning. By thus refusing closure, the poem denies even the semblance of consistency and coherence to the Law that has animated Cornelia's life; she remains a reproachful and bitter ghost who haunts Rome's vision of itself as "the most moral of nations" with the spectre of a cruel deadlock it would prefer to forget.[65]

CHAPTER TEN

Dreaming Rome

Le città e il desiderio. 5.

Di là, dopo sei giorni e sette notti, l'uomo arriva a Zobeide, città bianca, ben esposta alla luna, con vie che girano su se stesse come in un gomitolo. Questo si racconta della sua fondazione: uomini di nazioni diverse ebbero un sogno uguale, videro una donna correre di notte per una città sconosciuta, da dietro, coi capelli lunghi, ed era nuda. Sognarono d'inseguirla. Gira gira ognuno la perdette. Dopo il sogno andarono cercando quella città; non la trovarono ma si trovarono tra loro; decisero di costruire una città come nel sogno. Nella disposizione delle strade ognuno rifece il percorso del suo inseguimento; nel punto in cui aveva perso le tracce della fuggitiva ordinò diversamente che nel sogno gli spazi e le mura in modo che non gli potesse più scappare.

ITALO CALVINO

moenia namque pio coner disponere versu

PROPERTIUS 4.1.57

The preceding pages have sought to demonstrate that desire's elusive and tantalizing insinuation in Rome is crucial to understanding the imaginative contours of the Eternal City as they took shape in Propertius' verse. Specifically, the frequently remarked palindrome *amor/ Roma* traces a nexus of ideas crucial to understanding Propertius' poetry: *Roma* and *amor* mirror one another, not just as words, but as structurally and functionally identical forces that organize the subject. Love and the state revolve around a common axis of desire that intersects citizen and lover, falsely promising wholeness beneath the aegis of culturally weighted signifiers. Seeing this makes sense of apparent incoherencies in Propertius' work, places where too-hasty analysis of the erotic and the political as fundamental antitheses has fashioned an insensible instrument with which to rack his poems. Naturally, I urge the usefulness of the model of understanding outlined in this book to the rest of Propertius' corpus—even to its more lucid passages: relative cohesion may have beguiled us into false complacency before we have fully probed the poet's drift. Yet my methodology approaches his poems not as an idiolect, but as responses to logical impasses inherent in symbolization itself (albeit responses stamped with his peculiar genius). Consequently, I believe it adaptable to understanding other puz-

---

Italo Calvino, *Le città invisibili* (Turin, 1972), 51. Reprinted by the kind permission of Arnoldo Mondadori Editore.

zlements of seemingly irreconcilable discordance in Latin poetry that have preserved their cunning mysteries unto our own day.

In particular, such an approach will help us reconsider the dichotomies that have long informed our understanding of Roman letters. We need to reflect on how, and whether, presumed antitheses such as Augustanism/anti-Augustanism can usefully analyze the poetry of the late Republic and early Empire. Scholars such as Duncan Kennedy and Charles Platter have already pointed out that such a dichotomy cannot accurately capture Roman elegy, marked as it is by the ambivalence of self-styled dissent under quasi-official patronage.[1] They remind us that politics assuredly informed Roman poetry in general and elegy in particular, but that to frame the political as binary opposition does too little justice to the complexity of its dissonances. The same skepticism helps us to reassess other social and institutional forces that shape ancient culture, and perforce its literary expressions. Important work by contemporary classicists has reformulated the tensions that traverse Roman thought, seeing them less as stable, rigid, and oppositional dyads than as fluid borderlines crossed and recrossed in a process of continual redefinition. Denis Feeney on Roman religion,[2] Duncan Kennedy on Augustan lyric poetry,[3] Paul Allen Miller on Roman erotic elegy,[4] Carlin Barton on Roman popular culture,[5] are a few of the scholars representative of a much larger cohort (too numerous to cite exhaustively) whose work traces the specific dynamics of Rome's unremitting ideological "border war." Lacan's work advances the trajectory of such scholarly contributions by showing how conceptual binaries meet and contend elastically in shaping a subject structured by language—that is, by a purely differential system unanchored by any pre-symbolic ground, and thus infinitely (and anxiously) plastic. He helps us describe with precision what ancient literature reveals about subjects' attempts to align themselves with such cardinal signifiers as *Romanitas,* because he accounts for the inherent fragility and tenuousness that vitiate both signifier and subject.

Conceptual fragility thrown into relief by historical vicissitudes helps explain Propertius' special fascination with Woman—not just as mistress, but as the myriad *dramatis personae* from *lenae* to mythological heroines who figure prominently in his elegies. Aptly so: Woman (as Lacan's work shows) iconically marks the point at which logical systems break down. Where the signifying systems that constitute us *as* subjects come to grief—where the naked scandal of another truth impinges upon our dreams—She is the sibyl who marks the unpleasant revelation. Lacan's concept of Woman thus subsumes the instabilities of the forces that intersect and shape the subject, a subject who, in Propertius' elegies, wavers, shifts, scatters under the pressure of cultural contradictions.

Using gender as a tool with which to sift classical poetry has, by this last decade of the twentieth century, a substantial and honorable (though comparatively short) scholarly history, one that has recently sought to understand Woman less as a function of anatomy than as a sign within ancient cultural systems—as, for example, a bridge over tensions within hierarchical male relationships,[6] or an ever-available, oddly internalized, foil against which even an undermined masculinity may define itself,[7] or an icon of "lost" masculinity and power that summarized the fears of a disenfranchised male elite.[8] Following in the footsteps of these studies that emphasize semiotics over biology, I hope by unfolding Propertius' strategic deployment of Woman in his poetry to have sketched some new paths that this already well-launched inquiry may follow in the future. As I have argued in the preceding pages, gender can usefully be rethought as two types of logical impasse: on the feminine side, the impossibility of drawing a limit (such as produces the implausible heterogeny of qualities attributed to the elegiac mistress, who is alternately fetishized and sadistically reviled); on the masculine side, the necessity of drawing a limit that is then negated (such as shapes the envied excess of the poet-lover's impossibly fortunate rivals). These impasses mark some of the ways in which discursive practices falter in ancient Rome (especially, but not exclusively, in erotic poetry); understanding them enriches and broadens the repertoire of approaches that retrieve from a literature molded by the hands of men something of significance for understanding ancient women. Intellectually so armed, we can map with greater precision the complex sign system inhabited by *Romanae*, a system that bore upon the lives both of those who did, and who did not, read or hear Propertius.[9]

Nonetheless, I advance no claim to Propertius as prescient feminist, at least as that word signifies today. Rather, I see his poetry as disenchanted observance of his times, recording with shrewd reflection exactly where and how the institutions and practices that implicate the Roman subject break down logically—fissures thrown into particular relief as the pressure of change in Augustan Rome worried inherent contradictions. His work discloses logical schisms within the way Roman culture mapped gender over seemingly unrelated areas—politics, foreign relations, the division of the world into public and private spheres. Insofar as his poems reveal the clandestine dependency of masculine "norm" on feminine "deviation," Propertius makes recuperating the feminine (as that which falls outside, and challenges, cultural categories of understanding) a much larger venture, with higher stakes, than many of us have suspected. He compels us to rethink entirely what it means to rescue Creusa from the burning city.[10]

In this context, both the recrimination and apology that have marked contemporary debate over Propertius' "feminism" need reframing. Scholars have tended either to stress those details of the poetry that affirm the poet's control over his mistress, and thus to brand him as unreflective sexist,[11] or, noting on the other hand particulars that grant his mistress puissance, to champion him as natively sympathetic to women.[12] Assuredly, these readings have added a dimension to Propertius studies difficult to overvalue, given that contributions from both sides of the debate have deepened the way we now read his work: they have brought to the fore details previously overlooked or dismissed and placed them in compellingly fresh interpretive frameworks. However, I would urge a reconsideration of the question based on remarking the particulars of the way Propertius represents women, not simply as data bereft of context to be entered as evidence for or against the poet, but as narrative strategies. The movement and structure of each elegy—indeed, of the corpus as a whole—potentially ironizes, complicates, and contests these details' import. The syntax of reading these elegies' complex cross-references describes an elegant dance that confounds any traditional understanding of gender. Sex emerges in this poetry from the inherent limits of signification, defining two positions (habitable by *any* body) that bear principally upon epistemology, not anatomy—feminine skepticism that knowledge can ever be complete, and masculine "bad faith" that makes knowledge complete by repressing whatever does not fit a rationale. Accordingly, Propertius does not champion Woman so much as reveal Her to be the concomitant of our own unexamined habits of mind; her startling appearances in his corpus scatter the bits of sleepy dogmatism that cling to thought.

It seems appropriate, therefore, to conclude with Propertius' wry assessment of Woman's role in his own work, an assessment that proceeds from the mouth of his creation Horos. The Babylonian astrologer counters Propertius' dreams of an implicitly androcentric, quasi-epic monument to Rome's past (57–70) by reminding the poet of the essential status his verse has always granted the feminine, the object he pursues with all his intellectual and artistic powers and yet can never grasp: "'nam tibi victrices quascumque labore parasti / eludit palmas una puella tuas'" ("'no matter what victories your efforts have gained you, one girl evades your conquest,'" 140). Horos' comment conjures up a vision of Woman's presence within the walls of Rome scheduled to arise in Propertius' "reverent verse" as a seductive dream always disappearing round a corner of those walls, always just beyond the poet's grasp in a race he can neither win nor ever wish to abandon. The pursuit itself becomes his—and our—most demanding askesis, and best reward.

NOTES

INTRODUCTION

1. The term "subject" (and "subjectivity," the corollary abstract noun for the condition of being a subject) has gained popularity in the last half of the twentieth century over cognate terms with a similar range of references—for example, "person," "individual," "self," "agent"—as the more comprehensive and flexible concept. The traditional terms imply a consciousness completely self-aware, self-controlled, and autonomous. They thus resist accounting for the effects of forces that someone neither originates nor controls. The subject, on the other hand, is conceived as a site through which social, cultural, institutional, and unconscious forces move. The model is the grammatical subject, governed from outside itself by rules of grammar and syntax making up a linguistic structure—rules that grant the "I" its meaning. The subject is thus the vector product of all the forces in play at the site of consciousness at any one time (cf. Leicester 1990, 14).

2. As I shall demonstrate especially in my expositions of poems 4.3, 4.4, and 4.11.

3. I date the principate of Octavian from approximately 30 B.C.E.—the defeat of his one remaining serious rival for power, Mark Antony—to his death in 14 C.E. The exact beginning of the principate is difficult to specify, however, given that the title *princeps* was never an official one, and that the formal constitutional bases for Octavian's rule inadequately indicate the extent of his real power. He himself attests to the gap between his de jure and de facto power: his sixth and seventh consulships saw him in possession of "complete control of all affairs by universal consent" ("per consensum universorum potitus rerum omnium," *RG* 34)—underlining the fact that his supremacy has no specified legal basis. After he hands over control of Rome to the senate and people in 27 B.C.E., he still "excelled all in influence, though I possessed no more official power than others who were my colleagues in the various magistracies" ("potestatis autem nihilo amplius habui quam ceteri qui mihi quoque in magistratu conlegae fuerunt," *RG* 34).

4. *RG* 21.

5. Zanker 1988.

6. Livy 1.23.1–3. Rome's war with Alba Longa reduced the mother-city at last to a deserted ruin whose population Rome forcibly incorporated (Livy 1.29.1–6).

7. I owe a deep debt of gratitude to my learned colleague Diskin Clay for first drawing my attention to the many contradictions captured in the Forum Augustum's summation of Roman history and identity, and for suggesting the relevance of Zanker's writings on the monument to my own work on Propertius.

8. The *spolia opima* (literally, "best/richest spoils") were those a Roman general stripped from an enemy commander defeated in single combat and dedicated to Jupiter Feretrius in the god's temple.

9. "An attitude of dutiful respect towards those to whom one is bound by ties of religion, consanguinity, etc." (OLD, s.v. *pietas*, 1a).

10. "The qualities typical of a true man, manly spirit, resolution, valour, steadfastness, or sim." (OLD, s.v. *virtus*, 1a).

11. Livy 1.10.

12. Each of the *summi viri* arrayed on either side the Forum's central long axis is a *triumphator*—i.e., a Roman general who celebrated the triumph, an official ceremonial recognition of his defeat of an enemy people—with two exceptions: L. Albinius and Appius Claudius Caecus (Lahusen 1983, 24n150).

13. The phrase, customary in referring to the Forum's statues, is borrowed from Lampridius, who says that Augustus erected marble statues of the most illustrious men (*summorum virorum statuas*) in his forum, accompanied by inscriptions (*SHA*, Alex. Sev. 28).

14. Cf. *RG* 35.

15. The younger of the two *Africani*.

16. Zanker 1968, 18; Zanker 1988, 211.

17. His bitter quotation of Athene's condemnation of Aegisthus (*Od.* 1.47) upon hearing of Tiberius' death—"so perish also all others who on such evil venture"—implies as much: the goddess responds to Zeus' tale of Aegisthus' having murdered Agamemnon and married his wife. Scipio Aemilianus thus quotes Homer's condemnation of a destroyer and usurper of legitimate authority—precisely the assessment of Tiberius voiced by his senatorial peers, who accused Tiberius of attempting to confuse the body politic, foment revolution, and ultimately establish himself as tyrant (Plutarch *Gracchi* 9.3, 19.3).

18. As censor, Numidicus tried to refuse to seat Saturninus and Glauca in the Senate, and he later chose exile over swearing to support legislation framed and passed by Saturninus. Historians such as Rutilius Rufus and Posidonius view this as anti-demagoguery (see Malitz 1983, 380–81)—nor are they alone in doing so. Cicero regularly construes Numidicus' exile as parallel to his own engineered by Clodius Pulcher—each the result of a brave man's principled, if doomed, opposition to demagoguery. See, for example, *De Domo Sua* 31, in which Cicero characterizes Saturninus and Glauca as "homines seditiosissimi" who retaliated vindictively against Metellus, one of the *optimi ac fortissimi cives* opposed to a politics Cicero regards as little more than rabble rousing.

19. Livy and Valerius Maximus do not expand upon Camillus' dictatorships as Plutarch does, but both concur in emphasizing his circumspect regard for deferring both to the prerogatives of others, and of tradition, in executing his office. Livy records the fact that, after the defeat of Veii, Camillus deferred to the Senate on the question of how to divide the spoils, even though he, as dictator, would have been within his rights to decree unilaterally how they were to be apportioned (Livy 5.20.1–3). Both Livy (5.46.4–11) and Valerius Maximus (Val. Max. 4.2.1) cite with approval Camillus' reluctance to be recalled from exile in Ardea and made dictator until the Senate had given its formal approval, even though, under the circumstances of a besieged Rome, that scrupulous punctilio costs considerable effort

and time. Plutarch follows the precedent of these earlier historiographic sources in emphasizing Camillus' modest wielding of his power (cf. *Camillus* 24.3, 31.3, 39.2).

20. Plutarch *Camillus* 1.3, concurring with the earlier, but terser, portrait drawn by Livy (Livy 5.20.1–3, 9).

21. The word *Romanitas* ("Romanness"), though admittedly postclassical (from Tertullian *De Pallio* 4), marks with useful succinctness the powerful ideology of "the Roman way" so evidently at work throughout Roman history.

22. See, for example, Griffin 1985, Wiseman 1985.

23. Veyne 1988.

24. *Mollitia* means both "effeminacy" and "licentiousness."

25. *Servitium amoris* = "love's slavery," i.e., the lover's emotional bondage to his mistress' whims.

26. Kennedy 1993.

27. Miller forthcoming; a foretaste of Miller's analysis of all of Roman elegy can be seen in his fascinating essay on Tibullus (Miller 1999).

28. Catullus' claim to the status of Roman elegist is admittedly controversial; he is often considered a precursor to elegy—though an important one—rather than a Roman elegist in his own right.

29. Understandably, given that his patron was the politically astute and aloof Messalla, whose career bespeaks a cordial but politic distance between himself and Augustus. On Messalla, and Tibullus' relation to him, see Little 1982, 311–16.

30. Ovid, like Tibullus, was also Messalla's client, at least in his early years (*Pont.* 1.7.27ff.), and never enjoyed Augustus' patronage.

31. Miller forthcoming.

32. The Ara Maxima was an altar located in the Forum Boarium, the oldest and most venerable cult center of Hercules in Rome. See Richardson 1992, s.v. *Herculis Invicti Ara Maxima*.

33. Cf. Žižek 1997, 217.

34. By which I do not mean simply "anti-Augustan"; the poetry is far too complex to be subsumed under such a reductive and narrow rubric. See below, chapter 1, "A Preliminary Test Case: The Gallus Poems."

CHAPTER ONE: THEORETICAL PRELIMINARIES

1. Of the major Latin poets, only Catullus suffers from a worse attested and later manuscript tradition, as Margaret Hubbard notes (Hubbard 1974, 5).

2. *Od.* 9.534 (translation based on Richmond Lattimore's).

3. Butrica 1984, 4, quoting Lachmann 1829, ad 1.9.9 (Lachmann's 1.10.9): "9 DUCERE CARMEN. 21 TOTIS] Immerito obtrusas Propertio elegantias his ostentat exemplaria. Alterius commenti TOTIS MEDULLIS auctor exstat Janus Dousa filius: DUCERE CARMEN Ant. Volscus jam dedit MCCCCLXXXII, non obsequente Beroaldo. Scripti omnes, ne uno quidem dempto, habent:

Quid tibi nunc misero prodest grave Dicere carmen?
Quam pueri TOTIENS arcum sentire medullas

Quis jure impugnet? quis tanti ducat defendere."

4. E.g., Williams 1968, 557–59 ("This is the world in which Propertius sets his love-poetry: it is created out of a tension between the real world of politics and the private microcosm

of his love-affair," 558); Hallett 1971; Commager 1974, 37–77; Sullivan 1976, 56–61, 70–73; Little 1982, 293–308; Sauvage 1983; Della Corte 1986.

5. Stahl 1985 well exemplifies this dichotomy between the erotic and the political, though the sensitivity of his readings often overcomes what I regard as oversimplistic theoretical premises.

6. Thomas Benediktson notes that "there is an almost direct correlation between the classicism of an age and its ability to understand Propertius," meaning a negative correlation: the poet reacts against classical language and structure, depending instead upon vivid imagery to create an associative logic in his poetry. While Propertius was enthusiastically taken up by Renaissance writers, "they read him as though he were Tibullus or Ovid and consequently allude to his themes and even to passages, but without really seeing what he represented"; the even more glaring "enlightenment" of the eighteenth-century shrinks Propertian allusions almost to nothing. But Benediktson makes clear that he includes in his definition of "classicism" the confidence in reason that founds the chief ideal models of the polity in ancient and modern times, so that misunderstanding of, and disaffection from, Propertius correlates to prevailing political as well as literary thought (Benediktson 1989, 129–30).

7. The subject is split by

1. the orders of existence Lacan calls the Real, the Imaginary, and the Symbolic. He elaborates their relations in SXXII, but they are present in Lacan's thought long before that seminar. (See Macey 1988, 228–29 for a brief account of the order's definitive emergence in the course of Lacan's career; for an explanation of the orders themselves, see Janan 1994, 16–21).

2. language—self-evident in the fact that the subject who speaks is never exactly coincident with the subject of the speech. The person who says "I laughed" may or may not be laughing at the moment she speaks, and thus obviously differs from the subject, the "I," of the sentence (Cf. SXI, 127–30/138–42, where Lacan illustrates this concept by means of the Liar's Paradox; I discuss this passage from SXI more fully in chapter 5.)

The polarity Conscious/Unconscious overlies both modes of division, but not such that any one realm can be said to be completely coterminous either with the Conscious or Unconscious.

8. *Écrits* 793–827/292–325. See also Žižek 1989.

9. Cf. e.g. *RG* 8.5.

10. Under "social upheaval," I include the relatively peaceful, but nonetheless profound and unsettling, changes the early Empire wrought at the largest institutional levels (in the courts, the Senate, and, of course, the government itself, as it changed from republic to principate).

11. J. P. Postgate (Postgate 1881, liii-liv), seconded by P. H. Damsté (Damsté 1928, 214–19) both propose the "weak" and the "strong" theory of Book IV's oddity (i.e., as "posthumously edited" and "the work of a later poetaster" respectively), with Damsté inclined particularly to the latter belief. Léon Herrmann (Herrmann 1951, 137–65) elaborates on Damsté's conviction that Book IV is fraudulent by naming a suspect for the crime ("Passennus Paullus Propertius, qui les a conçues sous Titus," 168).

12. Both Rothstein and Camps construe *prisca* closely with *sacra diesque* as well as *cognomina*, even though grammatically it only modifies the latter: these will be "ancient" rites and

their designated days of celebration documented in this poetry, as well as ancient place-names (Rothstein 1966, ad loc.; Camps 1965, ad loc.).

13. E.g., literary epistle (4.3), epicedion (4.11), hymn (4.6, 4.9), satire (4.8). For general discussion of Callimachus' influence on Propertius, see e.g. Boucher 1965, 194–203; Pillinger 1969, 171–99; Miller 1982, 380–96.

14. Gutzwiller 1992.

15. Berenike and Ptolemy were, in fact, cousins, but the lock describes Berenike's sorrow at her husband's departure as owed to a sisterly regard for her "brother," according to the evidence of Catullus 66.21–22. For Catullus' poem as reliable witness to the content of Callimachus' (now only fragmentarily extant) poem, see Marinone 1984, 45–76.

16. Vertumnus claims, for example, the ability to emulate that quintessential object of amorous interest, a *non dura puella* (4.2.23).

17. Wyke 1987a, 154.

18. *Evocatio:* the ritual whereby the gods of a conquered city were induced to leave it with the promise of a cult in Rome at least as good as that offered by the enemy city.

19. Pinotti 1983.

20. 4.6: Apollo quickly tires of bellicosity at Actium and doffs his military gear in favor of a drinking party; 4.10: the discussion of the *spolia opima* treads the burning coals, not only of Rome's military abuse of the Etruscans again (at Veii), but of Augustus' petty refusal of the *spolia opima* to M. Licinius Crassus on the sophistical grounds that his (Crassus') command derived from Augustus and so Augustus alone deserved the honor (Cassius Dio 51.24.4). See below, chapter 6, "Double Vision," and note 13.

21. On 4.1's double agenda, see, e.g., Grimal 1952; Nethercut 1968; Wyke 1987a.

22. Deremetz 1986, 130. He draws attention to ancient interest in etymology as veridical instrument—a claim that Plato's Cratylus passionately argues (see, e.g., *Crat.* 383a). Varro also attests that—for a later era in Rome—etymology strongly engaged the serious attention of philosophers (*LL* V.1–3).

23. 4.4: Propertius plays on the homoiophony between the traitorous Tarpeia's name—eventually bequeathed to the Tarpeian Rock—and *turpe*, "shameful."

24. Bing 1988, 70–71; Zanker 1986, 121–23.

25. Tissol 1997, 201–202; cf. Edwards 1996, 16–18.

26. Though 1.22 does not explicitly say that its subject, Propertius' dead *propinquus*, is the same as the "Gallus" of 1.21, the majority of scholars accepts the identification. H.-P. Stahl includes a useful survey of previous opinion in his discussion of this issue (Stahl 1985, 111–12).

27. King 1980, Cairns 1983.

28. See Ross 1975, 82–84, King 1980, Cairns 1983.

29. Tränkle 1960, 23. Ross and Cairns follow suit (Ross 1975, 68n3, 83, 95n3; Cairns 1983, 85).

30. The most extensive analyses of Propertius as anti-Augustan are Commager 1974; Sullivan 1976, esp. 54–73; Stahl 1985. Nethercut 1983, 1836–52 and Viparelli 1987, 20–28 usefully survey scholarship on the question of Propertius' Augustanism.

31. Benediktson draws attention to the influence of nineteenth-century intellectual revolution on the appreciation of Propertius (Benediktson 1989, 130).

32. Livy eloquently expresses this despair: "haec tempora quibus nec vitia nostra nec remedia pati possumus," *Ab Urbe Condita*, Praefatio 9. He echoes Sallust's despondency over Rome's seemingly irremediable corruption by "primo pecuniae, deinde imperi cupido" (*BC*

10.3). Among the poets must be noted the pessimism of Catullus, who concludes c.64 with an apocalyptic vision of the gods turning away in disgust from a world infected by incest, greed, and murder (64.397–408); of Vergil and Horace, who, as Douglas Little has noted, believe Romans (or, sometimes, humanity in general) to be stained with an "original sin" that repeats itself as bloodshed—especially fratricidal or civil bloodshed—from generation to generation ("Laomedonteae luimus periuria Troiae," *G.* 1.502; "priscae vestigia fraudis," *Ecl.* 4.31; Romulus' murder of Remus, *Epod.* 7.17–20; cf. Little 1982, 260, 277); of Tibullus, who contrasts the current Jovian age of bloodshed with Saturn's benevolent reign (1.3.35–50; n.b. "nunc Iove sub domino caedes et vulnera semper / nunc mare, nunc leti mille repente viae," 49–50); of Propertius himself, who sees avarice as the root of Rome's present evils:

> at nunc desertis cessant sacraria lucis:
>   aurum omnes victa iam pietate colunt.
> auro pulsa fides, auro venalia iura,
>   aurum lex sequitur, mox sine lege pudor.
>   (3.13.47–50)

Even Ovid, generally a cheerful advocate of his times, sometimes paints a sour picture of modernity (e.g., the contemporary rule of wealth, especially that wrested by violence, depicted in *Amores* 3.8.53–56). The elegists may invoke the theme of deterioration in the present age more lightly than other writers, but their frequent recurrence to it shows that the topos had currency for a contemporary audience.

33. To speak only of the plastic arts: B. A. Kellum stresses the way in which Augustus shaped his building program—the *Aedes Concordiae Augustae* being the particular example—to reflect a putative "new world order" of harmony and prosperity (Kellum 1990, esp. 279–80). W. Mierse extends the conspectus to the provinces brought within the scope of "the newly established political unity of the West" via imperial building projects that visibly symbolized unity and integration (Mierse 1990).

34. Cf. Williams 1990.

35. Propertius was hardly blind to Augustus' failings, and neither should we be. I only wish to emphasize that the structure and purpose of the *princeps*' and poet's enterprises mirror one another.

36. In my account of this problem, I have relied heavily on Joan Copjec's eloquently lucid exposition of it (Copjec 1994, 205).

37. See Saussure 1983, [159–69], [176–84] (page numbers in square brackets refer to the standardized pagination of the French editions from 1922 onwards, printed in the margins of most modern editions and translations).

38. Plato *Timaeus* 42b5–6; Ar. *GA* 737a28; Cic. *Tusc.* 2.43; Val. Max. 5.3.1; Sen. *Ad Helv.* 16.

39. Lloyd 1984, 3.

40. Lacan 1975, 31.

41. Žižek 1991a, 112. Throughout this book, I have availed myself not only of Lacan's work per se, but of that of his most brilliant disciples—such as Žižek, Joan Copjec, and Luce Irigaray—wherever I felt their writings could help either shed light on an obscure sector of Lacan's legacy or extend the trajectory of his reflection on critical problems beyond where it stood at the time of his death in 1981. The writings I have used from these authors are extensions of Lacan's thought that are nonetheless compatible with its fundamental principles.

42. On Cynthia's guises in the Monobiblos, cf. Richardson 1977, 3–4 (quoted below in full in chapter 7).

43. Lacan 1975, 35.
44. Cf. Slavoj Žižek on the concept of nationality (Žižek 1991a, 109–10). Žižek's discussion draws upon Hegel (principally the *Wissenschaft der Logik*) as Hegel rethinks both Fichte (*Wissenschaftslehre*) and Kant.
45. I capitalize Law in order to emphasize its status in my arguments as the principle of imposing constraint upon the subject rather than as a particular set of juridical codes; obviously, though, Law-as-the-idea-of-constraint subsumes its own more concrete articulations in particular statutes.
46. Frier 1985, esp. xi–xvi, 185–96.
47. A premise principally elaborated in SVII, esp. 197–209/167–78 ("Tout exercice de la jouissance comporte quelque chose qui s'inscrit au Livre de la dette dans la Loi," 208).
48. On Cynthia as conqueror, note the references to her initial furious burst through his doors as being "no less astonishing a sight than when a city is captured" ("spectaclum capta nec minus urbe fuit," 4.8.56); her rejoicing in the "spoils" ("exuviis") she tears from Phyllis and Teia (63); Propertius' description of himself as a "captive" ("captus eram," 70); his begging for a "treaty" ("foedera," 71) and her imperiously dictating (and his accepting) "terms" ("formula legis," 74; "'legibus utar,'" 81); her rejoicing in the "command" yielded her ("imperio . . . dato," 82).
49. Freedom of will is a central problem for ancient philosophy, with which Aristotle, Epicurus, Carneades, and the Stoics wrestled. For Aristotle, see Irwin 1980; for Epicurus (and Aristotle as a witness to his thought) see Englert 1987 and Long 1986, 56–61; for Carneades and the Stoics, see Long 1986, 101–104, 167–68.
50. Ronald Syme sums up succinctly the Roman emphasis on freedom (*libertas*)—as well as the cynical uses to which this catchphrase was put in both Republic and Empire (Syme 1939, 154–56).
51. Lacan 1998, 69. (The French reads: "C'est une façon tout à fait raffinée de suppléer à l'absence de rapport sexuel, en feignant que c'est nous qui y mettons obstacle," Lacan 1975, 65.)
52. "Sexuation" is Lacan's coinage, and means "the assumption of the position of Man or Woman *solely as a relation to a signifier* (i.e., to the phallus)"—which is, according to Lacan, the only way the subject *can* assume either gender position.
53. Commentaries on Books II and III succeeded the initial two efforts in 1966.
54. Camps 1965, v.
55. Nethercut 1983, 1850–52.
56. Nethercut 1983, 1852.
57. Not that Acanthis confines herself entirely to criticism of Book I, but that that book is paradigmatic of the "bad faith" she finds at the heart of Propertius' elegiac doctrine. Laura Celentano, for example, has noticed that Acanthis implicitly taxes Propertius with not extrapolating the logical consequences of his own precepts: the *lena*'s observations on the ephemerality of the roses at Paestum echoes the vivid image of dying rose petals that summarizes mortality in 2.15.51–54. Propertius concludes from this that lovers should make love while they can; Acanthis sees that while dalliance with a poor man may make youth interesting, it will do nothing to provide for her charge's comfortable old age (Celentano 1956, 56–57).
58. Many scholars have accepted and expanded upon Propertius' invitation, implied in Acanthis' skepticism, to reread his work with an alertness to questions of gender, and none more so than feminist classicists. Recently, Maria Wyke has supplied an excellent overview and genealogy of feminist work on Propertius that has appeared within the last three decades

(Wyke 1994). She traces an "optimistic" view of Propertius as de facto feminist to Judith Hallett's provocative article that appeared in *Arethusa* more than 25 years ago (Hallett 1973; however, since Hallett's observations on Propertius in *Arethusa* drew heavily upon her Harvard dissertation [Hallett 1971], her views on Propertius were even more precocious than the article's publication date makes apparent). According to Hallett, the Roman elegists in general, and Propertius in particular, embody a "counter-cultural feminism" insofar as they assume traditionally feminine roles of subservience, faithfulness, and deference to a masterful (and correspondingly "mannish") elegiac mistress (*domina*). By flouting conventional gender roles, the elegists reveal these roles to be nothing more than convention, not rooted in any stratum of "nature" or "right."

About two decades later, Barbara Gold redevelops Hallett's idea of elegy crossing gender boundaries in the context of Alice Jardine's "gynesis," paying strict attention to the way that Woman is produced as a sign. Gynesis names a methodology through which Jardine sought a way to analyze texts that combined the idea of Woman as a process that disrupts symbolic structures with attention to ethics, practice, and sexual identity; building upon this concept, Gold argues that the Propertian corpus consistently puts into play the concepts of Woman and the feminine as problematic, and consequently opens up a space in which one can question anew the representations of women in these texts (Gold 1993a). Wyke herself has brought into feminist discussions of Propertius the idea that the beloved girl (*puella*) of elegiac poetry is discursively produced and symbolizes specifically the act of writing itself. That allegorical reading of the *puella* has its roots in non-feminist criticism of the early seventies, such as Steele Commager's *Prolegomenon to Propertius* (Commager 1974, 3–12, 21–24), although it has proven useful to feminists who wish to emphasize the gap between representations of women in elegiac poetry and the historical lives of actual Roman women (Kathleen McNamee, for example, attacks the problem of the Monobiblos' inconsistent representations of Cynthia by exhaustively analyzing them as symbols for writing [McNamee 1993]). Such emphasis is necessary because the "romantic" tendency to assimilate fiction to fact lives on, especially in the service of ferreting out a real woman's history behind the *puella* (Wyke cites the recent efforts of Oliver Lyne and Jasper Griffin as evidence; she could with justice have added Hans Peter Stahl's *Propertius,* wherein "Cynthia's" status as a married woman of noble rank actually named Hostia is firmly asserted [Stahl 1985, 28, 143–48]).

However, though Wyke's emphasis on the puella's discursive production aligns her with Gold's methodology, she is far from entertaining Gold's—or Hallett's—optimism as regards the first three books of the Propertian corpus. Rather, Wyke cites with approval the work of Paul Veyne and Duncan Kennedy, a "pessimistic" strand of Propertius analysis that, while not explicitly declaring itself feminist, holds interest for those who read from a feminist perspective (Veyne 1988, Kennedy 1993); Veyne and Kennedy see the dynamics of love elegy (Propertius' being no exception) as reducing the female beloved to a passive object. Much of Wyke's own work has also striven to elucidate the various ways in which the poet-narrator of the Propertian corpus exerts discursive mastery over the beloved (Wyke 1987b, 1989a, 1989b). Nonetheless, in passing from an analysis of Propertius Books I-III to Book IV's anomalous array of female speakers who seemingly wrest the narrative away from the male poet-narrator's exclusive control, Wyke moves away from a purely "pessimistic" viewpoint and towards agreement with Gold's and Hallett's optimism, albeit with some reservations (Wyke 1987a, 1994). She can say of Book IV both that "when the elegiac poet gives a point of view and a voice to female characters, he still exercises discursive mastery over them" and that "when Propertian elegy is engendered as female, when it 'plays the other,' the poet's prior self-representation as the male *ego* is opened up to question" (Wyke 1994, 123, 124).

My own work on Propertius, as represented in this book, has most in common with Gold's theoretical perspective; even though she works from Jardine's "gynesis," and I from a Lacanian perspective, we share the idea that Woman in elegy is constructed from signifying practices and has nothing necessarily to do with anatomy or historical women, that even the male poet-narrator may assume the position of Woman; both of us press the analysis of Woman-as-sign beyond reading Her as an allegory for writing elegiac verse. I hope to build upon Gold's insights into Propertius by applying in a principled fashion the Lacanian idea of Woman where it exceeds any reference to historical women, or anatomy or biology, and refers *tout simple* to the gaps in any logical system; analyzing the Propertian text will not then be limited to problematizing and questioning representations of women. Lacan's broad concept of Woman is crucially relevant to, say, the logical incompatibilities that prevent us from assimilating the Gallus poems of the Monobiblos either to one coherent Gallus or many Galluses (as I shall show in chapter 1), even though representations of elegiac *puellae* fade into the background in these elegies.

I also incline toward Gold's (and Hallett's) optimism. Although Wyke rightly draws attention to Acanthis' mocking quote from the Monobiblos, and reads it (as do I) as Propertius' implicit command to reevaluate his own earlier work with skepticism, I cannot agree with her that the entire first three books exemplify Propertius' exercise of "discursive mastery" over the elegiac puella. For one thing, I doubt that complete "discursive mastery" is possible. Lacan's persuasive development of the idea that every system has its point of logical breakdown—an idea upon which his conceptualizations of *jouissance*, Woman, and *objet a* center—undermines the premise that anyone can assume the position of Master with complete effectiveness, especially mastery of a signifying system. Even in theory, gaps and resistances would be expected in the most carefully premeditated stratagem of domination; in practice, I find more in Books I-III that disturbs and resists the dominant Roman ideology of gender than can easily be assimilated to the idea of the poet's "discursive mastery" (such as Cynthia's dramatic disruption of his fantasies about her in Prop. 1.3).

However, my differences with Wyke are more of degree than of kind. I agree with her reading of Propertius that sees him, in Book IV, questioning his own work, and elegy in general, along lines of interest to feminists; I simply do not consider this to be grounds for reading Books I-III as though they were devoid of such questioning.

CHAPTER TWO: "SHADOW OF A DOUBT"

1. Propertius only implies that Gallus is a rake in 1.5, by portraying him as used to having his way with women; Cynthia will be quite another kettle of fish, Propertius assures his friend. Elegy 13 confirms Gallus as an (ex-)philanderer: "dum tibi deceptis augetur fama puellis, / certus et in nullo quaeris amore moram"—"while your reputation increases because of the women you have deceived, and you are sure to seek no lingering in love" (5–6).

2. Stahl 1985, 111–12.

3. Cairns, for example, must ignore the subtle differences among the types of love in the poems (promiscuity versus enslavement versus the most tenuous of holds on the beloved) in order to pronounce Gallus a "successful lover" throughout, thus the same Gallus throughout

(Cairns 1983, 91–92). Fedeli reconciles the obvious differences as evidence of one Gallus' rising, then falling, fortunes in love, a trajectory designed by Propertius to culminate in "anticlimax" (Fedeli 1983, 1911). King argues, with considerable subtlety, for reading the entire series as an allegory: she analyzes the poems surrounding the Gallus elegies, as well as Vergil's tenth Eclogue and some poems of Callimachus, in order to trace a theme of poetic rivalry between Cornelius Gallus and Propertius represented as erotic rivalry (King 1980, esp. 219–30).

4. See discussion and bibliography in King 1980, esp. 212–13; Cairns 1983, 83–96.

5. Nicolas Heinsius (Heinsius 1742, 333) for example, believed that both poems were incomplete, while Friedrich Leo (Leo 1960, 169–78) restricted the unfortunate fragmentation to 1.22; E. Courtney, and R. I. V. Hodge and R. A. Buttimore, on the other hand, consider the last poems to be Propertian juvenilia that he was nonetheless unwilling to discard (Courtney 1968, 254; Hodge-Buttimore 1977, 10). Paolo Fedeli and Hans-Peter Stahl examine the problem, with useful discussion of previous bibliography (Fedeli 1983, 1914–19; Stahl 1985, 122–23).

6. For the purposes of this book, I accept as a working definition Clifford Geertz' definition of ideology as a shared cultural system for organizing values and inspiring action. "Whatever else ideologies may be . . . they are, most distinctively, maps of problematic social reality and matrices to the creation of collective conscience" (Geertz 1964, 64). I shall concentrate, however, on the subject's individual interest in this—on what is offered to her as an inducement to collectivity.

7. Cf. Wyke 1989b, 29.

8. For more on Cynthia's inconsistent portraiture in the Monobiblos and its relation to her portrayals in Book IV, see chapter 7 below.

9. Nigel Nicholson analyzes the Gallus portraits in the Monobiblos in a perceptive essay, arguing—as do I—that their simultaneous disjunctiveness and overlap are a calculated textual strategy (Nicholson 1999). His reading, however, differs from mine in concluding only that the poems urge upon their audience a semiotic rather than a mimetic mode of reading, one that would see that Gallus "exposes the agreement behind the mimetic reading that characters act and exist like real people, and reveals them instead as effects of the text, not existing prior to it." This is certainly a valuable insight, and I have benefited greatly from Nicholson's work, but it leaves aside the (to me) more interesting question, pursued in this chapter, of the ideology that makes a mimetic reading possible in the first place.

10. An identification first proposed by Franz Skutsch and revived by Luigi Alfonsi (Skutsch 1906, 144–46, Alfonsi 1943, 54–56). The latest advocates of this position are Commager 1974, 12n23; Sullivan 1976, 33n17; Ross 1975, 82–84; Thomas 1979, 203–205; King 1980; Cairns 1983, 83–96.

11. See, for example, Butler-Barber 1933, 163; Boucher 1965, 271; Hubbard 1974, 24; Richardson 1976, ad 1.7.1; Fedeli 1980, 138, 188–89.

12. See Butler–Barber 1933, 162; Stahl 1985, 83 and 329n10 (the latter usefully, if briefly, surveys the literature pertaining to the identification).

13. Cairns 1983.

14. Thomas 1979, 203–205.

15. Skutsch 1906, 144–45.

16. Benjamin 1965.

17. Zetzel 1977, 260. His remarks are specifically aimed at Ross 1975.

18. Even the scholars who originally published the newly discovered fragment are tactful but unenthusiastic. See the remarks of Parsons and Nisbet on the metrical peculiarities of

verses 2–5, the best-preserved section, and on the whole fragment's "austere diction and involuted style" (Anderson–Parsons–Nisbet 1979, 141–43, 148–49). The evaluations of other scholars have ranged from scornful to apologetic: Giuseppe Giangrande waspishly pronounces them "singularly ugly"—so much so that he declines to believe that they can be by the Gallus held in such high esteem by Vergil and Propertius (Giangrande 1980, 152). Among the many who do not doubt their authenticity, the highest praise they seem capable of mustering for the verses is that they are "competent"; the oddest, that they are deliberately bad—Janet Fairweather assumes that Gallus mimes the loser in an amoebaic song contest. See Barchiesi 1980–1981, 164–65; Verducci 1984, 119–21; Fairweather 1984; Merriam 1990, 447, 452.

19. Zetzel 1977, 259. Zetzel demonstrates this with particular forcefulness in Propertius' case, by pointing out that his echoes of Gallus' poetry—if they are echoes—contain refinements of detail available only from the *Eclogues*. See his analysis of Propertius 3.3 (Zetzel 1977, 258).

20. As Franz Skutsch first noted (Skutsch 1901, 13).

21. All citations from Vergil are, unless otherwise noted, from Mynors 1969.

22. Noted by King 1980, 222.

23. Thus far Ross, who draws upon Tränkle's analysis of the style change (Tränkle 1960); he strengthens Tränkle's argument by analyzing the additional situational correspondences mentioned and explains their appearance in Vergil and Propertius as stemming from a common source in Gallus' poetry (Ross 1975, 61–68). Zetzel cautiously agrees: "That the archaic language of the Milanion exemplum points to a Gallan model had already been suggested by Tränkle, and the analyses of both Tränkle and Ross seem to me to demonstrate that as conclusively as the nature of the evidence permits" (Zetzel 1977, 253).

24. King 1980, 221–22.

25. The passage from Servius and Servius Auctus runs as follows; I have put in italics what belongs to Servius Auctus.

72. GRYNEI NEMORIS DICATUR ORIGO Gryneum nemus est in finibus Ioniis, Apollini *A Gryno filio consecratum: vel a Grynio, Moesiae civitate, ubi est locus arboribus multis iucundus, gramine floribusque variis omni tempore vestitus, abundans etiam fontibus. quae civitas nomen accepit a Gryno, Eurypyli filio, qui regnavit in Moesia, qui adversus Troianos Graecis auxilium tulit: Eurypylus namque filius Telephi, Herculis et Auges filii, ex Astyoche, Laomedontis filia, fuit, qui Grynum procreavit. is cum patris occupasset imperium et bello a finitimis temptaretur, Pergamum, Neoptolemi et Andromaches filium, ad auxilium de Epiro provocavit: a quo defensus, victor duas urbes condidit, unam Pergamum de nomine Pergami, alteram Grynium ex responso Apollonis. in hoc nemore Calchantem vites serentem quidam augur vicinus praeteriens dixit errare: non enim fas esse novum vinum inde gustare. at is opere absoluto vindemiaque facta cum ad cenam vicinos eumque ipsum augurem invitasset, protulit vinum, et cum diis libare in focum vellet, dixit se non solum poturum, sed etiam diis daturum et convivis; cui ille eadem, quae ante, respondit. ob hoc deridens eum Calchas adeo ridere coepit, ut repente intercluso spiritu poculum abiceret. Varro ait, vincla detrahi solita, id est compedes catenasque et alia, qui intrarunt in Apollinis Grynei lucum et fixa arboribus.* in quo luco aliquando Calchas et Mopsus dicuntur de peritia divinandi inter se habuisse certamen; et cum de pomorum arboris cuiusdam contenderent numero, stetit gloria Mopso: cuius rei dolore Calchas interiit. hoc autem Euphorionis continent carmina, quae Gallus transtulit in sermonem latinum: unde est illud in fine, ubi Gallus loquitur, <X 50> ibo et Chalcidico quae sunt mihi condita versu carmina: nam Chalcis civitas est Euboeae, de qua fureat Euphorion.

26. Ross 1975, 79–80. Even Zetzel, Ross' most stringent critic, admires the deduction as "brilliant" (Zetzel 1977, 253).

27. Unless we could discern in Martial 11.6.9–16 a veiled reference to the Juventius poems:

misce dimidios, puer, trientes,
quales Pythagoras dabat Neroni,
misce, Dindyme, sed frequentiores;
possum nil ego sobrius; bibenti
succurrent mihi quindecim poetae.
da nunc basia, sed Catulliana:
quae si tot fuerint, quot ille dixit,
donabo tibi passerem Catulli.

Passer has been interpreted by some scholars (beginning with Politian) as obscene slang for the penis, which would make Martial's offer a pederastic proposition (Politian 1489, cap. vi; Genovese 1974, 122; Giangrande 1975, 137; Nadeau 1980, 880; Hooper 1985, 168–70). However, this gloss of *passer* is controversial (see Jocelyn 1980, 422–25)—and in any case, Martial models his request upon the phrasing of Catullus c.5, which demands kisses from Lesbia using the imperative mood. C.48 (addressed to Juventius) rather more mildly fantasizes an orgy of kissing (in a future-less-vivid conditional sentence). The inference that Martial 11 depended, at least in part, on the audience's recognizing a reference to Catullus' Juventius poems would depend upon 11's pederastic context.

28. Tränkle 1960, 23. Ross and Cairns follow suit (Ross 1975, 68n3, 83, 95n3; Cairns 1983, 85).

29. See especially the wording of *Ecl.* 10.28–29, with its similar rhetorical strategies of statement *a contrario* and personification.

30. See Kunihara's survey of previous opinion and his argument in favor of the sister as the speaker's beloved (Kunihara 1974, 240)—though I have reservations about his conclusion that the sister is Propertius' own mother.

31. A twist of fate brought Cornelius Gallus even closer to the disasters pinned to his name by both his Augustan portraitists: as Joy King points out, the historical Gallus became a victim of *insanus amor duri . . . Martis* just as did the Gallus of Vergil's tenth *Eclogue* (King 1980, 229–30). His suicide after his fall from Octavian's grace also brings him closer to his Propertian namesake from Perusia: Octavian's honored friend became Octavian's enemy, at least in the *princeps'* own eyes. Though both the *Eclogues* and the Monobiblos predate Cornelius Gallus' fall, Propertius, at least, may have welcomed this windfall of irony. In any case, Cornelius Gallus' fate must have influenced the reading of the Monobiblos poems shortly after its publication—a reading further prompted by the fact that the name "Gallus," so prominent in Propertius' first book, is mentioned only twice, and that but in passing, in the subsequent three books.

32. Hans-Peter Stahl (Stahl 1985, 3–129) best exemplifies this line of argument and provides, in addition, a useful guide to previous scholars' attempts to trace such a tension in the Monobiblos.

33. This is only one view presented in the dialogue, to be sure, and it receives ample scorn from Socrates; however, as Martha Nussbaum has shown, the dialogue's final speech, from Alcibiades, strongly supports Aristophanes' view while it undermines Socrates' disdain for the erotic specificity implied in seeking one's "other half" ("The Speech of Alcibiades: A Reading of the *Symposium*," in Nussbaum 1986, 165–99).

34. Cf., e.g., 2.1; 2.34, esp. 93–4; 4.7.77–78.
35.

> laus in amore mori: laus altera, si datur uno
> posse frui: fruar o solus amore meo!
> (2.1.47–48)

36. 2.13.39–42; 2.20.17–18; 2.28.39–42. The Platonic lovers' mutually entwined fates even informs (parodically?) Propertius' grimmest ideas of how he and his mistress will attain and spend eternity: cf., e.g., 2.8.21–28 (murder-suicide); 4.7.93–94 (grinding away at each other in the same funeral urn).

37. See Lacan's essay "The Subversion of the Subject and the Dialectic of Desire" (Lacan 1977b, 292–325) and Slavoj Žižek's lucid discussion of it (Žižek 1989, 87–129).

38. Tibullus never credits his mistress Delia (whose name derives from Apollo of Delos) with inspiring him poetically, much less with being divine, despite her name; Nemesis, who reigns in his second book, appears demonic rather than divine. She inspires Tibullus to steal rather than write verses for her: she wants money, not poems (Ti. 2.4.13–26). Lycoris, Gallus' mistress—named for Apollo *Lykôreos* as King notes (King 1980, 226)—does seem capable of exacting improved verse from poets, as evidenced by *Eclogue* 10 ("pauca meo Gallo, sed quae legat ipsa Lycoris, / carmina sunt dicenda," *Ecl.* 10.2–3) and the Qaṣr Ibrîm fragment ("tandem fecerunt c[ar]mina Musae / quae possem domina digna mea," 6–7). Unfortunately, not enough is left of Gallus' poetry to tell whether either Vergil or the Egyptian fragment reflects a preoccupation with Lycoris as *divina puella*–Muse to match Propertius' artistic obsession with Cynthia. The definitive study of the *divina puella* motif remains Lieberg 1962.

39. Cf., e.g., elegies 3.1, 3.2, and 3.3: as a series, they argue that Propertius has achieved fame and Apollo's approval because he lauds Cynthia in amorous verses. On faithful love as virtuous discipline, see 2.1.47–48.

40. *Phaedrus* 246d3–253c1. The lover is "whole" in the pre-corporal state in the sense that he has not yet lost his soul's "wings," whose restoration *erôs* allows.

41. Ann Carson shrewdly notes that libidinal language surrounds Lysias' non-lover's speech eliciting sexual favors from a beautiful boy; the speech is the rhetorical showpiece that motivates the entire dialogue:

> Desire stirs Phaedrus when he gazes at the words of this text (epethumei, 228b) and visible joy animates him as he reads it aloud to Sokrates (234d). Phaedrus treats the text as if it were his paidika or beloved boy, Sokrates observes (236b), and uses it as a tool of seduction, to draw Sokrates beyond the city limits for an orgy of reading in the open countryside (230d-e; cf. 234d). The reading elicits from Sokrates an admission that he himself is a "lover of logos" (andri philologô, 236e; cf. tô logôn erastou, 228c). (Carson 1986, 123)

The *Phaedrus* thus paints rhetoric as an essentially erotic art.

42. Cf. *RG* 6.1: ". . . nullum magistratum contra morem maiorum delatum recepi"; *RG* 8.5: "Legibus novis me auctore latis multa exempla maiorum exolescentia iam ex nostro saeculo reduxi et ipse multarum rerum exempla imitanda posteris tradidi."

43. Propertius' near-contemporary Vergil expresses the intimate relationship between the political and the erotic clearly when he invokes Erato, Muse of Love(-poetry), in *Aeneid* 7.37–45; she is to preside over a narrative that designates Rome the master signifier of a providential history, in the face of the ever-accelerating human cost of this mission. As Michael Putnam

has pointed out in his analysis of the poem (Putnam 1985), Evander plays a part in this by allying his interests in defeating the Latins with Aeneas' interests, and sealing their pact by handing over his son Pallas to Aeneas' care. His gesture formally reproduces between his son and Aeneas the pederastic relationship that once bound himself to Aeneas' father, Anchises. The epic represents the relationship between Aeneas and Pallas consistently as one with erotic overtones, and in fact the epic's final gesture—Aeneas' dispatching Turnus in an accession of *furor* over Pallas' death—is motivated by possessive passion for the young boy (n.b. *meorum* in 12.747).

44. Oliensis 1997, 157–62.

45. The arch reference to bodies of water as dangerous to comely youths probably warns, allegorically, against the notoriously flirtatious Roman watering places (cf. Propertius' concerns for Cynthia, sojourning at Baiae, in 1.11).

46. See Žižek 1991a, esp. 99–140 ("Hegelian Llanguage").

47. For a thorough discussion of these land redistributions and their effect on the citizenry, see P. A. Brunt's analysis ("Land allotments in Italy in the first century B.C." in Brunt 1971, 294–344).

48. Louis Althusser, who devoted much of his intellectual energy to marrying Lacanian psychoanalysis to Marxist concepts, invented the term "interpellation" to crystallize Lacan's conceptualization of the social production of the subject. Althusser defines his coinage as follows:

> ideology "acts" or "functions" in such a way that it "recruits" subjects among the individuals (it recruits them all), or "transforms" the individuals into subjects (it transforms them all) by that very precise operation which I have called interpellation or hailing, and which can be imagined along the lines of the most common everyday police (or other) hailing: "Hey, you there!"
>
> Assuming that the theoretical scene I have imagined takes place in the street, the hailed individual will turn round. By this mere one-hundred-and-eighty-degree physical conversion, he becomes a *subject*. Why? Because he has recognized that the hail was "really" addressed to him, and that "it was *really him* who was hailed" . . .
>
> Naturally for the convenience and clarity of my little theoretical theatre I have had to present this in the form of a temporal succession. . . . But in reality these things happen without any succession. The existence of ideology and the hailing or interpellation of individuals as subjects are one and the same thing. (Althusser 1971, 174–75)

Tityrus' lands cry out for their master—and he returns *as* a master, having redeemed himself from slavery and gained a waiver that, together with his freedman status, now allows him legal possession of his land.

49. On the oddity of the way Tullus frames his questions, see, e.g., Putnam 1976, 94; Nethercut 1971a, esp. 412n3 and 1971b, 465n4; Stahl 1985, 99–102.

50. See Nicolet 1980, 17–47 (the chapter titled "*CIVITAS:* The Citizen and His City").

51. Consider, in this context, Cicero's concept of the "two fatherlands": the first is one's place of birth, described metaphorically as a parent by birth, and the second is Rome, one's "adoptive" parent (*Leg.* 2.25). According to the terms of his suggestive metaphor, the relationship with one's homeland is organic, as if to a biological parent; that with Rome, which subsumes the homeland relationship, is notional or abstract (Nicolet 1980, 44, discusses this passage).

52. The *adunata* ("impossibilities") passage (*Ecl.* 1.59–63) and Meliboeus' lament (*Ecl.* 1.64–72) are juxtaposed and similar in structure, to underline the unnaturalness and "impossibility" of allowing foreigners and strangers to possess a Roman's ancestral lands.

53. Cicero *Second Phillipic*, esp. *Phil.* 2.76 (dresses in Gallic costume), 2.58, 2.106 (travels around like an eastern potentate, with an entourage and in fashionably luxurious vehicles); 2.110 (plays the priest, in Hellenistic fashion, to a deified human being, the "divine" Julius). Suetonius records Octavian's accusation that Antony had behaved in a fashion unbefitting a "Roman citizen" because he treated Cleopatra as his wife by bestowing legacies on their children: "M. Antoni societatem semper dubiam et incertam reconciliationibusque variis male focilatam abrupit tandem, *et quo magis degenerasse eum a civili more approbaret*, testamentum, quod is Romae etiam de Cleopatra liberis inter heredes nuncupatis reliquerat, aperiundum recitandumque pro contione curavit" (*Aug.* 17). More generally, Catharine Edwards has shown that a persistent trend in Roman culture arrays vice and virtue on an imaginary geographical grid: practices regarded as vicious are traced to foreign origin and influence, while "virtue" belongs to native Roman practices (Edwards 1993, esp. 80, 100–103, 147–48, 157, 176–78, 186–87). The question "who is a Roman?" thereby becomes even more comprehensive and central, largely subsuming the question "who is the best human being?"

54. Thomas Habinek provocatively and incisively analyzes the struggle to answer the question "who is a Roman?" from a slightly different vantage point; he sees much of Latin literature as a progressive attempt to found Roman identity on the suppression of Italian identity (Habinek 1993, 88–102).

55. The term *novus homo* has two meanings in the late Republic, designating both the first man of a family to reach the Senate, and, in a special sense, the first to attain the consulate (the latter a much greater accomplishment that conferred *nobilitas* upon his family, and so the right to display ancestral deathmasks at their funerals).

56. See Syme 1939, 242–47; Keith Hopkins and Graham Burton have also analyzed the motives and effects of voluntary political withdrawal under the Emperors in greater detail, though with a specific focus on accession to the senate (Hopkins 1983, 120–200, esp. 120–23, 149–55, 166–98).

57. On Augustus' perceived power, see Fergus Millar, "State and Subject: The Impact of Monarchy" (Millar–Segal 1984, 37–60). On the larger question of Augustus' theoretical versus his actual power, and the exercise thereof: the essays collected by Fergus Millar and Erich Segal focus generally upon Augustus' symbolic and practical powers and show that these often exceeded his constitutional powers, following a line of thought eloquently and cogently argued in a variety of venues by Sir Ronald Syme (notably Syme 1939). At the other end of the spectrum of opinion on Augustus' power stands the recent collection by Kurt A. Raaflaub and Mark Toher, which dissents to varying degrees from Syme's portrait of Augustus as a virtual monarch, and seeks to represent him as more restrained by the observances of Roman republican government. Yet even from the heart of this "apologist" collection, Christian Meier's "C. Caesar Divi Filius and the Formation of the Alternative in Rome" does not hesitate to discuss Augustus' reign as a bona fide monarchy (Raaflaub–Toher 1990, 54–70).

58. Syme 1939, 233.

59. Millar 1984, esp. 53–54.

60. *Ecl.* 1.6–8, for example, allegorically expresses gratitude for Octavian's protection of Vergil from the full impact of the confiscations by referring to Octavian as a god whose gracious act deserves his beneficiary's worship: "O Meliboee, deus nobis haec otia fecit / namque erit ille mihi semper deus, illius aram / saepe tener nostris ab ovilibus imbuet agnus"; Horace imagines Octavian as Mercury having taken human shape and come to be the savior of Rome (*C.* 1.2.41–52).

61. Augustus' ill-fated attempts to secure among his own younger kinsmen a successor to himself as *princeps*—first choosing his nephew Marcellus, then his grandsons Gaius and Lucius—indicate a reconceptualization of Rome's supreme position of power along dynastic lines: "blood" took precedence over other considerations.

62. See Hegel 1942, 179–88 (esp. 181–86) and 287–89; Hegel 1976, vol. 8, p. 264 (*Jenenser Realphilosophie*). The entire *Jenenser Realphilosophie* has now been translated and copiously annotated, along with a lucid introductory essay, in Taminiaux 1984. See also Slavoj Žižek's analysis of Hegel's concept of monarchy (Žižek 1991a, 19–20, 81–85).

63. Žižek 1991a, 19–20, 83.

64. Sextus Tarquinius, the king's youngest son, pretends to have fled from his father's cruelty to Gabii, where he eventually brings the entire city under his father's domination (1.53–55).

65. Such as constructing the seats in the Circus and excavating the sewers (1.56.2).

66. Turnus Herdonius, for example, is accused of planning a violent *coup d'état*; weapons smuggled into his house without his knowledge and concealed there provide the "evidence" for his conviction and subsequent execution (1.50–51).

67. On the slogans, see Ogilvie 1965, ad 1.59.9.

68. As Stahl rightly points out, other "sealing poems" such as would inform our expectations for this poem also promise a story of one's life and origins as a *sphragis* to their books, but they ask a wider range of questions. He summarizes these as: "when born?" (under consuls x and y); "where?" (Sulmo); "which people?" (Paelignians); "place of residence while writing?" (Naples); "family?" (father a freedman). Horace *Ep.* 1.20.20–28, *C.* 3.30.10–14, Ovid *Am.* 3.15, and Vergil *G.* 4.559–66 fairly exemplify such *sphragis* poems. Putnam 1976 on Propertius 1.22 usefully cites bibliography on Greek examples of *sphragis* poems that inform expectations of the genre.

69. Accepting, as does Barber, "*sic*" at 1.22.6 (the reading of the *deteriores*) over O's *sit*.

70. "A Triumviris praepositus fuit ad exigenda pecunias ab his municipiis, quorum agri in Transpadana regione non dividebantur," Servius Auctus on *Ecl.* 6.64. For the details of this portion of Gallus' career, see Broughton 1952, 377–78.

71. Koenen–Thompson 1984, 131–42.

72. My thanks to Marilyn Skinner for drawing my attention to the importance of Cornelius Gallus' biography and its implications for the interpretation of Propertius' Gallus poems.

CHAPTER THREE: THE ETHICS OF EVIL

1. Merklin 1968; Dee 1974; Maltby 1981; Poliakoff 1987. Poliakoff and Maltby are essentially notes—skillful and illuminating, though brief—on a proposed interpretation of small sections of the text.

2. Thomas Benedikston is an exception, yet his subtle and discerning discussion focuses chiefly on the poem's modernist *Nachleben* in Robert Lowell's translation (Benedikston 1989, 135–42).

3. I leave aside the considerable literature devoted to speculation on whether Propertius or Ovid first invented the elegiac epistle as being irrelevant to my analysis of 4.3.

4. See, for example, Alfonsi 1945, 84; La Penna 1951, 83–84; Grimal 1952, 438–39; Celentano 1956, 55; Becker 1971, 469; La Penna 1977, 173–74; D'Anna 1986, 72.

5. Hubbard 1974, 144. Michael Poliakoff concurs: "that Arethusa is slightly muddle-headed is undeniable" (Poliakoff 1987, 94). Erich Reitzenstein is even more condescending: "Für die vielleicht großen Aufgaben und Pflichten des Mannes hat sie keinerlei Verständnis. Sie ist nur die verlassene, liebende Frau" (Reitzenstein 1936, 22). Hallett gives Arethusa better credit for resilience, noting that she has endured and managed a Roman household for many years with her husband absent, but even so describes her character as "young, innocent, and naïve" (Hallett 1971, 142).

6. Weeber's interpretation of the poem, also lengthy and detailed, falls more or less into the anti-militarism vein. He observes that "die Thematik der Elegie sich nicht besonders gut mit der Konzeption eines echt römisch-augusteischen virtus-Ideals vereinbaren läßt, wie es etwa Horaz in der zweiten Römerode entwirft," yet will not countenance the wholehearted antipathy that Hallett and Wyke see (Weeber 1977, 87).

7. Hallett 1971, 141–47; Wyke 1987a.

8. I thank Marilyn Skinner for bringing this line, and its implications for Arethusa's canniness, to my attention.

9. See, in addition to the passage from Hubbard quoted above, Rothstein 1966, 228–29; Hubbard 1974, 143–45; Dee 1974, 84–85, 93; Weeber 1977, 87 ("Nicht Logik, sondern Affekt ist das dominierende Prinzip dieses Gedichts"); Poliakoff 1987, 94.

10. The "learned girlfriend" is a stock figure in elegiac poetry, a woman accomplished enough not only to capture the poet-narrator's heart and fire his imagination, but sufficiently learned as to appreciate the verse she purportedly inspires (see Lilja 1978, 133–43). The *docta puella* is not typically portrayed as a legitimate wife in a loving marriage, however—a convention that sets Arethusa's learning slightly at odds with her marital status and her affection for her husband.

11. Augustus greatly tightened the restrictions governing senior officers' visits to their wives, permitting such leaves only during winter, the nadir of military activity (Suet. *DA* 27.1). On the law forbidding enlisted men to marry, see Treggiari 1991, 47, 64.

12. Butler and Barber 1933, ad 7 ("Propertius flatters Roman imperialism by anticipating exploits far beyond the point yet reached by Roman arms"); Richardson 1976, 429. The majority of other scholars, if not denying the catalogue's veracity altogether, take it *cum grano salis* (e.g., Camps 1965, ad 7–10; Poliakoff 1987, 93). Some, such as Dee, believe that the catalogue can be very loosely reconciled with Augustan military forays, if we allow for the "notoriously casual" attitude of poets toward geography (Dee 1974, 83). Dee cites no evidence to back up this contention, but Hallett observes that Augustus planned an invasion of Britain in 26–25 B.C.E. (though he never got that far) and that Prop. 2.10.15 associates Aelius Gallus' expedition to Arabia in 24 B.C.E. with India, so that "Indus" in 4.3.10 might metonymically point to that foray (Hallett 1971, 144–45). Yet, even if we accept readings that require such extraordinarily generous interpretations of the poem's terms, the import of that exaggeration for interpreting the elegy should not be overlooked.

13. K.-W. Weeber sees the parallel between Catullus 11 and Propertius 4.3, but does not develop its implications (Weeber 1977, 85n15).

14. Shackleton-Bailey discusses the reasons for adopting the emendation (Shackleton-Bailey 1956, ad loc.).

15. Cf. Janan 1994, 64.

16. I owe this observation to Marilyn Skinner.

17. Janan 1994, 65.

18. "It is perhaps a little suspicious that the activity attributed to Lycotas should be so systematically and widely distributed" (Camps 1965, ad 7–10).

19. "Krieg erzeugt Krieg," as Rothstein puts it (Rothstein 1966, ad 4.3.21).

20. On Arethusa as jealous, see Dee 1974, 86–87; on the supposed romantic motivation behind her imagining Lycotas as *puer,* see Camps 1965, ad 4.3.24, Richardson 1977, ad 4.3.23–24; Weeber 1977, 87.

21. According to Schmeisser 1972, *carbasus* makes up the Vestal Virgin Aemilia's robe, beneath which she miraculously rekindled Vesta's hearth (4.11.54), while *odoratus* describes Roman women's hair (3.14.28) and Bacchus' seductively smooth (*levis*) neck, dripping with "fragrant unguent" (3.17.31). The noun *odor* is associated with expensive perfumes required by desirable women (3.13.8) and perfumes bested by Cynthia's even more seductive fragrance (2.29.17).

22. E.g., in 2.15.17–18 and 3.21.8, Cynthia's clothing bars his lovemaking, but he manages (in the first case) to get rid of the obstacle over her playful objections; in the second case, she remains cold and clothed, to his torment. In 3.8.8, her tearing *his* clothing, though immediately motivated by jealousy, will still (in his eyes) be proof of love.

23. On lovemaking as "battle" worthy of epic treatment, cf. 2.1.12–13.

24. Edwards 1993, 20–22.

25. Cf. Sall. *Cat.* 9–10, Livy *Praef.* 8–12. See also the discussion of Roman concepts of virtue in Lind 1989 and 1992, and note the emphasis on self-denial and distinction in military prowess that runs throughout his exegesis of the terms (esp. of such canonical excellences as *virtus* and *fortitudo*).

26. Griffin 1986, 7–8.

27. Jameson 1988 (Jameson analyzes specifically Weber's *The Protestant Ethic and the Spirit of Capitalism*).

28. Žižek 1991a, 182–85. Lacan speaks most directly to the notion of *méconnaissance* in the origin and conceptualization of ethics in SVII, esp. 93–97/76–80.

29. Cicero *Catil.* 1.26–27; *Cael.* 12–13; Sallust *Cat.* 5.1–5. Paul Veyne observes that, by contrast, the Romans were rather more forgiving of "energetic laxity" when it succeeded in attaining authority: Scipio Africanus, Sulla, and Julius Caesar were rumored to combine public efficiency with contemptible private lives, and yet their careers garnered nothing like the execration heaped on poor failed Catiline (Veyne 1988, 161–62).

30. Edwards 1993, 19–20.

31. "Ad illa mihi pro se quisque acriter intendat animum, quae vita, qui mores fuerint, per quos *viros* quibusque artibus domi militiaeque et partum et auctum imperium sit" (Livy, *Praef.* 9).

32. On the women of the family spinning in Augustus' household, see Suetonius 64.2, 73; on the emperor's rumored debaucheries, see Suetonius 71.

33. On passages connecting *vir* and *virtus,* see Edwards 1993, 20 and 20n70.

34. Much as the women of Augustus' household bear the weight of establishing the congruence of that household with his announced design to return to the *mos maiorum* when they spin the *princeps'* clothing.

35. *SE* 13:1–162, esp. 140–61.

36. Žižek (Žižek 1991b, 23–24) draws upon and expands Lacan's observation—also made in discussing *Totem and Taboo*—that Law begins with a founding act of Crime (Lacan 1977a, 42–44).

37. Thomas Habinek assesses Ovid's exile poetry as demonstrating this same conundrum: his exilic poems (falsely) construct the place to which he was relegated, Tomis, as backward, barbarian, a geographical *and* cultural periphery to Rome, a portrait that reassures Rome of its centrality and civilization. Rome, and the Roman subject, thus paradoxically need Tomis (and "Barbary" generally) for self-definition (Habinek 1993, 151–69).

38. Žižek 1993, 58.

39. "This [passage in 4.3] is almost our only evidence that private individuals might be likely to have [maps]" (Richardson 1977, ad 37). For information on the making and use of maps in the Augustan period, see Dilke 1985, 39–54; 1987a, 1987b, 1987c; for mapmaking in the ancient world generally, see Dilke 1985, Harley–Woodward 1987.

40. Nicolet 1991, esp. 95–114.

41. In this respect, Arethusa's map echoes the climatic astrological doctrine that divided the world into a frigid northern, temperate middle, and torrid southern zone. The action of climate upon the inhabitants of these zones made the northerners brave but witless and the southerners crafty but cowardly. The temperate zone constituted the perfect balance of a climate conducive to brains and bravery; Romans and those friendly to Roman interests found it convenient to equate this zone with Italy. The notion first appeared in Hippocrates' *On Climates, Waters, and Places,* but won over even so rational a mind as Aristotle's (*Politics* 1327b19–36). See Walbank 1972, 156–57; Thompson 1989, 100–104.

42. Though rarely acknowledged openly in "official" accounts (such as the *Res Gestae*) a number of areas within and without the empire were similarly refractory to Roman control—Britain being an obvious example. Cf. Nicolet 1991, 128.

43. Dee 1974, 88.

44. Richardson 1977 ad loc.

45. Examples of *doctus* as "sophisticated, recherché": "librorum tuos, docte Menandre sales," 3.21.28. Also, "docta puella/doctae puellae" occurs in a number of places—2.11.6; 2.13.11; 1.7.11—all in contexts that show a woman has to be "docta" to appreciate the subtleties of Propertius' verse. "Docti . . . Calvi" appears in a list of the canonical forerunners of erotic verse, the very Calvus to whom Catullus addresses that undecidable poem 50, a poem that suggests both "real" homoeroticism and spoof—thus positing an unanswerable riddle to the reader, the essence of learned irony expressed by *doctus*. True that in other contexts in Propertius *doctus* obviously means "learned" or "knowing how to." Yet this sense would be odd or otiose when describing a god—why, as a god, would he have to learn anything, or why would we have to be told that he "knew how to do" what he did?

46. For a discussion of irony in the context of the influence of Callimachean aesthetics (a large factor in Propertius' poetry: cf., e.g., Pillinger 1969), see Janan 1994, 4–5, 44–45.

47. Nicolet 1991, 189–204.

CHAPTER FOUR: "BEYOND GOOD AND EVIL"

1. Zofia Gansiniec offers a useful conspectus both of the ancient evidence for, and previous scholarship on, the legend of Tarpeia—though, rather surprisingly, she dismisses Propertius' version from consideration in a contemptuous footnote (Gansiniec 1949, 22n53).

2. E.g., Alfonsi 1945, 78 (with some caution: he attributes to all of Propertius' work, including Book IV, the same reservations about the Augustan program that the *Aeneid* reveals

to have haunted Vergil); Grimal 1951; Grimal 1952, 315–18; Boucher 1965, 148 (who in fact sees the whole of Book IV as the flowering of a patriotism that he argues was always present, though more muted, in Propertius' verse); Weeber 1977, 101–102.

3. E.g., Paratore 1936, 130; R. J. Baker 1968, 342–44; Hallett 1971, 115–21 (with some reservations: Hallett argues that Propertius despises Tarpeia's actual betrayal of Rome and her "materialistic beliefs" that lead her to try to win Tatius with the gift of the city rather than herself); Sullivan 1976, 136–37; La Penna 1977, 87; Sullivan 1984, 31; Stahl 1985, 279–305.

4. Duncan Kennedy's work makes the very assumptions behind the conceptual division "pro-" versus "anti-Augustan" seem appallingly naïve. Assessing whether a given text supports, opposes, or is neutral towards Augustus involves us in logical contradiction: "a situation deemed historically determined is studied in accordance with terms and criteria thought not to be so determined" (Kennedy 1992, 26). Take, for example, his analysis of Ovid's flippant agnosticism: "expedit esse deos et, ut expedit, esse putemus" (*Ars* 1.637) is usually taken as ironic and "anti-Augustan" insofar as it interprets moral crusades as a cynical form of social control.

> However, Ovid's statement, although rhetorically resisting its own implication in this logic of explanation, cannot be exempted from its effects, for Ovid's ironic and flippant appropriation is part of what gives this logic its social meaning and force, and so helps to render legitimate the moral and religious programme of Augustus. This is the discursive context which both enables the *Ars Amatoria* as witty and sophisticated text *and* constitutes it at the same time as what-must-be-repressed. This is the logic that helps to generate the "necessity" of an "Augustus," and thus plays an integral part in creating and sustaining the position of Augustus (Kennedy 1992, 45).

Kennedy does not claim to be able to avoid the dilemma he has so well elucidated; language functions pragmatically on the basis of binary oppositions, an inescapable impasse. He does, however, put the key dyads that have long governed the analysis of "Augustan" poetry into question as a tactical maneuver designed to defamiliarize seemingly "well-known" territory. I, too, aware that the shifty properties of binaries cannot be evaded, nonetheless hope to raise questions in this chapter either never posed, or posed with insufficient force, about Propertius' text.

5. I do not wish to pass over lightly the split between Irigaray and Lacan that resulted in her expulsion from the *École freudienne* in 1974. However, the only difference between them that is relevant to the present discussion is that she elaborated the possible conceptual content of the feminine as a category of thought, while his last seminars largely abandoned the project in favor of articulating the exact relationship between the registers of the Real, the Symbolic, and the Imaginary. Her meditations are an original extension of Lacan's thought on the feminine, compatible with its principles, and at the same time a brilliant innovation on its fundamental assumptions. Margaret Whitford incorporates, in her discussion of Irigaray's thought, an evenhanded assessment of its debt to Lacan (Whitford 1991).

6. For a discussion of the ancient manifestation of conceptual chaos associated with Woman, see Lovibond 1994 on the Pythagorean table of opposites. I also discuss the Pythagorean table's implications for gender conceptualization at greater length below.

7. Baehrens 1880, Postgate 1894 (as indicated by their texts and *apparatus critici*; both rearrange the relevant lines, while Postgate prints "exili" for "ex illo" in 4.4.14); Rothstein 1966, ad 4.4.15; Richardson 1977, ad 4.4.15; Marr 1970, 167–69; Walsh 1983, 75.

8. So Enk 1911, 311–12 (*montem* for *fontem* in 7, after Heinsius); Richmond 1928 (*furtim* rather than *fontem* in 15); Camps 1965 (*contra* for *fontem* in 7).

9. For example, Wellesley 1969, 97–98 (following Karsten 1915) makes the barricade three-sided, leaving one approach open; similarly, Hanslik 1962, 237–39, declares that "praecingit" (7) means "bordered," so that Tatius does not fully enclose the *fons*.

10. E.g., Butler–Barber 1933, 344–45.

11. Rutledge 1964, 70–71; Warden 1978, 177–78; Brenk 1979.

12. On fire or heat as metaphors for love, see Nisbet–Hubbard 1970, ad Horace *Odes* 1.19.5, 1.33.6, Onians 1951, 151–52.

13. Lloyd 1984, 3. For more on the Pythagorean table of opposites, see chapter 1 ("Citizens and Lovers").

14. Here and in the previous paragraph, I have summarized the ideas of Irigaray 1985, 106–18, but Irigaray 1991 takes up these thoughts again and expands on them. The best guide to Irigaray's thought on these and other matters remains Whitford 1991.

15. Joshel 1992, 117–21; Edwards 1993, 173–75. Support for the idea that greater liquidity, weakness, deviance, and propensity for irrationality characterized the feminine was also available to Romans from a "scientific" quarter, i.e., from medicine. Heinrich von Staden and Monica Green have both demonstrated, for example, that Celsus (writing in the first quarter of the first century C.E., under Tiberius) inherits the prevalent Greek conceptualization of women attested throughout the Hippocratic corpus' gynecological writings: women are wetter than men, and their health (including their mental health) depends upon the proper management of their bodily fluids (Staden 1991; Green 1985). The overabundance or improper situation of women's bodily fluids—particularly menstrual blood—may result in delirium. Though Celsus was no slave to Greek medical ideas, he does bring into Roman discourse a muted version of the Greek view of female physiology as damp chaos. For an overview of Greek gynecological beliefs, see King 1983, Hanson 1990 and 1992.

16. On truth as solid and stable, see, e.g., *Tusc.* 2.21.48 (the part of the soul devoid of reason is *mollis*), 4 passim, esp. 4.5.10–6.11 (*placida quietaque constantia* characterizes the rational soul), 4.10.23 (by contrast, corrupt beliefs are like bad blood or an overflow of phlegm or bile); 4.13.31 (the essence of virtue is consistency of beliefs and judgments, firmness and stability [*firmitas, stabilitas*]). On truth as measurable, see, e.g. *Off.* 1.59 (ethical duty can be calculated, like a problem in accounting), 3 passim, (which focuses entirely on comparing two goods in order to distinguish the true from the apparent good—e.g. 3.3.11: measuring one good against another is like comparing weights in a balance scale).

17. *Tusc.* 2.18.43.

18. Carneades visited Rome in 155 B.C.E., about a century before Propertius' birth; however, Cicero features a précis of Carneades' addresses to the city in *De Republica*, finished in 51 B.C.E., which indicates that the philosopher's ideas were still matters of lively debate in Propertius' youth.

19. For Heraclitus' views on change, see the fragments collected and discussed by Kirk–Raven 1957 (esp. pages 196–202). Though assessing Heraclitus' cosmology on the basis of our scanty fragments is a matter of controversy, the ancients certainly believed that his views denied a stable substrate to phenomena: see Plato *Cra.* 401d, *Tht.* 160d, 179e–180b; Aristotle *de An.* 405a25, *Metaph.* 987a33, 1005b25. Indeed, Heraclitus' conviction that binary opposition is an illusion drives Aristotle to distraction: he returns repeatedly to this doctrine, trying to refute it (see *Top.* 159b30, *Ph.* 185b20, *Metaph.* 1010a13, 1012a24, 1012a34, 1062a32, 1063b25). See also Cherniss 1935, esp. 380–82; Kirk 1954 (who offers a bolder and—to my mind—more satisfying interpretation of the fragments than that found in Kirk–Raven 1957); Guthrie 1962, 435–69 (whose notes usefully summarize previous bibliography); Kahn 1979

is also a useful companion to the fragments (though I believe him mistaken in interpreting the crucial fr. D90 as a record of Heraclitus' belief in periodic cosmic conflagration). As for Carneades' views: Cicero, in *De Republica*, has "Philus" painstakingly summarize a speech Carneades is said to have made defending ethical relativism (*Rep.* 3.8–31). Although "Laelius" refutes the argument, it must have seemed a formidable threat to merit the considerable trouble Cicero takes both to redact and refute it.

20. Plut. *Rom.* 18.1.

21. Richardson construes the *limina* as indicating the temple of *Iuppiter Feretrius* (Richardson 1977, ad 4.4.1–2). But Propertius himself thinks of "Tarpeian" Jupiter as having no temple on the Capitoline at this time ("Tarpeiusque pater nuda de rupe tonabat," 4.1.7); he must, therefore, be thinking of *Iuppiter Capitolinus*.

22. W. A. Camps emends *nemus* to *lucus* outright (Camps 1965, 21 and ad 4.4.1); Shackleton-Bailey preserves the vulgate reading, but calls Krafffert's conjecture "tempting" (Shackleton-Bailey 1956, 234). Among those who take *nemus* in 4.1 to be identical with the *lucus* of 4.3: Butler–Barber 1933, 344; Wellesley 1969, 96; Marr 1970, 170–71; King 1990, 226.

23. Stahl remarks upon the conflict between martial and pastoral imagery (Stahl 1985, 281).

24. Among Propertius' near-contemporaries, Lucretius emphasizes this necessary intentionality when he intricately imbricates the physiology of perception and erotic love (*DRN* IV). Some objects impinge upon the sight willy-nilly, but perception of others requires active projection of the subject's will (4.805–17): desire and perception influence one another (4.1061–67, 1153–70). For an illuminating discussion of relations between perception and desire in Lucretius, see Nussbaum 1989; for a sophisticated application of ancient theories of the imbrication of vision and desire to Propertius 2.31/32, see Hubbard 1984.

25. On the jarring effect of this passage's mixing of pastoral with military imagery, that brings their assumed mutual exclusion into question, see the subtle analysis of Miller–Platter 1999.

26. Sissa 1990, esp. 127–77.

27. Sissa 1990, 127–29, discusses Tuccia's miracle as recorded in V. Max. 8.1.5 and D.H. 2.69.

28. Sissa 1990, 127–34, 162–63, 171–72.

29. Instances of this calumny are too numerous in classical literature to list here, but as representative examples consider: Catullus 70; Horace *Odes* 2.8 and Nisbet–Hubbard 1970's introductory note citing parallel examples of women forsworn in love; Propertius 2.16.47–48; Ovid *Amores* 3.3.

30. Konstan 1986, 198–201.

31. Joplin 1990, Joshel 1992, discussing *Ab Urbe Condita* 1.57–60, 3.44–48 (the story of Appius and Verginia receives further attention in chapter 9 of this book, because of its importance to understanding Prop. 4.11, the Cornelia elegy). Joplin 1991 analyzes the Tereus–Procne–Philomela story from Ovid's *Metamorphoses*, further illuminating the way Roman literature allegorically links women's body boundaries to the limits of the state.

32. Grimal 1951, 1952, 315–18.

33. Joseph Rykwert notes that a quasi-apotheosized Tarpeia, albeit a traitor of legendary stature, received state sacrifice at the opening of the Parentalia, the Roman feast of All Souls. Such dubious heroines regularly figure in foundation stories; Tarpeia is to be identified, Rykwert declares, as "the virgin at the sacred hearth [by whose] guilty or substitute intercourse with god or hero, as well as its punishment, a new city, a new alliance, a new nation, a new

state are founded" (Rykwert 1976, 160). Miles 1992 deftly uses Rykwert's observations to explicate Tarpeia's significance for the Roman conceptualization of marriage (183–84).

34. Lucia Beltrami and Pierre Grimal both see the similarity between the aim of Tarpeia's project and the Sabines', though neither expands upon the observation (Grimal 1952, 316n3; Beltrami 1989, 270–71).

35. The principal late Republican and Imperial accounts of the Sabine women's abduction all report legitimate marriage to Roman men as the outcome; cf. Cicero *Rep.* 2.7; D.H. 2.30–31; Livy 1.9.14–16, 13.1–5; Ovid *Fasti* 3.202–28. For an insightful analysis of the rape of the Sabines as represented in these and other ancient texts, see Miles 1992.

36. Noticed by King 1990, 239.

37. A tradition upon which Propertius himself regularly draws: cf. 3.14.13–14, 4.3.43–44 (Warden 1978, 179).

38. Warden 1978, 177–80; he points to Vergil (*Aen.* 4.300–301) and Propertius himself (3.8.14) as examples of Latin writers who compare women in erotic distress to Bacchants (Miller 1995, 227, aptly cites *Aen.* 7.385–405 as another instance).

39. Warden 1978, 182.

40. See MacNally 1978, 121–24; Lissarague 1990, esp. 62–64. Literary sources also echo this theme of the Bacchant as inviolate, even—or especially—when most vulnerable in sleep: see Plutarch *Moralia* ("Mulierum Virtutes") 249e-f.

41. Warden 1978, 179.

42. On the Amazons' worship of Ares and Artemis, see Bennett 1967, 30–72; duBois 1982, 34; Tyrrell 1984, 16, 55, 77, 86–87. The myths of the Amazons' divine attachments offers yet another curious parallel to the maenads: some accounts have it that the Amazons, too, followed the maenads' god as Dionysus' martial allies when he conquered the East (cf. D.S. 3.71.4); others that Dionysus was their enemy initially, but pardoned them when they became his suppliants (cf. Paus. 7.2.7–8, Tac. *Ann.* 3.61 and W. R. Halliday's discussion of Plut. *Quaest. Gr.* 56 [Halliday 1928, 210–11]).

43. Tyrrell 1984, esp. 40–63.

44. Various strands of the Amazons' myth indicate their hostility to men: they mutilate male children for slaves, or send them away to their fathers; they will have sex with men, but they steadfastly reject marriage; sometimes they are reported to refuse even cohabitation, choosing to live in a single-sex society. See duBois 1982, 34; Tyrrell 1984, 53–55.

45. For the Amazons' homelands as always at civilization's borders, see Tyrrell 1984, 56–58; for their propensity to be drawn into war with "civilized" peoples (such as the Greeks), see duBois 1982, 32–36.

46. Regarding the ambiguity of "permisit bracchia," see Richardson 1977, ad loc.

47. On Vesta as tutelary deity of the community, see Latte 1960, 108. To enable a breach in the walls that protect that community—in this case, Rome—abrogates her peculiar function.

48. On Vesta's flame as Trojan in origin, see Ovid *F.* 3.417–18, 6.365, 455–56. Aeneas, according to legend, was charged with conveying the goddess' fire from Troy to Rome (*Aen.* 2.296–97).

49. On Vesta's ambiguity, see Miller–Platter 1999, Miller 1995, 226.

50. Warden notes the peculiarity, but sees it only as a reference to the woman's Amazon associations: the Strymon bordered Thrace, a legendary haunt of the Amazons (Warden 1978, 177).

51. I follow Richardson's suggestion in my translation (who takes *per* to stand for *super*), but the puzzling phrase "per flavas . . . iubas" has provoked a wide range of interpretations.

Butler and Barber offer a fair summary of the possible readings (Butler–Barber 1933, ad loc.); I have not concerned myself to argue the case here, as the phrase's exact meaning does not impinge on my interpretation of the poem.

52. Her admiration for the shields curiously echoes another version of the Tarpeia legend in which she remains, despite appearances, loyal to Rome. She acted (so the story runs) as Rome's double agent, sending a message to Romulus that she would lead them into the city, and then demanding the Sabines' shields as her reward once she has them inside the city. However, the messenger betrays her to Tatius, and the Sabines crush her with their shields (L. Calpurnius Piso in his *Annales*, as recorded by Dion. Hal. 2.38–40).

53. Stahl 1985, 286.

54. Stahl 1985, 287.

55. "Instead of the simple, 'the horse that Tatius rides,' Tarpeia throws into sharp relief the enviable luck of the steed, which is tended by Tatius himself; a type of feeling that is familiar to ancient eroticism, as it is to modern" (Rothstein 1966, ad 4.4.37).

56. A bad faith familiar to antiquity: Lucretius, after Epicurus, expounds eloquently on desire's ability to create an object for itself (see above, note 24) and his conviction finds a distinct echo in Prop. 3.24, for example, when Propertius tells Cynthia that his poetry granted her the appearance it purported to record.

> mixtam te varia laudavi saepe figura,
>   ut, quod non esses, esse putaret amor;
> et color est totiens roseo collatus Eoo
>   cum tibi quaesitus candor in ore foret
> (3.24.5–8)

Note that in this passage, he does not contrast his verse's praise of her beauty with any real ugliness—"candor" is only another type of beauty; rather, he contrasts the projection of his desire onto her (seeing her with a rosy complexion, and with whatever other permutations "varia figura" implies) with her shaping of her appearance (she makes herself up to be pale, but he simply dismisses *her* cosmetic standards as if unworthy of aesthetic evaluation, saying simply: "what you were not, love thought you were"). I discuss this passage further in chapter 5.

57. On the Amazons as reversing the bride's traditional passivity in their liaisons—demanding, for example, that their husbands be the ones to bring a dowry, move where the Amazons feel most comfortable, and attend to all household tasks—see Tyrrell 1984, 41–43, 53–55, 66, 71, 77. On the ambiguity of *pactis*, and the way that it implies Tarpeia's marriage pact with Tatius, see Richardson 1977, ad 4.4.82.

58. Another famous crux: Butler–Barber and Shackleton-Bailey between them fairly summarize the problems and the solutions proffered to date (Butler–Barber 1933, ad 4.4.55; Shackleton-Bailey 1956, ad 4.4.53). I follow Butler's text and (in the main) his and Barber's interpretation; but the precise translation of this distich does not affect my argument.

59. Miller–Platter 1999.

60. *SE* 17:179–204.

61. "Ce que serait une syntaxe de féminin, ce n'est pas simple, ni aisé à dire, parce que dan cette «syntaxe» il n'y aurait plus ni sujet ni objet, le «un» n'y serait plus privilégié, il n'y aurait plus de sens propre, de nom propre, d'attributs «propres».... Cette «syntaxe» mettrait plutôt en jeu le proche, mais un si proche qu'il rendrait impossible toute discrimina-

tion d'identité, toute constitution d'appartenance, donc tout forme d'appropriation" (Irigaray 1985/1977, 134/132; ellipsis in original).

62. On consent as the logical fulcrum that divides rape from adultery, see Livy 1.58.9.

63. Despite the influence Roman women could, and undoubtedly did, exert over the marriages of their children, they had no legal right to do so. Moreover, as Emile Benveniste has shown, the very language of the marriage ceremony constructs men as its agents, women as its object: a father gives his daughter in marriage (*filiam dare in matrimonium*), a man leads someone's daughter in marriage (*alicuius filiam ducere in matrimonium*), but a woman enters into marriage (*ire in matrimonium*), as into a place constructed for her by someone else (Benveniste 1969, 1:239–44).

64. Nor can we seek comfort in an allegorical reading of a goddess fixing Tarpeia's determination, as we might if she were Venus rather than Vesta: Vesta does not traditionally personify passion.

65. Dido's affair with Aeneas is consistently referred to as a *culpa* in *Aeneid* 4 (cf. *Aen.* 4.19, 4.172), not only as a breach of faith with her former husband Sychaeus, but also implicitly as the beginning of all the trouble she brings upon herself and her city. Nonetheless, the affair was inspired in (forced upon?) Dido by two powerful gods, Venus and Cupid (*Aen.* 1.657–722).

66. Miller 1995 insightfully analyzes the Roman conceptualization of women as a potentially destructive, but necessary, force to be contained both literally (within the domestic space) and metaphorically (within the boundaries of decorum).

67. Butler–Barber 1933, ad 93–94, gives a fair summary of the possible interpretations of the vulgate reading of these lines, as well as some suggested emendations.

CHAPTER FIVE: THE RETURN OF THE DEAD

1. The chief discussions of 4.5 during the last few decades have been: Celentano 1956, 56–60; Tränkle 1960, 105–108, 175–78; Lefèvre 1966, 100–108; Hallett 1971, 158–63; Hallett 1973; Hubbard 1974, 136–42; Weeber 1977, 114–25; Puccioni 1979; Gutzwiller 1985; Fedeli 1987; Wyke 1987a, 165–67.

2. Judith Hallett notices the relation of these three poems based on the fact that they report "the words of a woman dead at the time that [the poet] was writing," but she finds the central focus of the three poems to be "the most important event in [Propertius'] life, his personal experience with Cynthia," not the return of the dead (Hallett 1971, 139–40).

3. Gutzwiller 1985.
4. Gutzwiller 1985, 105.
5. Weeber 1977, 114; Wyke 1987a, 165–66.
6. Butler and Barber hesitate to identify the mistress positively with Cynthia (Butler–Barber 1933, 350); Camps disposes of both problems, Acanthis' anomaly and the identity of the mistress, by declaring, without explanation, that "there is no ground for supposing that the *lena* is a real person; or that the *amica* of line 63 is Cynthia" (Camps 1965, 97).

7. Acanthis repeats the famous opening lines of 1.2 ("'Quid iuvat ornato procedere, vita, capillo / et tenuis Coa veste movere sinus?'"—"what avails it, my life, to appear in public with carefully dressed hair, and to create gauzy billows in Coan dress?" 4.5.55–56 = 1.2.1–2), judging them to be miserliness masquerading as simplicity. "Qui versus, Coae dederit nec munera vestis, / istius tibi sit surda sine arte lyra!" ("the one who gives you poetry instead

of Coan dress—let him be a broken lute to your ears!" 4.5.57–58) sums up her sober view of the matter.

8. Weeber lists the correspondences between Acanthis' hetaira-catechism and other poems of the corpus (Weeber 1977, 116–17).

9. Laura Celentano has also noted that Acanthis implicitly taxes Propertius with not extrapolating the logical consequences of his own precepts, though Celentano does not develop her thesis to the degree that Gutzwiller does. She observes, though, that the *lena*'s lament over the ephemerality of the roses at Paestum echoes the vivid image of dying rose petals that summarizes mortality in 2.15.51–44. Propertius concluded, in 2.15, that dying roses urge lovers to make love while they can; Acanthis sees that, while dalliance with a poor man may make youth interesting, it will do nothing to provide for her charge's comfortable old age (Celentano 1956, 56–57). In short, both Celentano and Gutzwiller conclude that Acanthis turns Propertian elegy against itself; the *lena* quotes the poet to demonstrate the "bad faith" she finds at the heart of elegiac doctrine.

10. Hermann Tränkle comments on the lover's rage, comparing this passage to its closest analogue, Ovid's sketch of the *lena* Dipsas (*Am.* 1.8.5–20): "aus allen diesen Beispielen [von 4.5] spüren wir den Ingrimm des Dichters über die Macht der lena, während bei Ovid nur scheues Staunen hier und dort anklingt, im übrigen aber der äusere Vorgang geschildert wird" (Tränkle 1960, 107).

11. *Aeneid* 4.487–91, Tibullus 1.2.43–52.

12. Cf. Hor. *Ep.* 5.

13. Gutzwiller 1985, 107.

14. See Gutzwiller 1985, esp. 108–109, 111–12.

15. A feature that has even struck Propertius' textual critics and informs their sober work of emendation. For example: emendations offered to the problematic distich 19–20 frequently work toward a comparison between Acanthis' speech and the effect of some persistent force (water, a mole) working its way through stone, the parallel resting upon the idea of wearing away resistance through slow but constant application. Also, Richardson urges the reading *sine aere* over *sine arte* in 58 guided by repetition: "though this is repetitious [after the twice-iterated *aurum* in 53], it is in character with Acanthis" (Richardson 1977, ad 58).

16. Cf. Richardson 1977, ad 4.5.45–46.

17. To name but one of several examples: 1.3.41–46 finds her waiting with Lucretia-like modesty and spousal devotion for Propertius' return from revelry. Cf. also her description of her own exemplary faithfulness in 4.7.51–54, and her residence among the Good Beauties of the Underworld (4.7.63–70; discussed more fully in chapter 6).

18. Fedeli 1987, 93–107, offers the most complete overview of the *lena*'s stereotypical traits in previous literature.

19. Cf. Weeber 1977, 116–17.

20. Some have doubted the authenticity of these lines, convinced by the many arguments of Ulrich Knoche that they must be an interpolation (Knoche 1936). However, Reitzenstein 1936, 94–108 cogently refutes Knoche's contentions.

21. "Ein Hetärenkatechismus, eingekleidet in die Form eines Nachrufes für eine vor kurzem verstorbene Kupplerin, die durch die schlimmen Lehren, die sie der Geliebten des Dichters gegeben hat, ihn unglücklich gemacht und sich seine bitteren Haß zugezogen hat" (Rothstein 1966, 260); "Propertius curses an old procuress named Acanthis, now dead, for thwarting his love by corrupting the mind of his mistress" (Butler–Barber 1933, 350); "Such is the retribution merited by an individual with Acanthis' values, proof of how debased the

attitudes which Propertius condemns in Rome's public policies are when applied to private affairs" (Hallett 1971, 163); "[Acanthis] made [Propertius'] life hell by urging his mistress, her pupil, to faithlessness and almost daily demands of presents and cash" (Richardson 1977, 441).

22. Cf., e.g., 1.8, 1.14, 2.1, 2.7, 2.14, 2.16, 3.5, 3.7, 3.11.

23. "Hippomanes" designates either a mucous secretion from mares in heat, or a fleshy growth on the forehead of a foal that its mother bites off; both substances are credited with aphrodisiac powers. See Shackleton-Bailey 1956 ad 4.5.17 and Fahz 1904, 134.

24. As Shackleton-Bailey points out (Shackleton-Bailey 1956, 241n2), Vergil provides the only exception that hints at possibly poisonous effects for hippomanes:

hic demum hippomanes vero quod nomine dicunt,
pastores, lentum destillat ab inguine virus,
hippomanes, quod saepe malae legere novercae,
miscueruntque herbas et non innoxia verba.

(*G.* 3.280–83)

25. On Cynthia's covetousness, cf. 1.8 (a praetor's fortune fails—just barely—to tempt Cynthia to Illyria); 2.16 (the same moneyed praetor now gains her favors); 2.24.11–14 (she riles him by asking for whatever exotic luxuries capture her eye in the marketplace).

26. The phrase is Malcolm Bowie's (Bowie 1991, 105).

27. Žižek 1993, 200–37, esp. 203.

28. Christopher Spelman has well analyzed the workings of *objet a* in 2.3, and my use of that poem depends upon his groundbreaking work (Spelman 1994).

29. Jacques-Alain Miller, "Extimité," unpublished lecture, Paris, November 27, 1985; quoted in Žižek 1993, 203. Žižek quotes from one of the lectures in the course on "Extimité" that Miller gave over the course of the academic year 1985–1986 in the Department of Psychoanalysis at the University of Paris VIII. The extremely condensed version of that course now translated into English (Miller 1988) does not contain the remarks quoted by Žižek.

30. *Écrits*, 691/286–87; SXI, 127/139.

31. SXI, 127–30/138–42.

32. On *jouissance* as non-meaning, see SXX, esp. the passages in which he sets *jouissance* at odds with significance, the suspect representation of Woman, and experience for which there is no account ("Il y a une jouissance à elle, à cette *elle* qui n'existe pas et ne signifie rien. Il y a une jouissance à elle dont peut-être elle-même ne sait rien, sinon qu'elle l'éprouve—ça, elle le sait. Elle le sait, bien sûr, quand ça arrive," 69/74; "Et de quoi jouit-elle [Sainte Thérèse]? Il est clair que le témoignage essentiel des mystiques, c'est justement de dire qu'ils l'éprouvent, mais qu'ils n'en savent rien," 70–71/76; "Là où ça parle, ça jouit, et ça sait rien," 95/104). Illuminating discussions of SXX's connections among *jouissance*, that which escapes significance, and non-knowledge may be found in Lee 1990, 171–99, and Copjec 1994, 201–36.

33. As a representative sample of poems that detail losing his love to a rival, consider: 1.8 (almost—Cynthia relents at the last moment), 2.9, 2.16, 4.8. Propertius only explicitly mentions his patrimony's partial confiscation late in his work (4.1b.126–30); however, his claims to poetic "poverty" as a foil to Cynthia's "greed" form a consistent thread throughout the corpus, especially as a combination that tempts his mistress toward a rival's riches (witness, e.g., 1.8, 2.16, 2.24, 3.5, 3.7, 3.13). As for poetic talent, Propertius generally sketches

himself (whether ironically or not) falling short of his more illustrious and ambitious epic predecessors and contemporaries, such as Ennius and Vergil (witness, e.g., 2.1, 2.34, 3.3, 3.9, 4.1). Elegy 3.3 constructs the comparison explicitly as an opportunity taken from him, albeit gently: Apollo and Calliope combine forces to redirect his ambition to follow in Ennius' footsteps and shepherd him back to erotic elegy.

34. Cf. Spelman 1994.

35. Tränkle's is still the definitive analysis of the elegy's breathtaking amalgam of styles and diction, but Giulio Puccioni offers some further refinements (though his overall assessment of the poem is unfavorable and, to my mind, quite unjust). See Tränkle 1960, 68, 81, 105–108, 110–14, 117, 123, 127, 129–32, 140–41, 175–78; Puccioni 1979, 614–23.

36. Propertius' picture has certain affinities with Lucretius' portrait of the world as it would be, were matter not made up of indestructible atoms: things could be destroyed by insubstantial forces, in the wink of an eye, without the relation of magnitude and appropriateness between cause and effect ordinarily observable in the world (*DRN* 1.215–24, 238–49). The powers imputed to Acanthis realize this absurd state of affairs in that Propertius alleges her magic to prevail against everything upright and solid, without exception or discrimination.

37. "The *object small a* designates precisely the endeavor to procure for the subject a positive support of his being beyond the signifying representation; by way of the fantasy relation to *a*, the [divided and decentered] subject ($) acquires an imaginary sense of his 'fullness of being,' of what he 'truly' is independently of what he is for others, i.e., notwithstanding his place in the intersubjective symbolic network" (Žižek 1993, 266n15).

38. Which is—as Maria Wyke points out—her central function in elegiac discourse: "The female is employed in the [elegiac] text only as a means to defining the male" (Wyke 1989b, 34).

39. Richardson 1976, ad 4.5.40; Camps 1965, ad 39–40. J. C. Yardley (Yardley 1976) argues convincingly that *lis* must be taken here as a quarrel, as against Camps' and Fedeli's (Fedeli 1965, ad 40) interpretation of the word as rough sexual play. Yardley does not, however, smooth the difficulty of linking *lis* to physical force.

40. *SE* 13:1–162, esp. 140–61.

41. Lacan had already articulated this point clearly in analyzing *Hamlet* during the course of SVI, "Desir et ses interpretations," the year before he addressed *Antigone* (Lacan 1981–1983, 30–31/1977a, 37–39), but he returned to and expanded his ideas in the later seminar (SVII 324–25, 329/278–79, 283).

42. Žižek 1991b, 23.

43. For the breaking of vessels as a rite to ensure the dead person's release from her or his earthly haunts, see Fedeli (1987), esp. 118–20. See also Lombardi Satriani–Meligrana 1982, esp. 172–75. On the broken-necked wine-jar as a useful object—worth making to order, in fact—see Cato, *Agr.* 88.1.

CHAPTER SIX: "THE BOOK OF REVELATION"

1. Although a terse couplet toward the end of the poem does show Apollo doffing his arms in favor of the cithara (4.7.69–70), the vast preponderance of the poem emphasizes Apollo's militancy.

2. Cf., e.g., the comically self-possessed Apollo's perching in a tree from which he delivers a mildly deflating, but hardly unfriendly, admonition to Propertius to abandon epic ambitions and stick to erotic elegy (3.3.13–24).

3. I owe the observation of this structural correspondence between 4.6 and 4.7, and its significance for the two poems, to Marilyn Skinner.

4. Cynthia describes herself as golden ("aurea Cynthia," 4.7.85), an epithet Apollo does not explicitly receive in 4.6; yet the poet envelops the god in a similar effulgence of fiery light ("nova flamma / luxit in obliquam ter sinuata facem," 4.6.29–30).

5. Even his one unsuccessful attempt at faithlessness, chronicled in elegy 4.8, he carefully constructs as a reaction to Cynthia's prior offense(s): she has deserted him for a rich fop (see chapter 7).

6. E.g., Lake 1937; Lefèvre 1966, 108–19.

7. Frances Muecke (Muecke 1974) finds in the surprising assertion of fidelity an index of Cynthia's own contradictory character. William Helmbold, P. J. Enk, Jean-Paul Boucher, and Karl Jäger all believe the statement to result either from Propertius' high-minded resolution to cover up Cynthia's lapses, or from wishful thinking (Helmbold 1949, 342; Enk 1957, 30; Boucher 1965, 95; Jäger 1967, 86). The second sphere of interpretation still burdens Cynthia with a dichotomy—the split between what she is, and what she "should" be—even though it shifts the immediate responsibility for the statement's contradiction from Cynthia's character to Propertius' (altruistic or delusional) prevarication.

8. Burck 1966, 417–18.

9. See, e.g., Grimal 1952, 446; Nethercut 1968, 461–64 (though he is anxious to grant 4.1 and 4.11 almost equal weight); Pillinger 1969, 190.

10. For a judiciously comprehensive review and evaluation of previous scholarship on 4.6, see Gurval 1995, 249–78.

11. Among those who see the poem as intentionally parodic are Sweet 1972, Johnson 1973, Connor 1978, and Gurval 1995, 249–78.

12. Witness the oddity of referring to Romulus as "Trojan Romulus" ("Teucro Quirino"); by thus referring to Romulus' Eastern heritage, Propertius blurs the distinction between Rome's founder and her Egyptian (thus stereotypically oriental and effeminate) enemies, as I shall discuss in greater detail in chapter 8.

13. Prop. 4.10 might seem, at first blush, to rival 4.6 as an embodiment of masculinist poetics. Elegy 4.10 undertakes an explanation of the unrelentingly martial cult of Jupiter Feretrius (including a speculative etymology of the god's cult name), depicting the three occasions on which a Roman general slew an enemy leader in single combat and was accordingly allowed to dedicate the "best spoils" (*spolia opima*, stripped from the defeated enemy commander) to Jupiter Feretrius in the god's temple. Describing the victories of Romulus over Acron of Caenina, Cossus over Tolumnius of Veii, and Claudius Marcellus over the Gaul Virdomarus, the elegy's patriotic tone, martial and nationalistic subject matter, and sole concentration on male achievement appear to press its claims as an instantiation of poetic masculinism. However, closer scrutiny reveals facets that cast doubt upon the very themes promoted, and that debar 4.10 from unquestioning self-assurance, which is 4.6's chief claim to masculinism. Take, for example, 4.10's terseness: the shortest poem in Book IV, it narrates each winning of the *spolia opima* more laconically than the last, a compression especially noticeable in the third episode. Although Propertius fleshes out Romulus' and Cossus' victories with eye-catching animadversions on the first Roman's tough, spare life (4.10.19–20) and the melancholy ruin into which Veii has fallen in Propertius' day (4.10.25–30), he concludes with a six-line perfunctory summation of Claudius' conquest, as though the subject ceased to hold interest even before the poem ended (cf. Richardson 1977, 476). In the concluding episode, only Virdomarus' description summons attention (4.10.40–43), chiefly

because it paints the Belgian commander as cliché barbarian, focusing on his outlandish striped breeches, his vast size, and boastfulness (cf. Weeber 1977, 213–14). Triumphing over such a clownish braggart subtly tarnishes Cossus' victory (just as, I shall argue in chapter 8, elegy 4.9's description of the cattle-thief Cacus—an admittedly more complex blend of triple-headed monster and effete shepherd—robs Hercules' victory of perfect lustre by making the Greek hero's poaching enemy seem implausible).

4.10's sad lines on Veii's contemporary decay as compared to its glorious past (25–30), when it could plausibly challenge Rome, work to similar effect; they bespeak sympathy with an ancient enemy of Rome at odds with a purely patriotic tone—especially where, as William Nethercut points out, they define Roman growth as brigandage ("necdum ultra Tiberim belli sonus, ultima praeda / Nomentum et captae iugera terna Corae," 25–26; Nethercut 1983, 1851). Moreover, the "then ... now" (*tum ... nunc*) structure of Veii's description echoes elegy 4.1's studied contrasts between ancient pastoral Rome and the glorious city of Propertius' day (Weeber 1977, 209). The structural similarity implies that Veii's vicissitudes of fortune can also be Rome's: even a city that now rules the known world may in future again see humble times.

Assuredly the Rome that Propertius knew was already diminished by the fact that it would not soon witness again the distinct military honor of the *spolia opima* awarded. In 29 B.C.E., Marcus Licinius Crassus killed Deldo, the king of the Bastarnae, in single combat, yet was denied the *spolia opima* on the grounds that since he derived his command from Augustus, he was not truly general in his own right and was therefore ineligible. The poem's subject matter cannot but bring to the reader's mind Augustus' jealous monopolizing of military glory, a pettiness that seconds the poem's implicitly gloomy imagination of Rome's history and future. Little wonder, then, that Propertius ends his poem in doubt when he etymologizes the cult name of the god to whom the *spolia opima* were dedicated: perhaps we call Jupiter "Feretrius," he says, because "helped by a sure omen, commander wounds [*ferit*] commander with his sword," or perhaps because "they bear [*ferebant*] these defeated arms upon their shoulders" to the god's temple. The two etymologies imply different views of the Roman victories commemorated in Jupiter's temple: the first underlines the conquests' status as divinely aided (*omine ... certo*, 4.10.45), the second preserves a diplomatic silence regarding heaven's supposed tutelage over Roman triumph. The poem's wavering between the two versions and their implied divergent *Weltanschauungen*, refusing to choose one over the other, aligns it with such examples of persistent "feminine" doubt as the Tarpeia elegy and the ambiguity as to which *vigilans* is the object of injustice in 4.4's closing lines (chapter 4).

The scant attention that scholarship has paid 4.10 ranges along a spectrum, from readings that see it as unproblematically patriotic in its ambitions to those that see it as bitterly anti-Roman; yet not even the most sanguine analysis argues that 4.10 even remotely rivals 4.6 in its realization of nationalistic tribute (the chief reflections on 4.10 within the last few decades poem are: Grimal 1952, 188–90; Burck 1966, 414–15; Nethercut 1968, 455–56; Becker 1971, 465–66; Hubbard 1974, 128–34; Weeber 1977, 203–16). In light of 4.10's details outlined above, both in themselves and in the way that they align 4.10 with the ambiguous "feminine" perspectives recorded elsewhere in Book IV, I consider elegy 4.10 too imbued with subtle self-interrogation to represent a masculinist poetics cleanly, and elegy 4.6 to stand alone as masculinism's purest representative within Book IV.

14. There are dissentient voices among the interpreters of 4.6, and these see more problematic details in the elegy than the "patriotic" interpretation will regularly allow (such as the fact that the poem ends on a note, not of martial triumph but of drunken bacchanalia,

more appropriate to erotic elegy than the supposedly "new" patriotic elegy that Propertius is forging). Yet even the most skeptical readings cannot entirely erase the significant presence of 4.6's patriotic trappings, even if they dismiss them as a mere superficies that covers over a more deeply ambivalent depth. 4.6 flaunts an array of pretensions at odds with the female-prominent and anti-martial elegiac ethos typical not only of Propertius' work, but of his fellow elegists', too (4.6 displays contempt for feminine dominance, for example, and revamps Apollo, the god of poetry, into an unambiguously, if temporarily, martial afflatus).

15. Elegy 4.5 cannot make the same claim to be an epicenter as can 4.7, because (1) its order with respect to 4.6 does not reproduce the pattern of assertion followed by direct riposte established in the programmatic opening poem, 4.1, where Horos scoffs at Propertius' quasi-epic, nationalistic program, (2) Acanthis—old, foul, sick, impoverished—hardly commands the numinous power that Cynthia's ghost does, even in the courtesan's post-mortem decrepitude, and so cannot constitute a worthy match to Apollo as the divine focus of elegy 4.6.

16. Of course, elegy is far from being the only conduit for stories of "good" and "bad" women, but the genre as a whole lavishes keen attention on developing exemplary histories of women at length, especially those drawn from myth—logically so, given that its declared subject matter is love, and chiefly the love of women. See Lilja 1978, 143–55.

17. See esp. the discussion of the imagery of rape in Cornelia's speech in chapter 9, "The Urns of the Danaids."

18. Cornelia's iron Hades in 4.11 condemns women to the extent that it can find no conceptual place for them, whereas Cynthia's Hades in 4.7 shows itself logically stymied in that it cannot seem to make good on its condemnations. Yet both the condemnation in 4.11, and the de facto suspended sentences of 4.7, rest upon *jouissance*, upon the same kernel of nonsense inherent in judging Woman upon an inadequate basis of thought.

19. In fact, as Theodore Papanghelis observes, Propertius suggests that, like a snake, she *secretes* her poisons: "arcanas tollat versuta *salivas*," 37 (Papanghelis 1987, 170).

20. See Allison 1984.

21. Cf., e.g., Antonio La Penna: "Ha giudicato duramente questa elegia Giosuè Carducci: «L'elegia di Properzio è indegna del bellissimo cominciamento»; vi si sente «un paganesimo vizioso» (vedi il commento alla canzone *Quando il soave mio fido conforto* nelle «*Rime di F. Petrarca*» commentate da G. Carducci e Severino Ferrari, Firenze, Sansoni, 1924—nuova tiratura—pag. 497). È facile vedere che il giudizio critico è stato traviato dal confronto fra l'elegia properziana e la canzone petrarchesca, di ispirazione diversissima. *Ma è giusta la notazione di una incongruenza estetica tra il motivo iniziale el altri motivi minori*" (La Penna 1951, 85n1; emphasis mine).

22. Serious: Postgate 1881, xxiv-xxvii; Butler–Barber 1933, xiv; Helmbold 1949; Enk 1957, 29–30; Hubbard 1974, 149–53; Lange 1979. Humorous: Lake 1937; Guillemin 1950, 189–91; Allison 1984.

23. E.g., Lefèvre 1966, 108–19; Muecke 1974; Papanghelis 1987, 145–98.

24. Margaret Hubbard observes that 4.7 takes place in "the Roman world of sordid and brutal actuality that by and large the poets prefer to neglect"; she does not, unfortunately, expand upon her observation (Hubbard 1974, 90). Jasper Griffin (Griffin 1985) makes it clear, in his careful tracing of the relationship between "real life" and poetry, that even in cases where the poets had (presumably) some knowledge of the facts, they were not averse to suppressing its more unpleasant elements (substituting an unintimidating *lena* for the more formidable *leno* ["pimp"], for example, though the latter was doubtless the more common custodian of a *meretrix* ["courtesan, prostitute"]).

David Konstan has elucidated a parallel instance of "voyeurism" in Greek poetry, when he discusses Herodas (Konstan 1994, 162–67). "The defining characteristic of Herodas' mimes would seem to be precisely the absence of male heads of household, or just those figures who define the social norms in official comedy" (163); with the exit of the "official," the mime adopts a style of realism, focusing on women and other marginal figures engaged in the humbler details of life. Herodas' representation of women, however, is misogynistic, portraying women of independent status as dissolute stereotypes, whereas (I argue) Prop. 4.7 undermines such an attitude by its attention to economic constraints on women.

25. Jasper Griffin (Griffin 1985, 203–208) has traced the lineaments of comedy's stock collocation of clever slaves, irregular women, indigent young men, and upstart freedmen in the typical themes of elegy; he also provides useful references to previous scholarly explorations of this thesis.

26. E.g., Allison 1984; Warden 1980, 35; Komp 1988, 69–80.

27. Parker 1989.

28. Gutzwiller 1985, 110.

29. There are exceptions, of course, to the general picture of women's economic dependence on their lovers: Cicero, for example, virtually equates Clodia Metelli's alleged love affairs with the behavior of a *meretrix* (*Pro Caelio* 35, 38, 47–50, 57), and yet any extra-marital attachment so wealthy a woman had could not have been motivated by a need for money. If Clodia was, as so often alleged, the model for Catullus' Lesbia, that may explain why his corpus never records a question of money arising between them. At the other end of the spectrum, sex with slaves would be the master's legal right and customary prerogative, for which no remuneration would be expected; Propertius' Ponticus falls in love with his own slave (Prop. 1.9), and perhaps so does Horace's Xanthias (*C.* 2.4; Horace does not specify whether Xanthias owned his beloved Phyllis). Xanthias has, nonetheless, tried to ply his mistress with gifts, to which she has shown herself nobly indifferent (Horace *C.* 2.4.17–20). Jasper Griffin discusses the delicate question of dissimulating economics in Roman representations of "love" affairs (Griffin 1985, 112–41).

30. Amy Richlin makes a similar point in discussing the clash between the distracting aesthetic felicities and the gruesome content of Ovid's depictions of rape in the *Metamorphoses* (Richlin 1992b, esp. 159).

31. Cf. Tibullus 1.5.59–70 (a rich rival steals away Delia's affections); 2.3, 2.4 (a wealthy rival captures all Nemesis' attention); Propertius 1.8 (a praetor's fortune fails—just barely—to tempt Cynthia to Illyria), 2.16 (the same moneyed praetor now gains her favors); Ovid *Amores* 3.8 (Corinna shuts him out in favor of a rich soldier). Kathryn Gutzwiller shrewdly notes that Ovid rather gives the game away: "Ovid, who is especially good at showing the soft underside of any argument, concedes in *Amores* 1.10.53–56 that his mistress still needs a *dives amator* ('wealthy lover') to support her in the proper style," so that she can supply her favors *gratis* to the poor poet (Gutzwiller 1985, 111).

32. Cf. Gutzwiller 1985, esp. 110–11. For a conspectus of the evidence on prostitution's economic realities and the literary prevarication thereof, see Griffin 1985, 112–41.

33. Papanghelis notes the anomaly, but attributes it to Propertius' indulgent affection for any dead beauty, a love that supposedly suspends the poet's judgment (Papanghelis 1987, 178–79). But Propertius does not just withhold judgment here, he makes history's assessment of these women as types of feminine vice or virtue a problem; he calls into question the standards by which they have been judged (as I shall show). That is a different, and much deeper, affair than merely turning a blind eye to the dead queens' faults, while conceding that they *are* faults.

34. Noted by Warden 1980, 41.
35. Warden's subtly acute observation (Warden 1980, 43).
36. Rothstein, Allison, Komp, and Dimundo, for example, blandly compare 4.7's Underworld to that of *Aeneas* 6 and Tibullus 1.3, ignoring the fact that both Vergil's and Tibullus' Hades are far more orderly and sensible affairs of judgment than Propertius' aspires to be. Rothstein in particular makes a brave attempt to tidy up Propertius' eschatological omissions by assuming, anterior and posterior to the glimpse of Hades' workings afforded by the poem, a Prussian efficiency in winnowing good from evil: "die Verteilung der Toten auf diese beiden Wohnsitze geschieht schon vor der Überfahrt (s. zu III 18, 31), und auf getrennten Wegen und in besonderen Schiffen werden die Seligen und die Verdammten an den Ort ihrer Bestimmung gebracht" (Rothstein 1966, ad 55; Allison 1980, 333–34; Komp 1988, 86; Dimundo 1990, ad 57–58). Warden and Papanghelis, by contrast, notice the anomalies—Warden's is a particularly acute elucidation—but both attribute them to sentiment, either for Cynthia in particular or feminine beauty in general, that sways Propertius from harsh logic (Warden 1980, 39–50; Papanghelis 1987, 170–85).
37. OLD, s.v. *caudex/codex*, definitions 1b and 2a.
38. Cf. e.g. 2.5.26; 2.30.39; 4.1.62. Lawrence Richardson, Jr., makes the point in his sensitive commentary on Cynthia's injunction (Richardson 1977, ad 4.7.80).
39. Noted by Warden 1980, 59.
40. Noted by Warden 1980, 46–47 ("why are they weeping? Their sufferings are over long ago, and need not pursue them into the underworld"); Papanghelis 1987, 183 ("they just gather and narrate on and on"). Warden, Allison, and Papanghelis all emphasize, too, that the heroines of Hades preserve eternally their posture and looks from life in death (Warden 1980, 43, calling attention to Andromeda's bruises; Allison 1980, 334; Papanghelis 1987, 181—"the Propertian ladies can do little else besides affecting the same posture for all eternity recounting in statuesque immobility the highlights of their earthly adventures").
41. Enk argues on the basis of these endlessly flowing tears that the line needs emendation; obviously I disagree (Enk 1911, 336). D. R. Shackleton Bailey (Shackleton Bailey 1956, 252–53) objects that Propertius' thoughts need not be as orderly as his critic's, but I think we should be sure we have thoroughly plumbed Propertius' import before we accuse him of woolly-mindedness.
42. On the East as the mirror-inversion of Rome, see Quint 1993, 21–31.

CHAPTER SEVEN: CYNTHIA RETURNS FROM LANUVIUM (4.8)

1. Cf. Butler–Barber 1933, xiv, 365; Rothstein 1966, 307–308; Lefèvre 1966, 119–20 (who, though he takes issue with the estimate of 4.8 as Propertius' *only* humorous poem, thinks it the poet's *most* humorous poem); Pasoli 1967, 39–40; Hallett 1971, 128–29; Currie 1973, 616 (quoting Butler and Barber with approval); Sullivan 1976, 152–58; La Penna 1977, 96–97; Dee 1978, 41.
2. Komp's book is itself the most useful general guide to previous scholarship on both poems 4.7 and 4.8; in the following pages, I shall confine myself to citing critical analyses only as they pertain to specific questions of interpretation.
3. Scholars do often assume—with reason—that Cynthia's shadow falls on Horos' cryptic reference to the one girl whom Propertius cannot conquer (4.1.140) and that Acanthis addresses her in 4.5; however, neither of these constitutes anything like 4.7's and 4.8's detailed portraits of Cynthia.

4. Warden lists various opinions on the juxtaposition of 4.7 and 4.8 (Warden 1980, 80–81 and notes); to his discussion one may add Celentano 1956, 35–36, Jäger 1967, 95–98, Hubbard 1974, 153; Weeber 1977, 264–65; Papanghelis 1987, 196–97; Wyke 1987a, 169.

5. Most notably of late, scholars have organized the elegies' shared details under the idea that 4.7 and 4.8 respectively parody Patroklos' ghostly visit to Achilles in *Iliad* 23 and Odysseus' routing of Penelope's suitors in *Odyssey* 22. See Evans 1971; Currie 1973; Muecke 1974; Hubbard 1974, 149–56; Dalzell 1980; Komp 1988, 59–68, 122–28, 212–25.

6. See Lake 1937; Dalzell 1980, 33.

7. Postgate 1881, lv.

8. Nethercut 1968 discusses briefly the major voices within the history of claims for Book IV's unity; Hutchinson 1984, 100–103 updates the survey. See also Burck 1966, 405–409 and Weeber 1977, 250–60, both of whom evenhandedly discuss the larger question of the book's arrangement.

9. Aelian supplies further details: the cave was in a grove near the grove of "Argive Hera," the food barley-bread; a mysterious current guided the blindfolded young women. Ants revealed the iniquity of any unchaste young woman by carrying the refused food to the upper air, but (unlike Propertius) Aelian does not imply necessarily that her life was forfeit, only that she would be punished "by law" (*NA* XI).

10. José Turpin notes the contradiction (Turpin 1973, 160).

11. Dee (Dee 1978, 42) assimilates the poem to the aetiological program of the book, but at the cost of weakening the sense of "sacra diesque canam et cognomina prisca locorum" (4.1.69) to mean the mere presentation of antiquarian material *tout court*. His comparison of 4.8 to elegies 4.4 (on Tarpeia) and 4.9 (on Hercules), on the basis of these poems' "mingling of antiquarian and erotic aspects," ignores the fact that the latter two elegies are complete aetiologies, tracing the origins of the *Mons Tarpeia*'s name and of the Ara Maxima; no such aetiology graces the Lanuvium excursus in 4.8.

12. Rothstein 1966, ad 4.8.3; Pasoli 1967, 40.

13. Camps 1965, 3; Richardson 1977, 414.

14. E.g., H. MacL. Currie, in discussing the poem's structure, attempts to make the poem fall neatly into three parts by assimilating the description of the ritual to the general category of "Cynthia's absence," which ignores the ritual's stated irrelevance to her absence (16) (Currie 1973, 616–17). Tränkle unhelpfully but forthrightly contents himself with remarking upon the excursus' irrelevance without attempting an explanation (Tränkle 1960, 179).

15. Turpin 1973, Noonan 1983, 46.

16. A suspicion made all the more plausible by the fact that *impurus* regularly means "morally foul" or "infamous"; the OLD cites no passage from classical Latin aside from Prop. 4.8.22 in which *impurus* means "physically dirty."

17. Regarding *concubitus*, Richardson comments: "[the word's] use here for *accubitio* or *accubitus* is in part to point out how tight they were squeezed together, in part comical anticipation" (Richardson 1977, ad 36). J. D. Noonan is the source of the interpretation of *impuros locos* cited: "Cynthia's choosing the crowded and trampled-on path also suggests a vulgar, used-up quality, or the opposite of that virtue possessed by Juno's maidens" (Noonan 1983, 46). Marion Komp notices the significance of *Venerem quaerente* (Komp 1988, 143). *Respondi* is interpreted sexually by Rothstein, (Rothstein 1966, ad 87), both *respondi* and *solvimus* by others, most recently Smyth, who expands on a suggestion of Passerat's (Smyth 1951, 78–79; cited with approval by Fedeli 1965, ad 88). Hot debate rages, however, over the interpretation of these last two examples of sexual innuendo. The battle is joined between schol-

arly daring and shocked modesty: Shackleton-Bailey, for example, finds the idea of sexual innuendo in these phrases scandalous (Shackleton-Bailey 1956, 258).

18. Žižek 1994, 127.
19. Copjec 1994, 201–36.
20. Copjec 1994, 204.
21. On the subject's division perceived as lack, see chapter 5's discussion (under ". . . and Desire") of the "theft of enjoyment."
22. Copjec 1994, 205, 226.
23. Richardson 1977, 3–4.
24. Richardson 1977, 462.
25. On Propertius' irritation with Cynthia's changefulness, see, e.g., 1.8, 2.9, 2.16, 2.17, 2.22b, 2.24b.
26. Dee 1978, 46; Rothstein and Fedeli had earlier commented on the signs of the *nepos'* effeminacy, though they drew no specific conclusions from these regarding his sexual habits or means of income (Rothstein 1966, Fedeli 1965, both ad 8.23).
27. On depilation as associated with aging pathics, see Richlin 1992a, 41.
28. My discussion of Lacan's conceptualization of sexuality is heavily indebted both to Žižek 1994, 137–64, and Copjec 1994, 201–36.
29. Quite aside from the contradictions that accrue to Cynthia, mentioned above, Propertius often involves himself in blatant illogic, as when he professes himself jealously suspicious not only of other men who might visit Cynthia's house, but of the painted portraits and even the names of men, of babes in arms, her mother, and her sister (2.6.9–12).

Or again, having made of his exclusive devotion to Cynthia a crown of thorns, in 2.22a he suddenly announces himself a catholic lover who has cut a wide swathe among the beauties of Rome. The theme of his "other women" returns in 2.23 and 24, but in a form now difficult to reconcile with 2.22a: he says he pursues common streetwalkers because (a) he has grown impatient with the difficulty of conducting an affair with a married woman and (b) his mistress is unfaithful and greedy. The latter reasons might be traced to Cynthia, but construing her as a *matrona* can hardly be reconciled with the evidence of other poems (that she consorts openly with her admirers, for example, even offering to go off with the Illyrian praetor on his next journey); no further poems take up again this theme of "preferring other women to Cynthia"—the obscurities of 2.22a, 23, and 24 remain a single inexplicable eruption in the corpus.

In short, the bases of the affair—the grounds for Propertius' jealousy, the assumed social status of his mistress(es), his fidelity or promiscuity—keep shifting in ways that are sometimes blatantly comic in their illogic, but more often just puzzlingly irreconcilable between one version and another.

30. Richardson notes the contradiction (Richardson 1977, ad 4.8.17).
31. Cf., e.g., 2.22a, esp. 13–16, where he compares love to the masochistic religious furor that drives devotees to self-mutilation.
32. On the illogic of Cynthia's rancor against Lygdamus in 4.8, see, e.g., Richardson 1977, ad 4.8.79; Dee 1978, 51–52. On the illogic of her demand for her "poisoner's" torture in 4.7, Richardson remarks: "in her passion for revenge the ghost of Cynthia assails all those she conceives to be possible enemies without concerning herself about logic in the reconstruction of the deed" (Richardson 1977, ad 4.7.37).
33. 2.9.23–24, 2.14.19–20 versus 1.17 and 18.
34. 1.8.1–26, 2.16 versus 1.8.27–46, 2.26b.

35. 1.8.39-42, 2.26b.21-26 versus 3.24.

36. "Fulminat illa oculis et quantum femina saevit, / spectaclum capta nec minus urbe fuit," 55-56; "Cynthia gaudet in exuviis victrixque recurrit," 63. Komp places the diction that characterizes Propertius' description of Cynthia's entry and rout of her rivals in the context of other roughly contemporary Latin poetry and shows that such terms as "furibunda" (52) and "fulminat oculis" invoke the tones appropriate to the imperial (and often excessive) rages of tragedy's and epic's queens, goddesses, and maenads (Komp 1988, 134-41).

37. Elster 1993, 2-5.

38. Žižek 1994, 135n15.

39. I do not, of course, read her gesture as amounting to a theory of human voluntarism.

40. Cf., e.g., Paul Veyne: "So Ego was unhappy over Cynthia? If so, it was simply because women are fickle, and even if they are kept under lock and key, the slightest opening is enough for them to slip out (IV.1)" (Veyne 1988, 138).

41. Cf. Žižek 1994, 122.

42. Lacan 1998, 69 (translating Lacan 1975, 65).

43. See Richardson 1977, ad 3.8.3.

44. Cf. Horace *C.* 1.13.12, Tibullus 1.6.13-14, Ovid *Am.* 1.8.98.

45. Žižek 1994, 125-62. The distinction drawn here—body-depth as cause and surface-sense as effect that belong to heterogeneous orders—was already apparent to the Stoics: knowledge for the Stoics was neither the complete materialism of Epicureanism (for which sense impressions are *tout court* the avenue to substance as the embodiment of truth) nor the complete idealism of Platonism (which sees surface-sense as an avenue to truth only if guaranteed by the Forms—Forms that are thus, oddly enough, hypostasized into sublime Bodies, as if idealism were a closet form of vulgar materialism). Stoic knowledge depends upon the coming together of sense impression and mental patterns already in existence (πρόληψις), types of "idea-forming hexis" common to us all (κοιναὶ ἔννοιαι) (Watson 1966, 24; on the whole question of Stoic knowledge, see Watson 1966, 22-54, Annas 1980, Frede 1983). The division the Stoics thus draw in knowledge roughly corresponds to the division between Being and the Symbolic, the body's imagined depth falling on the side of Being and its culturally-mapped surface on the side of the Symbolic.

46. *Nota* is the regular word for a bruise made in amorous play. Cf. 4.3.26; Horace *C.* 1.13.12; Tibullus 1.8.38.

47. Lacan 1981, 263.

48. Žižek 1991b, 31-32 (cf. Miller 1987, 19).

49. E.g., Tränkle: "Venus als Ursache, daß Cynthia zu dem Fest fährt, wo ein Mädchen ihre Jungfräulichkeit beweisen muß! Verkehrte Welt!" (Tränkle 1960, 179).

50. I have borrowed Richardson's elegant translation of this line (Richardson 1977, ad 4.8.4).

51. James Dee (Dee 1978, 43) notes the "tourist-guide-like appraisal of Lanuvium" in 4.8.4.

52. For a sketch of the temple and its porticus, see Coarelli 1987, 142, fig. 37. Coarelli also remarks upon the use of temple porticus as shelters for markets in his discussions of the sanctuaries at Gabii (15) and at Tibur (88), whose principal architectural features—large gathering place(s) surrounded by porticus—Lanuvium shares. Lawrence Richardson thoughtfully discusses the use of porticus in general as shelters for markets, (Richardson 1992, 310-11, s.v. *porticus*); see also his remarks on particular porticus and their markets (s.v. *Porticus Aemilia, Porticus Argonautarum, Porticus Margaritaria, Porticus Pompeii*). Coarelli makes it clear that Lanuvium's accommodation of sanctuary space to more secular interests was not

unparalleled; he analyzes the sanctuary at Praeneste, for example, as comfortably encompassing an area devoted generally and unblushingly to "attività commerciali" (52).

53. Though "fraud" implies simple cynicism where I suspect attitudes were far more complex (Gordon 1938, 38). Consider Mary Beard's and Michael Crawford's brief but insightful remarks on the Roman attitude toward religion (Beard-Crawford 1985, 25–39), and Denis Feeney's more detailed observations (Feeney 1998, esp. 12–46).

54. On Cynthia's resemblance to Juno Sospita, see Hubbard 1974, 155.

55. Hegel 1977, 288 (§§ 475). Cf. Žižek 1994, 148.

56. On the two possible interpretations of *solvere arma*, see Smyth 1951, 78–79.

CHAPTER EIGHT: HERCULES IN ROME (4.9)

1. Warden 1982.

2. See, e.g., Grimal 1952, 191–92; Heinze 1960, 367–69 ("dieser Hercules ist nicht der strahlende begnadete Heros und künftige Gott, den der Epiker Virgil feiert, sondern der mühselig Beladene," 368); Rothstein 1966, ad 4.9.65 ("auch sonst erscheint Hercules in dieser Elegie als ein von der Last der Arbeit niedergedrückter Mann; eine trübe, beinahe verdrießliche Stimmung herrscht in dem ganzen Gedicht"); Karl-Wilhelm Weeber (who specifically combats Anderson's "comic" interpretation—Weeber 1977, 170–86).

3. So Anderson 1969; Pillinger 1969, 182–89; Galinsky 1972, 153–56; La Penna 1977, 88; Warden 1982; Lefèvre 1966, 92–97; Sullivan 1976, 135–36.

4. Cairns 1992 is a welcome exception to the rule of polarizing readings of 4.9: he painstakingly traces the threads of various genres, from serious to comic, that he sees as informing the elegy (*pace* Anderson 1992, who expresses reservations about the generic contexts Cairns has adduced as appropriate to 4.9). However, having lavished scholarly care on elucidating the contexts that may influence the reading of 4.9, Cairns defers the attempt at detailed interpretation of the elegy (quite justifiably, given the scope of the groundwork he has already laid out in his essay). This chapter shall—though from rather different methodological premises—attempt such an interpretation.

5. On historiography as an instrument of cultural identity—especially as set against Hellenic culture—see Beard and Crawford 1985, 17; Rawson 1985, 215–32; Gruen 1992, esp. 6–51. Some Greek historiographers under the Empire (such as Dionysius of Halicarnassus) take a slightly different slant, emphasizing Rome's Greek origins, yet their project remains the same: defining who is (the best) Roman (Gabba 1984).

6. Propertius cannot be aligned in any simple or straightforward sense with any of the contemporary or preceding sources of the myth, but he follows *Aeneid* 8 most closely in both major and minor details (such as the use of the weighty patronymic *Amphitryoniades*, the representation of Cacus as a monster, the breaking down of the doors to Cacus' cave, the exact order of events). Warden 1982 details these and other points of rapprochement that confirm Propertius' close engagement with Vergil—details that make the differences between the two versions all the more significant (Sbordone 1941 argues, to the contrary, that Propertius' elegy stems from an entirely independent source of the myth, but he misses many of the correspondences Warden cites and seems to demand that cognizance be proven by an exact mirror relationship between the epic and elegiac passage). The relationship among the various literary redactions of Hercules' encounter with Cacus is discussed in: Winter 1910, 193–250; Münzer 1911; Nagore-Perez 1981.

7. See Galinsky 1972, 131–41; Buchheit 1963, 116–33, esp. 131–32; Binder 1971, esp. 2–3, 141–49.

8. Cf. Williams 1973, ad 184f.; Galinsky 1972, 136.

9. The bibliography on the "dark voice" of the *Aeneid* is too vast to be surveyed here, but some of the classic discussions are: Brooks 1953; Parry 1963; Clausen 1964; Putnam 1965; Johnson 1979. Some more recent additions to this school of thought are: Hanson 1982; Lyne 1987; Henry 1989; Quint 1993, 21–96 (notice must also be taken of Putnam 1995, a collection of essays that spans the 1980s).

10. Quint 1993, 23.

11. H.-P. Stahl cogently argues this point in his discussion of the *Aeneid* as political allegory (Stahl 1990, 178).

12. Richardson 1977, ad 4.9.19; Warden 1982, 240.

13. *LL* 5.146. Richardson expresses skepticism of Varro's etymology, but dismisses Propertius' version as wholly "tongue-in-cheek" (Richardson 1992, 162–63).

14. Heinsius and Richmond emend to "Sancus" ("the purifier"), for reasons discussed below.

15. Calling him the "Purifier" (*Sancus,* which governs Heinsius' and Richmond's emendations) presents similar problems, and for the same reason.

16. Butler–Barber 1933, ad 4.9.71–74.

17. Richmond is enthusiastically seconded by Robson 1973, 235–36—an endorsement especially interesting to my argument, since Robson wants to see a circular order of reading reinforced by the transposition.

18. Richardson 1977, ad 73–74.

19. Aristotle (*Poetics* 1450b), Cicero (*De Oratore* 2.325), and Horace (*Ars Poetica*) all, in turn, adopt Plato's metaphor of the body's organic logic—only one right order—as the logic that ought to control the artistic and persuasive uses of language. See Fantham 1972, 164–75. See also Quint 1993, 140–47, who uses this equation of body to "classical" poetic order in order to elucidate the counter-classical aesthetic and subversive sympathies of Lucan's *Pharsalia,* with its ghoulish concentration on bodies broken by civil war into incoherent pieces.

20. See 2.12.21–24; 3.2.17–18; 3.24.3–8.

21. Camps simply concludes that the poet nodded, while Richardson makes a brave (and mildly tongue-in-cheek) attempt to save the poet's chronology:

> In 67–8 *infra* we discover that the Ara Maxima at the southeast end of the Forum Boarium has also now been built by Hercules as a victory monument, though its construction is passed over without a word. It appears that in P.'s version the building of the massive altar has diverted the river and created the band of Tiber bank that includes the Forum Boarium. Suppression of this important action is only one of the puzzling ellipses in the poem. (Richardson 1977, ad 4.9.19)

22. Bostock 1994, 25.

23. Bostock 1994, 25–26. Plato's other famous inquiry into the workings of language, the *Cratylus,* points—though far less strongly—to similar conclusions when Socrates refutes Cratylus' mimetic theory of language. That leaves the philosopher with the idea that convention, rather than resemblance, determines the meaning of words. Convention ultimately points, logically, to a structuralist conceptualization of how language works—yet Socrates does not extrapolate to quite the same hair-raising linguistic *mise en abîme* in the *Cratylus* as in the *Theatetus*. On the *Cratylus*' theory of language, see Schofield 1982, Williams 1982.

24. On ancient theories of the natural origins of language, see Everson 1994; Glidden 1994, esp. 134–35.

25. Varro wishes to derive the name from *vehere* and/or *velum*, insisting that a ferry between the Aventine and the Forum Romanum once landed there (*LL* 5.43–44, 6.24; Butler-Barber 1933 and Richardson 1977, both ad 4.9.5, point to the relevant passages in Varro).

26. *LL* 5.53; Rothstein points to Varro's speculation (Rothstein 1966, ad loc.)

27. Saussure 1983, [164–65], [179–80]. See Harris 1987, 124–33; Culler 1986, 27–64. Culler summarizes the idea with admirable clarity and simplicity: "We have considerable latitude in the way we utter *bed*, so long as what we say is not confused with *bad, bud, bid, bode; bread, bled, dead, fed, head, led, red, said, wed; beck, bell, bet*. In other words, it is the distinctions which are important, and it is for this reason that linguistic units have a purely relational identity" (Culler 1986, 37).

28. Cf. Lycotas' simple spear and shield (23–24) with his enemies', the expensive arms of the cataphract ("munito Sericus hostis equo," 8) and the Briton's gay chariot ("pictoque Britannia curru," 9). On the wealth necessary to the cataphract, see 3.12.12 (where the warrior even gilds his horse's armor!) and Richardson's note on that line (Richardson 1977 ad loc.).

29. The theme of the brothers' rivalry runs like a subtle red thread throughout the poem. Propertius alludes obliquely (4.1.49–50) to Remus situating himself on the Aventine hill, Romulus on the Palatine hill, to take the omens for the founding of Rome, *and* to Remus' death: "si modo Avernalis tremulae cortina Sibyllae / dixit Aventino rura pianda Remo"— "since the tripod of the trembling Sibyl of Lake Avernus said that the countryside would have to be purified by [the blood of] Remus" (sc., because he had desecrated Romulus' walls by jumping over them; cf. 3.9.50 and Richardson's note [1977] on that line).

30. Clearly my discussion of the (impossibility of) *Romanitas* relies upon Hegel's ideas of boundary (*Grenze*) and limit (*Schranke*) as articulated in his *Wissenschaft der Logik* (particularly 103–17) and *System der Philosophie: Der Logik* (particularly §92 and §92, Addition). Slavoj Žižek summarizes these Hegelian concepts with admirable clarity (Žižek 1991a, 109–10):

> *Boundary* is the external limitation of an object, its qualitative confines which confer upon it its identity (an object is "itself" only within these confines, in so far as it fulfills a set of qualitative conditions); whereas *limit* results from a "reflection-into-itself" of the boundary: it emerges when the determinateness which defines the identity of an object is reflected into this object itself and assumes the shape of its own unattainable limit, of what the object can never fully become, of what it can only approach into (bad) infinity—in other words, limit is what the object *ought to* (although it never actually *can*) become. In the course of the dialectical progression, every boundary proves itself a limit: apropos of every identity, we are sooner or later bound to experience how its condition of possibility (the boundary that delimits its conditions) is simultaneously its condition of impossibility.

Hegel did not invent these notions, though: Fichte sketches virtually the same mechanism of a contrastive definition that fundamentally vitiates its subject in his Jena lectures' discussions of Ego, and in *Über den Begriff der Wissenschaftslehre* and *Grundlage der gesamten Wissenschaftslehre*.

31. The expression cannot be merely accidental, because it is so unusual: Romulus is not distinguished for his connection to Troy, though obviously he was a descendant of the original Trojan Aeneadae. Scholars have struggled to explain the locution; Gurval 1995, 260–62 has a good summary of previous scholarship on these lines.

32. See Ralph Hexter's thoughtful essay on Roman perceptions of the Other (Hexter 1992); Rawson 1985 is also useful on the subject of ancient ethnography in Rome.

33. Ralph Hexter notes that Diodorus Siculus, for example, gave as much space to non-Greek as to Greek history in the six books on pre-Trojan War history (Hexter 1992, 345–46). For the significance of Greek culture in particular to the construction of Roman identity, see Gruen 1992. For a general overview of the function of ethnography and the construction of the Other in the ancient world, see Sordi 1979 (the essays by Alberto Grilli, Luisa Prandi, Cornelia Cogrossi, and Gian Guido Belloni—all listed separately in my bibliography—are of particular interest for the way they analyze various aspects of the Roman confrontation with ethnic difference); Thomas 1982; Fornara 1983. Horsfall 1970 and Hexter 1992 both make compelling cases for ethnography as essential to the understanding of the pre-eminent Augustan national epic, Vergil's *Aeneid*—which makes it unsurprising that Propertius would engage the same tensions when composing his version of the Roman ethos, especially in taking up a mytheme (Hercules' encounter with Cacus) previously deployed by the *Aeneid*.

34. Evander, before beginning his tale, seats Aeneas on a lionskin, the emblem of Hercules (*Aen.* 8.177), and exhorts Aeneas to emulate Hercules' humility in accepting the hospitality of a poor people (*Aen.* 8.362–65).

35. Servius ad *Aen.* 8.190.

36. D. S. 4.21.2. Servius Auctus also records an even more thoroughly inverted strand of the legend, that paints Cacus as hospitable, and cheated for his pains by one Geranes or Recoranus ([Servius] ad *Aen.* 8.203).

37. Livy 1.7, 3–15; Ovid *Fasti* 1.543–86.

38. Warden 1982, 232. Warden unfortunately dismisses these effects as meaningless *sprezzatura* on Propertius' part; they merit more serious attention, as I shall show.

39. Though Vergil balances Evander's decidedly oversimplified account of Cacus as nothing but aboriginal monster with sympathetic portrayals not only of Mezentius, but of Polyphemus, another native victim of a not-quite-innocent intruder's *furor* and therefore another "double" to Cacus (Hercules is, after all, a cattle thief and murderer, too: the cattle he drives through Cacus' land he stole from Geryon after murdering their owner). See Glenn 1971, Gotoff 1984.

40. Winter 1910, 225. For an account of Cacus' (Etruscan "Cacu"'s) varied representations that pays more attention than Winter to the evidence available from visual works of art, see Small 1982, esp. chapter 1.

41. Itself a refinement of several refrains in the *Eclogues*—e.g., 1.74 ("ite meae, felix quondam pecus, ite capellae"—"get along, my nanny-goats, my once-happy flock") and 7.44 ("ite domum pasti, si quis pudor, ite iuvenci"—"get along home, you bull-calves, if you've any decency, now that you've pastured"). Both Pillinger (Pillinger 1969, 185–86) and Warden (Warden 1982, 233n11) note the echoes of *Ecl.* 7.44 and 10.77, but overlook 1.74.

42. Warden notes the change, but considers it a preparation for the Bona Dea episode *tout court* (Warden 1982, 233n11).

43. Žižek 1991a, 111–12.

44. On *lalangue*, see Lacan SXX, 126–27; Miller 1975.

45. Technically, the poem focuses on Aeneas' band of exiled *Trojans*, but seen always in the light of their destiny as proto-Romans, in preparation for which they progressively lose all markers of "Trojanness." For example, David Quint shows that Aeneas' band—relict of a people whose fatal mistake was to accept the gift of a (wooden) horse from foreigners—symbolically turn around their fate and abandon their identity as history's quintessential los-

ers by leaving behind various treasures culled from Troy's wealth. They bestow them as gifts (usually fatal ones) on the foreign peoples *they* encounter, while by contrast, they themselves receive (real) horses as gifts from their hosts. The horse still portends war (*Aen.* 3.537–40), but this time a war that Aeneas' men can win; these horses of flesh and blood foreshadow the formation of Roman identity around conquest and a martial ethos (Quint 1993, 65–66).

46. Paul Allen Miller points out to me that 4.9.7–8 can also be read, at first glance, as "but they remained safe with Cacus as their not-untrustworthy host"; only the second half of the pentameter renders this a contextually inappropriate translation. Propertius' ambiguous grammar keeps the reader momentarily in suspense as to precisely what ethical coloring his portrait of Cacus will take on, another ambiguity in relation to the aborigine that Vergil's Evander never entertains.

47. On the Symbolic mechanism for manufacturing mythic icons that organize, in a purely formal way, pre-existing free-floating anxieties, see Žižek 1992, 131–34.

48. Warden 1982, 234.

49. Warden 1982, 240–41 (the pattern would be *sanx . . . sic . . . Sanc . . . Tat . . . com . . . Cur . . . Sanc . . . pat . . . sal . . . sanc*, if one were to accept Schneidewin's transposition, but that makes no difference to my argument).

50. "Es ist, als wollte der Elegiker absichtlich ein Gegenstück zu der virgilischen *ekphrasis* der schauerlichen Mörderhöhle des Cacus liefern" (Heinze 1960, 368).

51. Warden 1982, 236, with references on the use of *puniceus* to describe blood (to which should be added: Plautus *Ps.* 229; Ovid *Met.* 13.887).

52. Warden 1982, 239.

53. Warden 1982, 242.

54. Slavoj Žižek (Žižek 1994, 116) discusses the skin as the "dress of the flesh"—i.e., as that to which we address our attention when relating to any particular body, while "suspending" knowledge of the body's depth (the muscles, blood, organs, veins that would strike us as a revolting chaos if brought to the forefront of consciousness). The Symbolic makes this suspension possible, by rendering the surface of the body "legible," a bodily reality structured by language (as, say, belonging to a particular race or gender, beautiful or ugly, aged or young, the token of a particular discrete identity).

55. So Lefèvre 1966, 94; Pillinger 1969, 187–88; McParland 1970, 352; Galinsky 1972, 155. Anderson 1969 adds that Hercules' transvestitism aligns him with Clodius Pulcher's recent scandalous entry into the Bona Dea rites, disguised as a woman, in order to pursue a love intrigue (cf. Richardson 1977, ad 4.9.49, who quotes Cicero's horrified vituperation of Clodius' cross-dress).

56. Cairns 1992, 90. Propertius may have had available to him a poetic version of Tiresias' history that recorded not one, but six, sex changes, which would make the prophet even more an icon of gender-crossing than the canonical version that limits him to two. See O'Hara 1996.

57. Gantz 1993, 529. Gantz' admirably encyclopedic work documents virtually all literary and artistic sources for the Teiresias myth (as for most other Greek myths).

58. Aristotle *GA* 737a. On gynecology's role in the ancient world as the mirror of culturally constructed gender oppositions, see Dean-Jones 1994, esp. 1–40, 225–53; von Staden 1991, esp. 272. Dean-Jones discriminates between the Hippocratic corpus and its followers, who see Woman as a different species from Man, and the Aristotelians' model of the female as an inferior instance of the same species as the male—but that distinction does not affect the fact that ancient gynecology (like versions of the female in other fields) saw Woman as "what Man is not."

59. Anderson (drawing upon Pichon 1902, 264, 281) notes that "thirst" (*sitis/sitire*) is a common metaphor for lovers' passionate longing, and argues cogently for the relevance of that trope to 4.9; he is seconded by Warden (Anderson 1969, 11–12; Warden 1982, 239n30).

CHAPTER NINE: THE PHENOMENOLOGY OF THE SPIRITS (4.11)

1. Although nearly every Propertius scholar has directed her or his attention at some time to the Cornelia elegy, I have confined my citations in this chapter to a representative sample of opinion on the principal enigmas, rather than attempt an exhaustive inventory of previous scholarship.

As for Scaliger's enthusiastic evaluation of the poem, it may not, in fact, have been original to himself. Emil Hübner credits "Scaliger oder Valckenaer" with originating it (Hübner 1877, 98).

2. Though scholars debate over the precise ratio of the tribunal's function in the poem between judging Cornelia and inducting her into Hades as its "naturalized" citizen; Pirrone's copious annotation of this *locus conclamatus* with parallels drawn from Latin literature and inscriptions offers a useful conspectus of the bases for varying translations (Pirrone 1904, ad 4.11.18). Hertzberg (Hertzberg 1843–1845, III.508–509) argued that *iura dare* meant to assign privileges or status in a state, and thus that judging Cornelia (denoted by the phrase *ius dicere*) did not come into question; Postgate and Butler both agree (Postgate 1881, ad 4.11.18; Butler 1905, ad 4.11.18). Shackleton-Bailey, on the other hand, demurs: "no doubt *iura dare* and *ius dicere* normally mean different things, but I cannot think that *iura* means anything but judgment here" (Shackleton-Bailey 1956, ad 4.11.18); and Sandbach, while agreeing with Hertzberg's formal distinction between the two phrases, points out that "this can imply a previous inquiry into merit; and it may be doubted whether the author of *carm. epigr* 1109.23, *nec Minos mihi iura dabit*, sharply distinguished *ius dicere* and *iura dare*" (Sandbach 1962, 274n2).

3. Stahl 1985, 262.

4. Wyke 1987a, 171–72.

5. Plessis 1884, 288–89; Alfonsi 1945, 84–86; Grimal 1952, 449; Highet 1957, 98–105; Celentano 1956, 53–54; Luck 1959, 115; Soría 1965; Reitzenstein 1969. K.-W. Weeber also sees the poem as a paean to Cornelia, but considers its admiration to be for an embodiment of early Roman ideals, rather than for Augustus' attempt to revive those ideals—hence, the poem does not (for Weeber) mark any detente in Propertius' skepticism toward Augustus (Weeber 1977, 217–49).

6. Richardson 1977, 481; Curran 1968.

7. La Penna 1951, 86–88 and La Penna 1977, 94–95; Hallett 1971, 163–75; Hubbard 1974, 145–49; Sullivan 1976, 44.

8. Williams 1968, 398–99 (Mynors' OCT text reads "fas obstat, tristisque palus inamabilis *undae* / alligat et *novies* Styx interfusa coercet," but Williams accepts readings that Mynors assigns to the *apparatus criticus*); Curran 1968, 135.

9. On Law as implicated with enjoyment, see SVII, esp. 225–41/191–217; on *jouissance* as non-meaning, see SXX; the relevant passages are cited above in chapter 5, note 32, along with scholarly discussions of the concept.

10. This is another way of putting the question Lacan formulated as Is there an Other of the Other?—i.e., is there a foundation or anchor of meaning in signification beyond signification itself? To this he answers a resounding "No!" (as in the title and subject matter of

his sixth *Séminaire*'s fourth session devoted to *Hamlet:* "Hamlet: il n'y a pas d'Autre de l'Autre" [Lacan 1981–1983, 25:26–36]).

11. Frier traces the transition to casuistry in (for example) the Roman judicial system's shift away from dependence on rhetorical advocacy toward reliance on juristic *responsa* (Frier 1985, esp. xi-xvi, 185–96).

12. The *comitia centuriata* was a political assembly based on the centuries, the smallest units of the Roman legion (a legion contains sixty centuries); the assembly's constituency was not strictly military, however, since five centuries of non-combatants were also included among its ranks.

13. Epicurus *Kuriai Doxai* 33.

14. Testimony to the content of Carneades' speech is found in Cicero *Rep.* 3, and Lactantius *Div. Inst.* 5. Anthony Long thoughtfully discusses the evidence (Long 1986, 104–106).

15. My discussion is heavily indebted to R. M. Ogilvie's excellent analysis of the legal fine points that allow Verginia's entrapment; he illustrates his commentary with meticulous references to the Twelve Tables, as well as to further helpful bibliography (Ogilvie 1965, 481–83).

16. Livy 3.45.2.

17. Just as the repeated imagery of urns in Cornelia's speech—both the urns that receive jurors' votes (4.11.19, 49) and the urns that punished the Danaids for crime (4.11.28)—ostensibly symbolize the Law's impartial and unbending judgment, but in fact impugn the Law as nothing more than the prejudice of its executors. I discuss these passages more fully below ("*Objet a:* Patching the (W)hole").

18. "Cum promptum hoc ius velut ex oraculo incorruptum pariter ab iis summi infimique ferrent, tum legibus condendis opera dabatur" (Livy 3.34.1).

19. Livy 3.34.8–3.35.1.

20. "decem Tarquinios," Livy 3.39.3.

21. Livy 3.40.11–13. See especially Ogilvie's commentary ad 3.40.11, with its discussion of the shrewdly dilatory demand for a *praeiudicium* (a judicial proceeding for examining a preliminary question upon which the decision of a case depends) put forward by Lucius Cornelius Maluginensis, brother to one of the decemvirs and thus Appius' clandestine supporter.

22. Sulla and Julius Caesar: Ogilvie 1965, 454, with references; Second Triumvirate: Ogilvie 464, ad 3.36.3.

23. "Factione respectuque rerum privatarum," Livy 2.30.2.

24. "Civitas secum ipsa discors intestino inter patres plebemque flagrabat odio, maxime propter nexos ob aes alienum," Livy 2.23.1–2.

25. Plutarch also records the anecdote (*Coriolanus* 6.2–4). Emily Gowers shrewdly analyzes these and other "digestive" metaphors for the harmonious or inharmonious body politic (Gowers 1993, esp. 1–49).

26. Just as Woman's sexuality, in Cornelia's speech, becomes both the "cause" and "cure" for social harmony, depending on whether it is "properly" channeled toward chaste reproduction, or not. I discuss this point further below.

27. Acanthis, in 4.5, similarly assumes the function of *objet a* when her hetaira-catechism "explains" everything about Cynthia that enrages Propertius; Acanthis, despite the fact that she infuriates Propertius and that he blames her for all Cynthia's "bad" behavior, proves essential to him, insofar as she allows him to preserve his fantasies about Cynthia as (in herself, apart from Acanthis' putative influence) the "perfect" object of desire.

28. See Ogilvie 1965, 390 on *libertas* as the central theme of Livy's third book, and the tale of the decemvirs and Verginia as its focal point.

29. "Et, ne gratuita crudelitas esset, bonorum donatio sequi domini supplicium," Livy 3.37.8.

30. Similarly, the constant refrain of hysterical terror in Cornelia's speech makes it clear that the demands of the tribunal she faces are intrinsically unsatisfiable, because wholly arbitrary; nothing she can bring before the court can possibly satisfy them of her innocence. The subject of the tribunal's implacability is discussed further below ("The Urns of the Danaids").

31. The deteriores offer *tonsa* ("shorn") for *tunsa*, but, as Butler and Barber note, this "is a needless alteration" (Butler-Barber 1933, ad 4.11.38).

32. On "qui" as Aemilius Paullus, see, e.g., Rothstein 1966, ad loc.; Richmond 1928, ad loc. (reading *Achive* instead of *Achille* in the pentameter, thus making it refer to Paullus' military exploits in Greece); Camps 1965, ad loc.

33. "As Aeacus was the founder of the dynasty over which Cornelia's forebears had triumphed, his examination of her case might be expected to be the most severe" (Richardson 1977, ad 4.11.19).

34. For Perses cited only as conquest, rather than witness, see Santen 1780; Munro 1876, 53–62 (who conjectures that a distich has dropped out between 38 and 39); Richmond 1928.

35. Cf. Joplin 1990, 1991, Joshel 1992, both discussed in greater detail in chapter 4 ("A Bend in the Wall").

36. "Censura Planci et Paulli acta inter discordiam neque ipsis honori neque rei publicae usui fuerat, cum alteri vis censoria, alteri vita deesset, Paullus vix posset implere censorem, Plancus timere deberet nec quidquam obicere posset adulescentibus aut obicientes audire, quod non agnosceret senex" (Velleius Paterculus 2.95.3). Richardson offers an attractive reading of l.41 that has Cornelia herself imply as much by calling upon her ancestors to witness "me neque censurae legem mollisse"—"that *I* was not the one who softened the rule of censorship" (Richardson 1977, ad loc.).

37. Consider, for example, their wholesale condemnation of marriage as such (not just marriage with the Aegyptioi) in *Supp.* 104–11, and their twice-repeated wish to remain forever virgin (*Supp.* 141–43, 151–53). Caldwell 1974 and Gantz 1978 both argue the case for the Danaids' misandry and misogamy (*contra* Friis Johansen-Whittle 1980, 1.29–33, who see the Danaids' revulsion as limited to their cousins). Garvie 1969, 215–24 judiciously lays out the evidence for both sides of the question, with an admirable conspectus of previous scholarship.

38. Cf. Sissa 1990, 127–46, discussed above in chapter 4 ("In a Strange Land").

39. Of *rapina*, Richardson notes: "a strong word, almost in accusation of the court she faces" (Richardson 1977, ad 4.11.62).

40. Curran 1968, 138. Lacan discusses the idea that Law springs from an inaugural act of Crime—so that Crime, far from being an aberration from Law, in fact logically founds Law—in his only partially published SVI (*Le désir et son interprétation*); he bases his analysis chiefly on Freud's *Totem and Taboo*, which sketches the germ of the idea. See Lacan 1981–1983, 26/27:34–36/1977a, 42–45.

41. Cf. Copley 1956, 80–82.

42. Cf. Curran 1968, 135—though he oddly misses the parallel to Persephone, instead identifying Cornelia with Eurydice.

43. Cf., as a representative sampling, Curran 1968, esp. 136, 138; Paduano 1968; Reitzenstein 1969; Richardson 1977, 481–82.

44. See Paduano 1968.

45. The Romans have, of course, no word for this concept, which would have been at odds with the dominant paradigm of masculinity as above obsessive fascination with something so unimportant as a woman—hence I must fall back on Holt Parker's neologism *unifeminus* (from Parker 1992).

46. As Paduano notes (Paduano 1968, 26–27).

47. Hermann Fränkel, in the context of discussing Ovid, also notes that "a strange sense of propriety forbade the Romans to publicize even the most innocent details of their family life," and cites Cornelia's silence on the subject of her love for her husband as an example (Fränkel 1956, 184n43). Saara Lilja demonstrates, however, that this reticence is not as uniform as Fränkel suggests, so that Cornelia's taciturnity is not entirely explained by the Roman sense of *comme il faut* (Lilja 1978, 237–38).

48. *Alc.* 305–10.

49.

"seu tamen adversum mutarit ianua lectum,
    sederit et nostro cauta noverca toro,
coniugium, pueri, laudate et ferte paternum:
    capta dabit vestris moribus illa manus;
nec matrem laudate nimis: collata priori
    vertet in offensas libera verba suas."
                (4.11.85–90)

These lines paint the stepmother as on her guard (*cauta*), thus likely to interpret words of praise for Cornelia as damaging to herself; this could be the worse for the children. Cornelia's image of her seems to imply as much: the stepmother, properly handled, offers her hands to the children like a captured barbarian (Richardson 1977, ad 88)—but a slighted "barbarian" could be savage to them. Otherwise, it is hard to see why Cornelia should care what her children say to their stepmother: what to the former wife are her successor's emotional wounds?

50. Given the often-fatal dangers of childbirth for women in the ancient world, bearing three children was to risk one's life to repopulate the state—a quite reasonable claim to virtue. On the dangers of reproduction for women, see Burn 1953, 10–13.

51. See Gardner 1986, index s.v. "ius liberorum"; Dixon 1988, 71–72 and also 98n2 on ancient evidence, and modern scholarly analysis, of the specific content of the laws.

52. Purcell 1986.

53. The institution of *clientela* ("clientship") tied people (as *clientes* ["clients"]) to their superiors in wealth, power, and status (as *patroni* ["patrons"]) in a relationship of exchange. The *cliens* was expected to reciprocate his *patronus* for favors and benefits received by supporting the latter in his political and social life. See Brunt 1988, 382–442.

54. Dixon 1983.

55. Dixon 1988, 71–103; Purcell 1986, 85–93.

56. My discussion of the Cornelia elegy in the light of *The Phenomenology of Spirit* is heavily indebted to Slavoj Žižek's analysis of *Bildung* and the subject in Hegel (Žižek 1993, 22–27).

57. See, for example, Borch-Jacobsen 1991.

58. Hegel 1977, 362.

59. Žižek 1993, 25.

60. Žižek points to Lacan's riposte to Dostoevsky in his second Seminar as also illustrating this point. Lacan cites the passage in Dostoevsky's *The Brothers Karamazov* where the

brothers' father responds in horror to his son Ivan's atheistic speculations, "If God doesn't exist, then everything is permitted!" To the contrary, Lacan says: "If God doesn't exist, then nothing at all is permitted any longer" (SII 156/128)—meaning that, if "God" has failed as Master Signifier, as the supreme quilting point that "made sense" of everything and that granted the subject a place in the world, then the subject's sense of deficiency can no longer be assuaged; his perception of his own lack is universalized and becomes oppressive, unanswerable, paralyzing guilt (Žižek 1991a, 9).

61. Richardson 1977, ad 4.11.84.
62. Cicero *Off.* I, 54; Lucretius *DRN* 5.1011–27.
63. Cf. Lacan: "Il n'y a pas *La* femme, article défini pour désigner l'universel. Il n'y a pas *La* femme puisque—j'ai déjà risqué le terme, et pourquoi y regarderais-je à deux fois?—de son essence, elle n'est pas toute" (Lacan 1975, 68). Being "pas toute"—unable to be organized into a Whole according to a single principle—She cannot guarantee Man's consistent and coherent identity.
64. Cf. 4.7.89–90.
65. Livy offers eloquent tribute to Rome's notion of its own moral superiority, though he is hardly the first or last Roman to do so: "Nulla umquam res publica nec maior nec sanctior nec bonis exemplis ditior fuit, nec in quam civitatem tam serae avaritia luxuriaque immigraverint, nec ubi tantus ac tam diu paupertati ac parsimoniae honos fuerit" (*Praef.* 11). Catharine Edwards shrewdly analyzes Roman claims to preeminence in virtue (Edwards 1993, esp. 1–33).

CHAPTER TEN: DREAMING ROME

1. Kennedy 1992, Platter 1995 (Platter also gives additional useful bibliography on the ambivalence of the Augustan elegists).
2. Feeney 1998.
3. Kennedy 1992, 1993.
4. Miller 1994, 1999, and forthcoming.
5. Barton 1993.
6. Oliensis 1997.
7. Fredrick 1997.
8. Skinner 1993.
9. Amy Richlin elegantly argues the case for the relevance of a male-authored ancient literature to ancient women's lives (Richlin 1992b), though she views this literature with suspicion; see also Gold 1993a, who makes a somewhat more optimistic case for sympathetic feminist readings of ancient Roman poetry.
10. On gender-division as subsuming other divisions within Roman culture, see Edwards 1993; Quint 1993, 3–93; Skinner 1998.
11. E.g., Betensky 1973, 1974; Wyke 1987b, 1989b; Gold 1993b. Saara Lilja, though she credits Propertius with a degree of appreciation for women's accomplishments and character as well as physical beauty, nonetheless convicts him overall of "selfishness" and "possessiveness" with regard to his lady love(s) (Lilja 1978, esp. 192–205).
12. E.g., Lilja 1978; Hallett 1971, 1973, 1974, 1993; Wyke 1987a, Wyke 1994 (though Wyke expresses reservations in both articles); Gold 1993a. For more on both sides of the debate over the feminist import of Propertius' verse, see chapter 1, note 58.

BIBLIOGRAPHY

Alfonsi, Luigi.
    1943.   "L'elegia di Gallo." *Rivista di Filologia* ns 21:46–56.
———.
    1945.   *L'elegia di Properzio.* Milan.
Allison, June.
    1980.   "Virgilian Themes in Propertius 4.7 and 8." *CP* 75:332–38.
———.
    1984.   "The Cast of Characters in Propertius 4.7." *CW* 77.6:355–58.
Althusser, Louis.
    1971.   *Lenin and Philosophy.* Translated by Ben Brewster. New York.
Anderson, R. D., P. J. Parsons, and R. G. M. Nisbet.
    1979.   "Elegiacs by Gallus from Qaṣr Ibrîm." *JRS* 69:125–55.
Anderson, William S.
    1969.   "*Hercules Exclusus:* Propertius, IV, 9." *AJP* 85:1–12.
———.
    1992.   "The Limits of Genre: Response to Francis Cairns." In Gotthard Karl Galinsky, ed., *The Interpretation of Roman Poetry: Empiricism or Hermeneutics?* 96–103. Frankfurt.
Annas, Julia.
    1980.   "Truth and Knowledge." In Malcolm Schofield, Myles Burnyeat, and Jonathan Barnes, eds., *Doubt and Dogmatism: Studies in Hellenistic Philosophy,* 84–104. Oxford.
Auerbach, Eric.
    1953.   *Mimesis: The Representation of Reality in Western Literature.* Translated by Willard Trask. Princeton.
Baehrens, E.
    1880.   *Sex. Propertii elegiarum libri IV.* Leipzig.
Baker, R. J.
    1968.   "*Miles annosus:* The military motif in Propertius." *Latomus* 27:322–49.

Barber, E. A.
　1960.　　　*Sexti Properti Carmina.* 2nd ed. Oxford.
Barchiesi, Alessandro.
　1980–1981.　"Notizie sul «Nuovo Gallo»." *Atene e Roma* 25–6:153–66.
Barton, Carlin.
　1993.　　　*The Sorrows of the Ancient Romans: The Gladiator and the Monster.* Princeton.
Beard, Mary, and Michael Crawford.
　1985.　　　*Rome in the Late Republic.* Ithaca, N.Y.
Becker, Carl.
　1971.　　　"Die Späten Elegie des Properz." *Hermes* 99:449–80.
Belloni, Gian Guido.
　1979.　　　"Figure di stranieri e di barbari nelle monete della Repubblica Romana." In Sordi 1979, 201–28.
Beltrami, Lucia.
　1989.　　　"Properzio 4, 4: La colpa della Vestale." In Giuseppe Catanzaro and Francesco Santucci, eds., *Tredici secoli di elegia latina: Atti del convegno internazionale, Assisi, 22–24 aprile 1988,* 267–72. Assisi.
Benediktson, Thomas.
　1989.　　　*Propertius: Modernist Poet of Antiquity.* Carbondale, Ill.
Benjamin, Anna S.
　1965.　　　"A note on Propertius 1.10. *O iucunda quies.*" *CPh* 60:178.
Bennett, Florence Mary.
　1967.　　　*Religious Cults Associated with the Amazons.* New York.
Benveniste, Emile.
　1969.　　　*Le vocabulaire des institutions indo-européennes.* 2 vols. Paris.
Betensky, Aya.
　1973.　　　"Forum." *Arethusa* 6:267–69.
———.
　1974.　　　"A Further Reply." *Arethusa* 7:217–19.
Binder, Gerhard.
　1971.　　　*Aeneas und Augustus: Interpretationen zum 8. Buch der Aeneis.* Meisenheim am Glan.
Bing, Peter.
　1988.　　　*The Well-Read Muse: Present and Past in Callimachus and the Hellenistic Poets.* Göttingen.
Borch-Jacobsen, Mikkel.
　1991.　　　*Lacan: The Absolute Master.* Stanford.
Bostock, David.
　1994.　　　"Plato on Understanding Language." In Stephen Everson, ed., *Language,* 10–27. Cambridge.
Boucher, Jean-Paul.
　1965.　　　*Études sur Properce: Problèmes d'inspiration et d'art.* 2nd ed. Paris.
Bowie, Malcolm.
　1991.　　　*Lacan.* Cambridge, Mass.
Brenk, Frederick E.
　1979.　　　"Tarpeia among the Celts: Watery Romance, from Simylos to Propertius." *Studies in Latin Literature and Roman History* 1:166–74.

Brooks, R. A.
1953. "*Discolor Aura:* Reflections of a Golden Bough." *AJP* 74:260–80.
Broughton, T. Roberts.
1952. *The Magistrates of the Roman Republic: Volume II: 99 B.C.-31 B.C.* New York.
Brunt, P. A.
1971. *Italian Manpower, 225 B.C.-A.D. 14.* Oxford.
———.
1988. *The Fall of the Roman Republic.* Oxford.
Buchheit, Vinzenz.
1963. *Vergil über die Sendung Roms: Untersuchungen zum Bellum Poenicum und zur Aeneis.* Heidelberg.
Burck, Erich.
1966. "Zur Komposition des vierten Buches des Properz." *WS* 79:405–27.
Burn, A. R.
1953. "*Hic Breve Vivitur:* A Study of the Expectation of Life in the Roman Empire." *Past and Present* 4:1–31.
Butler, H. E.
1905. *Sex. Propertii opera omnia.* London.
Butler, H. E., and E. A. Barber, ed.
1933. *The Elegies of Propertius.* Oxford.
Butler, Judith.
1993. *Bodies That Matter.* New York.
Butrica, James.
1984. *The Manuscript Tradition of Propertius.* Toronto.
Cairns, Francis.
1983. "Propertius 1,4 and 1,5 and the 'Gallus' of the *Monobiblos*." *PLLS* 4:61–102.
———.
1992. "Propertius 4.9: '*Hercules Exclusus*' and the Dimensions of Genre." In Gotthard Karl Galinsky, ed., *The Interpretation of Roman Poetry: Empiricism or Hermeneutics?* 65–95. Frankfurt.
Caldwell, Richard S.
1974. "The Psychology of Aeschylus' *Supplices*." *Arethusa* 7:45–70.
Camps, W. A.
1965. *Propertius: Elegies, Book IV.* Cambridge.
Carson, Ann.
1986. *Eros the Bittersweet: An Essay.* Princeton.
Celentano, Laura.
1956. "Significato e valore del IV Libro di Properzio." *Annali della Facoltà di Lettere e Filosofia* 6:33–68.
Cherniss, Harold.
1935. *Aristotle's Criticism of Presocratic Philosophy.* Baltimore.
Clausen, Wendell.
1964. "An Interpretation of the *Aeneid*." *HSCP* 68:139–47.
Coarelli, Filippo.
1987. *I Santuari del Lazio in Età Repubblicana.* Rome.

Cogrossi, Cornelia.
 1979. "Preoccupazioni Etniche nelle Leggi di Augusto sulla 'Manumissio Servorum'?" In Sordi 1979, 158–77.
Commager, Steele.
 1974. *A Prolegomenon to Propertius*. Cincinnati.
Connor, P. J.
 1978. "The Actian Miracle: Propertius 4.6." *Ramus* 7:1–10.
Copjec, Joan.
 1994. *Read My Desire: Lacan Against the Historicists*. Cambridge, Mass.
Copley, F. O.
 1956. *Exclusus amator*. TAPA Monograph 17. Madison, Wis.
Courtney, E.
 1968. "The Structure of Propertius' Book I and Some Textual Consequences." *Phoenix* 22:250–58.
Culler, Jonathan.
 1986. *Ferdinand de Saussure*. 1st ed. 1976. Ithaca, N.Y.
Curran, Leo.
 1968. "Propertius 4.11: Greek Heroines and Death." *CPh* 63:134–39.
Currie, H. MacL.
 1973. "Propertius IV.8—A Reading." *Latomus* 32:616–22.
Dalzell, A.
 1980. "Homeric Themes in Propertius." *Hermathena* 129:29–36.
Damsté, P. H.
 1928. "De Propertii Elegiarum libro quarto." *Mnemosyne* 56:214–19.
D'Anna, Giovanni.
 1986. "Il Quarto Libro delle Elegie di Properzio." *Cultura e Scuola* 25:68–74.
Dean-Jones, Lesley Ann.
 1994. *Women's Bodies in Classical Greek Science*. Oxford.
Dee, James.
 1974. "Arethusa to Lycotas: Propertius 4.3." *TAPA* 104:81–96.
 ———.
 1978. "Elegy 4.8: A Propertian Comedy." *TAPA* 108:41–53.
Della Corte, Francesco.
 1986. "Properzio, l'elegiaco della trasgressione." In *Bimillenario della morte di Properzio: Atti del convegno internazionale di studi properziani, Roma–Assisi, 21–26 maggio 1985*, 21–51. Assisi.
Deremetz, Alain.
 1986. "L'elegie de Vertumne: L'Oeuvre trompeuse. *REL* 64:116–49.
Dilke, O. A. W.
 1985. *Greek and Roman Maps*. Ithaca, N.Y.
 ———.
 1987a. "Itineraries and Geographical Maps in the Early and Late Roman Empires." In Harley–Woodward, 234–57.
 ———.
 1987b. "Maps in the Service of the State: Roman Cartography to the End of the Augustan Era." In Harley–Woodward, 201–11.

1987c. "Roman Large-scale Mapping in the Early Empire." In Harley–Woodward, 212–33.

Dimundo, Rosalba.
1990. *Properzio 4.7: Dalla variante di un modello letterario alla costante di una unità tematica.* Bari.

Dixon, Suzanne.
1983. "A Family Business: Women's Role in Patronage and Politics at Rome 80–44 B.C." *Classica et Mediaevalia* 34:91–112.

———.
1988. *The Roman Mother.* Norman, Okla.

duBois, Page.
1982. *Centaurs and Amazons: Women and the Pre-history of the Great Chain of Being.* Reprint 1991. Ann Arbor.

Edwards, Catharine.
1993. *The Politics of Immorality in Ancient Rome.* Cambridge.

———.
1996. *Writing Rome: Textual Approaches to the City.* Cambridge.

Elster, Jon.
1993. *Political Psychology.* Cambridge.

Englert, Walter.
1987. *Epicurus on the Swerve and Voluntary Action.* Atlanta.

Enk, P. J.
1911. *Ad Propertii Carmina Commentarius Criticus.* Reprint 1978. New York.

———.
1957. "De vero Propertii erga Cynthiam amore." In *Miscellanea Propertiana.* Primo Comizio (Atti, Lett., Scienze), ed. Atti dell'Accad. Properziana del Subasio V,5,1957. Assisi. 25–30.

Evans, S.
1971. "Odyssean Echoes in Propertius IV.8." *G&R* 18:51–53.

Everson, Stephen.
1994. "Epicurus on Mind and Language." In Stephen Everson, ed., *Language,* 74–108. Cambridge.

Fahz, Ludwig.
1904. *De poetarum Romanorum doctrina magica quaestiones selectae.* Giessen.

Fairweather, Janet.
1984. "The 'Gallus Papyrus': A New Interpretation." *CQ* 34:167–74.

Fantham, Elaine.
1972. *Comparative Studies in Republican Latin Imagery.* Toronto.

Fedeli, Paolo.
1965. *Properzio: Elegie, Libro IV.* Bari.

———.
1980. *Sesto Properzio: Il primo libro delle elegie.* Florence.

———.
1983. "*Propertii monobiblos*: Struttura e motivi." *ANRW* II.30.3:1858–1922.

———.
1987. "Acanthis e la sete dei morti." In Renato Raffaelli, ed., *Rappresentazioni della morte,* 93–129. Urbino.

Feeney, Denis.
   1998.   *Literature and Religion at Rome: Cultures, Contexts, and Beliefs.* Cambridge.
Fornara, Charles.
   1983.   *The Nature of History in Ancient Greece and Rome.* Berkeley.
Fränkel, Hermann.
   1956.   *Ovid: A Poet Between Two Worlds.* 2nd ed. Berkeley.
Frede, Michael.
   1983.   "Stoics and Skeptics on Clear and Distinct Impressions." In Myles Burnyeat, ed., *The Skeptical Tradition,* 65–93. Berkeley.
Fredrick, David.
   1997.   "Reading Broken Skin: Violence in Roman Elegy." In Judith P. Hallett and Marilyn B. Skinner, eds., *Roman Sexualities.* Princeton.
Freud, S.
   1953–1973.   *The Standard Edition of the Complete Psychological Works of Sigmund Freud* [= *SE*]. Ed. James Strachey. 24 vols. London.
Frier, Bruce.
   1985.   *The Rise of the Roman Jurists: Studies in Cicero's Pro Caecina.* Princeton.
Friis Johansen, H., and Edward W. Whittle.
   1980.   *Aeschylus: The Suppliants.* 3 vols. Copenhagen.
Gabba, Emilio.
   1984.   "Augustus and the Historians." In Fergus Millar and Erich Segal, eds., *Caesar Augustus: Seven Aspects,* 61–88. Oxford.
Galinsky, Gotthard Karl.
   1972.   *The Herakles Theme.* Totowa, N.J.
Gansiniec, Zofia.
   1949.   *Tarpeia: The Making of a Myth.* In Kazimierz Majewski, ed., *Acta Societatis Archaeologicae Polonorum 1.* Wrocław.
Gantz, Timothy.
   1978.   "Love and Death in the *Suppliants* of Aischylos." *Phoenix* 32:279–87.
———.
   1993.   *Early Greek Myth: A Guide to Literary and Artistic Sources.* Baltimore.
Gardner, Jane.
   1986.   *Women in Roman Law and Society.* Bloomington, Ind.
Garvie, A. F.
   1969.   *Aeschylus' Supplices: Play and Trilogy.* Cambridge.
Geertz, Clifford.
   1964.   "Ideology as a Cultural System." In D. Apter, ed., *Ideology and Discontent,* 47–76. New York.
Genovese, E. N.
   1974.   "Symbolism in the *Passer* Poems." *Maia* 26:121–25.
Giangrande, Giuseppe.
   1975.   "Catullus' Lyrics on the *Passer.*" *MPhL* 1:137–46.
———.
   1980.   "An Alleged Fragment of Gallus." *QUCC* 34:141–53.
Glenn, Justin.
   1971.   "Mezentius and Polyphemus." *AJP* 92:129–55.

Glidden, David K.
1994. "Parrots, Pyrrhonists and Native Speakers." In Stephen Everson, ed., *Language*, 129–48. Cambridge.
Gold, Barbara.
1993a. "'But Ariadne Was Never There in the First Place': Finding the Female in Roman Poetry." In Nancy Sorkin Rabinowitz and Amy Richlin, eds., *Feminist Theory and the Classics*, 75–101. New York.
———.
1993b. "'The Master Mistress of My Passion': The Lady as Patron in Ancient and Renaissance Literature." In Mary DeForest, ed., *Woman's Power, Man's Game: Essays on Classical Antiquity in Honor of Joy K. King*, 279–304. Wauconda, Ill.
Gordon, A. E.
1938. "The Cults of Lanuvium." *University of California Publications in Classical Archaeology* 2.2:21–58.
Gotoff, Harold C.
1984. "The Transformation of Mezentius." *TAPA* 114:191–218.
Gowers, Emily.
1993. *The Loaded Table: Representations of Food in Roman Literature*. Oxford.
Green, Monica.
1985. *The Transmission of Ancient Theories of Female Physiology and Disease through the Early Middle Ages*. Diss. Princeton University.
Griffin, Jasper.
1985. *Latin Poets and Roman Life*. Chapel Hill, N.C.
Grilli, Alberto.
1979. "L'Approccio all'etnologia nell'antichità." In Sordi 1979, 11–33.
Grimal, Pierre.
1951. "Études sur Properce, II: César et la légende de Tarpéia." *REL* 29:201–14.
———.
1952. "Les intentions de Properce et la composition du livre IV des 'Élégies.'" *Latomus* 11:183–97, 315–25, 437–50.
Gruen, Erich S.
1992. *Culture and National Identity in Republican Rome*. Ithaca, N.Y.
Guillemin, A.
1950. "Properce, de Cynthie aux poèmes romains." *REL* 28:182–93.
Gurval, Robert Alan.
1995. *Actium and Augustus: The Politics and Emotions of War*. Ann Arbor.
Guthrie, William Keith Chambers.
1962. *A History of Greek Philosophy. Vol. I: The Earlier Presocratics and the Pythagoreans*. Cambridge.
Gutzwiller, Kathryn.
1985. "The Lover and the Lena: Propertius 4.5." *Ramus* 14.2:105–15.
———.
1992. "Callimachus' Lock of Berenice: Fantasy, Romance, and Propaganda." *AJP* 93:359–85.
Habinek, Thomas.
1993. *The Politics of Latin Literature*. Princeton.

Hallett, Judith.
    1971.   *Book IV: Propertius' Recusatio to Augustus and Augustan Ideals.* Diss. Harvard.

———.
    1973.   "The Role of Women in Roman Elegy." *Arethusa* 6:103–24. Reprinted in John Peradotto and J. P. Sullivan, eds., *Women in the Ancient World*, 241–62. Albany, N.Y., 1984.

———.
    1974.   "Women in Roman Elegy: A Reply." *Arethusa* 7:211–17.

———.
    1993.   "Martial's Sulpicia and Propertius' Cynthia." In Mary DeForest, ed., *Woman's Power, Man's Game: Essays in Classical Antiquity in Honor of Joy K. King*, 322–53. Wauconda, Ill.

Halliday, W. R.
    1928.   *The Greek Questions of Plutarch.* Oxford.

Hanslik, R.
    1962.   "Textkritisches in Properz Buch IV." *RhM* 105:236–52.

Hanson, Ann Ellis.
    1990.   "The Medical Writer's Woman." In David M. Halperin, John J. Winkler, and Froma I. Zeitlin, eds., *Before Sexuality: The Construction of Erotic Experience in the Ancient Greek World.* Princeton. 309–37.

———.
    1992.   "Conception, Gestation, and the Origin of Female Nature in the *Corpus Hippocraticum.*" *Helios* 19:31–71.

Hanson, John Arthur.
    1982.   "Vergil." In T. James Luce, ed., *Ancient Writers: Greece and Rome*, 2:669–701. New York.

Harley, J. B., and David Woodward, eds.
    1987.   *The History of Cartography. Vol. 1: Cartography in Prehistoric, Ancient and Medieval Europe and the Mediterranean.* Chicago.

Harris, Roy.
    1987.   *Reading Saussure: A Critical Commentary on the Cours de Linguistique Générale.* La Salle, Ill.

Hegel, G. W. F.
    1942.   *The Philosophy of Right.* Translated by T. M. Knox. Oxford.

———.
    1976.   *Gesammelte Werke.* Ed. Rolf-Peter Horstmann and Johann Heinrich Trede. Hamburg.

———.
    1977.   *The Phenomenology of Spirit.* Translated by A. V. Miller. Oxford.

Heinsius, Nicolas.
    1742.   *Adversaria.* Harlingen.

Heinze, Richard.
    1960.   "Ovids Elegische Erzählung." In Erich Burck, ed., *Vom Geist des Römertums*, 308–403. Stuttgart. Reprinted from *Sitzungsberichte über die Verhandlungen der Sächsischen Akademie der Wissenschaften zu Leipzig*, phil.-hist. Kl., Bd. 71, H.7, 1919.

Helmbold, William C.
1949.   "Propertius IV.7: Prolegomena to an Interpretation." *University of California Publications in Classical Philology* 13.9:333–43.
Henry, Elisabeth.
1989.   *The Vigour of Prophecy: A Study of Virgil's Aeneid.* Carbondale, Ill.
Herrmann, Léon.
1951.   *L'âge d'argent doré.* Paris.
Hertzberg, W. A. B.
1843–1845. *Sex. Aur. Propertii elegiarum libri quattuor.* 3 vols. Halle.
Hexter, Ralph.
1992.   "Sidonian Dido." In Ralph Hexter and Daniel Selden, eds., *Innovations of Antiquity.* New York.
Highet, Gilbert.
1957.   *Poets in a Landscape.* New York.
Hodge, R. I. V., and R. A. Buttimore.
1977.   *The "Monobiblos" of Propertius.* Cambridge.
Hooper, Richard W.
1985.   "In Defence of Catullus' Dirty Sparrow." *G&R* 32:162–78.
Hopkins, Keith.
1983.   *Death and Renewal. Sociological Studies in Roman History.* Cambridge.
Horsfall, Nicholas.
1970.   "Numanus Remulus: Ethnography and Propaganda in *Aen.*, ix, 598 f." *Latomus* 30:1108–16.
Hubbard, Margaret.
1974.   *Propertius.* London.
Hubbard, Thomas.
1984.   "Art and Vision in Propertius 2.31/32." *TAPA* 114:281–97.
Hübner, Emil.
1877.   "Zu Propertius." In *Commentationes Philologae in Honorem Theodori Mommseni Scripserunt Amici*, 98–113. Berlin.
Hutchinson, G. O.
1984.   "Propertius and the Unity of the Book." *JRS* 74:100–103.
Irigaray, Luce.
1977.   *Ce sexe qui n'en est pas un.* Paris.
———.
1980.   *Amante marine: De Friedrich Nietzsche.* Paris.
———.
1985.   *This Sex Which Is Not One.* Translated by Catherine Porter. Ithaca, N.Y.
———.
1991.   *The Marine Lover of Friedrich Nietzsche.* Translated by Gillian Gill. New York.
Irwin, Terence H.
1980.   "Reason and Responsibility in Aristotle." In Amélie Oksenberg Rorty, ed., *Essays on Aristotle's Ethics*, 117–55. Berkeley.
Jäger, Klaus.
1967.   *Zweigliedrige Gedichte und Gedichtpaare bei Properz und in Ovids Amores.* Diss. Eberhard-Karls-Universität zu Tübingen.

Jameson, Fredric.
    1988.   "The Vanishing Mediator, or Max Weber as Storyteller." In *The Ideologies of Theory*, vol. 2, 3–34. Minneapolis.
Janan, Micaela.
    1994.   *When the Lamp Is Shattered: Desire and Narrative in Catullus*. Carbondale, Ill.
Jocelyn, H. D.
    1980.   "On Some Unnecessarily Indecent Interpretations of Catullus 2 and 3." *AJP* 101:421–41.
Johnson, William Ralph.
    1973.   "The Emotions of Patriotism: Propertius 4.6." *CSCA* 6:151–80.
    ———.
    1979.   *Darkness Visible: A Study of Vergil's Aeneid*. Berkeley.
Joplin, Patricia Klindienst.
    1990.   "Ritual Work on Human Flesh: Livy's Lucretia and the Rape of the Body Politic." *Helios* 17:51–70.
    ———.
    1991.   "The Voice of the Shuttle is Ours." In Lynn A. Higgins and Brenda R. Silver, eds., *Rape and Representation*, 35–64. New York.
Joshel, Sandra.
    1992.   "The Body Female and the Body Politic: Livy's Lucretia and Verginia." In Amy Richlin, ed., *Pornography and Representation in Greece and Rome*, 112–30. Oxford.
Kahn, Charles H.
    1979.   *The Art and Thought of Heraclitus*. Cambridge.
Karsten, H. T.
    1915.   "Propertii Elegia IV 4." *Mnemosyne* ns 43:357–64.
Kellum, B. A.
    1990.   "The City Adorned: Programmatic Display at the *Aedes Concordiae Augustae*." In Raaflaub–Toher, 276–307.
Kennedy, Duncan.
    1992.   "'Augustan' and 'Anti-Augustan': Reflections on Terms of Reference." In Anton Powell, ed., *Roman Poetry and Propaganda in the Age of Augustus*, 26–58. London.
    ———.
    1993.   *The Arts of Love: Five Studies in the Discourse of Roman Elegy*. Cambridge.
King, Helen.
    1983.   "Bound to Bleed: Artemis and Greek Women." In Averil Cameron and Amélie Kuhrt, eds., *Images of Women in Antiquity*, 109–27. Detroit.
King, Joy.
    1980.   "The Two Galluses of Propertius' *Monobiblos*." *Philologus* 124:212–30.
King, Richard.
    1990.   "Creative Landscaping: Inspiration and Artifice in Propertius 4.4." *CJ* 85:225–46.
Kirk, G. S.
    1954.   *Heraclitus: The Cosmic Fragments*. Cambridge.
Kirk, G. S., and J. E. Raven.
    1957.   *The Presocratic Philosophers*. Cambridge.

Knoche, Ulrich.
    1936.   "Zur Frage der Properzinterpolation." *RhM* 85:8–63.
Koenen, Ludwig, and Dorothy B. Thompson.
    1984.   "Gallus as Triptolemos on the Tazza Farnese." *BASP* 21:111–56.
Komp, Marion.
    1988.   *Absage an Cynthia: Das Liebesthema beim späten Properz*. Frankfurt am Main.
Konstan, David.
    1986.   "Narrative and Ideology in Livy: Book I." *ClAnt* 5:198–215.

———.
    1994.   *Sexual Symmetry: Love in the Ancient Novel and Related Genres*. Princeton.
Kunihara, Kichinosuké.
    1974.   "Propertiana: 1,21." *REL* 52: 239–50.
Lacan, Jacques.
    1966.   *Écrits*. Paris.

———.
    1973.   *Séminaire XI: Les quatres concepts fondamenteux de psychanalyse*, 1969 [=SXI]. Paris.

———.
    1975.   *Séminaire XX: Encore, 1972–73* [=SXI]. Paris.

———.
    1977a.   "Desire and the Interpretation of Desire in *Hamlet*." In *Literature and Psychoanalysis: The Question of Reading: Otherwise* (Yale French Studies 55/56, 11–52). Translated by James Hulbert.

———.
    1977b.   *Écrits: A Selection*. Translated by Alan Sheridan. New York.

———.
    1978.   *Séminaire II: Le moi dans la théorie de Freud et dans la technique de la psychanalyse, 1954–55* [=SII]. Paris.

———.
    1981.   *The Four Fundamental Concepts of Psychoanalysis*. Translated by Alan Sheridan. New York.

———.
    1981–1983. "Hamlet." *Ornicar?* 24:7–31; 25:13–36; 26/27:7–44.

———.
    1986.   *Le séminaire de Jacques Lacan, livre VII: L'éthique de la psychanalyse, 1959–1960* [=SVII]. Paris.

———.
    1991.   *The Seminar of Jacques Lacan, Book II: The Ego in Freud's Theory and in the Technique of Psychoanalysis, 1954–55*. Translated by Sylvana Tomaselli. New York.

———.
    1992.   *The Seminar of Jacques Lacan, Book VII: The Ethics of Psychoanalysis, 1959–1960*. Translated by Dennis Porter. New York.

———.
    1998.   *The Seminar of Jacques Lacan, Book XX: On Feminine Sexuality, the Limits of Love and Knowledge (Encore!), 1972–1973*. Translated by Bruce Fink. New York.
Lachmann, Karl.
    1816.   *Sex. Aur. Propertii Carmina, emendavit ad codicum meliorem fidem et annotavit C. Lachmannus*. Leipzig.

———.
    1829.   *Propertii Elegiae ex recensione C. Lachmanni.* Berlin.

Lahusen, Götz.
    1983.   *Untersuchungen zur Ehrenstatue in Rom: Literarische und epigraphische Zeugnisse.* Rome.

Lake, Agnes Kirsopp.
    1937.   "An Interpretation of Propertius IV,7." *CR* 51:53–55.

Lange, Dorothy.
    1979.   "Cynthia and Cornelia: Two Voices from the Grave." *Latomus* 1:335–42.

La Penna, Antonio.
    1951.   *Properzio.* Florence.

———.
    1977.   *L'integrazione difficile: Un profilo di Properzio.* Turin.

Latte, Kurt.
    1960.   *Römische Religionsgeschichte.* Munich.

Lee, Jonathan Scott.
    1990.   *Jacques Lacan.* Amherst, Mass.

Lefèvre, Eckard.
    1966.   *Propertius Ludibundus.* Heidelberg.

Leicester, H. M., Jr.
    1990.   *The Disenchanted Self: Representing the Subject in the Canterbury Tales.* Berkeley.

Leo, Friedrich.
    1960.   *Ausgewählte kleine Schriften.* 2 vols. Rome.

Lieberg, Godo.
    1962.   *Puella divina.* Amsterdam.

Lilja, Saara.
    1978.   *The Roman Elegists' Attitude Toward Women.* New York. Reprint of 1965 Helsinki edition.

Lind, L. R.
    1989 and   "The Idea of the Republic and the Foundations of Roman Morality" (I
    1992.   and II). *Studies in Latin Literature and Roman History* 5:5–34 and 6:5–40.

Lissarague, François.
    1990.   "The Sexual Life of Satyrs." In David M. Halperin, John J. Winkler, and Froma I. Zeitlin, eds., *Before Sexuality: The Construction of Erotic Experience in the Ancient Greek World.* Princeton. 53–81.

Little, Douglas.
    1982.   "Politics in Augustan Poetry." *ANRW* II.30.1:254–370.

Lloyd, Genevieve.
    1984.   *The Man of Reason: "Male" and "Female" in Western Philosophy.* Minneapolis.

Lombardi Satriani, Luigi M., and Mariano Meligrana.
    1982.   *Il Ponte di San Giacomo: L'ideologia della morte nella società contadina del Sud.* Milano.

Long, Anthony A.
    1986.   *Hellenistic Philosophy: Stoics, Epicureans, Skeptics.* 1st ed. 1974. Berkeley.

Lovibond, Sabina.
    1994.   "An Ancient Theory of Gender: Plato and the Pythagorean Table." In Léonie Archer, Susan Fischler, and Maria Wyke, eds., *Women in Ancient Societies: An Illusion of the Night,* 88–101. New York.

Luck, Georg.
    1959.   *The Latin Love Elegy*. London.
Lyne, R. O. A. M.
    1980.   *The Latin Love Poets: From Catullus to Horace*. Oxford.
———.
    1987.   *Further Voices in the Aeneid*. Oxford.
Macey, David.
    1988.   *Lacan in Contexts*. London.
Malitz, Jürgen.
    1983.   *Die Historien des Posidonios*. Munich.
Maltby, Robert.
    1981.   "Love and Marriage in Propertius 4,3." *Papers of the Liverpool Latin Seminar* 3:243–47.
Marinone, Nino.
    1984.   *Berenice da Callimaco a Catullo*. Rome.
Marr, J. L.
    1970.   "Notes on Propertius 4.1 and 4.4." *CQ* ns 20:160–73.
McNally, Sheila.
    1978.   "The Maenad in Early Greek Art." *Arethusa* 11:101–35.
McNamee, Kathleen.
    1993.   "Propertius, Poetry and Love." In Mary DeForest, ed., *Woman's Power, Man's Game: Essays in Classical Antiquity in Honor of Joy K. King*, 215–48. Wauconda, Ill.
McParland, Elizabeth.
    1970.   "Propertius 4.9." *TAPA* 101:349–55.
Meier, Christian.
    1990.   "C. Caesar Divi Filius and the Formation of the Alternative in Rome." In Raaflaub-Toher 1990, 54–70.
Merklin, Harald.
    1968.   "Arethusa und Laodamia." *Hermes* 96:461–94.
Merriam, C. U.
    1990.   "The New Gallus Revisited." *Latomus* 49:443–52.
Mierse, W.
    1990.   "Augustan Building Programs in the Western Provinces." In Raaflaub-Toher, 308–33.
Miles, Gary B.
    1992.   "The First Roman Marriage and the Theft of the Sabine Women." In Ralph Hexter and Daniel Selden, eds., *Innovations of Antiquity*, 161–96. New York.
Millar, Fergus.
    1984.   "State and Subject: The Impact of Monarchy." In Millar-Segal, 37–60.
Millar, Fergus, and Erich Segal.
    1984.   *Caesar Augustus: Seven Aspects*. Oxford.
Miller, Jacques-Alain.
    1975.   "Theorie de Lalangue (Rudiment)." *Ornicar?* 1:16–34.
———.
    1987.   "Les réponses du réel." In Marcos Zafiropoulos, ed., *Aspects du malaise dans la civilisation*. Paris.

———.
    1988.   "*Extimité.*" *Prose Studies* 11:121–31.
Miller, John F.
    1982.   "Callimachus and the Augustan Aetiological Elegy." *ANRW* II.30.1:371–417.
Miller, Paul Allen.
    1994.   *Lyric Texts and Lyric Consciousness: The Birth of a Genre from Archaic Greece to Augustan Rome.* New York.

———.
    1995.   "The Minotaur Within: Fire, the Labyrinth, and Strategies of Containment in *Aeneid* 5 and 6." *CP* 90:225–40.

———.
    1999.   "The Tibullan Dream Text." *TAPA* 129:181–224.

———.
                Forthcoming. *Subjecting Verses: Latin Love Elegy and the Emergence of the Real.*
Miller, Paul Allen, and Charles Platter.
    1999.   "The Crux as Symptom: Augustan Elegy and Beyond." *CW* 92:445–54.
Mitchell, Juliet, and Jacqueline Rose.
    1985.   *Feminine Sexuality: Jacques Lacan and the école freudienne.* 1st ed. 1982. New York.
Muecke, Frances.
    1974.   "Nobilis Historia? Incongruity in Propertius 4.7." *BICS:* 124–32.
Munro, H. A. J.
    1876.   "The Last Elegy of the Third or Second Book of Propertius." *Journal of Philology* 6:28–69.
Münzer, Friedrich.
    1911.   *Cacus der Rinderdieb.* Basel.
Mynors, R. A. B.
    1969.   *P. Vergili Maronis Opera.* Oxford.
Nadeau, Yvan.
    1980.   "O passer nequam (Catullus 2,3)." *Latomus* 39:879–80.
Nagore, Josefina, and Elena Perez.
    1981.   "El Episodio de Hércules y Caco en Cuatro Autores Latinos." *Argos* 5:35–51.
Nethercut, W. R.
    1968.   "Notes on the Structure of Propertius Book IV." *AJP* 89:449–64.

———.
    1971a.   "Propertius 3.11." *TAPA* 102:409–43.

———.
    1971b.   "The ΣΦΡΑΓΙΣ of the Monobiblos." *AJP* 92:464–72.

———.
    1983.   "Recent Scholarship on Propertius." *ANRW* II.30.3:1813–1857.
Nicholson, Nigel.
    1999.   "Bodies Without Names, Names Without Bodies: Propertius 1.21–22." *CJ* 94:143–61.
Nicolet, Claude.
    1980.   *The World of the Citizen in Republican Rome.* Translated by P. S. Falla. Berkeley.

———.
    1991.   *Space, Geography, and Politics in the Early Roman Empire.* Ann Arbor.

Nisbet, R. G. M., and Margaret Hubbard.
1970.   *A Commentary on Horace, Odes, Book I.* Oxford.
Noonan, J. D.
1983.   "*Sacra canam:* Ritual in the Love-Elegies of Propertius IV." *CB* 59:43–47.
Nussbaum, Martha.
1986.   *The Fragility of Goodness: Luck and Ethics in Greek Tragedy and Philosophy.* Cambridge.

———.
1989.   "Beyond Obsession and Disgust: Lucretius' Genealogy of Love." *Apeiron* 22:1–59.
Ogilvie, R. M.
1965.   *A Commentary on Livy, Books 1–5.* Oxford.
O'Hara, James J.
1996.   "Sostratus Suppl. Hell. 733: A Lost, Possibly Catullan-Era Elegy on the Six Sex Changes of Tiresias." *TAPA* 126:173–219.
Oliensis, Ellen.
1997.   "The Erotics of *Amicitia:* Readings in Tibullus, Propertius, and Horace." In Judith P. Hallett and Marilyn B. Skinner, eds., *Roman Sexualities,* 151–71. Princeton.
Onians, Richard Broxton.
1951.   *The Origins of European Thought.* Cambridge.
Otto, A.
1880.   "De Fabulis Propertianis: Particula Prior." Diss. U. of Breslau.

———.
1886.   "De Fabulis Propertianis: Particula II." *Program des königlichen katholischen Gymnasiums zu Gross-Glochau* 171:3–21.
Paduano, Guido.
1968.   "Le reminiscenze dell'Alcesti nell'Elegia IV, 11 di Properzio." *Maia* 20:21–28.
Papanghelis, Theodore.
1987.   *Propertius: A Hellenistic Poet on Love and Death.* Cambridge.
Paratore, Ettore.
1936.   *L'Elegia III. 11 e gli atteggiamenti politici di Properzio.* Palermo.
Parker, Holt.
1989.   "Crucially Funny or Tranio on the Couch: The *Servus Callidus* and Jokes about Torture." *TAPA* 119:233–46.

———.
1992.   "Wo(men) in Love." Paper given at the American Philological Association Convention, New Orleans.
Parry, Adam.
1963.   "The Two Voices of Vergil's *Aeneid.*" *Arion* 2:66–80.
Pasoli, Elio.
1967.   *Sesto Properzio: Il Libro Quarto delle Elegie.* 2nd ed. Bologna.
Pichon, R.
1902.   *De Sermone Amatorio apud Latinos Elegiarum Scriptores.* Paris.

Pillinger, Hugh.
    1969.   "Some Callimachean Influences on Propertius, Book 4." *HSCPh* 73:171–99.
Pinotti, Paola.
    1983.   "Properzio e Vertumno: Anticonformismo e restaurazione augustea." In *Colloquium Propertianum (tertium). Assisi, 29–30 maggio 1981*, 75–96. Assisi.
Pirrone, Nicolò.
    1904.   *L'epicedio di Cornelia*. Milan.
Platter, Charles.
    1995.   "Officium in Catullus and Propertius: A Foucauldian Reading." *CP* 90.3:211–24.
Plessis, Frédéric.
    1884.   *Études critiques su Properce et ses élégies*. Paris.
Poliakoff, Michael.
    1987.   "The Weapons of Love and War: A Note on Propertius IV.3." *ICS* 12:93–96.
Politian (Angelo Poliziano).
    1489.   *Miscellanea*. Florence.
Postgate, John Percival.
    1881.   *Propertius: Select Elegies*. London.
    ———.
    1894.   *Sexti Properti Carmina*. London.
Prandi, Luisa.
    1979.   "La 'Fides Punica' e il pregiudizio anticartaginese." In Sordi 1979, 90–97.
Puccioni, Giulio.
    1979.   "L'elegia IV 5 di Properzio." In *Studi di poesia latina in onore di Antonio Traglia*, 609–23. Rome.
Purcell, Nicholas.
    1986.   "Livia and the Womanhood of Rome." *CPhS* 32:78–105.
Putnam, Michael.
    1965.   *The Poetry of the Aeneid*. Cambridge, Mass.
    ———.
    1976.   "Propertius 1.22: A Poet's Self-Definition." *QUCC* 23:93–123.
    ———.
    1985.   "Possessiveness, Sexuality and Heroism in the *Aeneid*." *Vergilius* 31:1–21.
    ———.
    1995.   *Vergil's Aeneid: Interpretation and Influence*. Chapel Hill, N.C.
Quint, David.
    1993.   *Epic and Empire: Politics and Generic Form from Vergil to Milton*. Princeton.
Raaflaub, Kurt A., and Mark Toher.
    1990.   *Between Republic and Empire: Interpretations of Augustus and His Principate*. Berkeley.
Rawson, Elizabeth.
    1985.   *Intellectual Life in the Late Roman Republic*. Baltimore.
Reitzenstein, Erich.
    1936.   *Wirklichkeitsbild und Gefühlsentwicklung bei Properz*. Leipzig.
    ———.
    1969.   "Die Cornelia-Elegie des Properz (IV 11)." *RhM* 112:126–45.

Richardson, Lawrence, Jr.
    1977.   *Propertius: Elegies I-IV.* Norman, Okla.
———.
    1992.   *A New Topographical Dictionary of Ancient Rome.* Baltimore.
Richlin, Amy.
    1992a.   *The Garden of Priapus: Sexuality and Aggression in Roman Humor.* First edition 1983. New York.
———.
    1992b.   "Reading Ovid's Rapes." In Amy Richlin, ed., *Pornography and Representation in Greece and Rome,* 158–79. Oxford.
Richmond, Leigh Oliffe.
    1928.   *Sex. Propertii quae supersunt opera edidit novoque apparatu critico instruxit.* Cambridge.
Robson, Arthur G.
    1973.   "The Enfolding Couplets: Their Relation to the Problems of Propertius IV 9, 71–74." *Mnemosyne* 26:234–38.
Ross, D. O.
    1975.   *Backgrounds to Augustan Poetry.* Cambridge.
Rothstein, Max.
    1966.   *Propertius Sextus Elegien.* 1st ed. 1898. 2 vols. Dublin.
Rutledge, Harry C.
    1964.   "Propertius' *Tarpeia:* The Poem Itself." *CJ* 60:68–73.
Rykwert, Joseph.
    1976.   *The Idea of a Town.* Princeton.
Sandbach, F. H.
    1962.   "Some Problems in Propertius." *CQ* 56:263–76.
Santen, L.
    1780.   *Sex. Aur. Propertii elegiarum libri IV. Cum commentario perpetuo P. Burmanni Secundi et multis doctorum notis ineditis. Opus Burmanni morte interruptum L. Santenius absolvit.* Utrecht.
Saussure, Ferdinand de.
    1983.   *Course in General Linguistics.* Ed. Charles Bally and Albert Sechehaye, with Albert Riedlinger. Translated by Roy Harris. La Salle, Ill.
Sauvage, André.
    1983.   "Properce e l'idéologie masculine." *Latomus* 42:819–43.
Sbordone, Francesco.
    1941.   "Il ciclo italico di Eracle." *Athenaeum* 19:72–180.
Schmeisser, Brigitte.
    1972.   *A Concordance to the Elegies of Propertius.* Hildesheim.
Schofield, Malcolm.
    1982.   "The dénouement of the *Cratylus.*" In Malcolm Schofield and Martha Craven Nussbaum, eds., *Language and Logos,* 61–81. Cambridge.
Shackleton-Bailey, D. R.
    1956.   *Propertiana.* Cambridge.
Sissa, Giulia.
    1990.   *Greek Virginity.* Translated by Arthur Goldhammer. Cambridge, Mass.

Skinner, Marilyn.
1993. "*Ego Mulier:* The Construction of Male Sexuality in Catullus." *Helios* 20.2:107–30.

———.
1998. "*Quod multo fit aliter in Graecia . . .*" In Marilyn B. Skinner and Judith P. Hallett, eds., *Roman Sexualities*, 3–25. Princeton.

Skutsch, Franz.
1901. *Aus Vergils Frühzeit*. Leipzig.

———.
1906. *Gallus und Vergil*. Leipzig and Berlin.

Small, Jocelyn Penny.
1982. *Cacus and Marsyas in Etrusco-Roman Legend*. Princeton.

Smyth, W. R.
1951. "Interpretationes Propertianae." *CQ* 45:74–79.

Solmsen, Friedrich.
1961. "Propertius in his Literary Relations with Tibullus and Vergil." *Philologus* 105:272–89.

Sordi, Marta, ed.
1979. *Conoscenze etniche e rapporti di convivenza nell'antichità*. Milan.

Soría, Claudio.
1965. "S. Propercio IV, 11 y la Moral Tradicional de la Matrona Romana." *Revista de Estudios Clasicos* 9:29–50.

Spelman, Christopher.
1994. "Propertius 2.3: The Disgusting Subject of Desire." Paper read at the Classical Association of the Atlantic States Annual Conference, Carlisle, Penn. (April 1994).

Staden, Heinrich von.
1991. "*Apud nos foediora verba:* Celsus' reluctant construction of the female body." In Guy Sabbah, ed., *Le Latin médical: La constitution d'un langage scientifique. Réalités et langage de la médecine dans le monde romain*, 271–96. Actes du IIIe colloque international "Textes medicaux latins antiques" (Saint-Étienne, 11–13 Septembre 1989). Saint-Étienne.

Stahl, Hans-Peter.
1985. *Propertius: "Love" and "War"—Individual and State under Augustus*. Berkeley.

———.
1990. "The Death of Turnus: Augustan Vergil and the Political Rival." In Kurt A. Raaflaub and Mark Toher, eds., *Between Republic and Empire: Interpretations of Augustus and His Principate*. Berkeley.

Sullivan, John P.
1976. *Propertius: A Critical Introduction*. Cambridge.

———.
1984. "Propertius IV: Themes and Structure." *ICS* 9:30–34.

Sweet, Frederick.
1972. "Propertius and Political Panegyric." *Arethusa* 5:169–75.

Syme, Ronald.
1939. *The Roman Revolution*. Oxford.

Taminiaux, Jacques.
1984.   *Naissance de la philosophie hégélienne d'état: Commentaire et traduction de la Realphilosophie d'Iéna (1805–1806)*. Paris.
Thomas, Richard.
1979.   "New Comedy, Callimachus, and Roman poetry." *HSCPh* 83:179–206.
———.
1982.   *Lands and Peoples in Roman Poetry. The Ethnographical Tradition*. Cambridge Philological Society, Suppl. vol. 7. Cambridge.
Thompson, Lloyd A.
1989.   *Romans and Blacks*. London.
Tissol, Garth.
1997.   *The Face of Nature: Wit, Narrative, and Cosmic Origins in Ovid's Metamorphoses*. Princeton.
Tränkle, Hermann.
1960.   *Die Sprachkunst des Properz und die Tradition der lateinischen Dichtersprache*. Wiesbaden.
Treggiari, Susan.
1991.   *Roman Marriage: Iusti Coniuges from the Time of Cicero to the Time of Ulpian*. Oxford.
Turpin, José.
1973.   "Cynthia et le dragon de Lanuvium: Une élégie cryptique (Properce, IV,8)." *REL* 51:159–71.
Tyrrell, William Blake.
1984.   *Amazons: A Study in Athenian Mythmaking*. Baltimore.
Verducci, Florence.
1984.   "On the Sequence of Gallus' Epigrams: *Molles Elegi, Vasta Triumphi Pondera*." *QUCC* 45:119–36.
Veyne, Paul.
1988.   *Roman Erotic Elegy*. Chicago.
Viparelli, Valeria.
1987.   "Rassegna di studi properziani (1982–1987)." *BStudLat* 17:19–76.
Walbank, F. W.
1972.   "Nationality as a Factor in Roman History." *HSCPh* 76:145–68.
Walsh, T. J. R.
1983.   "Propertius' Tarpeia Elegy (4.4)." *LCM* 8.5:75–76.
Warden, John.
1978.   "Another Would-Be Amazon: Propertius 4,4,71–72." *Hermes* 106:177–87.
———.
1980.   *Fallax opus: Poet and Reader in the Elegies of Propertius*. Toronto.
———.
1982.   "Epic into Elegy: Propertius 4,9,70ff." *Hermes* 110:228–42.
Watson, Gerard.
1966.   *The Stoic Theory of Knowledge*. Belfast.
Weeber, Karl-Wilhelm.
1977.   *Das 4. Properz-Buch: Interpretationen zu seiner Eigenart und seiner Stellung im Gesamtwerk*. Diss. Ruhr-Universität Bochum.

Wellesley, Kenneth.
    1969.   "Propertius' Tarpeia Poem (IV 4)." *Acta Classica Univ. Scient. Debrecen.* 5:93–103.
Whitford, Margaret.
    1991.   *Luce Irigaray: Philosophy in the Feminine.* London.
Williams, Bernard.
    1982.   "Cratylus' theory of names and its refutation." In Malcolm Schofield and Martha Craven Nussbaum, eds., *Language and Logos*, 83–93. Cambridge.
Williams, Gordon.
    1968.   *Tradition and Originality in Roman Poetry.* Oxford.
———.
    1990.   "Did Maecenas Fall from Power? Augustan Literary Patronage." In Raaflaub–Toher, 258–75.
Williams, R. D.
    1973.   *The Aeneid of Vergil.* London.
Winter, J. G.
    1910.   *The Myth of Hercules at Rome.* London.
Wiseman, T. P.
    1985.   *Catullus and His World: A Reappraisal.* Cambridge.
Wyke, Maria.
    1987a.   "The Elegiac Woman at Rome." *PCPhS* 213 n.s. 33:153–78.
———.
    1987b.   "Written Women: Propertius' *Scripta Puella*." *JRS* 77:47–61.
———.
    1989a.   "In Pursuit of Love, the Poetic Self, and a Process of Reading: Augustan Elegy in the 1980s." *JRS* 79:165–73.
———.
    1989b.   "Mistress and Metaphor in Augustan Elegy." *Helios* 16:25–47.
———.
    1994.   "Taking the Woman's Part: Engendering Roman Love Elegy." *Ramus* 23:110–28.
Yardley, J. C.
    1976.   "Lovers' Quarrels: Horace Odes 1,13,11 and Propertius 4,5,40." *Hermes* 104:124–28.
Zanker, Graham.
    1987.   *Realism in Alexandrian Poetry: A Literature and Its Audience.* London.
Zanker, Paul.
    1968.   *Forum Augustum.* Tübingen.
———.
    1988.   *The Power of Images in the Age of Augustus.* Ann Arbor.
Zetzel, J. E. G.
    1977.   "Gallus, Elegy, and Ross." Review of D. O. Ross, *Backgrounds to Augustan Poetry. CJ* 72:249–60.
Žižek, Slavoj.
    1989.   *The Sublime Object of Ideology.* London.
———.
    1991a.   *For They Know Not What They Do: Enjoyment as a Political Factor.* London.

———.	
1991b.	*Looking Awry: An Introduction to Jacques Lacan through Popular Culture.* Cambridge, Mass.
———.	
1992.	*Enjoy Your Symptom: Jacques Lacan in Hollywood and Out.* New York.
———.	
1993.	*Tarrying with the Negative: Kant, Hegel, and the Critique of Ideology.* Durham, N.C.
———.	
1994.	*The Metastases of Enjoyment: Six Essays on Woman and Causality.* London.
———.	
1997.	*The Plague of Fantasies.* London.

GENERAL INDEX

Aelian, on Lanuvian snake ritual, 202n9
Aeneas, in *Forum Augustum*, 5
Aeschylus, 157
aetiology: and anxiety over cultural continuity, 16; in Catullus' *Coma Berenices* (The Lock of Berenice), 13–14; and language as purely differential system, 133; as preserving conceptual oppositions in Propertius Book IV, 15; as reflecting Rome and Roman history, 14, 15, 134–35; as search for essence of phenomena, 129, 130, 133, 135
Alexandrian poets, 16
Alfonsi, Luigi, 147
Althusser, Louis, 182n48
Amazon: and Bacchant, 76–78, 191n42; iconography of, 76; and Man, 77, 80; and the state, 77, 80
Anderson, W. S., 209n55
Apollo: as Callimachus' patron god, 15; as Propertius' patron god, 15, 196n2; as Rome's champion in Propertius 4.6, 104
Aristotle, 20, 41, 144
Augustus (Octavian): and Battle of Actium, 101; and *capitonnage* (quilting), 50; and Cornelius Gallus, 51–52; as divinely aided leader in Propertius 4.6, 102; and divinity, 48, 183n60; and domestic asceticism, 63; and *Forum Augustum*, 4–6; and Hercules, myth of, 128–29; and legislation on reproduction (*ius trium liberorum*), 160; on Mark Antony, 46; and marriage legislation, 54, 60; and monarchy, 23, 47, 183n57; moral and political program of, 19, 70; and principate, dating of, 169n3; Propertius' "dissaffection" from, 12; in Propertius' poetry, 18, 33, 34; as reformer, 129; and Roman militarism, 54; and Roman state, attempts to unify, 19; and Rome, public vision of, 4; and succession, attempts to secure, 184n61

Bacchant: Cynthia as, 107; iconography of, 76; and Man, 77, 80; and the state, 77, 80
Barber, E. A., 11, 155
Barton, Carlin, 165
Bassus, 35, 36–37
Beard, Mary, 205n53
Benediktson, Thomas, 172n6
Benjamin, Anna S., 37
Benveniste, Emile, 193n63
Bing, Peter, 16
Bostock, David, 133
Brenk, F. E., 71
Burck, Erich, 101
Butrica, James, 11
Butler, H. E., 155

Caesar, Julius, 47, 151
Cairns, Francis, 36–37, 128, 143, 177n3, 205n4
Callimachus, 13, 14, 16, 37, 178n3
Camps, W. A., 28, 29, 94, 96, 115, 132
capitonnage (quilting): and citizenship, 46; as conceptual link between the political and the personal, 4, 18; and desire, 41, 164; and divided/lacking subject, 12, 18, 36;

237

GENERAL INDEX

capitonnage (continued)
in Gallus poems, 41, 44–45, 50; and ideology, 18, 36, 42; and *objet a*, 152; and the phallus, 118; and Propertian subject, 42; and signification, 152–53
Carneades, 73, 150, 190n19
Carson, Ann, 181n41
cartography: as administrative tool in Roman Empire, 68; in ancient world, 187n39; and knowledge, 66–67; in Propertius 4.3, 54, 65–66; and Roman imperialism, 66
Catiline (Lucius Sergius Catilina), 62
Catullus (Gaius Valerius Catullus): c. 11 and Propertius 4.3, 56, 57, 58; c. 66, 14, 15, 173n15; and divided/lacking subject, 3; and homosociality, 43; Lesbia cycle of, 3; pederastic poems of, 40, 180n27; and politics, 47; and Propertius' Gallus poems, 43; and Roman erotic elegy, 103, 171n28; on Rome's moral deterioration, 174n32; as translator of Callimachus, 13–14
Celentano, Laura, 175n57, 194n9
Celsus, 144
Cicero (Marcus Tullius Cicero): on Carneades, 190; on Catiline, 61–62; on citizenship, 46, 182n51; on Clodia Metelli, 200n29; on ethics as epistemology, 72–73; on Mark Antony, 46, 183n53; on marriage, 162; on natural law, 149; and Roman jurisprudence, 149; on virtue as masculine province, 20
citizenship: and Roman conceptualization of, problems in, 46; and Roman expansionism, 46
Clay, Diskin, 170n7
Coarelli, Filippo, 204–5n52
Commager, Steele, 176
Copjec, Joan, 117, 120
Copley, F. O., 158
Cornelia (daughter of Augustus' first wife, Scribonia), 146–63
Cornelius Nepos, 136
courtly love, 123, 125
Crassus (Marcus Licinius Crassus), 198n13
Crawford, Michael, 205n53
Curran, Leo, 147, 148, 158
Currie, H. MacL., 125
Cynthia: as Acanthis' protegée, 85–99; as Bacchant, 77; and causality, 121–22; contradictory portrait of, in Monobiblos (Propertius

Book I), 35, 119; contradictory portrait of, in Propertian corpus, 21; as disordering principle, 23; and expedition to Lanuvium, 114–27; as master-signifier, 42; and *objet a*, 27, 95, 123–24; as paradigmatic free Roman, 24; as revenant, 25, 110–13

Danaids, 74–75, 157
Dean-Jones, Lesley-Ann, 209n58
Dee, James, 66, 120
Deremetz, Alain, 15
Diodorus Siculus, 137

Edwards, Catharine, 59, 62, 72, 183n53
Elster, Jon, 122
Enk, P. J., 112
Epicurus: on desire's influence on perception, 192n56; on friendship, 41; on justice, 149–50; on knowledge, 204n45
the erotic, and the political, relation between, 11, 12, 17–19, 23, 41, 164
the erotic rival: and Lacan's formulae of sexuation, 166; as *objet a*, 96; and the phallus, 120; as "thief of enjoyment," 95–96
ethnography, ancient: and geography, 66, 187n41; and Roman national identity, 136
etymology, as guide to essence of phenomena, 15, 133
Euripides, *Alcestis* and Propertius 4.11, 158–59, 160, 161–62

fantasy: and *objet a*, 95; and sexual non-relation, 97; and subjectivity, 83; and Woman, 97
Fantham, Elaine, 206n19
Fedeli, Paolo, 28, 29, 178n3
Feeney, Denis, 165, 205n53
feminism: and Propertius, 175–77n58; and Propertius studies, 166
Forum Augustum, as contradictory vision of Roman identity, 4–6, 8
Foucault, Michel, theory of *épistémè*, 7
free will, in ancient philosophy, 175n49
Freud, Sigmund, 64, 83, 96–97, 117
Frier, Bruce, 24, 149

Gallus (Gaius Cornelius Gallus): and land redistributions, 51; and Octavian, relationship with, 180n31; and Parthenius, 39; and Propertius' Gallus poems, 18, 34, 36, 39, 40, 41, 44, 45, 51–52, 178n3; provincial equestrian

background of, 40; and Qaṣr Ibrîm fragment, 37, 178–79n18
Gansiniec, Zofia, 187n1
Gantz, Timothy, 144
Geertz, Clifford, 178n6
gender: as formal logical relation, 120, 166; and knowledge, 65–68, 118, 145, 167; and *lalangue* (llanguage), 141; as purely differential system, 23, 144; and signification, 165, 167
geography: sexualization of, in Catullus c. 11, 57, 58; sexualization of, in Propertius 4.3, 58
Gold, Barbara, 175–177n58, 214n9
Gordon, A. E., 126
Green, Monica, 189n15
Griffin, Jasper, 60, 176n58, 200n25,29
Grimal, Pierre, 75, 147
Gutzwiller, Kathryn, 14, 86, 87, 109, 194n9

Habinek, Thomas, 183n54, 187n37
Hallett, Judith, 54, 147, 175–177n58
Hanson, Ann, 189n15
Harrauer, Hermann, 53
Hegel, G. W. F.: on *Bildung*, 160; on external boundary (*Grenze*), 207n30; on external terror, 161; on internal limit (*Schranke*), 207n30; on Jacobin Reign of Terror, 161; on monarchy, 48, 49; on "sacrifice of the sacrifice," 160–61; on Woman as "eternal irony of the community," 126
Heinze, Richard, 141
Heraclitus, 73, 189n19
Herodotus, 66, 67
Highet, Gilbert, 147
hippomanes, 90
history: as ideological instrument, 129, 132; as retrospectively constructed fiction, 17
homosociality, 43
Horace, 46, 72, 87, 174n32, 200n29
Hubbard, Margaret, 54, 55, 147
Hubbard, T. K., 190n24

identity: as effect of discourse, 35; erotic perfection of, 42; and external boundary (*Grenze*), 23, 135–36, 207n30; in Gallus poems, 16, 29, 34–36, 43–44, 46–52; and internal limit (*Schranke*), 23, 135–36, 207n30; and monarchy, 48; of Propertius and *jouissance* (enjoyment), 95, 97; of Propertius and *objet a*, 95, 97
identity, Roman: and aetiology, 135; and conceptual dependence on the Other, 65, 75, 139; and differentiality, 64, 135, 136, 138, 139, 140; and domestic austerity, 63; and the East as inversion, 113; and ethnography, 136, 208n33; and etymology, 134; and external boundary (*Grenze*), 23, 136; and feminine desire, 78; and *Forum Augustum*, 5; and Hercules/Cacus myth, 136; and imperialism, 16, 58, 64, 68; and internal limit (*Schranke*), 23, 135, 136; and land redistributions, 49, 51; and language, 134; and militarism, 61, 63–64; and Roman ethics, 61, 64; and state offices, 46–47, 49, 51; in transition to principate, 23; and transsexuality, 26, 144; unquestioned, in Propertius 4.6, 102; in Vergil's *Aeneid*, 138
identity, sexual: as formal logical relation, 65, 118–19; and Roman militarism, 58, 63–64; unquestioned, in Propertius 4.6, 102
Irigaray, Luce: on epistemology, 71; on "feminine" knowledge, 72; on "feminine" syntax, 83; and Jacques Lacan, 188n5

McNamee, Kathleen, 176n58
Maecenas (Gaius Maecenas), 12
Man: and false certitude, 65, 67, 103; and Lacan's formulae of sexuation, 120, 127; as principal subject of thought, 21
Man/Woman: as failed binary, 22, 57, 73, 81, 93, 117, 119, 144; and knowledge, 65–68, 108, 142; as master binary, 20, 22
marriage, Roman: soldier's, regulated by the state, 55; women's traditional role in, 81
Martial, 180n27
Meier, Christian, 183n57
Messalla (Marcus Valerius Messalla), 171n29,30
Mierse, William, 174n33
Miles, Gary, 190–91n33
militarism, Roman, and decadence, 59, 60
Millar, Fergus, 47, 183n57
Miller, Jacques-Alain, 92–93
Miller, Paul Allen, 7–9, 82, 165, 190n25, 193n66, 209n46

Nethercut, W. R., 28, 29, 198n13
Nicholson, Nigel, 178n9
Nicolet, Claude, 66
Noonan, J. D., 116
Nussbaum, Martha, 180n33, 190n24

objet a: and *capitonnage* (quilting), 152; and causality, 26–28, 124, 152; and desire, 91–92, 93, 95;

objet a (continued)
    and fantasy, 95, 153; and hatred, 27, 91, 95; and identity, 93; and ideology, 153; and the Law, 152, 154; and logical impasse, 177n58; and the Real, 125; and sexual non-relation, 26–27, 123; and signification, 152, 153; and subjectivity, 91; as unspecifiable, 92; and violence, 123, 124; and Woman, 95, 154, 156
Ogilvie, R. M., 151
Oliensis, Ellen, 35, 43, 44
Ovid: *Amores* 1.8, on Dipsas the bawd, 87, 88; on Hercules-Cacus myth, 132, 137; and Roman erotic elegy, 103; on Roman expansionism, 62; on Rome's moral deterioration, 174n32

Papanghelis, Theodore, 200n33, 201n36
Parker, Holt, 107, 213n45
Pasoli, Elio, 115
perception, cultural construction of, 74, 80
pietas, represented in *Forum Augustum*, 5
Pinotti, Paola, 14
Plato: and *capitonnage* (quilting), 41; on erotic love as philosophical askesis, 41–42; on ethics as epistemology, 72; on knowledge, 204n45; on language, 133, 206n23; on "organic" model of rhetoric, 131; on women's souls, 20
Platter, Charles, 82, 165, 190n25
Plutarch, 136, 170n17, 171n19
Polybius, 60
Ponticus, 35, 36–37
Posidonius, 170n18
Propertius (Sextus Propertius): and Augustus' conservatism, 54; and Plato, 41; poetry of, and binarism, 22; poetry of, difficulties of, 9, 11, 13; rereading affair with Cynthia, 89, 90, 97, 100, 101; rewriting affair with Cynthia, 86; on Rome's moral deterioration, 174n32
property ownership, and social identity, 46
Protestantism, and capitalism, 61
Putnam, Michael, 181–82n43
Pythagorean table of opposites, 21, 72

Quint, David, 129, 206n19, 208n45

Raaflaub, Kurt, 183n57
the Real: and divination, 125; and *objet a*, 91, 125; and racial hatred, 91; as rupture in the Symbolic, 9, 94, 99; and Woman, 99

repetition: and Acanthis, 88, 89; and the dead, return of, 88, 112; and the Symbolic's failures, 98; and textual criticism of Propertius 4.5, 194n15; and Woman's desire, 98
rhetoric: body as metaphor for, 131; and *capitonnage* (quilting), 42
Richardson, Lawrence, Jr.: on contradictory representation of Cynthia in Propertius' poetry, 119; on Propertius 4.5, 90, 94, 96; on Propertius 4.8, 115; on Propertius 4.9, 130, 131, 132; on Propertius 4.10, 197n13; on Propertius 4.11, 147, 159
Richlin, Amy, 200n30, 214n9
Roman erotic elegy: contradictory nature of, 3; and *docta puella* (learned girlfriend), 185n10; and representation of Woman, 103, 106, 107, 108, 109, 111, 112
Roman imperialism: and "decadence," 59–62; and Propertius 4.3, 185n12; and state administrative reorganization, 68
Romanitas: and aetiology, 134–35; displaced by sensuality, 25, 60, 63; and female chastity, 27, 155–56; as *point de capiton* (quilting point), 12; and Roman ethics, 61
Roman/non-Roman: as failed binary, 22, 57, 75, 136–38, 144, 197n12; as master binary, 20, 22
Roman Republic, martial conflicts in, 19
Rome, and belligerence toward non-Romans, 14
Romulus: in *Forum Augustum*, 5; and portrait of Battle of Actium, in Propertius 4.6, 136
Rothstein, Max, 80, 115, 131, 201n36
Rutilius Rufus, 170n18
Rutledge, Harry, 71
Rykwert, Joseph, 190–91n33

Sallust (Gaius Sallustius Crispus): on Catiline, 62; on Roman morality, 59, 60, 72, 173n32
Saussure, Ferdinand de, 134
Sbordone, Francesco, 205n6
Scribonia (Augustus's first wife, mother of Cornelia), 146
Segal, Erich, 183n5 7
Seneca, 20, 72
Servius, 38
Servius Auctus, 39
sexuality, 117, 120
sexual non-relation: and Books I and IV, 29; and double entendre, 116, 120–21; and illogic,

121; and return of the dead, 97; and violence, 124
Shackleton-Bailey, D. R., 90
Sissa, Giulia, 74
Skeptics, 149–50
Skinner, Marilyn, 184n72, 185n8,16, 197n3
Skutsch, Franz, 37
sleeplessness (*agrupnia*): theme of, in Catullus c. 50, 37; theme of, in Propertius 1.10, 37
Sophocles, 145
Soranus, 144
Spelman, Christopher, 195n28, 196n34
Staden, Heinrich von, 189n15
Stahl, H. P., 80, 147, 176n58, 184n68
Stoics, 41, 72, 204n45
the subject: and *capitonnage* (quilting), 36, 43, 46, 47; and causality, 25, 122; as divided/lacking, 3, 4, 17, 18, 19, 23, 42, 97, 172n7; and history as retrospective reconstruction, 17; and linguistic ambiguity, 83; and *objet a*, 91, 93
subjectivity: and ambiguity in language, 82; in ancient Rome, 12; defined, 169n1; problematization of, 26, 33, 41; and Propertius' Gallus poems, 23, 33, 41; in transition to principate, 8
Suetonius, 183n53
Sulla (Lucius Cornelius Sulla Felix), 151
Sullivan, J. P., 147
the Symbolic: and causality, 94; as containing the Real, 9; and differentiality, 93; and return of the dead, 98; and sexual non-relation, 97
Syme, Ronald, 47–48, 183n57

Tarquinius Superbus, 48
Thomas, Richard, 37
Tibullus, 40, 87, 103, 174n32
Tiresias: and knowledge, 142, 143, 144, 145; and transsexuality, 142, 143, 144, 209n56
Tissol, Garth, 16
Toher, Mark, 183n57
Tränkle, Hermann, 40
Transsexuality, 142, 143
Tullius (identified as L. Volcacius Tullus), 35, 36, 46, 50
Turpin, José, 116

Valerius Maximus, 20, 170n19
vanishing mediator, 61

Velleius Paterculus, 156
Vergil: *Aeneid*, Dido and witchcraft in, 87; *Aeneid* VII, Muse Erato in, 181n43; *Aeneid*'s Dido, and Propertius 4.3, 76–77, 83; *Eclogue I*, and land redistributions, 45–46; *Eclogue I*, and Propertius' Gallus poems, 45–46; *Eclogue 10*, and Propertius' Gallus poems, 178n3; *Eclogues*, Cornelius Gallus in, 37, 41; *Eclogues*, and Gallan elegy, 38, 40; *Eclogues*, and Propertius 4.9, 138; *Georgics IV*, and Propertius 4.11, 148; on Hercules-Cacus myth, 129, 130, 132, 136, 137, 138, 139, 140, 141, 142, 205n6, 208n39; and Roman history, ethical mission of, 142; and Roman "manifest destiny," 139; on Rome's moral deterioration, 174n32; Underworld, description of, and Propertius 4.11, 148, 163
Vessels, as symbols of female chastity, 74, 156, 157
Veyne, Paul, 7, 176n58, 186n29, 204n40
virtus, represented in *Forum Augustum*, 5

Warden, John: on Propertius 4.4, 71, 76, 77; on Propertius 4.7, 201n36; on Propertius 4.9, 130, 137, 140, 141, 205n6
Weber, Max, 61
Weeber, K. W., 87, 198n13
Whitford, Margaret, 188n5
Williams, Gordon, 148
Williams, R. D., 129
Winter, J. G., 137
Woman: and the body, 55, 69, 108; and *capitonnage* (quilting), 43, 44; and causality, 122; as conceptual deadlock, 23, 177n58; contradictory representation of, 104, 119; and courtly love, 145; as divine Muse/mistress in Roman erotic elegy, 42, 181n38; and epistemological uncertainty, 79; ethical evaluation of, 98, 99, 104, 109, 110–11, 112, 113, 126, 156, 157, 162; as exposing the Symbolic's failings, 44, 71, 78, 126, 165, 176n58, 177n58; as fantasy, 94–95, 113; as figuring logical breakdown, 9, 17; as found lacking, 24, 72–73; as guarantor of the Law, 156, 157; as guarantor of Man's identity, 63, 75, 93, 111, 123, 144, 162, 166; as guarantor of Roman national identity, 155–56; as guarantor of the state, 125, 162, 166; Her desire as incalculable, 78; Her desire as undermining conceptual

Woman *(continued)*
    categories, 79, 81; Her representation in Roman erotic elegy, 103, 106, 107, 108, 109, 111, 112; inadequate conceptualization of, 21, 95, 108; and knowledge, 65–68, 144; and Lacan's formulae of sexuation, 118, 127; as lacking an essence, 94–95; and the Law, 24, 96–97, 156; as Man's antithesis, 64, 95; as mediating homosociality, 43; and *objet a*, 95, 154, 156; and the phallus, 119; as *point de capiton* (quilting point), 12; as sign, 165; and skepticism, 29, 65, 66, 67, 68, 102, 103; and the state, 156, 160
women, Roman: mores of, 86, 146–47
Wyke, Maria, 54, 147, 163, 175–77n58

Zanker, Graham, 16
Zanker, Paul, 4
Zetzel, James, 37, 38, 179n19
Žižek, Slavoj: on body inscribed by the Symbolic, 209n54; on causality in human behavior, 122; on the construction of mores, 61; on divination, 125; on external boundary (*Grenze*) and internal limit (*Schranke*) in Hegel, 207n30; on "Father of Enjoyment," 64; on Hegel's assessment of Woman, 126; on language, 138; on the Law and internal terror, 214n60; on return of the dead, 98; on "sacrifice of the sacrifice," 161; on sexual non-relation, 116–17, 124; on Woman as conceptual deadlock, 21, 22–23

INDEX OF PROPERTIAN POEMS CITED

Propertius 1.1, 38, 39
Propertius 1.2, 28–29, 89
Propertius 1.3, 77, 107
Propertius 1.5: and *capitonnage* (quilting), 42–43; and Gallan elegy, 39, 40; and male mirroring, 43, 44
Propertius 1.5, 1.10, 1.13, 1.20, 1.21, 1.22 (Gallus poems): and defining Roman citizen-subject, 23; disjunctive nature of, 17, 18, 33–34; divided subject in, 18, 43; Gallus(es)' erotic history in, 39; general discussion of, 33–52; and male mirroring, 45; and problematization of identity, 16, 29, 34–36, 43–44, 46–52
Propertius 1.8, 38
Propertius 1.9, 200n29
Propertius 1.10: and *capitonnage* (quilting), 42–43; and homosociality, 43; and male mirroring, 44; and Propertius as *praeceptor amoris*, 43
Propertius 1.13: and male fusion, 43; and male mirroring, 44
Propertius 1.14, 40
Propertius 1.16, 34
Propertius 1.19, 109
Propertius 1.20: and *capitonnage* (quilting), 43; and Cornelius Gallus, 44; and Gallan elegy, 39; and male mirroring, 43, 44
Propertius 1.21: and Cornelius Gallus, 40; and siege of Perusia, 40, 41; unexpected narrator of, 34

Propertius 1.22: and *capitonnage* (quilting), 50–51; and Cornelius Gallus, 40; and siege of Perusia, 40, 41; and social identity, 46
Propertius 2.6, 203n29
Propertius 2.22a, 203n29
Propertius 2.23, 203n29
Propertius 2.24, 203n29
Propertius 2.29, 107
Propertius 2.34, 51
Propertius 3.8, 123–24
Propertius 3.15, 151–52
Propertius 3.19, 152
Propertius 3.22, 77
Propertius 3.24, 192n56
Propertius 4.1: and Book IV's aetiological program, 102; and Book IV's erotic elegiac program, 102, 103; contradictory program of, 15, 102–3; and discontinuity with Roman past, 16, 135; and etymology, 133–34; and patriotism, 101; and Roman identity, 134, 135; and Romulus/Remus legend, 207n29
Propertius 4.2, 14, 15
Propertius 4.3: as elegiac epistle, 54; and feminization of Roman ego-ideals, 23; general discussion of, 53–68; and *jouissance* (enjoyment), 108; and Roman identity, 29–30, 61–65, 135; and Roman imperialism, 102, 185n12; and Roman militarism, 56, 186n18
Propertius 4.4: and binarism, 22, 30, 72, 73; as contradictory portrait of the past, 16, 71, 72, 73;

Propertius 4.4 *(continued)*
and the feminine, inadequate conceptualization of, 77–78, 81, 106, 111; general discussion of, 70–84; and *jouissance* (enjoyment), 55, 108; and the Law, 24; and Propertius 4.10, 198n13; water imagery in, 71, 72, 74, 76, 78

Propertius 4.5: and Acanthis as *objet a*, 27, 95; and courtly love, 26; as epicenter of Book IV, 199n15; and the erotic rival, 26, 95–96, 120; as "feminine" rereading of Book I (Monobiblos), 29, 89; general discussion of, 85–99; and *jouissance* (enjoyment), 55, 104, 105; and the Law, 24, 96–97; and *objet a*, 95–96, 104, 152; as repeating opening lines from Propertius 1.2, 28–29, 89; and return of the dead, 85–86, 88–89, 98–99, 100; and witchcraft, 88, 94; and Woman as *objet a*, 95, 104, 152, 211n27; and Woman's inadequate conceptualization, 30, 99; and women's economic vulnerability, 87, 89, 108, 109

Propertius 4.6: and Augustus' conservatism, 54; on Battle of Actium, 100–101; as center of Book IV, 102; and divine moral order, 104; and masculine "knowledge," 103, 108; and "masculinist" poetics, 197–98n13; and patriotism, 108, 198–99n14; its relation to Propertius 4.7, 103, 108; and Roman identity, 136; and Romulus, 136

Propertius 4.7: as center of Book IV, 104; and courtly love, 26; and Cynthia's contradictory portrayal, 119; and Elysian Fields, 109, 112, 113, 163; and ethical evaluation of Woman, 98, 110–11; and the feminine, representation of, 108; general discussion of, 100–113; and the Law, 24; and *objet a*, 27; and Propertius 4.8, poems' relation to Homer, *Iliad* 23 and *Odyssey* 22, 202n5; and reconstructing the past, 16–17, 100, 101; relation to Propertius 4.8, 115; and rereading Propertius' affair with Cynthia, 97, 100, 101; and return of the dead, 85–86, 162; and Roman comedy, 107; and sexual non-relation, 98; suspension of moral judgment of, 25, 110, 112–13; and Woman's inadequate conceptualization in erotic elegy, 30–31, 108, 113

Propertius 4.8: body as locus of suppressed truth, 55; and courtly love, 26, 122–23; and Cynthia's contradictory portrayal, 119; and the erotic rival, 26, 114–16, 120; on extrarational in religion, 31, 124–25; on extrarational in the sexual non-relation, 31, 124–25; and feminine "illogic," 24–25, 119, 121–22; and feminization of Roman ego-ideals, 23; general discussion of, 114–27; and *objet a*, 27, 123–24, 152; and relation between courtly love and religion, 28, 125; relation to Propertius 4.7, 115; and sexual non-relation, 28, 116–21

Propertius 4.9: and binarism, 31, 136, 144; and body as locus of suppressed truth, 55; and Bona Dea shrine, 16, 128, 130, 142–45; as contradictory portrait of the past, 16, 132; and feminization of Roman ego-ideals, 23; general discussion of, 128–45; and *jouissance* (enjoyment), 105, 141; and *lalangue* (llanguage), 111, 139, 140, 141; transsexuality in, 26, 142–45

Propertius 4.10: and etymology, 15, 198n13; and "masculinist" poetics, 197–98n13

Propertius 4.11: and Danaids, 156–57; and ethical evaluation of Woman, 98, 158; general discussion of, 146–63; and Hercules' apotheosis, 162; and inadequate conceptualization of the feminine, 111; and *jouissance* (enjoyment), 104, 105; and the Law, 31–32, 147, 148–52, 154–63; and murder of the Aegyptioi, 157; and *objet a*, 27, 152–56; and rape, 157, 158; and reevaluating the Roman matronal ethos, 97, 147; and return of the dead, 85–86, 162; and sexual non-relation, 98; and suspension of moral judgment, 25, 163

Text: 10/12 Baskerville
Display: Baskerville
Composition: Impressions Book and Journal Services, Inc.
Printing and Binding: Sheridan Books, Inc.

www.ingramcontent.com/pod-product-compliance
Lightning Source LLC
Chambersburg PA
CBHW031252230426
43670CB00005B/150